Mary Carpenter and the Children of the Streets

MARY CARPENTER AND THE CHILDREN OF THE STREETS

Jo Manton

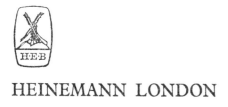

HEINEMANN LONDON

Heinemann Educational Books Ltd

LONDON EDINBURGH MELBOURNE AUCKLAND TORONTO
HONG KONG SINGAPORE KUALA LUMPUR
IBADAN NAIROBI JOHANNESBURG
LUSAKA NEW DELHI

ISBN 0 435 32569 8

Published by Heinemann Educational Books Ltd
48 Charles Street, London WIX 8AH
Printed in Great Britain by Butler & Tanner Ltd
Frome and London

CONTENTS

ILLUSTRATIONS

To

JOHN SCUPHAM

of the
British Broadcasting Corporation
and the
Open University

ACKNOWLEDGMENTS

This book is indebted to a large number of people and institutions. Any student of Mary Carpenter must be grateful for the devotion with which her nephew, J. Estlin Carpenter, compiled his *Life and Work of Mary Carpenter* in the year following her death. As a distinguished scholar in the field of comparative religion he was chiefly interested in her spiritual life, while the conventions of a hundred years ago forced him to deal discreetly with her public controversies. Moreover he was bound by a well-defined framework of church and family loyalties, and his portrait of his aunt has appeared to some readers unduly softened. Nevertheless his book remains a prime source for many documents which have since been censored or destroyed; it is referred to throughout the footnotes as *Life and Work*. Full bibliographical references will be found under *Sources* pp. 257–261.

Thanks are due to the following authorities who allowed me to copy and quote from documents in their keeping; the Trustees of the Huntington Library, San Marino, California, and of the Public Library Boston, Massachusetts, the Principal and Fellows of Manchester College, Oxford, the Master and Fellows of Trinity College, Cambridge, the Librarian, Birmingham University Library and the University Librarian, Liverpool, the Keeper of Manuscripts, Victoria and Albert Museum and the Archivist of the Dorset County Record Office. Special thanks are due to the authorities at Bristol, Mary Carpenter's almost lifelong home: Bristol Public Library and its staff, the City Archives and Miss Mary Williams, Assistant Archivist, the City Art Gallery and Miss Clare Crick, Assistant Curator, and the Red Lodge Museum.

Librarians have been generous of their time and specialized knowledge at Dr Williams's Library, Manchester College, Oxford, Trinity College, Cambridge, Cambridge University Library, the Wellcome Institute of the History of Medicine, the University of London Periodicals Library, the State Paper Room at the British Museum, and the Public Record Office. To all of these, as well as to the always helpful staff of the West Sussex County Council's Reference Library at Chichester, I offer appreciative thanks. Very many people have answered questions and provided personal information. In particular I should like to thank W. H. Fordham Esq. of Odsey for his long memory of the past, the Rev. G. Lant Carpenter, who greatly simplified the early stages of the work by lending me his full family tree, and the late Dr Ida Macalpine F.R.C.P.

Work of this nature is now almost impossible without financial help. I am greatly indebted to the Social Science Research Council for the Research Award which made it possible for me to trace and collate such widely scattered sources, and to Girton College, Cambridge, especially the Bursar and her Clerk, for administering the grant: I should also like to give my personal thanks to Sir Leon Radzinowicz. Finally, I should like to thank my husband for his professional help and criticism, and Kathleen Kahler who prepared the manuscript for the press.

Chichester 1976

CHILDREN OF THE STREETS

THE CHILDREN OF THE STREETS

'No sight so bad as that of a naughty child,' said 'black marble' Mr Brockle-hurst to small Jane Eyre. Here he spoke for his contemporaries, united in determination not to spare the rod and spoil the child. Naughtiness seldom went unpunished in nineteenth-century Britain, except by occasional unhoped-for good luck. Early in the century, children were taken to watch public hangings, and then were soundly whipped afterwards, it is said, 'that they might remember the example they had seen'.[1] *The History of the Fairchild Family*, published in 1818 by the popular evangelical authoress Mrs Sherwood, and in its fourteenth edition by 1840, tells how Mr Fairchild took his children, who had been quarrelling, to see the gibbet where the corpse of a man who had murdered his brother was hanged in chains. 'The face of the corpse was so shocking that the children could not bear to look at it,' and Mr Fairchild felt comfortably certain that they would remember this improving experience for the rest of their lives. Later in the century, a child of the middle classes, caught in an orchard or a jam cupboard, was liable to be whipped if a boy, or if a girl, sent to bed for the rest of the day, a punishment of loathed and lonely tedium. The new proprietary boarding schools, middle-class imitators of the seven original public schools, put their faith in corporal punishment. 'I was flogged every day of my life at school,' said Sir John Lawrence, hero of the Indian Mutiny, 'except one—and then I was flogged twice.'

Canon Woodard, in his Tractarian schools, favoured fasting, replaced after parental protests with a diet of bread and cheese. At Rugby and its numerous imitators, prefects had fagging and flogging powers; Shrewsbury claimed with simple pride that its headmaster Moss held the record, at eighty-seven lashes in one session. Because of the great distress it caused to parents, expulsion, with the appalling interview and the lonely journey in the cab to the nearest railway station, was the supreme public school punishment.[2] Private schools for both sexes resorted to bread and water; readers of *Dombey and Son* will remember that at Dr Blimber's this was served, in the interests of gentility, with a silver fork. Punishing girls, or rather young ladies, was not easy, but curious punitive rituals evolved, such as learning by heart a chapter selected at random from the Bible, or walking round the garden a given number of times with a bean bag on one's head. From all this we can see that punishment was a traditional Victorian institution; very few people questioned that it was right, proper, and for the child's own good. Yet, with all this, young people of the respectable classes enjoyed an essential security. Rules of conduct were laid down, faults and punishment contained within the

[1] Radzinowicz, L. *A History of English Criminal Law*, I, 176n.
[2] Bamford, T. W. *The Rise of the Public Schools*, 66–7.

safe, familiar framework of home and school. Severity carried with it love, and concern for the child's welfare; the trouble would be lived through, and the boy or girl grow up to a hopeful future.

The situation of the children in the streets was very different. These were the children of the gutter, sent out by their parents, as soon as their legs would carry them, to scavenge a living in the streets. One of Henry Mayhew's collaborators described them as they appeared in London in the 1860s. They wore 'an old greasy grey or black cap, with an old jacket rent at the elbows, and strips of the lining hanging down behind; others have an old, dirty pinafore, while others have petticoats.' Presumably these last were girls, though filthy matted hair, and red, chilblained feet were common to both sexes. In spite of neglect, he noticed, 'They are generally very acute and ready-witted and have a knowing twinkle in their eye.'[3] They begged, they sold matches, they sang ballads or turned cartwheels for money, they pilfered from open shops or market stalls, not daring to go home empty-handed. Some traded rags and old iron with the toffee-maker, whose handcart they followed, wrote an observer of the Manchester streets in the 1840s, 'as cats followed the cats meat man'.[4] The crimes of these small marauders, in a different social setting, would hardly have been considered crimes at all. In the 1850s, thirty-three juveniles were seen at a single sitting of a magistrate's court, charged with stealing sweets or fruit; the youngest of them was 6 years old. The eldest, a boy of 13, 'little more than skin and skeleton' had snatched a hunk of meat from a butcher's stall and was so famished that he crammed it into his mouth raw.[5]

These wild children belonged essentially to large towns and everyone agreed that their number grew prodigiously in the first half of the nineteenth century; it may well be, as we shall see, that the towns created them. The very speed of the change when the factory drew families from the village to fast-growing towns which could not provide houses, schools, clean water or safe streets, strained the structure of society to its utmost.[6] It was hardly surprising that the new population engulfed the old towns, when it increased in England and Wales from just over six million in 1751 to almost eighteen million by 1851. Children, one of the most vulnerable social groups, showed the strain most. Many had to fend for themselves from earliest childhood, and those who could not find work or friends, stole. A constant complaint up to the 1850s was the growing army of juvenile beggars and delinquents.

The background to these children's lives emerges from a multiplicity of documents, police court news, the papers of refuges and ragged schools, prison chaplains' reports. They reveal the dark underside of triumphant Victorian achievement, an abyss of poverty, neglect, brute ignorance and dangerous violence, into which most people, understandably, preferred not

[3] Quoted in Tobias, J. J. *Crime and Industrial Society in the Nineteenth Century*, 93.
[4] Neale, W. B. *Juvenile Delinquents*, contemporary pamphlet.
[5] Waugh, B. *The Gaol Cradle*, 21.
[6] The effect of industrial change on crime, especially juvenile crime, is fully examined in Tobias, J. J. *Crime and Industrial Society in the Nineteenth Century*.

to look. The chaplain of Preston Gaol summarized the history of nine boys, reconvicted to his prison in 1844, within a year of their previous sentence. 'Two of the six', he wrote, 'were orphans, a third had lost one parent by death and the other by desertion, the fourth was altogether neglected by his father and mother, the fifth and sixth had parents who encouraged them to steal. Only two of the nine have well-conducted parents.'[7] Good parents were sometimes forced by the struggle to make a living to neglect their children and went out leaving them locked in the house alone. 'When I was about the age of 8,' said a Lancashire girl, 'my father and mother worked in the mill, and left me to take care of the house and four children.' 'I've always left my children to theirselves,' said a woman in an agricultural labour gang, 'but, God be praised, nothing has happened to them.'[8] Small children left alone were all too often burnt or scalded to death.

Those who survived grew up in gross ignorance. Of twenty-five young prisoners at Preston in 1843, none could repeat the names of the months or say in what month Christmas or New Year's day fell. None of the girls knew the date or even the year, nor could any of them count to a hundred. The world must have seemed to them a strange, baffling place as they struggled to survive in it. 'Ah've heerd 'em say they gets iron out of t'ground,' said one sturdy sceptic, 'but ah never believe 'em.' A young girl construed 'Hallowed be thy name' rather touchingly in her own dialect, as 'Ah be wed i' thy name,' to the scandal of the chaplain. 'Can't tell how many week in the year,' said a Black Country boy, 'but I know there are eight pints in a gallon of ale.' 'No,' said Eliza Coats, aged 11, finally, 'I don't know where I shall go if I'm a bad girl.'[9]

The primitive resourcefulness of these children in fending for themselves was often amazing. Gangs of small children were sent out into the streets to sell watercress, like Mayhew's famous watercress girl, or bundles of firewood, and were told they must bring home a set sum. Manchester children stole pet dogs, hens from roosts, pigeons from lofts and washing from clothes-lines.[10] In ports like Liverpool or Bristol, stealing from the docks was the quickest way, and numbers of children supported themselves by this alone. The Bristol police, first established in 1836, found that nothing came amiss to little boys of 6 and 7, bits of old iron, copper, brass, ropes left lying on the quays, even doormats left out on the front steps of houses while the owner swept inside. At Liverpool they conducted their own market in the cellars of empty houses, where they sold their swag to scrap-merchants and ran off for more. Others robbed drunken people who fell unconscious in the streets, or stole lead and gas-pipes from housing sites. Two boys who appeared in a London police court, lived alone in the garret of a tall, dingy house. They were visited once a month by a woman who paid the rent and may have been their mother; she made her living 'no one knew how'. The boys did quite

[7] Clay, W. L. *The Prison Chaplain*, 445.
[8] Briggs, T. *An Enquiry into the extent and causes of Juvenile Depravity*, 61.
[9] *Ibid.*
[10] Neale, W. B. *Juvenile Delinquents passim.*

well by picking up lumps of coal from the Thames mud at low water, but when in a hard winter the river froze over, the elder stole from a coal-yard, and was caught.[11] They were ragged, dirty and defiant, never washed unless they were sent to gaol. Such children were described by Dickens in *Household Words*. 'They hop about like wild birds, pilfering the crumbs which fall from the table of the country's wealth.' They had no more idea of crime than the blackbirds among the currant bushes. 'They certainly have no more idea of what we call justice,' he added, 'than blackbirds have of nets, scarecrows and guns.'

Those who did not blame the children agreed to blame their parents. The poor lived, wrote a magistrate, in a pattern of shifting concubinage, in which violent quarrels were a commonplace, and children often found themselves unwanted by a new parent. The same phrases recur again and again in their histories. 'Father gets drunk every Saturday night,' said J.C., aged 16, 'then he beats mother and me, because I'm a *chance child*.' 'I never knew I had a mother,' said J.B., aged 14, 'until I got wages at the factory. Then she came and fetched me from the old woman that kept me.' A., aged 14, had been three times in Liverpool Gaol in twelve months; 'his father lives with a woman who is always beating him.' H., three years older, had been in prison seven times. 'Father alive, a boiler-maker, but stepmother beat him, so he ran away from home.'[12] The schoolmaster at Preston Gaol took down an extraordinary tale from a boy of 11, serving eighteen months for stealing money from a shop. His father, a railway porter, drank heavily. 'One night he came home very drunk when James and I were in bed; he made us get up and said he would take us to the canal and drown us. He asked my stepmother for our shoes, but she said, "If you're going to drown them, you might as well leave the shoes for Johnny." He threw me into the canal a good way, but a boatman jumped in with his clothes on and got me out. Then the boatman took out his knife and said to father, "If you don't let them alone, I'll stick you." ' This sounded so wild, that the prison officials made inquiries, but neighbours confirmed the boy's story.[13] The respectable classes, hearing such stories, blamed the improvidence, drunkenness or immorality of the poor. Many people felt strong conscientious objections to free schools or free meals for these children, as 'unjust to the self-denying and industrious poor', encouraging parental neglect, or even 'interfering with the Universal Law of Providence'.[14] Those who knew these families best, however, condemned them least. The mothers especially were often worn out by malnutrition and incessant child-bearing. 'Occasionally they take three penn'orth of gin,' wrote the founder of the Society for the Prevention of Cruelty to Children. 'On the whole, however, they seem quiet women, willing to let dirt, indecency and disease have their tyrannical way.'

These children had homes, however wretched: but there was another class

---

[11] Waugh, B. *The Gaol Cradle*, 18–19.
[12] Clay, W. L. *The Prison Chaplain*, 80–1.
[13] Carpenter, M. *Juvenile Delinquents*, 60.
[14] Carpenter, M. *Reformatory Schools*, 40–2.

of child in even greater danger of delinquency. These were the children of the vagrants who conceived and bore families of children in common lodging-houses. In one of these, a room eighteen feet by ten housed twenty-seven adults of both sexes, thirty-one children and numerous dogs. The lodgers of necessity spent much of the day in public houses, where the children were dragged around by their mothers, dirty, poorly clad, half-starved and kept quiet with sips of beer or gin. A young lodging-house girl at Bristol had sixty-one convictions for drunkenness by the age of 16. Other children became addicted to what was euphemistically called 'a drop of quietness'. The Registrar General's report for 1842 records thirty-nine child deaths from overdose of opium drops. There was no opportunity to wash, or change clothing; whole families' heads, clothes and bodies were perpetually verminous. The children suffered most in wet weather, when they were forced to come in and lie down in soaking clothes. Many children of course died of rheumatic fever or pneumonia; but those who survived and grew up in common lodging-houses, were, in the opinion of a city missionary, 'practically irreclaimable'.[15]

The children who had the threepence to pay for a lodging-house bed were either with their parents or resourceful enough to fend for themselves. Others walked about the streets at night, lying under railway arches, in cellars or church porches or under tarpaulins in the docks. Lord Brougham, inquiring into the condition of these children in 1847, was scandalized to hear of a boy of 10, 'so wicked' that he actually preferred staying in prison to going out.[16] Another boy is quoted as saying, when he left prison: 'It's the most comfortable crib as ever I was in. I wish I'd a got three months instead o' three weeks.' This was commonly called 'juvenile depravity'; it might be called the instinct of survival.

Vagrants made their living largely by begging, and here of course children were an asset. A pretty, pale, woebegone infant, still better a sickly or crippled child was a valuable property; such children were hired by the week, or sometimes bought outright. Four little girls, sent out in the blackest midwinter in cotton frocks and nearly frozen to death in the streets of St Pancras, were reported to have kept a couple, possibly their parents, in comfortable idleness. Railway stations in all big towns were infested with tiny pestering urchins, plucking at the sleeves or scuffling under the feet of passers by. They were seen to be sought out by bedraggled women, who collected their takings at regular intervals.[17] Little girls were considered more appealing than boys, and if possible, were in greater danger. A little girl of 9, arrested for theft in Salford in the 1840s was found to be already infected with venereal disease. Between the ages of 9 and 13 this child earned her living as a juvenile prostitute and during that period she was imprisoned thirty times.[18] Another girl, Anne M., who did not know how old she was, was admitted to a

[15] Bullar, E. P. *Report to the Female Aid Society*, pamphlet, n.d.
[16] Carpenter, M. *Reformatory Schools*, 215.
[17] Chesney, K. *The Victorian Underworld*, 203–5.
[18] Neale, W. B. *Juvenile Delinquents*, 43.

refuge in Ipswich in 1852. She had been told her mother died when she was
five days old, but not who her father was. The grandmother who brought her
up died when she was about 12, leaving her homeless and destitute; from that
time she had supported herself by prostitution. 'She had sometimes slept in
lodging houses, at other times in stables, pigsties and sand holes. When
recommended to the institution,' reported the matron, 'she was one heap of
rags and disease.'[19] The sentimental tradition was that most prostitutes were
girls who had been seduced, 'ruined', and betrayed. In reality this was a
much less common cause than sheer need. Out of 550 penitentiary cases, 423
were dismissed servant-girls, unable to get another respectable job from lack
of references.[20]

So far we have considered the children of the unrespectable poor and the
children of vagrants, who became delinquents casually, from need or by
accident. There was a third class of children who were professional criminals
from an early age by heredity and training. These were taught and operated
in gangs, by specialists, known to the trade as 'kidsmen'. Some of these were
genial rogues, like the Professor of Fobology described by a London ragged
schoolmaster. He taught children to 'dip' watches from an old pair of trousers
hung from the ceiling, and rewarded promising pupils with a hilarious mock
trial, in which he acted as judge. On special occasions he would take the
children round to the nearest pub for a school treat of beer and skittles.
Women specialized in training girl pickpockets; one was known to have
trained at least fifty, who travelled from place to place in first-class carriages
and lived at inns or railway hotels.[21] Once trained, the little professionals
were neatly and decorously dressed and sent out to churches, big shops or
out-door gatherings, from a revivalist rally to a race meeting. Mr Rushton,
the Liverpool Stipendiary Magistrate, regretted that he had no legal power to
remove an intelligent boy of 10 from the mother, 'a convicted thief, who had
trained the child to dextrous picking of pockets. He would have turned out a
clever, useful man; now he will turn out a clever thief.'[22] Skilled child pick-
pockets were so valuable, that highly-feed counsel were sometimes retained
to defend them in court. The Recorder of Birmingham, where children stole
in the streets and from small metal or jewellery workshops, believed manual
labour was the most effective punishment, since it destroyed for ever the
sneak-thief's delicacy of touch.[23]

All these children, the street urchins, the vagrants, and the little gangsters,
were liable to be taken up by the police and brought before the magistrates
on a variety of charges. By 1850 there was still no specific law covering youthful offenders and no agreed policy towards them. There were few specialized
institutions for children. Isolated parishes had founded 'schools of industry'
for spinning or stocking-knitting. A Refuge for the Destitute at Hoxton

[19] *Report of the Ipswich Ragged School for 1852.*
[20] Waugh, B. *The Gaol Cradle,* 151.
[21] Carpenter, M. *Our Convicts,* II, 57.
[22] Carpenter, M. *Reformatory Schools,* 252-3, quoting from E. Rushton, *A Letter upon Juvenile Crime,* 1850.
[23] Hill, M. D. *Draft Report on the Principles of Punishment* 1847.

housed eighty juvenile offenders in a separate boys' section. In 1825 the hulk of the frigate *Euraylus* had been moored off Chatham, to receive up to four hundred boys under 16, some so young that they could hardly put on their own clothes. Life between decks became a hell of bullying and filth. 'A floating Bastille,' wrote Captain Brenton, late of the Royal Navy, 'children in iron cages who should have been in a nursery garden;—children pining in misery where the stench was intolerable.' Boys burnt themselves with red-hot buttons or broke their own arms to be sent to the Juvenile Convict Hospital.[24] The *Euraylus* was finally abandoned in 1846. Captain Brenton himself established voluntary asylums for boys and girls, but his Children's Friend Society was dissolved soon after his death for lack of funds. The Warwickshire magistrates maintained a small voluntary asylum at Stretton-on-Dunsmore, supported by local subscription, but it could never house more than thirty boys, and made no provision for girls.

Girls might be sent to the Magdalen Hospital founded in London by Jonas Hanway in 1758. Boys might be sent to the Marine Society for training under sail, or to the Philanthropic Society's Farm School at Redhill, to be trained to 'habits of cleanliness, industry and order'. This, the first reformatory school, had been founded in 1788 'for the protection of poor children, the offspring of convicted felons, and for the reformation of children who have themselves been engaged in criminal practises'. Children in Manchester or Liverpool or in Scottish cities might be sent to a new Industrial School, on the model founded by Sheriff Watson of Aberdeen in 1841. Here, he wrote, 'we have seventy-five children in process of cleansing, scrubbing, dressing and feeding', while they were taught a useful trade. These schools had, however, no legal authority to detain pupils. Selected boy prisoners might be sent to the Juvenile Prison at Parkhurst opened in 1838, for their 'effective punishment and timely reformation'. This patchwork of institutions dealt with only a handful of the boys and girls convicted by the courts.[25] The vast majority were sent, as they always had been, to county and borough gaols. The usual pattern was one of repeated short imprisonments. The Liverpool Stipendiary described a boy's record. 'At the age of fourteen, he has been twenty-four times in custody, he has been five times discharged, twice imprisoned for fourteen days, once for one month, once for two months, six times for three months . . . and twice whipped.'[26] His little brothers had been arrested, one eight times and the other six. All three would probably end by being transported.

In 1847 a Select Committee of the House of Lords on Juvenile Offenders heard what became of children in prison. In a given year, 11,000 young people between the ages of 10 and 20 would be in prison at any time, and of these 1,274 were less than 12 years old. On arrival, these children were subjected to an utterly impersonal, inflexible routine: name, age, height,

[24] Pinchbeck, I. and Hewitt, M. *Children in English Society*, II, 452–5, quoting from E. P. Brenton, *Observations on the Training and Education of the Children of Great Britain*.
[25] Young, A. F. and Ashton, E. T. *British Social Work in the Nineteenth Century*, 164–6.
[26] Rushton, E. *A Letter upon Juvenile Crime*, 7.

complexion, occupation noted, bathed, head shaven, stiff canvas prison clothes issued, locked in cell. Almost all witnesses agreed that prison harmed children. 'I am prepared to say', said Captain W. J. Williams, a Prison Inspector, 'that whenever a boy goes into prison he can never come out, in point of feeling, the same individual again.' Through their association with older prisoners the children, as everyone realized, were recruited for theft or prostitution. When discharged, the brand of a prison sentence cut off a boy or girl from hope of honest work. The Governor of Edinburgh Gaol agreed that 'the fact that a boy has been imprisoned goes far to ruin him for life'. The Committee was shocked to learn of sexual dangers to young prisoners. A returned convict, who had served thirty years in different penal settlements, spoke of assaults on boys, 'there being so great a number of men in the barrack room at night; they were not separated and the boys are among them.' A member protested that there should be 'a number of constables in the room'. 'In a penal settlement', said the convict shortly, 'it would not be safe to have constables there.' He added, 'I have seen men cut up in the barracks as you would cut up meat.' Conditions in England were equally damaging. At Newgate, the Governor admitted, 400 boys were locked into adult wards at five and unlocked at seven next morning. In winter they spent fourteen hours without lights, unsupervised among male convicts.

Solitary confinement, the penal panacea of the utilitarians, had an alarming effect upon children. Captain Williams described boys in close separate confinement at Wakefield. They suffered from 'debility and contracture of the joints', and if left became 'sluggish and feeble-minded'. He had ordered leap-frog and games for their health.[27] Elsewhere, the chaplain of Bath Gaol described a small boy, who, when locked in his cell, 'threw himself on the ground and beat his head against the iron grating of the wall.' His brother, a boy of 14, accustomed to lead their blind father about at fairs and markets peddling bootlaces, alarmed the prison doctor by his incessant nervous movements and his dilated staring eyes while in confinement. The chaplain of Preston Gaol believed separate confinement was less corrupting to children than the coarse brutality of crowded prison yards, but even he admitted that 'an unfortunate boy of fourteen showed great fear and excitability, when the usual sentence of twenty-eight days solitary confinement and a whipping had to be inflicted. His irritability became so excessive as to call for circumspection in this treatment.'

Many witnesses before this Committee thought corporal punishment the answer, though one revealingly admitted that it might be 'overdone by an ardent gaoler'. The Governor of Lancaster Gaol thought 'whipping a very satisfactory punishment for a boy of ten caught robbing an orchard'. The chaplain of Newgate thought it 'highly salutary as a punishment which boys dread very much'; and the Governor of Coldbath Fields was even more specific; he suggested 'for a trifling offence a dozen stripes with a birch rod'. A Middlesex magistrate proposed 'a whipping post at every police court'. The most enthusiastic advocate of flogging was Sergeant Adams of Middlesex

[27] *Parliamentary Papers*, 1847, xxiv, 1, 461.

Sessions, who described boys he had sentenced 'upon their knees blubbering and praying not to be flogged with a birch rod'. 'I often sentence a child to a month's imprisonment, and to be well whipped at the end of the first fortnight, so as to keep the terror in his mind for a fortnight; but,' concluded the Sergeant in honest bewilderment, 'I find these children continually coming again.' It is clear that whatever caused juvenile delinquency, it was not lack of punishment, yet no one seemed able to suggest any alternative. The report of the House of Lords' Committee reflected this impasse. It recorded an agreement that 'the contamination of gaols may often prove fatal and must always be harmful to boys committed for a first offence'; but as an alternative punishment it could only recommend transportation 'since it has terrors for offenders which none other short of death possess', together with 'a moderate use of corporal punishment'.[28]

Many charitable members of the public, clergy, the magistrates, the prison authorities themselves sincerely desired to rescue the children whom they saw drifting helplessly to a life of crime. Dickens, near as always to his public, provides a sensitive barometer of public opinion. Later, as will appear, his attitude hardened, but at this time, even his cautious self-censorship in the interest of family reading allowed him to show how helpless children were among the dregs of life. As an example of a homeless destitute child, he took the figure of Poor Jo from an actual crossing-sweeper, called to give evidence in a trial at the Guildhall in 1850.[29] The boy, George Ruby, 'appeared about fourteen'. He was asked, 'Do you know what an oath is? 'No.' 'Do you ever say your prayers?' 'No.' 'Do you know what prayers are?' 'No.' 'Do you know what God is?' 'No.' 'What do you know?' 'I knows how to sweep the crossings.' This boy becomes Jo. 'Here's the boy, gentlemen! Here he is, very muddy, very hoarse, very ragged,' from the 'black, dilapidated street', the 'crazy houses' let out in lodgings, the fever and stench of Tom-all-Alone's. The professional thieves are shown when innocent Oliver Twist joins a gang of pickpockets; the Artful Dodger, with his 'little, sharp, ugly eyes' and the boys who lounge around in Fagin's kitchen, 'four or five boys, none older than the Dodger, smoking long, clay pipes and drinking spirits with the air of middle-aged men'. The description of their learning to lift handkerchiefs from Fagin's pocket again comes from a policeman's evidence in court. As a popular novelist, writing for the family circle, Dickens was careful to rescue Oliver in the nick of time; even poor Jo died learning the Lord's Prayer, while young lady readers wept profusely. In real life, as everybody must have known, the boys were much more likely to become like the figure which started up from the gravestones at the beginning of *Great Expectations*: 'A fearful man, all in coarse grey, with a great iron on his leg', who 'limped and shivered and glared and growled' as he threatened to cut Pip's throat— Magwitch, the escaped convict. These nightmare figures made such a strong

---

[28] *Ibid.*, xxiv xxv, 1, 461.
[29] House, H. *The Dickens World*, 2nd ed., 32–3. The trial was printed in *The Household Narrative*, the monthly supplement to *Household Words*, which contained details of crime and police court cases.

appeal to Dickens's public, precisely because they reflected fears and anxieties already present in the common reader's mind.

These destitute and criminal children preyed on the public conscience. Education for children convicted by the courts came twenty-five years before the Act of 1870, which marks the beginning of modern State education. The Victorian conscience was most sensitive to moral danger, in society as in private life. The crisis of the 1840s made this sensitivity acute. The decade was called 'the hungry forties', with misery, hunger and filth the labourer's common lot. Edwin Chadwick, acting as a Poor Law Commissioner, found living conditions worse than in the unreformed prisons of the 1770s, attacked by John Howard. 'More filth, worse physical suffering and moral disorder than Howard describes', he wrote in 1846, 'are to be found among the cellar populations of the working people of Liverpool, Manchester or Leeds, and in large portions of the Metropolis.' The Church of England had formerly been inclined to leave this raw industrial proletariat to the celebrated conscience of the Nonconformists, but by the 1840s the spirit of evangelicalism had worked a profound change in the established clergy. They were no longer altogether at ease shooting over their own acres of glebe, or making themselves agreeable to young women at evening parties, in the manner of Jane Austen's heroes. Conscience drove them, and their middle-class congregations, into an increasing concern with the evils of the world. A wave of earnestness spread over the country. Pious and respectable citizens put aside gambling, the playhouse and brutal sports, along with their embroidered waistcoats; now, black cloth-coated, they turned to the condition of the poor. Their watchword, 'Every hour and every shilling for God', often meant a practical attack on social problems.

Less generous but equally pressing was the fear of revolution and 'the mob'. The national convention of the Chartist Movement, gathered at Westminster in 1839 with its monster petition for universal male, though not female, suffrage, had been an alarming spectacle. Pamphlets were sold in the streets on the best methods of building barricades, and the apprehensive smelt a whiff of revolutionary gunpowder in the air. During the 1840s, a decade of revolutions throughout Europe, the Chartists, though they lost the support of many solid working men, became increasingly violent in tone, reflecting the desperate condition of the poor. In 1848, when the Chartists marched to present their last abortive petition to Parliament, middle-class citizens were sufficiently alarmed to exchange their umbrellas for bayonets and turn out in their thousands as special constables.

The spirit of religious concern and political alarm prevented the public from forgetting the criminal classes. Their concern increased to dismay, as the wave of Irish immigrants, fleeing from the potato blight of 1845–6, began to arrive in overcrowded, bug-infested ships at every west coast seaport. The agonies of these starving, filthy and bewildered peasants, dumped by the shipload to survive as best they could in British slums, have been fully chronicled.[30] The hostility and hate they aroused in the English were

[30] Woodham Smith, C. *The Great Hunger*, Ch. 13.

frightening; on their ragged and verminous shoulders were unloaded all the social ills of an unregulated industrial revolution. The Irish brought no skills; it was not the custom in Ireland for a man to learn a trade, and once their strength for hard manual labour had been undermined by starvation they were almost unemployable. From bewilderment and misery in a strange land, they took refuge in drink, the traditional 'Irish disease'. Moreover, they bore children at an alarming rate, who grew up to run the streets, beg and pilfer. 'Wherever these abject, deplorably ignorant creatures colonize,' wrote a Medical Officer of Health in the Black Country, 'dirt, disease and misery are sure to follow.' To the English middle classes, the poor Irish represented a bottomless reservoir of crime.

One single event brought the British public finally face to face with the destitute and delinquent children in their midst. This was the end of transportation for convicts, largely suspended in 1846 and finally abolished in 1852. The reason was the refusal of the colonies, after experience since 1788, to serve any longer as dumping grounds for criminals from home. The Home Secretary addressed a circular letter to all colonial governments, obligingly offering them supplies of ticket-of-leave men free of charge, but no colony would receive this doubtful blessing. The appearance of a convict ship at the Cape of Good Hope almost provoked a revolt in the colony. Criminals could no longer be loaded into prison hulks, and shipped out of sight and out of mind. Penal reform now became one of the burning questions of the day. Controversy filled columns of newsprint and volumes of tracts. Laden with Blue Books, crammed with dubious statistics, overflowing with theories, an army of amateur reformers addressed itself to the subject of crime. The silent workshop, the solitary cell, hanging, flogging, the treadmill, hard labour, low diet and the learning by heart of biblical texts, all had their devotees. Their dogmatic assurance, their overbearing zeal, their crudely biased use of statistics and their self-righteous acrimony make wearisome reading now. Yet on one point all were agreed. If criminals could ever be reclaimed, it was in childhood. However oddly described, as 'perishing juveniles', 'depraved youth' or even 'infant felons', children formed the first target for attack.

All this formed the background to the work of Mary Carpenter, the Bristol minister's daughter, who, after years as a schoolmistress, became in her middle-age a national authority on children in need. To all outward appearances, she was that quintessential Victorian figure, the formidable spinster given to good works. Nothing in her prim appearance suggested the fiery spirit within. Mary Carpenter's family believed that she was universally beloved, and that the spread of ragged, industrial and reformatory schools represented the triumph of her ideas. The reality was perhaps almost the opposite. Mary Carpenter was disliked, not without reason, in official circles. Her ideas ran directly counter to some of the most cherished beliefs of the age, with its insistence on individual responsibility and self-help. In some ways she was the first of the moderns; for she refused to see child offenders except as part of the great, ragged army of children in need. 'I have a great objection to calling them even semi-criminal,' she said, 'because the word has a moral meaning. I consider the condition they are in as that of *extreme neglect*.' Against the whole tide of the times, she held society itself responsible for them. 'If Society leaves them knowingly in the state of utter degradation in which they are,' she wrote, 'then I think it absolutely owes them reparation, far more than they could be said to owe reparation to it.'

These ideas are now unexceptionable. It is hard to realize the suspicion and ridicule they once aroused, or the bitterness with which this proud, passionate woman defended them. For the sake of children in need, Mary Carpenter sacrificed intellectual interests, a real talent for painting, all the minor pleasures of life; for their sake she lived very much alone. Yet the radicalism of one century becomes the accepted wisdom of the next, and now, wherever the needs of deprived children are recognized, or even sometimes met, one may imagine a ghost, umbrella and Blue Book in hand, eye and tongue devastatingly sharp, but heart tender—the approving ghost of Mary Carpenter.

PART ONE

DR CARPENTER'S DAUGHTER

I

FATHER AND DAUGHTER
1807-1820

'The meeting house of Protestant Dissenters', says Edward's Bristol Guide of 1801, 'is a large, elegant and costly place of worship.' The rich and influential Unitarian congregation of the city had rebuilt it at their own expense a few years earlier, a large square stone building with classical façade and portico. It still stands, darkened by smoke, forlorn and shabby, yet dignified, a monument to hopes of human perfectability, among the car-parks and office-blocks of the city's new commercial centre. Inside, it is still and deserted, the roar of traffic shut out. The square hall is lofty, with coffered ceiling and a severe frieze in the Greek key pattern; six tall Palladian windows let in the clear light; a temple of reason. Shafts of sunlight fall through the emptiness. Yet when the three galleries and the rows of box pews were filled, a thousand people could hear the preacher. The centre of the church, the meeting point for all eyes, is the pulpit on its lofty fluted plinth; panelled and canopied in gleaming mahogany it stands, a master cabinet-maker's tribute to the preacher's art.

In 1820 Lewin's Mead Meeting was always crowded for the sermons of the universally admired preacher, Dr Lant Carpenter, co-minister of the congregation. Regular worshippers would never miss a Sunday morning or evening, while visitors came from distant parts of the country, and even from abroad, to hear sermons so lucid, so learned, so remarkably long, delivered in a voice of such sweetness that it melted young and old alike. All eyes were fixed on the frail figure, in minister's black coat and white stock, framed by the dark canopy; all ears were attentive to the soft, silvery voice, which could yet carry with such thrilling intensity to the furthest corners of the gallery. Reading accounts of these sermons a hundred and fifty years later, it seems doubtful whether some members of the congregation were there to worship God or Dr Carpenter.

The minister's power was particularly spell-binding over young people. Harriet Martineau, as an elderly literary celebrity, remembered her girlhood visits to an aunt in Bristol, nearly sixty years before. One memory dominated all the others. 'There was a great furore among the Bristol Unitarians at that time,' she wrote, 'about Dr Carpenter who had recently become their pastor. ... I returned home raving about my pastor and teacher, with his instructions burnt in upon my heart and conscience.' As a direct result of her enthusiasm, her brother James was sent to the private school Dr Carpenter kept in Bristol. He in turn took his place amongst the enthralled listeners in the meeting house. Looking back in adult life on the crowded Sunday scene, James Martineau, a sensitive observer, found one figure especially clear in his mind. The minister's family pew was set at right angles to the congregation, close under the lofty pulpit. There, at the head of the six Carpenter children, he saw a strange little figure, pale, stiff and un-childlike, intelligent and profoundly serious. It was the minister's eldest daughter, Mary Carpenter, then 12 years old. She sat very quietly, gazing up at her father in the pulpit set so high above her head, 'lost to herself and all about her', wrote Martineau, 'in the pieties of that most winning voice'.[1]

As the years passed James Martineau, though he continued to love Dr Carpenter, moved far beyond him in religious thought. Harriet Martineau, his deaf, shy, awkward sister, grew into a middle-aged agnostic, who looked back on her youthful adoration of the minister with all the revulsion of disappointed love. She had been, she wrote, 'desperately and abominably superstitious. Dr Carpenter was a very earnest pietist; superficial in his knowledge, scanty in ability, narrow in his conceptions and thoroughly priestly in his temper.'[2] He was, she added sourly, just the man to be spoilt by 'the Pastor-Worship of his doting congregation'.

Miss Martineau waited fifty-nine years to put this condemnation on paper, and with good reason. No one would have dared to publish it while the Pastor's daughter, Mary Carpenter, was still alive. Her childhood fixed her character and beliefs for ever. The loss of faith, so marked in Harriet Martineau and many of their contemporaries, never touched her. The heart and centre of Mary Carpenter's work remained always her adoration for her father and his God. In the year of her death, when she was 70 years old, and an internationally famous authority, she went to lecture in the United States. Her host in Boston wrote in wonder. 'Old as she was to me, she used to give me the feeling that I was always talking with *someone's daughter*, her words had so much filial reference in them.' The equivocal, enigmatic figure of Lant Carpenter stands, for better or worse, at the centre of his daughter's achievement.

The Carpenters belonged to the aristocracy of English Puritanism. Both parents' families came from what was known as 'the old Dissenting Gentry', a tenacious cousinage of high principle and narrow rectitude. 'To them chiefly', wrote a member of this class with pride, 'we owe our liberty of thought'.[3] Both families had belonged in the Civil War period to Puritan congregations. When Charles II was restored to his father's throne, the Church of England, on the principle of 'no bishop no king', was restored with him. From 1662 an Act of Uniformity compelled all clergy to use the Church of England prayer book and no other. More than fifteen hundred clergy, who could not bring themselves in conscience to accept this, left their parishes.[4] A series of laws laid harsh penalties on Nonconformists, who were barred from the universities, the services and all public or civic office. They endured their disabilities with courage for conscience's sake, arguing that 'we ought to obey God rather

---

[1] *Life and Work*, 10.   [2] Martineau, H. *Autobiography*, 73.
[3] *The Christian Reformer*, 1856, XII, 145.
[4] Moorman J. R. H. *A History of the Church in England*, 252.

than man' and turning their abilities, often most profitably, to business and trade.

The eighteenth-century attitude to religious differences was tolerant and easy-going; among various congregations, Presbyterian, Baptist, Congregationalist, even Anglican, isolated individuals silently pursued their religious inquiries. The most radical among them, the extreme left-wing of belief, defied the law which made official worship of the Trinity compulsory. They returned to a belief known, they claimed, since Apostolic times and never wholly extinguished, that Jesus was in every respect a fully human being, and that following his example religious worship 'is properly to be addressed only to the one true God, the Father'. The first public meeting-house of these Unitarians was opened at Essex Street, London, in 1774. By 1810 there were at least twenty Unitarian congregations, and the number rapidly grew, although in Britain they never achieved the sweeping success that they enjoyed in New England, which caused the remark that Unitarians believed in the fatherhood of God, the brotherhood of man and the neighbourhood of Boston. To this church, an advanced minority of a minority, the Carpenters belonged. They were vowed to tolerance, but were socially and intellectually exclusive. High-mindedness, protest and reform were bred in their bones.

Lant Carpenter's ancestors owned and farmed a small estate called The Woodrow, near Bromsgrove, where they also served as dissenting ministers. His grandfather was mayor of Coventry, and his father a carpet manufacturer at Kidderminster. Lant was the youngest of nine children, and while he was still quite small his father's business failed. The household broke up and the family moved away, but Lant was left behind and handed over for adoption to Nicholas Pearsall, a distant relation of his mother's who had developed strong Unitarian views. Mr Pearsall was well-off, childless and wanted a son whom he could educate to become a Unitarian minister. This arrangement, so shattering to the entire world of a small child, was considered perfectly acceptable at the time, and was not particularly unusual. Elizabeth Fry's numerous children were distributed among various relations, and Richard Cobden was sent away for five years to an appalling Yorkshire boarding school, in each case as a result of business failures at home. No one seems to have doubted that the arrangement was in small Lant Carpenter's best interests. The Carpenter parents lived on for many years, the mother an old lady of forceful character, clinging to her self-respect in poverty and proudly polishing a silver teapot, the relic of more prosperous days. The father lived on until 1839, only a year before Lant himself died. Yet the child seems to have seen very little of them. For affection he depended on the kindness of a woman servant, until he was sent to boarding school. This was the excellent Dissenting Academy at Northampton, where the tutor, John Hersey, taught that 'Freedom of inquiry on all subjects is the birthright and glory of a rational being'.[5] Lant was an intelligent boy, but delicate, highly

---

[5] McLachlan, H. *The Unitarian Tradition*, 85.

sensitive and over-conscientious; the shock of his early loss affected him all his life.

At the same time, his talents were exceptional. At school he showed a gift for science and a strong wish to study medicine, but from sense of obligation to his guardian, entered Glasgow University, to read for the Unitarian ministry. Almost at once he suffered an attack of rheumatic fever, accompanied by 'despondency. During my illness.' he confessed, 'I often could not help thinking Christianity false,' and he ever after insisted on the need for 'a sound intellectual foundation'[6]. At Glasgow, Lant was an outstanding student, on whom the university later conferred an honorary Ll.D. After graduating he gave tuition in a wide range of subjects: 'Instruction in the Latin and Greek Languages, History, Geography, English Grammar and Composition, the Mathematics and the Elements of Natural Philosophy.'[7] In 1805 he was called to the duties of minister at George's Meeting, Exeter. With this security, he felt able to offer marriage to Anna Penn, whom he had known since childhood. Her background was very like his own, although she met the trials of life more forcefully. Her father died early, leaving his wife and daughters in poverty. Mrs Penn, who came from a family of ministers, and bore the Puritan Christian name of Budget, trained her daughters as governesses; a family friend described 'a youth of many trials, in which the sisters maintained themselves by tuition'.[8] Anna was conditioned to habits of hard work and rigid self-denial, which she passed on to her own children. No one ever heard her complain. It was this courage in hardship which won Lant's love, when he visited the frugal but spotless and orderly household of the Penns. The young couple were married on Christmas Day 1805, and at once took seven pupils as boarders into their own house. Lant quickly learnt to rely on his young wife's strong character, and her ability to create around him the calm, perfectly ordered household that was essential to his peace of mind. His health was not good, and though an excellent teacher, he found the racket and muddle of active boys, added to parish duties, exhausting, and after two years he suffered a complete loss of voice, which prevented him from preaching for months. He was convinced he had consumption, although the family doctor assured him 'his case was nervous'. In these somewhat ominous circumstances, on 3rd April 1807, Lant and Anna's first child was born. She was not christened, since her father considered the rite of baptism superstitious, but was simply called by the name Mary.

Even as a small child, Mary had an extraordinary memory and a strong character. She could remember being driven in a chaise up St David's Hill in Exeter when she was only sixteen months old. Anna noticed that as soon as she could walk, the baby 'had her father's sense of order and busied herself a good deal putting things in their places'. When Mary was eighteen months old, her sister, another Anna, was born. The young mother noticed how

[6] Carpenter, R. L. *Memoir of Lant Carpenter*, 34.
[7] Reid, J. *My Life of Walter Reid of Liverpool*, c. 1860. MS.
[8] *The Christian Reformer*, 1856, III, 448.

determinedly Mary held her own against this competition. 'The little sweet lamb would engage all my attention,' she wrote, 'did not the young doctor, with her funny ways and curious speeches make me attend to her whether I will or not. You may wonder at my giving her that name, but she gave it herself.' She explained that the child was first called Mary, then Miss Mary; next she insisted on Miss Carpenter, then firmly told their nursemaid, 'No Miss Carpenter!' 'What am I to call you then?' '*Dr* Carpenter!'[9] The nickname stuck, for Mary, as she grew older almost comically resembled her father. Dr Carpenter recovered from his illness and threw himself with his old enthusiasm into teaching, preaching, and a variety of good causes, all of the most advanced and liberal description. 'All Dr Carpenter's opinions,' noted a friend, 'were in favour of freedom and reform.'

It was hard for Mary to secure the notice she longed for, from this high-minded parent. His attentions had to be shared with the pupils who lived in the house, and a growing family of brothers and sisters. Anna was born in 1808, Susan in 1811, William in 1813, Russell Lant in 1816 and Philip, the youngest, in 1819.[10] Dr Carpenter needed quiet for his work; he got up long before the rest of the family for 'perfect stillness'; his study was guarded by his wife and kept 'sacred from all intrusion', while on principle he treated his own children and his pupils exactly alike, allowing 'no special favours'.[11] Mary learnt that she was never allowed to demand her father's attention; her only hope was to deserve it. To win his praise needed considerable effort. While Mary was still under 5, Lant took her and her baby sister Anna into a field of new-mown hay. Anna, whose temperament declared itself from the first as gay, affectionate and wholly feminine, rolled and tumbled among the haycocks, but Mary demanded to help the haymakers at their work. 'I want to be useful! I want to be useful!' she begged, until her father cut her a forked stick from the hedge to use as a toy rake. The parents were satisfied at this evidence of early training, but there is something pathetic in the little girl's anxious longing for approval.

Indeed the early upbringing of Mary Carpenter was a rigorous moral steeplechase. During her childhood her father was composing a book on the principles of education, and, as the eldest child, she was the natural testing-ground for all his theories. These Lant Carpenter published in 1817, with two other clerical schoolmasters, W. Shepherd and J. Joyce, under the title *Systematic Education*. Since individual chapters are signed with their authors' initials, it is possible to reconstruct the methods he used to mould the character of this most sensitive and intelligent child. Like James Mill, who was educating his small son John Stuart at exactly the same time, Lant Carpenter was strongly influenced by Hartley's *Observations on Man*. Indeed he later gave it to Mary as an improving 21st birthday present. Hartley attempted to find a physiological basis for the association of ideas, and suggested that 'vibrations' in the nerve fibres set up permanent connections between

[9] *Life and Work*, 2.
[10] Family tree in the possession of the Rev. G. Lant Carpenter.
[11] Carpenter, R. L. *Memoir of Lant Carpenter*, 490.

different centres in the brain. From this followed the Utilitarian theory of learning, in which sensations and ideas were mechanically linked. As John Stuart Mill bitterly expressed it, the child was regarded as 'an intellectual machine set to grind certain tunes'. It followed that the process of education could not start too early. Dr Carpenter noted 'the vast importance of early impressions, of early attention to the early culture of habits and dispositions'. So, just as John Stuart Mill could write, 'I have no remembrance of the time when I began to learn Greek. I have been told it was when I was three years old,' little Mary Carpenter could not remember the beginning of her training in self-sacrifice. At $3\frac{1}{2}$ she preferred a horse cut out of paper to a rocking-horse whose dappled gloss and flaring nostrils she had desired, 'because it cost nothing and "Mama would have more to give to the poor"'. It is no exaggeration to say that Mary Carpenter learnt her overmastering, sometimes overpowering, sense of social duty while she learnt her letters.

The Carpenter children however were not forced to endure the joyless grind of an education according to James Mill, deprived of toys, games, picture-books or holidays. The effect of Mary's early training was so indelible, because her education was happy; as she later said, it was the most wonderful experience of her long life. Lant Carpenter, for all his theories, had a natural love of small children, and a gift for entering into their feelings. Dissenting Academies were the most progressive schools in the country, and he was one of the most progressive of dissenting schoolmasters. He insisted that 'those who have the care of education should seize the *Happy Moment*' to implant important ideas.[12] 'Thus virtuous associations may be formed, so vigorous and so permanent as to bid defiance to time and to temptation.' He would often take one of his children in front of him on a horse, and ride slowly through the deep, leafy lanes around Exeter, pointing out the flowers by the wayside and the birds in the hedgerows. Two of his boys became celebrated naturalists, and to Mary the countryside was an abiding delight. The little girls he took to play in the garden, noting that 'sensations of *colour* are in the early parts of life very vivid and assist very considerably in the formation of our mental pleasures'. Mary was never a pretty or a gay child, but she was allowed ribbons of floss silk, a gaily bound book of fables, and a family of wax dolls. She and her sisters were taught to dance, both for health, to cultivate a love of music and 'because dancing will introduce cheerfulness into the mind'. Many Nonconformists affected an exaggerated plainness of dress or manner but as Lant sensibly pointed out, in a sermon on *Ornaments of the Female Sex*, one could be just as vain about ostentatious simplicity as about the most frivolous elegance. Religion, he said, is 'not to take us out of the world, but to guard us from abusing its good things'. His own black tail-coat and white stock were always, it was noted, immaculate.

Mrs Carpenter neither expected nor received the adoration lavished on her husband. She was a quick, clever, capable person, who seemed, said a boy in the school, 'to have the world and all that happened in it at her fingers' ends'. Nothing was allowed to disturb the perfection of her management, or to

---

[12] Carpenter, L. *Systematic Education*, 271-2.

escape her sharp eye. Her wit was ironic, she ridiculed stupidity, in or out of class, and the same boy felt that even her excuses for less competent people were 'something like contempt'. Her husband and the whole household depended upon this apparently cool, self-sufficient woman, and one feels that Mary feared her mother's judgments. 'Her rule over her children was strict,' wrote one of her sons. 'Only in later life was the tenderness of her heart revealed to them.' Only after her death they found a touching secret journal, in which their mother recorded the intellectual interests and spiritual ardours, which she had sacrified for a whole lifetime to the duties of headmistress and minister's wife. Unsentimental as she was, Anna Carpenter early felt an extraordinary quality of mind in the everyday behaviour of her eldest child, even when occupied in 'the grand affairs of her dolls. I never saw such a little animal,' wrote the mother in 1815, when Mary was 8. 'Mary may have difficulty in getting her sum done, or her multiplication table learnt, but her attention is soon occupied with some plan for converting the heathen, or turning her dolls' frocks into pelisses. She is now as intent upon dressing wax dolls and making wax candles as if she never had an idea beyond, and yet her little mind is capable of more than most of our lads are capable of.'

Early childhood, a golden age, 'the very house where we lived, the dear old chapel,' which she remembered as 'a joy unmixed with any painful feeling', belonged to Exeter. It ended in 1817, when Mary was 10 years old, and the whole family moved to Bristol. The family move was bound up with far-reaching plans for the future. Its immediate cause was a letter from members of the Lewin's Mead Meeting, referring in flattering terms to Dr Carpenter's 'talents and general excellence of character', and inviting him to take charge of their 'very important congregation in a very critical state'. Bristol dissenters were rich and powerful. By the middle of the nineteenth century they owned eighty-six chapels among their various sects; but Bristol bigotry was notorious, and the feuds within congregations were notorious also, to the ribald amusement of the ungodly. The challenge to Lant Carpenter's liberalism was irresistible, and in the summer of 1817 he accepted the invitation. His early days as minister of Lewin's Mead were hard, and the children were alarmed to see their father sink into an exhausted sleep one Sunday evening, during the course of a service. His reformist sermons outraged those Bristolians who believed in the sacredness of property, and his work for Roman Catholic emancipation affronted their Protestant prejudices. However, he told his family, 'I should cheerfully go over the same track again; the cause of religious liberty is too dear to admit of holding back.'[13] After a time his extraordinary charm had its usual effect. As Harriet Martineau noted, he persuaded the congregation to adore him. At his request they built a lecture room and Sunday School behind the chapel, where 11-year old Mary was set to teach a class of boys not much smaller than herself.

To the curious eyes of children, Bristol was a magical place. Great George Street, their new home, is a wide and handsome avenue of Georgian houses, one of which is now preserved as a museum of eighteenth-century Bristol.

[13] Carpenter, R. L. *Memoir of Lant Carpenter*, 193.

The street leads steeply upwards, and the far end opens through iron gates on to the slopes of Brandon Hill. Here since Tudor times the washerwomen of Bristol had enjoyed commoners' rights to dry and bleach their linen on the bushes. Once they had climbed the hill, the children were high above the tallest steeple in the city. Below them lay a tight knot of narrow streets, leaning gables, twisted chimneys, the medieval city; behind them white classical terraces clung in graceful curves to the slope of Clifton Hill. The great bend of the tidal river swept through its deep gorge, carrying a forest of masts into the heart of the city. A fifty-gun ship of war could sail up the Avon as far as Bristol Bridge. Snatches of music from passing pleasure boats echoed between the rocks and woody ravines of the gorge. On half-holidays they were taken to Clifton Downs to collect fossil shells, ferns, and the rare wild fritillary. From the observatory at the summit they could see on a clear day far into Somerset.

The Carpenter family moved into 2 Great George Street, a town-house of sober elegance, with room for some twenty-five people. It is now demolished, but survives in drawings as a classical building in the local stone, with rusticated doorways and a balustrade along the roof. Opposite rose in 1823 the elegant temple of St George's Church, designed by Robert Smirke, architect of the British Museum. It was a neighbourhood of urbanity, civilized restraint, enlightenment, all virtues embodied in the household of Dr Carpenter. The headmaster's family lived in a two-storey wing at the side of the main house. Ivy and creeper covered the back, which looked out on a large walled garden sloping downhill towards College Green, with coach-house and stables at the bottom. There was a grass plot, large enough for the boys to play games, and individual gardens where the children planted their own seedlings, and tall elm-trees, noisy with rooks, in which schoolboys could climb. In the stables was a woodwork shop, where young William Carpenter made a model of a full-rigged ship. The young children played endlessly with a box containing a thousand one-inch wooden cube bricks, which introduced them to measurement and number. William, when he became a celebrated scientist, compared the satisfaction of these early experiments with the futility of compelling children to learn multiplication tables they do not understand. 'This plaything of our nursery', he added, 'has been of the greatest value to me throughout life.' The Carpenter children were reared according to their father's belief that 'Home is the great teacher.'

With the birth of Philip in 1819, whom Mary bathed and nursed as tenderly as a mother, the family circle was complete, and the parents had to provide for the future of six children. For the present the school, increased to fifteen pupils, continued, but already Lant intended changes for the future. 'The plan to which I look forward,' he wrote, 'as a future resource for my elder girls, and affording me the power of confining myself to the ministry and directly related objects, is a school for girls, in which my elder girls might be directed by their mother, who could also superintend the household affairs until they had experience, and in which I might take some share with the pupils of greatest ability or age. This, I have thought, would enable me to relinquish my own school.'[14] Mary was only 10 years old when this future burden was laid on her shoulders, but her father was confident that he could mould her character and abilities to carry it without complaining. 'I was early taught to be useful,' was her humble judgment on her childhood. The early stages of the plan brought her nothing but good, since, to prepare for a teaching career, Mary and Anna were entered as pupils alongside the boys in their father's school. They thus received, not only an exceptional education for girls, but an outstandingly good education by any contemporary standards.

Ever since the seventeenth century Unitarian ministers had played a leading part in offering university learning to Nonconformists. Long before the public schools, they introduced modern studies.[15] Dr Carpenter offered chemistry and physics, with simple laboratory apparatus for practical experiments and a course in physiology which he taught himself. Mathematics included geometry, trigonometry and conic sections. Latin and Greek were the staple subjects in all grammar schools, but Dr Carpenter also taught New Testament Greek, as an introduction to philosophy. There were unusual courses in modern history, geography and modern languages. English literature, under the title of Belles Lettres, was an important subject, virtually unknown in the public schools.[16] Dr Carpenter's pupils even read living poets, Wordsworth and Coleridge.

A striking account of Mary Carpenter as a school girl, was written down sixty years later by her class-mate, James Martineau, who was to become a life-long friend of the family. He arrived at the school as a shy, sensitive boy of 14, a few months after his sister Harriet's visit to Lewin's Mead meeting, and on her enthusiastic recommendation. The boy had been at Norwich School where he hated the bullying and thrashing. James came to the Carpenters, pale, overgrown, and deeply disturbed by his unhappy experiences. To the distress and alarm of the family he walked in his sleep, and while asleep attempted to force another boy out of a third-floor window.[17] Mrs Carpenter took special care of his health, and hastily moved him to a room by himself, where he gradually grew calmer. James Martineau came to look on his time at Dr Carpenter's as 'rebirth', the start of his career as one of the founders of modern religious inquiry. The quiet, even days, the perfect order and neatness of the household, the gathering in the morning, when family and pupils shook hands, read a passage from the Bible, then joined in friendly conversation round the breakfast table, where Mrs Carpenter managed the coffee urn—all soothed him like a charm. The other boys considered him rather sentimental, but his adoration of Dr Carpenter was soon, he said, 'absolute'.

The school was essentially an enlargement of the Carpenter family, with its family tone of calm order, high ideals and civilized pleasures. The boys were given a measure of self-government, with their own debating society,

[14] Carpenter, R. L. *Memoir of Lant Carpenter*, 209.
[15] McLachlan, H. *The Unitarian Movement in England*, 131, 2. William Carpenter gave evidence to the Public Schools Commission of 1862 on the value of Sciences to train the mind.
[16] *Ibid.*, 131.
[17] Carpenter, J. E. *James Martineau*, 16.

their own voluntary work for the poor in the parish and their own charity fund. Dr Carpenter forbade cruel sports, like ratting or cockfighting, but encouraged 'cheerful activity', games in the paddock, country rambles and picnics.[18] His school was a remarkable personal creation, at a time when English public schools were a desert of barbarism. Christ's Hospital still had dungeons, 'little square Bedlam cells, where a boy could just lie his length upon straw'. A public schoolboy, wrote Sidney Smith, 'is alternately tyrant and slave', while Southey described Charterhouse as 'a sort of hell on earth for younger boys'. To Mary Carpenter, her father's school remained a life-long model and ideal of a community for young people, a substitute family, which could heal the unhappy child, as her father had healed James Martineau. It is doubtful whether she ever fully recognized, or would admit to herself, the exceptionally favourable circumstances at Great George Street. For a start, the school, at a hundred guineas a year, was among the most expensive in the country. The pupils, sons of rich, well-educated, professional families, were an enlightened minority of a minority. Her mother was a manager of exceptional calibre and her father a teacher of near genius. Among Mary's class-mates were the future Earl of Suffolk and his two brothers, Benjamin Heywood, F.R.S., founder of the Manchester Mechanics' Institution, and Sir Thomas Potter, founder of the *Manchester Guardian*. Among these clever boys, Mary's ability was outstanding. She loved the exactness of scholarship, on which her father insisted, the constant search for first prin-ciples, the rigorous training in order and method. As a model pupil, she might have been unpopular, but her relationship with the boys was simple and natural. 'Mary and Anna,' wrote their mother in the summer of 1820, 'have for some time past been two complete schoolboys, and it is to their honour that, though each has been the head of their respective classes, they are very much beloved by their schoolfellows.'[19]

The purpose of Mary Carpenter's early upbringing had been to form character through family affection. In the same way, school lessons at Great George Street served a purpose, to lay the intellectual foundations of Unita-rian belief. It is difficult, now that time and tolerance on both sides have done their work, to realize how far, not only from the Church of England, but also from orthodox Dissent, the Unitarians took their stand. While Mary was at school, Lant Carpenter himself came under attack from Thomas Burgess, the thunderous Bishop of Salisbury, for 'atrocious libels of infidelity and blasphemy'.[20] The Unitarian view of man was as radical as their view of God. Jared Sparks put the position clearly when he wrote: 'We do not believe that the guilt of Adam's sin was conveyed to posterity, or that there is in man any "original" corruption. This doctrine would make God the author of sin. . . . *We believe men have in themselves the power of being good or bad.*'[21] According to Unitarians, even the worst character could be improved by the right

[18] Carpenter, L. *Sermons on Practical Subjects*, 234.
[19] *Life and Work*, 6.
[20] Burgess, T. *The Divinity of Christ*, 1820, xxvi.
[21] Sparks, J. *The Unitarian Miscellany*. Boston, Mass.

treatment. In this doctrine, learnt from earliest childhood, lay the whole philosophical basis for Mary Carpenter's future work.

These doctrines seem unlikely to interest normal children, but there is rather engaging evidence that the small Carpenters took them to heart. One of Philip's favourite amusements was to play at religious services, with himself as minister and his sister Mary as devout, adoring congregation. One day their mother overheard them at this game, and described the scene. 'P. is now preaching and M. is his audience; but I perceive he is a sad heretic already, for, far from preaching the doctrine of the original sin, he said, "Mankind is *very good*; so nobody would talk to Cain, and he had to go away and live all by himself".'[22]

Lant Carpenter never 'disgusted young people with religion by emotional appeals'; instead he continually related it to everyday and public life. One of the chief duties of a Christian, he taught, was 'social justice, the regulation of our conduct by a steady regard for the rights of others'. Nor did he allow any compromise on public questions; 'expediency must *always* give way to right'. The whole household used to read the newspapers aloud, adults and children together, sitting round the dining-room table, and discussing each item in turn. This was Mary Carpenter's earliest education for public life. She had been born during the Napoleonic wars, and was 8 years old at the time of Waterloo and the passing of the Corn Laws. She learnt, in these family readings, of the radical movement and its repression, of the hunger and distress of the working classes, of machine-breaking and rick-burning. She was 12 years old when her father read aloud to school and family the account of Peterloo, 'the Manchester massacre, kindling his generous indignation as he drew on constitutional history to defend the right of popular petition.' He also read them Grattan's great speech in the Commons on Roman Catholic emancipation, which, James Martineau said, 'early thrilled into me true love of religious liberty'.[23]

During these years Mary Carpenter acquired for better or worse the characteristic tone of the English nineteenth-century Unitarians. Their following was small, only about 37,000 at the religious census of 1851, but publicly influential out of all proportion to its size. Everyone, but perhaps especially themselves, considered Unitarians socially superior to common Dissent with its army of self-educated artizans and shopkeepers. When Dissenters were finally admitted as Members of Parliament, four-fifths of them proved to be Unitarians, many from Dr Carpenter's school. In movements for public health, university reform and prison reform, Unitarians took the lead. Sometimes it was a long lead. Sir John Bowring, a close friend of the Carpenters, introduced the florin in 1841, as the first step towards a decimal currency which, he felt convinced by reason, must follow shortly. Unitarians did not share the philistine opposition of most Dissenters to a state school system; many supported the movement for secular schooling. Their distinguished scientists took the lead in research, and in the application

[22] Carpenter, R. L. *Memoir of Philip Pearsall Carpenter*, 18.
[23] Carpenter, J. E. *James Martineau*, 18.

of science to humanitarian ends. While literal-minded Bible readers of church and chapel denounced the use of chloroform in childbirth as contrary to God's will, Unitarians welcomed it as an example of 'knowledge and improvement'.[24] As employers they built model places of work, like the mill of the Greg family at Styal in Cheshire, now preserved by the National Trust. In Derbyshire, at Belper, the family of the inventor Jedediah Strutt created a complete industrial community, with sound cottages, where infectious diseases were almost unknown, a Unitarian Chapel, Lancastrian Schools, a choir and orchestra, allotments at a penny a week. Moreover many Unitarians, like the Quakers, were remarkably rich in a solid, unostentatious manner.

They would hardly have been human if they failed to feel their own importance. Certainly, although Lant Carpenter, in the great Unitarian tradition, was wholly admirable in his liberal principles, yet it must be said that there sometimes crept into his tone a bland assumption of superiority, which set an unfortunate example to his children. The rest of Lant Carpenter's family accepted his teachings implicitly. William, in a moment of insight, recalled how conversation at home tended to become 'a series of monologues on topics in which each member was interested'. 'Tolerance of things as they are,' confessed another brother, 'is a state of feeling hard for Carpenters to learn.' Mary was almost a middle-aged woman before she discovered that her father's opinions on politics, society and education were not necessarily shared by every right-thinking person.

This was the home and the family which shaped Mary Carpenter's character, the high-minded tradition of protest and the duty to reform bred deeply in the bone. The child, so hungry for affection, was particularly receptive to this early training, while to the father it seemed permissible, even right, to exploit his daughter's anxious love. 'Filial Love,' he wrote, 'becomes the *Leading Affection* in the child's life' and 'where gratitude and submission have been formed towards the earthly parent they will easily be transferred to a Heavenly Father.[25] Dr Carpenter wrote more truly than he knew. The results of his rigorous early training manifested themselves throughout his daughter's life in austere self-discipline, morbid sensitivity, resentment of criticism, extravagant grief over the death of those she loved and a lonely hunger for sympathy. Yet this puritan childhood, with its blending of love and severity, was also her unfailing inspiration. Mary Carpenter never lost her sense of 'the holiness of the heart's affections', and her hunger for love, though it cost her some bitter griefs, kept her heart fresh for seventy years.

[24] *The Christian Reformer*, 1840–1845, *passim*. They found an unexpected ally in Queen Victoria who received chloroform at the birth of Prince Leopold in 1853, after which anaesthesia became respectable.
[25] Carpenter, L. *Systematic Education*, 283.

2

A GOVERNESS ALONE
1820-1830

Although James Martineau was two years older than Mary, they shared lessons in science, history, geography and Greek Testament. When asked, sixty years later, he had at first some difficulty in describing his old class-mate. Other figures, Lant Carpenter with his beguiling manner, and Anna, 'so gleeful and kindling', were brighter in his memory; but finally he recalled, moving in the shadowy background of the scene, 'the sedate little girl of twelve, who looked at you so steadily and always talked like a book'. Already Mary seemed older than her age; she did not skip or run or play, but moved about quietly, 'so that she seemed to be no longer a child'. She evidently did not seem to be a girl either, for there was something stiff and angular about her, 'a want of suppleness and natural grace'. The now elderly scholar, seeking for a word which would combine precision with propriety, described her figure as 'somewhat *columnar*'. She had her father's build, thin, stoop-shouldered, frail, his rather pinched features and receding chin, dominated by a long, sensitive, inquisitive nose. Only after a time did one notice that she had also inherited his fine grey eyes and sweet voice. This appearance, redeemed in Lant by his charm, was totally incongruous in a girl of the Romantic Period. Muslins, ribbons and chip-straw bonnets merely made a plain girl more of an oddity. As though aware of this, Mary showed no interest in feminine accomplishments, dancing, playing the piano or fine needlework. Only when she took out her water-colour box and made fresh, delicate sketches of flowers, ferns or landscape, did her natural hunger for beauty reveal itself. To James Martineau there seemed to be 'signs of inward con-flict' upon her grave, set little face; she often worried that her own behaviour was not good enough to please her parents. He soon found this odd child could outshine him in class on any modern subject. He felt himself a fool when she 'picked up my dropped answers and corrected my mistakes', but he was grateful when she helped him, in a modest, unassuming way, to escape her formidable mother's ridicule. In classics her translations were conscien-tious and accurate, but stiff. Most revealing of all was James Martineau's memory of Mary with her father, how 'lost to herself and all around her' she listened to his sermons, how in class 'by voice, by eye, by the very mode of holding her book' her whole mood and bearing reflected his. On Sunday evenings, at whatever cost to the kitchen department, Dr Carpenter kept open house for supper to all his young friends; when the juniors had gone to bed the older boys and visitors stayed on for half an hour's candlelit talk with their host, and James remembered Mary 'privileged to sit with her arm in her father's', a silent, spell-bound listener. 'To his daughter', concluded James Martineau, 'he was prophet as well as parent.'[1] Long after his death, Lant Carpenter maintained this inspiring, but dangerous hold over his eldest child.

By the time they were 16 and 14 the two young scholars had an opportunity to serve their beloved master, for several times a warning attack of exhaustion confined Dr Carpenter to his room. In 1820 he was unable to preach or teach for three months. James Martineau took his place on the dais, with Mary to assist him at the monitor's desk, and they were able to send a message to the invalid that the schoolroom was as quiet, orderly and industrious as if he had been there in person.[2] Mrs Carpenter, preoccupied with nursing and management, yet had time to appreciate her daughter's quality. 'Mary has a very great influence among the boys,' she wrote, 'and with her gentle voice, and mild but firm expostulation, can maintain an astonishing degree of order among them.'

The school years glided quietly by. James Martineau left in 1821 with a note of farewell to the three Carpenter sisters. 'My dear Mary, Anna and Susan,' he wrote, 'I cannot leave Bristol without begging the acceptance of a small token of my regard for you. I am aware that I can in this way repay but a small part of your kindness to me.'[3] He signed himself 'your ever affectionate friend'; and his was to be a life-long friendship towards the whole family. It is doubtful that Mary was able to read this note for herself, for she was suffering from the first of a series of painful and frightening attacks of illness, which recurred several times before she grew up, and decisively influenced her adult life. Accounts of the symptoms, as so often in nineteenth-century letters, are vague and variable. She seems to have suffered pain, fever and faintness, with acute inflammation of the iris, which twice threatened her sight. Many things: her age, her sex, familial inheritance from her father, the recurrent attacks, suggest the acute rheumatism which nearly killed her in middle-age. For weeks on end Mary was shut up in a darkened room, unable to use her eyes in any way, and Dr Estlin, the family doctor, warned her parents that the inflammation might lead to permanent blindness. The brightness of a sunny morning was agony to her eyes, the days empty and dreary, the nights sleepless and full of fear. Mary showed in these early illnesses a lion-like moral courage which was to last all her life. When she could not see to read or write, she learnt the entire complicated time-table of school and household by heart, to act as family time-keeper. She had a profound need to be needed.

Mary emerged from the sick-room a thin, tense girl, with stooping shoulders, sharp features and weary irritability. This irritability was to stay with Mary Carpenter all her life, a source of passionate regret and self-reproach, but woven into the fibre of her constitution. Even her most devoted relatives admitted it.[4] Her father advised her to keep a notebook, in which with unflinching honesty, she entered her failings week by week. She wrote

---

[1] *Life and Work*, 10.   [2] Carpenter, J. E. *James Martineau*, 20.
[3] Manchester College, Oxford, Library, C.2.   [4] *Life and Work*, 43.

that she knew herself to be clever, and this made her conceited. She could never be satisfied 'unless I become distinguished in some way', though she knew she ought to be resigned 'to being as unsuccessful as God pleases to make me'. She could not bear to admit herself in the wrong and 'I also feel a very unchristian satisfaction in imagining my own feeling of a superior cast to those of others.' As she grew up, Mary longed to be loved, to be a universal favourite as her lively sister Anna was; instead she felt a 'humiliating sense of want of attractive manner, so that I had a general feeling of being disliked'.[5] She also worried over her adored father. His three months' illness in 1820 had been the first of several warning attacks, which Lant himself described as 'hours of darkness and weakening despondence'. He believed that the burden of work he carried, preaching, teaching and writing, was 'plainly too much for my strength'. In 1824 and 1825 he put his affairs in order and wrote farewell letters to his children in case of his death.[6] To his eldest daughter this threat was unimaginably terrible. Lant Carpenter's illness was not imaginary; his sufferings were real. Yet with the unconscious skill of the neurotic he used his threatened breakdown to forward a scheme he had formed while Mary was still a child. If he could hand over the teaching to his wife and daughters, he would be free to devote his talents to the good causes, parliamentary reform, religious freedom, abolition of slavery, which he had sincerely at heart. Mary willingly fell in with the suggestion that her father must be 'relieved of the school and the toil transferred to her mother, Anna and herself'. Once recovered from her own illness, she took up the family duties which were to consume more than half her life.

Mary Carpenter always described the two years from 1824 to 1826 with simple pride as 'the time when I assisted my dear father with his classical school'. She was happy in the success of the school, but too humble to take any credit to herself. 'I glory', she wrote, 'in being my father's daughter,' as though she had no other claim on the world. Yet it is clear she became a superb teacher. In class she could maintain effortless discipline and hold the boys' interest whatever the subject; out of school she herself joined in collecting fossils or caterpillars with the enthusiasm of a small boy. Her young brothers Russell and Philip had their first lessons with her, and looking back remembered shared enjoyment. Mary had inherited her mother's cutting wit, and with adults was wary and defensive, but she loved and understood children. This golden time was brighter in memory, because it ended so abruptly in the disaster, long dreaded, of her father's breakdown. Lant Carpenter had struggled to stave off collapse as long as he could, and here perhaps lies the key to his incessant reforming activities. He armed himself with right-thinking, committees, and endless correspondence, apparently against the outside world, but in reality against a dark world of insecurity, weakness and dread within himself. The same process can be seen in Mary, who became in her turn a compulsive reformer who could not stop working. In her case the defence mechanism succeeded, but Lant Carpenter was defeated by the

[5] *Ibid.*, 20–5.
[6] Carpenter, R. L. *Memoir of Lant Carpenter*, 285–6.

enemy within. In 1826 he collapsed under acute depression. 'He dwelt too much', wrote his son, 'on his own inward state.' The habit of continual religious introspection paralysed him in everyday living. Contemporary medicine offered no help. He went to Dublin to consult the celebrated Dr Cheyne, but wrote home 'he told me that mine was an everyday case (I think he said). Dyspepsia acting on the head attended with a great deal of nervousness.' He came home and grew steadily worse. His symptoms were distressing to his family and terrifying to himself. Under the burden of meaningless despair a premature old age seemed to creep over him; 'though not yet fifty,' wrote his son, 'he considered himself, and was regarded by others as an old man'.[7] A deadly inertia blanketed action and feeling. He woke early, a prey to fearful thoughts, and fell into an exhausted sleep only at daybreak. Teaching was unendurable, nor could he face the ordeal of public appearances in the pulpit. He resigned from Lewin's Mead, but a deputation came from the congregation begging him to return as soon as he was recovered. They suggested a sea-voyage, for which Lant complained there was no money. Yet even now his extraordinary charm did not fail. A wealthy acquaintance, who hardly knew him offered not only to pay all expenses, but to accompany the patient for a journey to spend the winter of 1826–7 in the South of France.[8] Mrs Carpenter thankfully accepted. The two men set off for Hyères, leaving Mary anguished at the parting, but comforted by these striking proofs of love for her father 'now he is suffering and cast down in affliction'.

Meanwhile the family was threatened with the closing of the school which provided a livelihood for them all. Mary, not yet 20, could not hope to run it by herself and bitterly reproached herself for not being more useful in this crisis. 'I see everyone around me,' she wrote in November 1826, 'excelling me in something. My mother possesses a firm and lively faith; my sister Anna shows a far greater firmness and presence of mind in trial than I do.' She felt their courage shamed her weakness. Mrs Carpenter, in this crisis showed her usual prompt good sense, and wrote to their former pupil James Martineau, asking him to take charge of meeting-house and school until her husband's recovery, which she firmly maintained would not be long. James Martineau had just graduated in theology from Manchester College; he had felt a bitter sense of deprivation that as a dissenter he could not enter Oxford or Cambridge, but this in no way hindered his strong and daring intellect. He was proud to help his old master, who had first awakened his mind to philosophy and whom he still honoured. He returned as a man to the school he had left as a boy, took vigorous charge of the classes, and sat up all Saturday nights in the study, with a kettle and a caddy of green tea, preparing a series of original sermons for Lewin's Mead meeting.[9]

James Martineau represented a new generation of scholarship. 'The Scriptures,' he wrote as early as 1828, 'were written in languages now extinct, by people widely separated from us, not only by time and distance,

---

[7] Carpenter, R. L. *Memoir of Lant Carpenter*, 363.
[8] *Ibid.*, 327. This was General Pitman, a retired regular soldier and staunch Anglican.
[9] Carpenter, J. E. *James Martineau*, 55–8.

but by manners, character and condition. Hence there arises a necessity for human learning and research in order to understand them.' This learning he vigorously pursued, while teaching in the school, tutoring the younger Carpenter boys, and introducing Mary to 'the best of our modern poets', particularly Wordsworth whom she came to love as much as he did. Excursions with the school, to collect minerals or fossils, were transformed by his reading of passages from *Tintern Abbey* or *The Excursion*, and this encounter with a first-class mind affected Mary more powerfully than she or anyone else could have foreseen. James Martineau, at 22, was only at the beginning of his intellectual development and his thought was less obscure than it afterwards became. 'I *do* wish I could understand what Mr Martineau meant,' the hymn-writer Catherine Winkworth was later to exclaim, after one of his lectures.[10] His appearance was as striking as his intellect. Even in his forties he struck a casual acquaintance as 'a very tall, handsome fellow'. Tall and gaunt, with a shock of dark hair above a pale face, his rugged features took on, it is said, a strange high beauty in the pulpit, as he concentrated on the pursuit of some elusive truth. Martineau was an inspiring teacher; his influence on the young Carpenters was profound and lasting, as a lifetime's correspondence survives to prove. He opened Mary Carpenter's mind and perhaps her heart to ideas never before imagined.

Mrs Carpenter may have thought his influence too strong, for in the spring of 1827 she withdrew Mary from teaching in the school and sent her away as governess to some young girls in the Isle of Wight. Mary went like Jane Eyre, a governess, poor, plain and proud, but no Mr Rochester awaited her. She was lonely and unhappy, feeling her isolation acutely. For the first time among normally frivolous young girls, she saw herself by the world's standards, and could not help resenting the convention which judged a woman solely by appearances instead of by qualities of heart and mind. Although she tried not to, she despised the commonplace family in which she found herself. 'You cannot think,' she confided to Anna, 'what a change I find this from an intellectual point of view; here the subjects which at home are common topics of conversation are scarcely noticed, and I have been so long now with those who are acquainted with our best poets that it seems strange to find them scarcely known.' Her employer's wife claimed to be 'a great Wordsworthian', but Mary was disillusioned to find her favourite poem was the pedestrian *Peter Bell*. 'As I wish to continue a Wordsworthian,' wrote Mary, 'I do not mean to read his trash. It is as well Mr Martineau is not by!'[11]

Wordsworth proved her chief consolation in her loneliness; she carried a little volume in her pocket as she spent her few free days on solitary rambles round the shore, profoundly moved, as she would always be, by the sea. Her interest was not merely sentimental; she recorded flowers and shells, and, having climbed up Headon Hill, was delighted to find in the rock 'unbroken beds of fossil shells, lying as neatly as if they had been placed there'. In a few years' time she would be an enthusiastic early reader of Lyell's *Principles*

[10] Hudson, D. *Munby, Man of Two Worlds*, 50.
[11] *Life and Work*, 13–14.

of Geology. Meanwhile she lived for news from home, which included a brave
letter from her young brother William. He had always planned to be an
engineer, but realized that because of his father's illness there would be no
money to pay for his training. When the family doctor, Dr Estlin, offered to
take him as apprentice under the regulations of the Society of Apothecaries,
William accepted, returning home several times a week to give chemistry
classes in the school. 'Dear old Poll,' wrote the 15-year old medical student to
his sister, 'I am grown a good deal and look more of a man than I did. . . . I
can vaccinate children and pull out their teeth.'[12] With this brave example,
Mary could only buckle to her uncongenial job, in which she continued to
feel 'a very undetermined success'.

Alone, she celebrated her 21st birthday on 3rd April 1828. A parcel from
home brought letters from her mother, her sisters and her aunt, congratulating
her on becoming a 'female majoriarian'. James Martineau wrote that he felt it
'a privilege to be allowed to write with the family party'; he wished to send
her a present, with her mother's permission, and included some specimens
from his own collection of pressed flowers and ferns, choosing those with
'endearing associations of locality. Believe me,' he wrote kindly but non-
committally, 'it is with a feeling of Christian friendship that I join in the
anniversary duty of greeting you cheerfully as you emerge from the past and
bidding you God speed as you place the first step on an untried future.'[13] At
the same time came a letter from Dr Carpenter in Paris; he was much better
and was returning home with his generous companion. They would put in at
Ryde on their homeward journey, and spend some time at Newport to visit
her. He sent her as a 21st birthday present Hartley's *Observations on Man*,
which so strongly influenced Coleridge, and a characteristic letter. 'Twenty-
one years have passed,' he wrote, 'since I first had the appelation "Father".
I look back on the past with wonder that I have been spared so long, and
with gratitude that after a period of thick darkness I am spared still to delight
in my children.' He urged Mary to 'work for others the work assigned thee
and faithfully, calmly and perseveringly to do the Lord's will'. [14] A few weeks
later he was with her, and she was able to pour out her troubles to him. A
letter shows how shrewdly he was able to judge others, if not always himself.
'Be less solicitous about personal distinction, my child,' he wrote on leaving
her, 'than respecting the chief qualities of the heart and head; form the habit
of sensible, cheerful conversation, not forgetting but not displaying the
knowledge you actually possess on subjects connected with history and science.
Check everything that feels like envy and jealousy of those who have more to
obtain the attention of others.'[15] To a girl already painfully unattractive,
craving affection and suffering from 'a general feeling of being disliked', this
was hardly comforting advice. Yet Lant Carpenter must have been struck by
his daughter's loneliness and misery, for within a few weeks Mary was
allowed to give up her post and come home.

[12] Carpenter, W. B. *Essays and Memoir*, 7–8.
[13] Manchester College, Oxford, Library, C2.
[14] Carpenter, R. L. *Memoir of Lant Carpenter*, 493–4.   [15] *Ibid.*, 497.

Home, with her father, shrunken and aged yet visibly himself, had never seemed more precious. Lant Carpenter, although much better, was still not strong enough to teach, and James Martineau remained with the family for a time, probably until the school year ended. He and Mary took up their eager exploration of books again. They had 'a grand discussion' about the popular poems of Thomas Moore, whom Mary considered over-rated. 'I do not like a garden filled with nothing but gaudy flowers,' she protested. When they read Leigh Hunt's *Feast of the Poets*, she objected to the exclusion of Wordsworth and Byron,[16] and maintained that women writers 'should be allowed at least to be in the gallery'. She was acutely sensitive to everything she read, confessing that she dared not read books about wicked people, because they always returned to terrify her in nightmares.[17] Beneath her shy, self-effacing manner, she was intensely alive, feminine, impressionable and full of passionate feeling. Mrs Carpenter, knowing the family instability, always feared for her daughter; perhaps also, she considered Mary too much drawn to the brilliant young scholar. At all events, for whatever reason, after a short stay, she again sent Mary away, this time on a two days' coach journey into Hertfordshire, to a new post as governess.

Mary's employers, the Fordhams of Odsey House near Royston, were rich brewers and landowners. The family was a large cousinage, vigorous and notably independent of mind. One member had become a Unitarian after stumbling over a drunken man on his way home from the family brewery. Another, when the local vicar refused to guarantee him burial with a favourite horse, instituted a private, unconsecrated burying ground for himself and his horse in a grove of fir-trees on the family estate. A Unitarian journal described his funeral ceremony, with some understatement, as 'very peculiar and striking'.[18] The Fordhams gave the new governess a kindly welcome, taking her about with them like one of the family. She was to take charge of the two youngest girls, Martha aged 16 and Sarah who was 10. Mr and Mrs Fordham were surprised to find, however, that she was fully capable of coaching their student son Frank in classics. She took him through Virgil's *Eclogues*, astonished and delighted to find how beautiful they were, and how they suited the pastoral scene. For Odsey itself was beautiful in a reticent English way, a tall Georgian house of russet brick, with rows of shining windows, fine panelling, and shell-shaped cupboards filled with delicate porcelain. Mary's domain was the old nurseries on the top floor, looking out on the clear-cut skyline of Royston Downs. Here Mary taught Martha and Sarah their lessons; they proved kind, intelligent girls and she remained on affectionate terms with them all her life.[19] In this atmosphere of confidence and appreciation her bruised self-confidence gradually healed. Her father sent kind and encouraging letters. 'Take care of your health,' he wrote in November 1828. 'Do not overstrain your mind or allow it to be too much excited.' He feared her

[16] Evidently in an early edition; later editions of Hunt's satire gave considerable praise to both these poets.

[17] *Life and Work*, 15. [18] *The Christian Reformer*, Vol. 34, 1848, 495.

[19] Personal information from the present Fordham family.

temperament, so like his own. Even in this kindly family circle Mary lived a good deal alone, reading by candlelight when the children had gone to bed, or writing, in a delicate schoolmistress hand, in her solitary journals. No one, seeing the small, composed figure going about her work, or meeting the proud and habitual reserve of her manner could have guessed at the intense and passionate life within.

Reality could hardly compete with the force of her inner feelings. When the Fordhams on a visit to London took her, for the first time in her life, to the theatre, she was disappointed by Kean's Othello. It was, she wrote to her younger sister Susan, 'like seeing a picture on any subject unequal to the idea you have previously formed. Kean did not make me feel interested *for* Othello and he did not make my blood either freeze or boil.' While living her inner life of the imagination, Mary Carpenter was enough her father's daughter to maintain a well-informed interest in public affairs. The great question of 1829 was Roman Catholic emancipation, and she was dryly amused by the efforts of the vicar of Ashwell to organize a petition against it. His parishioners disliked him so much, she wrote, that they refused to sign 'for, as they justly observed, they should not have to pay any more tithes, even if the Pope did come over to England'. She disliked the Tory government of the Duke of Wellington, but thought him the right person to introduce emancipation, 'for he is a good strong stick that will cudgel the asses along the road he has chosen to travel'.

By the autumn of 1828 Dr Carpenter was strong enough to take up his old duties as minister of Lewin's Mead meeting. His keenness of mind and his charm as a preacher were quite unaffected by his long breakdown; he spoke and wrote with his old fluency, corresponded with fellow Unitarians all over the world and planned a new book. But he made it clear to his anxious family that he would never again be strong enough to face a class of boys. Lant Carpenter's style is so elliptical, so filled, in the manner of the time, with large references to the leadings of Providence, that it is difficult to tell exactly what his plans were. Certainly it would have suited him very well for James Martineau and Mary to carry the teaching load, as they had in his earlier illness, and for this arrangement to be made binding by 'other ties'. A convenient marriage was in his mind when he wrote to Mary, 'I am glad you have so much of family service; perhaps one day it will lead to more.'[20] He invited James Martineau to enter into partnership, join his household permanently and run the school for him, which seemed to all the family an ideal solution. To their surprise and dismay Martineau refused, and a fact emerged which had apparently been unknown to them all, unless shrewd Mrs Carpenter had guessed. For at least two years there had been an engagement between him and the charming daughter of a Unitarian minister in Derby. He had been in love with Helen Higginson since he was 19, and lodging with her family as an engineering student, but the etiquette of the time compelled him to protect his fiancée's name by silence until they were ready to marry.

[20] Carpenter, R. L. *Memoir of Lant Carpenter*, 496–7.

Now he had been offered the ministry of a Presbyterian Church in Dublin and could at last provide a home; he courteously but firmly declined the Carpenter's offer, married in December 1828 and went to live in Ireland.[21] Even the decorous language of the time makes it plain that he was passionately in love, and proud of his young wife's beauty. Their marriage was of inspiring happiness.

Mary was still at Odsey when the wedding took place, but evidently sent them a book, for the letter acknowledging it survives. 'You must allow me,' he wrote politely but cautiously, 'to accept it and place it on my shelves as the memory of a kindness which has made me in spirit your brother.'[22] He sent in return some volumes of his own as a thank-offering for her kindness 'which has infused into its happier hours a degree of domestic enjoyment, which during a year of solitary duty I had no right to expect. . . . Do not imagine that in requesting your acceptance of the accompanying books, I entertain any idea of relieving myself of my obligations to you. Believe that under all circumstances to hear of your welfare, still more to witness it, would be a real and pure satisfaction.'[23]

It was years before Mary Carpenter gave any hint of her feelings at this time, and then only in the most veiled terms.[24] As always, her father was ready with good advice. 'Carefully guard the *affections*,' he wrote, 'lest they should be placed on any object which duty and religion will not sanction.' Meanwhile practical problems weighed heavily on the whole family. 'As my father declined the proposal and went to Dublin instead,' explained Mary Ellen Martineau, 'Dr Carpenter decided on giving up his school as incompatible with his ministry.' There was no choice but his old plan of a girls' school run by his wife and daughters. This might have opened sooner, but for the unexpected illness of Mrs Carpenter, worn out by the strain and worry of the past three years. 'She bears it patiently and submissively,' wrote Lant to a fellow minister, characteristically relating it to his own sufferings, 'and it is not, blessed be God, such a darkness as hung over my path.' Yet even so she could not open her school before September. Her husband used this delay to withdraw Mary from Odsey and send her with Anna to board in a Huguenot family in Paris. Like the Brontë sisters in Brussels, they would gain extra qualifications as teachers of young ladies. The two girls made remarkably serious visitors to Paris. Bonnets and laces, the chestnut trees and the crowds strolling in their shade, all passed unremarked while they toiled over their dictées and lecture notes. They went to the Institut Royal to hear Cuvier, the great palaeontologist, and attended a lecture on the astronomy of Laplace. Mary attended a demonstration of 'animal magnetism', and went repeatedly to revisit her favourite pictures at the Louvre. On the whole, however, she was baffled by the sceptical, tolerant temper of the

[21] Manchester College, Oxford, Library, A3 Box B. Letter from Martineau's daughter Mary Ellen in reply to an inquiry by J. E. Carpenter, Mary Carpenter's nephew and first biographer.

[22] *Ibid.*,C2

[23] *Ibid.*

[24] See below p. 146.

French mind. Even French Protestants did not come up to the standard of moral earnestness her father had taught her to expect. She described an argument with the son of her hostess, a clever young avocat. 'He said that he thought religion a very good thing for women and children (he generally classed these two together) but it was quite unnecessary for men who study philosophy.' Mary took him to task and he admitted her answer to be très bien raisonné . . . I think a little good has been done, to show that religion can be supported by reason,'[25] she ended triumphantly. Already Mary Carpenter, so humble about her personal attractions, hated being worsted in an intellectual argument. More ominously for the future, she treated any criticism of her father's ideas as an act of lèse majesté. Here lay the germ of her future intransigence.

In September 1829 Mrs Carpenter's Boarding School for Young Ladies opened at 2 Great George Street. Mary, with Anna's help, undertook most of the teaching; Susan, aged 18, gave music lessons as well as playing the organ in chapel. All took their share of business, household chores and the endless duties of chaperonage. 'School keeping is certainly difficult work,' wrote Mary to her friends at Odsey, 'but we have been so long accustomed to have something useful to do, that I do not think we should be happy without regular employment.'[26] 'Responsibility is always pressing,' she wrote another time to William, explaining why her letter had been delayed. She never allowed herself to complain openly but the tone of her letters makes clear that she did not enjoy teaching the Y.Ls., as she privately called them. Her own education had fitted her to teach Latin and Greek, history, elementary mathematics and science; the Y.Ls. demanded French conversation, embroidery and piano playing. She felt she was frittering her time away. 'I long to leave behind me', she wrote, 'something which men should not willingly let die, something which would enable my thoughts to mingle with my fellow beings when I am lying in death. But this is a hope little suited to my powers.'[27] Secretly, in her limited free time, she wrote poems and painted dream landscapes of ideal beauty in delicate water-colour.

The girls of the school looked on Miss Carpenter as a prodigy of learning, a creature of a different order from themselves, who made them painfully aware of their own ignorance and lazy habits of mind. They would have been startled to know how intensely, beneath her composed professional exterior, she shared their feminine hopes and fears. They saw her only as the brilliant teacher which clearly she was. 'Miss Carpenter is delightful,' wrote a new girl in her home letter. 'She understands Greek, Latin, Italian, French and every other language for all I know to the contrary, for I only know of these, hearing her teach them. She is fond of poetry, geology and conchology, which two latter she understands very well. In short she seems to be universal. She possesses the quality of great kindness as do all the family.'[28] Few of the twittering flock of young ladies who passed through the Carpenter house in the next twenty years emerge as individuals. Mary wrote of the five

[25] *Life and Work*, 18.   [26] *Ibid.*, 19.
[27] *Ibid.*, 50.   [28] *Ibid.*, 19.

daughters of a Jewish merchant;[29] she was proud that the father of these girls had entrusted them to her school, confident that true religious courtesy would respect their faith. She was fond of Lucy Sanford, daughter of a rich Unitarian merchant in the City of London. Another pupil who became a life-long friend arrived at the school in its first year. This was pretty Anne Simpson, daughter of a farm labourer, who was sent to school for the first time in her twenties, as a preparation for marrying Richard Yates, son of a Unitarian minister.[30] Richard Yates became a leading citizen of Liverpool; Anne, while she kept her country ways with children, animals and plants, was an excellent companion to him in all his interests and an early worker for animal welfare. With a few pupils the barriers of Mary's reserve were lowered, but much of her daily work remained a necessary drudgery.

Mary Carpenter had travelled at one step from childhood to middle-aged responsibility with no time to be young. Money must be earned and her young brothers educated; she, and apparently everybody else, took her self-sacrifice for granted. Only in later life looking back, would Philip write, 'How you girls toiled that we boys might be well prepared for life; for which I am ever grateful to you.'[31] Mary rebuked herself sternly for the least sign of 'ill temper' or 'discontent' in this gruelling daily round. 'If I have performed any service well,' she wrote in the autumn of 1830, 'I profess not to think myself deserving of praise, but I have a secret consciousness of having performed it better than others would have done; this I hope I am correcting.' Two years later, at 25, she sat down with pen and paper to a remorseless self-scrutiny. It is a remarkable document for a woman so young, and superficially so sheltered from life. She recognized the dangers of living so much among intellectual inferiors. 'My occupations,' she wrote, 'render it necessary for me continually to bring forward my own opinions and wishes; this is a dangerous tendency. . . . In my memoranda I observe that from the commencement *pride* is spoken of as my great enemy.' She attempted to draw up a balance sheet of her intellectual qualities: quickness of perception, but a tendency to hasty judgment, a good memory and love of order, but want of 'elegance in expression'. She wrote that she knew Greek, Latin, French, Italian and German, that she had 'enough knowledge of natural sciences to enjoy learning more' and that she was making progress with mathematics and history. Above all, she loved beauty in nature, music and poetry, and although she lacked neatness and accuracy, she even went so far as to admit that 'I draw pretty well'.

When she moved on from the intellect to the emotions, Mary found the task of self-analysis more difficult. 'Indeed,' she wrote, 'it seems almost impossible to dive into the recesses of my heart, having first removed the veil of self-love and assign to each passion and emotion its place.' She recorded bitterly her humiliation at being so unattractive, and the fear of being disliked, which prevented her from showing her deepest feelings. 'The affections', she added, 'are sometimes a source of overwhelming delight to

[29] Boston Public Library, MS.9.2, Vol. 20, No. 70.
[30] Cobbe, F. P. *Autobiography*, 702–3.
[31] Carpenter, R. L. *Memoir of Philip Pearsall Carpenter*, 305.

me, while at other times they fill every leisure moment with sorrow and make me almost wish that mine were a heart of stone.' Here she makes her one open reference to the great grief of her early life, hinted at but never described in her letters, a love which had been in some way forbidden or unreturned. 'I have been made very unhappy by another branch of the affections. I try to guard against them, for they are a source of nothing but sorrow to me. I pray God to help me subdue them.' Another solitary spinster, Edith Simcox, who knew Mary Carpenter's work, described this early sorrow more plainly. 'She was also troubled by inordinate affections, a disposition to set her heart on persons or things with an abandon she knew to be wrong and felt to be painful, for the objects of her affection turned out to have affections of their own, set in quite other directions.'[32] Years later, when past middle life, Mary Carpenter revealed how she had longed for the happiness of being wife and mother; but seeing herself plain, angular, stiff, shy and irritable, she accepted that it would never be hers. Of such bitter experiences the acidulous spinster, so cruelly portrayed in Victorian fiction, was born. For Mary Carpenter, rejection bit so deep in youth, that a lifetime of activity could not cover the scar. Something had wounded her to the quick, and the bitterness of pain never quite left her. Her pride and her puritan code of conduct would not admit self-pity or resentment. Her stifled feelings were transferred to children in need, rejected by society and cast aside in life for an ugliness not of their making. She would fight for neglected children with a fierce tenacity and resentment she had never shown in her own cause. For the present, her life seemed bleak and empty, but, she told herself, there was perhaps a reason for this; her strength and self-discipline were being forged for a purpose. '*It is possible,*' she wrote in her journal on Sunday 6th October 1832 '*that some great duty is reserved for me.*'[33] She waited to learn what it would be.

[32] Simcox, E. *Fortnightly Review*, May 1880, 'Ideals of Feminine Usefulness'.
[33] *Life and Work*, 23–6.

3
TWO VISITORS AND A
VOCATION 1831-1839

Once the primary burden of earning a living was transferred to his wife and daughters, Lant Carpenter made a remarkable recovery. During the 1830s his fame as a liberal speaker and thinker spread far overseas, while his slight form and eager, proboscidean features were to be seen at every notable progressive gathering. It is easy enough now to recognize, and too easy to condemn, the anxious, self-protective egoism which looks out between the lines of his family letters. On all public questions Dr Carpenter continued to be more liberal, more fearless and outspoken than lesser men, while at home the devotion of his wife and daughters cocooned him in emotional and even in financial comfort. 'His liberal mind', wrote his son Russell, ingenuously, 'was always devising and executing liberal things, which made the continuance of a large income peculiarly desirable.'[1] This convenient income was provided by the drudgery of the Young Ladies Boarding School, of which Mary bore a major part. This arrangement, whatever unease it may cause us, was perfectly acceptable to the code of the times; Mary Russell Mitford's father lived in idleness on her earnings, and in New England the Transcendentalist Bronson Alcott financed his high-souled lectures from the royalties of his daughter's best-seller, *Little Women*. There is every evidence that Mary Carpenter was a willing partner in her own exploitation. Once she had given up any secret hope of love or marriage for herself, her father became the sole centre of her emotional life. Illness, which had made him appear so frail, only increased Lant Carpenter's power to charm and dominate his hearers. The cult of sensibility was at its height, and Lant Carpenter was its high priest; before this virtuoso manipulator of the emotions his unattractive, diffident daughter sank in adoration. In 1834, with his enthusiasm for all that was new and scientific, Dr Carpenter lectured in favour of the Great Western Railway extensions, which would, he said, 'contribute to the general improvement and welfare by increasing the facilities of social intercourse'. At the same time he took the opportunity to acquire G.W.R. shares in which his capital gradually increased to provide a substantial income.

In politics Dr Carpenter was able to point out to his children the gradual triumph of reforms he had been preaching, as he said, 'for more than thirty years, during most of this time in a minority, and hoping almost against hope'.[2] He had seen his unusual beliefs permitted by the Unitarian Toleration Act of 1813. In 1828 the Test and Corporation Acts, which had barred

[1] Carpenter, R. L. *Memoir of Lant Carpenter*, 325.
[2] *Ibid.*, 380.

Dissenters from public life for nearly a hundred and seventy years, were at last repealed, to be followed a year later by the repeal of the penal laws against Roman Catholic worship. The great parliamentary Reform Bill of 1832, was followed the next year by the Abolition of Slavery throughout the British Empire. The great essential, wrote Lant Carpenter, was never to compromise on a question of principle, for 'with constant reference to first principles as the first object in view', there must in time follow the 'steady dawn of liberty and knowledge'. 'Being as a Minister of the Gospel', he remarked at a public meeting in Bristol, with sublime complacency, 'out of the immediate influence of many of the narrowing connexions of society, and accustomed as from an eminence to view the more distant prospect, I may form a judgment more correct than those who are on the level ground. Of one thing I feel assured, that events are confirming the great doctrine of *benevolence*.'[3] Mary ever afterwards regarded the least compromise on principle as a betrayal of her father's sacred trust. She expected to be in a minority and, however distressed or agitated by opposition, remained confident in her own infallibility. Like so many members of the great English reforming tradition, the Carpenters were admirable and exasperating at the same time.

This high-minded, well-ordered belief in progress was breached in 1832 by two major social disasters, the Bristol riots and the cholera epidemic. Both taught Mary Carpenter something she had never experienced at first hand, the reality of poverty, brutal, squalid and dangerous. It was her first introduction to the world of her future work.

Bristol lay on marshy ground laced with waterways, in the hollow where the valleys of the Frome and Avon meet; at spring-tide or after a heavy rainfall, the cellars of the old houses filled with scummy water. A series of paintings records scenes of romantic, but dangerous dilapidation. Over the river Frome, a common sewer, high tenements lean crazily on an undercroft of brick arches; little houses crowd together on Bristol Bridge; Redcliffe Street shows dark at mid-day under its overhanging Tudor gables; in Bull Paunch Lane the muddy ground is littered with broken window panes, roof tiles and lengths of fallen guttering.[4] As the city grew, its gardens, back-lanes and open spaces were built over with a network of overcrowded alleys. The 'out Parishes', including Bedminster, with a working class population of over thirteen thousand not incorporated in the city until 1835, had no effective local government. Bristol's unreformed City Corporation was a fossilized relic of ancient glories, self-appointed, meeting in secret, jealous of power and largely devoted to picturesque ceremonial. They let the port, on which the city's greatness depended, decay; they left the work of sewering, paving, cleaning and lighting undone. The working people of Bristol clamoured for municipal and parliamentary reform.[5]

The reform party had high hopes when, late in 1830, Lord Grey's Whig ministry came to power. Dr Carpenter gave a public speech congratulating

---

[3] Carpenter, R. L. *Memoir of Lant Carpenter*, 358.
[4] City Art Gallery, Bristol, *Views of Bristol*.
[5] *Petition of the Burgesses to the Corporation of Bristol*, 1836.

the French on their successful revolution, though in practice aristocratic Whigs, frightened by events in Paris, proved as hostile to public agitation as the Tories had been. Still, people pinned their hopes on the Reform Bill. In October 1831, these hopes were temporarily dashed; the great Reform Bill, with the aid of twenty-one bishops who voted against it, was thrown out by the House of Lords. As a protest two London papers appeared in mourning, muffled church bells were tolled in Birmingham, and rioting broke out in the streets of Nottingham and Derby. Meanwhile in Bristol the Recorder, Sir Charles Wetherell, arrived to conduct the Sessions. He had been a member of the previous Tory Government and was known to have voted against the Reform Bill in the House of Commons; feeling against him in Bristol was so violent that he came escorted by special constables and three troops of horse. Lant Carpenter wrote to the press before the Recorder's arrival, begging respect for his office. 'I heartily dislike his political conduct,' he said, 'but I would be one of his bodyguard *as a judge*.' This appeal meant nothing to the angry crowd, which greeted the Recorder's coach with hisses, yells and stones. That night they attacked the Mansion House where he was lodged, shouting 'Give us the bloody Recorder; we'll murder him!' They smashed the windows and stove in the doors, while Sir Charles made a hasty and undignified escape down a ladder at the back. Next day, a Sunday, the mob broke into the various city gaols and lock-ups, releasing the prisoners and using the straw from their bedding to set fire to the buildings. Next they rushed to set fire to the Bishop's Palace, heaping smashed furniture on to flaming feather beds. By Sunday night forty-five houses were alight, and the glare of the flames in the night sky could be seen from forty miles away. In Queen's Square, the heart of the riot, the mob chopped up furniture with axes and flung it into the burning houses. They dragged out food from the larders and bottles from the cellars for defiant picnics in the select square, while a drunken man, waving an empty bottle, straddled the equestrian statue of King William III in the centre of the green.[6]

To Mary Carpenter it was a night of anguish, for her father, so prone to imaginary nervous fears, reacted to real danger with calm courage. As night fell, he went fearlessly out into the streets, among the roaring flames, the clouds of smoke and the crash of falling buildings, to visit the members of his congregation one by one. He was so confident in his safety as a well-known liberal, that he invited neighbours to put their valuables into his house for safe keeping.

He spent the night in Queen's Square itself, at the house of some women who had no male relative to protect them. By this time the middle classes, even the supporters of reform, were angry and frightened of that ever-present nineteenth-century terror, the mob. On Monday morning the troops were ordered out, and the cavalry swept through the city, slashing and slicing at the crowds with their sabres, in a series of indiscriminate charges, against

[6] Anon. 'A citizen', *The Bristol Riots, their causes, progress and consequences*, contemporary pamphlet.
[7] Radzinowicz, L. *A History of English Criminal Law*, IV, 136–40.

rioters and passers-by alike. Lant Carpenter, returning home, saw a man's head sliced clean from his shoulders, and was horrified to recognize the victim as a Unitarian merchant from Frenchay, who had come into the city that morning on lawful business. In a few hours the dragoons had cleared the streets, leaving a total of about five hundred dead from the three days' rioting.

In the aftermath of the riots, the Mayor of Bristol, Charles Pinney and nine aldermen of the city were tried for wilful neglect of their duty as magistrates. They had failed to organize a force of special constables; out of a population of a hundred thousand, only some hundred and fifty had reported for duty. Pinney, though he had authorized the commanding officer to disperse the mob, had also refused to ride with the dragoons. He was acquitted, as the duties of magistrates in an emergency were so ill-defined. One of the witnesses Pinney called in his own defence was Lant Carpenter, who had seen much of the fighting. Dr Carpenter maintained that the cavalry charge had done more harm than good, since the rioters had already gone off with their loot, so that when the troops attacked, 'the innocent suffered for the guilty'. He drafted an account of the riots for the benefit of liberal Unitarian readers generally, which was published in their national journal.[8] He followed the trials of alleged rioters by special commission, and became convinced that one man, a Roman Catholic labourer, had been wrongly convicted on the evidence. Here Lant Carpenter showed the best side of his strange and contradictory nature; for he made a personal journey to London to present fresh evidence and get a pardon from the Home Secretary. The accused man had already sailed on a convict ship for transportation, but cholera broke out in the noisome holds, forcing the ship to put in at Milford Haven, where a special messenger arrived with the pardon, in time to save the man from brutal penal servitude or death.[9] Mary Carpenter's first response to the riots was horror and fear; as an old woman she would still describe the contrast between the sunlit Sunday morning and the angry red glare of the fire-lit sky at night. Yet her father urged her to face the problems of human justice and to 'ponder the general causes of the outbreak'. Thus her full attention was turned, for the first time, to the dark world of the very poor, and among them, to the suffering and degradation of convicts.

The troubles of 1833 were not yet over. Cholera was the next disaster to strike Bristol. The city had no public water-supply or drainage; cesspools seeped into wells, and the inhabitants collected their polluted drinking water in jugs and cans from parish pumps. The Bristol death rate in an ordinary year was thirty-one per thousand, as heavy as the Black Country and double the national average. To this sitting target for disease came the warning of a world-wide cholera epidemic. It had raged in Asia during the 1820s, with a thousand cases among the troops in Central India. In 1830 the disease spread overland through Russia; with the spring weather it reached the Near East and Europe. Each region in turn made desperate attempts to contain the infection. In Russia troops surrounded stricken villages and fired on the

[8] *The Monthly Repository*, V, 840–52.
[9] Carpenter, R. L. *Memoir of Lant Carpenter*, 323–6.

peasants who attempted to flee; in Persia priests sounded gongs to frighten away malignant influences. In Britain also the clergy took a hand, with a prayer specially composed, and publicly read in the autumn of 1831. 'Oh, Almighty God who hast visited the nations near us with the sudden death of thousands, spare, we beseech Thee, this Thy favoured land.'[10] Divine partiality to Britain notwithstanding, the first known death from cholera, of a Sunderland keelman, was recorded in October 1831. The population, provided on the best advice with 'herbs, rags and leeches', dumbly awaited its fate. In 1832 the cholera spread to Scotland, where the first patient was an old woman who stoutly refused to take any remedy but whisky. By March the epidemic reached London, where in four weeks there were over a thousand cases, with five hundred deaths. In the same month the disease was carried to Bristol, probably by a seaman from Rotherhithe who travelled down on the outside of the London coach and collapsed in the street on arrival. Bristol, densely populated, low-lying and filthy, was a natural breeding-ground for infection. In the event it escaped more lightly than Plymouth and Devonport, which had a thousand deaths, or towns like Bilston, in the Black Country, which lost half its total population. Nevertheless in four months 694 people died in Clifton and Bristol, and coffins could not be made fast enough for their burial. The disease, hideous in its symptoms and lethal in its outcome, started in the hovels and alleys round the docks, where the poor lodged, but quickly spread to all parts of the city. It inspired general panic and terror, with wild rumours that the sea was infected, causing a slump in the bathing-machine business, and gruesome tales of victims dissected by the doctors before the life was out of them.[11]

In the school there does not seem to have been a single case, in spite of much anxiety, a tribute in itself to Mrs Carpenter's scrupulously clean housekeeping; but in the mean and dingy streets round Lewin's Mead, cholera raged. Once again, Mary Carpenter, in her peaceful, cultured home, saw the reality of her poor neighbours' lives. She never forgot it. A national day of fasting and prayer was decreed, which was observed by all denominations. Mary used it to record in her journal a solemn vow to serve humanity. Under Dr Carpenter's direction the family did what they could to supply stricken households with blankets, food and fuel. Mary wrote, 'I feel deeply moved, that I can do no more towards alleviating the distress of the poor, but I hope I shall be enabled to so do.' In November, when the epidemic died down and a public thanksgiving was declared, she secretly renewed her vow. 'I have never forgotten the determination I made on the day of public humiliation, nor has it at all weakened, but I have not yet had the means of putting it into effect. God grant that I soon may have them!'[12] She was 25, and this was the first time she had dared to express a wish for herself. During the next year, two visitors came from overseas, who were to shape the whole course of her future life and work.

[10] Longmate, N. *King Cholera*, 13.
[11] Gatherer, A. *A socio-medical study of the first cholera epidemic in Britain* (unpublished M.D. thesis).   [12] *Life and Work*, 23.

In September 1833 a magnificent figure appeared in the streets of Bristol. Ram Mohun Roy was the first Brahmin to risk defilement by travelling overseas, a prince of Bengal, with proud bearing and deep, flashing eyes, dressed in the flowing robes of his high caste, and attended by two Hindu body servants. He had been horrified as a young man by seeing his brother's widow burnt alive on her husband's funeral pyre. She attempted to escape, but relatives drove her back, while loud gongs and drums drowned her dying screams. The young man vowed never to rest until the custom of suttee was abolished.[13] He studied the Vedantas and Upanishads, becoming gradually convinced that this rite and many other Hindu traditions, were corruptions of what had once been pure ethical monotheism. Interest in comparative religion led him to learn first Persian, Arabic and Sanskrit, later Hebrew, Greek and English. He was led to believe that all religions were in essence one. 'Cows are of different colours,' he explained in a homely simile to his wife, 'but the colour of the milk they give is the same.' In 1820 he published *The Precepts of Jesus the Guide to Peace and Happiness* and found himself sharply attacked by Christian missionaries in India, since as a monotheist he rejected the divinity and the miracles of Jesus.[14] Unitarians, on the other hand, were naturally tempted to regard him as a convert to their own faith. Ram Roy corresponded with Lant Carpenter, who, musing on the 'cloud no bigger than a man's hand', indulged in the unlikely dream of an Indian sub-continent exclusively populated with sound Unitarians. It is clear now that Ram Roy's chief concern was with the reformed Hindu temple which he founded in Calcutta to study the ethical teaching of the Vedantas; this has been a lasting influence, especially in Bengal, where Ram Roy is justly honoured as one of the founders of modern India. He was critical of the Christian church, and wrote a letter to Bristol regretting 'those corrupt and absurd notions which have gradually disfigured genuine Christianity and brought it to a level with heathen mythology'. Nevertheless when he made the bold decision to visit England, and was asked what Englishman he most desired to see, he answered, 'Dr Carpenter'.

The arrival of a Rajah created a mild furore in England, where the Oriental romances of Byron and Tom Moore were still favourite reading. Ram Roy was received by William IV and visited by Jeremy Bentham, while the Court Journal noted that 'his felicitous manner of paying a compliment gained him many admirers among the high-born beauties of Britain'. His promised visit to Bristol alarmed even the highly-organized Mrs Carpenter; a prince and his entourage could hardly be expected to fit into a girls' boarding school. Dr Carpenter was guardian to the orphan daughter of a rich Unitarian merchant, who offered her Georgian country mansion, set in a grove of fine elm-trees. Here, at Stapleton Grove a large reception was held on 11th September, where clergy of various denominations took turns to harangue the courteous Rajah, who listened with every appearance of interest. Dr Carpenter felt

---

[13] The practice was forbidden by the India Act against Suttee of 1829.
[14] Collett, S. D. *Life and Letters of Ram Mohun Roy*, 39.

persuaded that he 'accepted the Divine Authority of Christ'. On Sunday 15th, Mary, inwardly excited but gravely composed in manner, was sent in a carriage to accompany Ram Roy to Lewin's Mead, where he joined with his friends in Unitarian worship and listened to a lengthy sermon by her father. As the horses jogged along the homeward road after meeting, Mary was far too deeply inhibited to speak what was in her mind, but from that morning dated a resolution, which had to wait more than thirty years, to visit and serve the women of India.

Four days later, Ram Roy fell suddenly ill, with headache, high fever and collapse.[15] For a week he lay looking out on the garden, while his friends took turns to sit with him. He was distressed to be nursed by ladies, which he considered most improper, but was reassured that this was the English custom.[16] On 26th September, he appeared to have a stroke and become paralysed; by next evening he no longer recognized his friends. Dr Carpenter was not present, as he had fallen ill himself under the strain; but fortunately for the patient's peace of mind, one of the company had been in Calcutta, and realized that if the Rajah lost caste, his sons might be disinherited and his work for India undermined. When Dr Estlin pronounced the Rajah sinking, it was agreed to ask his Hindu servants to observe the full prayers and rites for the death of a Brahmin. It was a beautiful night, and a full moon shone on the great trees as Ram Roy's breathing grew harsher and slowly failed. 'The Star in the East', as Mary called him, had set. She was one of the witnesses who signed a formal account of his burial, without religious ceremony and in unconsecrated ground. The two tall servants sobbed like lost children, as they carried their master's coffin along the shady walk under the peaceful elm-trees and laid it in the ground. Dr Carpenter directed the silent ritual, surely the only dissenting minister ever to have buried a Hindu in an English private garden. Later he preached, as though to make up for the silence, 'a discourse more than an hour and a quarter in duration' in which he gave 'a review of the labours, opinions and character of the Rajah, and his own friendship with the illustrious deceased'.[17] Mary was too distressed to do more than write some sad, pitifully inadequate sonnets. Many years later Ram Roy's body was transferred to an elaborate domed and pillared mausoleum in the Indian style, built for him at Arnos Vale cemetery, near the tombs of the Carpenters, by the grandfather of the poet Tagore. This is the scene of a small yearly pilgrimage by members of the Indian community, which includes a service at Lewin's Mead. 'Should the Race Relations Board ever need a patron saint,' wrote Naseem Khan who joined the pilgrimage in 1971, 'Ram Mohun Roy is the obvious candidate.'[18] To Mary Carpenter, he was always the patron saint of man's brotherhood.

The second visitor came from America. In 1830, at a meeting of the British

[15] Post mortem examination showed that he suffered from meningitis.
[16] Carpenter, M. *Last Day in England of the Rajah Rammohun Roy*, 32. This name was spelt by Europeans in a variety of ways.
[17] Carpenter, R. L. *Memoir of Lant Carpenter*, 377.
[18] *The Guardian*, 2nd October 1971, Naseem Khan, 'Ram Roy was Here', to which I am also indebted for much of the preceding information.

and Foreign Unitarian Association held in Manchester, W. J. Fox [19] proposed that they should study a remarkable series of reports on social work, issued by a Unitarian minister at Boston, Massachusetts. The Reverend Joseph Tuckerman came from a well-known Boston family. He was apparently a cheerful young man, who passed through the city's Latin School and Harvard College, said his room-mate, 'as though on holiday'. He married and went as minister to what was then a small and lonely parish on the shore at Chelsea, Massachusetts. After four years of marriage his young wife died, and he passed through one of those prolonged nervous crises, so frequent in the lives of Puritans. Like Lant Carpenter, he was frequently ill from overstrain, and his voice failed for public preaching. After years of self-searching, he became convinced that his call was to 'the neglected poor of our cities'. In 1826 he gave up his parish and moved into Boston, to found what he called 'The Ministry at Large', a city mission based on house-to-house visiting.[20] He had a fanatical belief in the importance of his work. 'The greatest thing in any city is Man himself,' he wrote. 'He is its end.' His annual reports are among the earliest documents of American social work.

Lant Carpenter was so struck with them, that he wrote, hoping Dr Tuckerman might visit him in England. Back came a long, fervent letter from his brother minister, on 'the obligation of a city to care for the moral health of its members' and 'the need for *Christian friends* of the poor'. 'I long to be with you,' wrote the enthusiastic Bostonian. 'How glad I shall be to see you and the other English friends! Then, too, if I were in England, I could embrace the Rajah Ram Mohun Roy.'[21] Tuckerman arrived in Europe in summer 1833, in time to see Ram Roy briefly in London, before departing on a tour of France, Ireland, Liverpool, Manchester and Birmingham. Everywhere he went he talked 'in season and some may think out of season', said one listener feelingly, of his '*glowing* interest in the poor' and 'our Christian duty to the unfortunate'. Young people were inspired; ladies wept. Only one or two dissident voices were raised. 'Like all men of one idea,' wrote observant Lucy Aikin,' he could neither speak nor suffer others to speak of anything else, which wore out the patience of even the best disposed.' On the whole, however, his was a triumphal progress. It was December 1833, and Ram Roy had already died, when Dr Tuckerman finally arrived in Bristol as guest of the Carpenter family. For Mary, his visit came as the climax of a year's intense experiences, the riots, the cholera epidemic, the death of Ram Roy, her own unfocused longing for service. She had always been acutely sensitive to atmosphere and influence; now she was seeking a direction for her life. Within a surprisingly short time Joseph Tuckerman fixed it for ever.

Contemporary accounts are remarkably frank about the impression he made. Even in the course of his funeral sermon, William Ellery Channing admitted that most people disliked Tuckerman on sight. Gaunt, black-clad, austere

---

[19] Celebrated preacher and author of South Place Chapel, later disowned by the Unitarians because he separated from his wife.

[20] Channing, W. E. *A Discourse of the life and character of the Rev. J. Tuckerman*, 27-30.

[21] Carpenter, M. *Life of Tuckerman*, 1848, 67.

in nature and sanctimonious in manner, he would glide into a room, and, wrote his nephew, 'take a stand distinctly clerical to the casual observer. He was ready to preach, argue, sympathize, counsel, rebuke, compassionate or pray as the occasion demanded.'[22] 'Whether in conversation or preaching,' said his brother-in-law frankly, 'he had affectations of manner and utterance which were painful and disagreeable.' On a previous visit to England he had consulted the great Dr Abernethy, with a long account of his ailments, and his 'little parish'. Abernethy, famous for wasting no words, cut off the flow of clerical small talk. 'Never mind your little parish! Go home and build a barn.'[23] His total absorption in his own affairs was notorious, though Mary Carpenter grew to rival him in this. His manner was insistent, dominating, compelling attention and his influence over women extraordinary. Fifty years after his death, a group of industrious ladies in Boston was still known as Dr Tuckerman's Sewing Circle. Mary was content to listen for hours to his nasal New England voice sawing on about slums and soup kitchens, prisons and district visiting. Just as Lant Carpenter's liberal ideals remained valid, although he manipulated people in his private life, so Tuckerman's obsessional personality could not detract from the value of his practical work.[24]

The two ministers struck up a friendship of such sensibility that they could not trust themselves to meet for a farewell interview, while the young ladies of the boarding-school hovered round in admiration. Tuckerman wrote home describing the other-worldly charm of the Carpenter household, 'the family gathering in the morning, the cordial shaking of hands, the heartfelt affectionate kisses, the reading of the Word, the simple prayers, the friendly gathering and conversation round the breakfast table'. This cheerfulness, like the orderly charm which so often strikes the visitor to a convent, was only achieved by the intense self-discipline of every individual member of the household. Tuckerman, like Lant Carpenter, was always in uncertain health, and while staying with the Carpenters he fell seriously ill with pneumonia, then a critical disease. They nursed him devotedly,[25] and he stayed over Christmas and into the New Year of 1834 to regain his strength. Mary was appointed by her mother to cheer his convalescence with interesting conversation and careful walks. As soon as he was strong enough to go out, he demanded to explore the network of mean streets around Lewin's Mead. On these walks, he clearly became a different person from the clerical monologist of platform and drawing-room. Tuckerman had a true vocation, and great skill in his work. He compiled the first index ever made of social services available to the needy in Boston, and planned to open a bureau where citizens could come for free advice and information.[26] All his affectations vanished when faced with direct human need. His courtesy and respect, his passionate concern, won the trust of the most hostile, and his suggestions were usually full of good sense. 'There are resources for human happiness everywhere,' he later wrote

[22] McColgan, D. *Joseph Tuckerman* (Dissertation submitted to Faculty of Social Work of Catholic University of America, 1940), 270–1.

[23] *Ibid.*, 156.   [24] *Ibid.*, 99.

[25] *Ibid.*, 219.   [26] *Ibid.*, 260.

to Mary. 'Look on every human being, however encrusted with dirt and covered with rags, however degraded by ignorance and debased by sin, as still retaining in his soul the image of the Creator. The poorest, lowest, meanest human being is a child of God.'[27]

One day they were passing along under the shadow of a tall tenement, in the district of common lodging-houses, where discharged sailors, tramps, beggars, prostitutes and the occasional escaped slave from the West Indies slept thirty to a small room. These houses swarmed with children, who played in the gutters, or raked over the ash heaps for cabbage leaves and potato peelings to eat. As they passed by, a wild, ragged boy dashed out of a dark entry and across their path. Tuckerman watched him vanish anxiously. 'That child', he said, 'should be followed to his home and seen after.' 'His words sank into my heart,' said Mary. Thirty-five years later, she still remembered that moment as the great turning-point in her life.[28]

The whole problem of neglected, vagrant and delinquent children was uppermost in Joseph Tuckerman's mind at exactly this time; his report for 1832 had been largely devoted to it. From long experience he had become convinced that the cost of educating them would be far less in the long run than allowing them to drift into delinquency in order to survive in the city jungle. Above all, children should not be allowed, for want of any other provision, to pass through the city gaols 'where a confinement of a fortnight or three weeks only is enough to insure moral ruin'. He suggested the appointment of an officer whose special responsibility should be the children of the city, seeing that the young ones attended school, and finding jobs or apprenticeships for the older ones. When this officer found children in moral danger, there should be a special school, in healthy country, where they could go, with their parents' consent, 'if possible before the guilt of crime has been incurred'.[29] Such was Tuckerman's determination, that as a result of his efforts, Thompson's Island, in Massachusetts Bay, was bought, and a Farm School for a hundred boys built, to the plan of the great architect Bulfinch, designer of the Boston State House. The first hundred boys had actually been admitted in the year of Tuckerman's meeting with Mary Carpenter; he was full of enthusiasm for his experiment, and overflowing with optimism about its success. He described the farm for outdoor work in summer, and the workshops where during the long New England winter the boys could learn a variety of crafts. He described the special help for slow or backward children, and the sympathetic counselling for disturbed boys. Above all, he dwelt on the philosophy of child reclamation. 'The school presents no vindictive or reproachful aspects. It threatens no humiliating recollections of the past. It holds no degrading denunciations for the future. It is to be regarded, not as a prison but as a *school*.'[30]

There is no need to look any further for the origins of Mary Carpenter's

---

[27] Carpenter, M. *Life of Tuckerman*, 81.
[28] *Life and Work*, 35.
[29] Tuckerman, J. *Seventh Annual Report of the Ministry at Large.*
[30] *Ibid.*

most distinctive ideas. She received these opinions, reinforced of course by her father's fervent approval, like Moses receiving the tables of the law. Like Moses, she held them immutably for the rest of her days. What she did not yet understand, and perhaps never understood, was how far they differed from most people's confused, contradictory, worried thoughts on the subject. Her ideas had set in the mould of her father's own style of advanced, enlightened piety, and she would have felt it wrong to adjust in any way to changing times or circumstances, or to make serious concessions to people of other opinions. For the present, she could only dream of visiting the Farm School one day. Dr Tuckerman departed with effusive farewells for a tour of Europe, promising to return before he finally took ship home to Boston. Mary was always to acknowledge him, with her own father, as the author of her work.

True to his promise, Tuckerman came for a second visit early in 1834. He confirmed Mary Carpenter's resolution; service to the children of the poor, direct, practical and face to face, was to be her life's work. Her father took the first step by founding a society, on the model of Tuckerman's mission in Boston, for social work in the slums round Lewin's Mead. He called it the Working and Visiting Society, with working in its contemporary meaning of a regular needlework group, to make warm clothes for the aged, sick and for the ragged, shivering children, turned out to run the streets in winter. As the ladies sewed, Dr Carpenter read aloud 'some interesting or instructive passage to excite their Christian efforts'. Mary became the first secretary of the Society, training herself to keep individual case records, make up accounts and write reports for the monthly committee, a voluntary service she carried out with the most scrupulous efficiency for the next twenty years, feeling that her father's special blessing lay on the work. Meanwhile Lant Carpenter undertook to edit and publish a selection from Tuckerman's Annual Reports on the work in Boston, which he brought out in 1839.[31] A complete set of the closely printed, brown-paper covered, dull-looking little volumes, took its place among the classics of Unitarianism on his study shelves. To Mary they became a second Bible, which she studied almost with a sense of guilt, because they meant so much more to her than anything else in the endless round of everyday chores. 'I must *never* allow them to interfere with my other duties,' she wrote, 'but only with my hours of relaxation.' Nevertheless they took the place in her life of Florence Nightingale's secret hospital studies, and in these reports may be found the germ of many of Mary Carpenter's most distinctive ideas. 'Act upon the principle that human nature is *never* to be given up,' wrote Tuckerman in his Second Annual Report on criminal families. 'There is no condition so desperate as to forbid recovery, nor does repeated failure justify discouragement . . . I should as soon think of sending a diseased man for his health to a Lazaretto for the plague, as of sending a convict to prison for reformation.' Above all he stressed the responsibility of society for all its children, including young offenders. 'In receiving sentence

[31] Carpenter, L. *Christian Service to the Poor in Cities.*

of law,' he wrote, 'they are treated as alone responsible for their transgressions. But are they so? Is their guilt any greater than that of society around them, which might have saved them and yet left them uncared for?' Mary Carpenter believed in these ideas as fanatically as Tuckerman himself; they were to be the foundations of her teaching.

On the last day of 1836 Mary sat down, as her habit was each year, to write her resolutions. 'It is my earnest and greatest desire, if God sees it well, to devote my life *entirely* to aiding the poor and destitute. I should most cheerfully give up for this all other employment.' Only to her favourite sister Anna did she tell her secret ambition, to give up the school, once and for all, to spend two years in Boston training herself for the work, and to devote her whole life to the destitute. Meanwhile she faced the fact that 'India itself was not further away than Lewin's Mead.' For fifteen years—the best working years of many peoples' lives—she was forced to wait.

The sense of frustration, of wasted time, gnawed her, as her twenties wore away into her thirties in a ceaseless round of classes, French dictées, correcting essays, and deportment, supervising dreary walks and counting linen. By the time the youthful Queen Victoria came to the throne, Mary Carpenter, at 30, felt, and by all accounts looked, like a middle-aged woman. 'On her' wrote a relative, as if such exploitation was the most natural thing in the world, 'fell the cherishing of parents, the care of the school and the education of her brothers.' These cares grew heavier, not lighter, as the boys reached university age. William, his apprenticeship to Dr Estlin finished, went to the Middlesex Hospital as medical and surgical clerk, and on to Edinburgh University, where he began to reveal his future brilliance as a natural scientist. Russell, small, courteous and gentle, but of formidably strong character, left home to study at Manchester College for the Unitarian ministry. Philip unselfishly agreed to save expense by entering an apprenticeship with an optical instrument-maker. He never complained, but Russell, discovering his secret disappointment at this choice, persuaded their father to send Philip to college as well. Both, like William, took first class honours; their father was only disappointed that as Dissenters they were refused admission to Oxford or Cambridge. They were all intensely serious young men; Russell indeed refused to join in a snowball fight, on the grounds that 'he had not come to college to play'. With a little more self-consciousness they might have been prigs; as it was they were too unworldly to realize there was anything unusual about their family code of behaviour.[32] Mary loved her brothers and was proud of them; but the cost of their privileged education weighed heavily upon her. In 1838 Mrs Carpenter had to be nursed through a long illness, and the housekeeping for the whole school fell on the sisters. Mary, always slight, grew angular and careworn. Her sense of humour grew sharper, usually at the expense of the young ladies. When they attended lectures by the poet James Montgomery, she wrote, 'I have been more busy than usual in consequence of the lectures, of which the Y.Ls. write *unmercifully* long

[32] Carpenter, R. L. *Memoir of W. B. Carpenter*, and *Memoir of Philip Pearsall Carpenter*, *passim*.

recollections.' When a returned missionary visited, 'He breakfasted with us and made all the young ladies wish to go to the Sandwich Islands.' She felt a continual inner conflict, which she was careful to hide from her father, but which appears again and again in her self-revealing notebooks. 'I cannot accuse myself', she wrote in 1839, 'of neglecting any of the duties of our school; on the contrary I conscientiously prevent anything from interfering with them. Yet I neither love these duties as I ought, nor do I feel that vivid interest in them, which I do in others, to which I am tempted to wish myself called.'[33] An evil temptation, to her rigid puritan temperament, would have been easy to resist; a temptation to do good threatened her as a greater sin. She later confessed this was the darkest period of her life. It ended with a tragedy which both broke her heart and set her free, the mysterious, never-explained death of her father.

[33] *Life and Work*, 44.

4

A DEATH IN THE FAMILY
1839-1844

After the age of 55 Lant Carpenter withdrew gradually from public life, and devoted himself increasingly to the composition of his chief theological work. This was an *Apostolical Harmony of the Gospels*, designed to reconcile contradictions in the gospel narratives which had emerged from the historical criticism of the young generation of scholars. Dr Carpenter formed the opinion that the active ministry of Jesus lasted little more than one year, 'the acceptable year of the Lord'. He published this novel conclusion in 1835 and, in spite of much criticism, repeated it in a second edition, dedicated by special permission to Queen Victoria, which led to much hostile criticism for associating the young Queen's name with 'so deadly a heresy'. Faced with the stresses of authorship and hostile reviews, Lant developed his usual warning symptoms of sleeplessness, sickness and fainting, but rallied and wrote to his doctor son William that 'the indisposition seems to have arisen from indigestion acting on the head'. Although Mary, watching him with anxious love, noticed that he tired easily, he continued to travel around the country, preaching, examining and attending meetings of various Unitarian Associations for the next three years. In February 1839 his own father died at the age of 91, and Lant Carpenter attended his funeral, meeting some members of his large and scattered family almost for the first time in thirty years. He had lived little with his parents or his eight brothers and sisters; there had been as he said 'no reciprocity of endearments' and in the language of piety 'all was for the best'. Yet the meeting by the graveside carried him back to memories of his broken home and lonely childhood, 'enhanced', he said, 'by many painful recollections.' He confessed that it distressed him more than his reason approved.

He was still active. On 19th May 1839, he preached on behalf of the Sunday Schools and girls' day school attached to Lewin's Mead Meeting. Mary had taught in the Sunday Schools since childhood, and many of its happiest activities were her own creation. She had started a lending library, in which the books were so eagerly read that they fell to pieces, and a museum in which the children were 'pleased and proud to display their treasured curiosities, shells, minerals, pressed and fresh plants, seeds, corals, birds' eggs, stuffed birds and reptiles' collected by them on nature walks in the country. She had introduced singing lessons, teaching not merely hymns, but cheerful songs 'into which the boys especially enter with great spirit. So,' she concluded her anonymous report, as secretary of the schools, 'a field of pure enjoyment is opened to these children, even those from poor and ignorant homes.'[1] Seeing them in the meeting-house gallery for their anniversary service, 83 girls, 77 boys and 116 infants, orderly, well-scrubbed, clean-pinafored and singing cheerfully, she had every right to be proud of her work. Yet she knew that these children of the respectable 'deserving' poor, so beloved of evangelical philanthropists, were not the children to whom Tuckerman had directed her, and whom she still longed to reach. For every child in chapel, three roamed the nearby quays and alleys begging and stealing. Secretly she renewed her vow to find them.

That school service was almost the last occasion on which Mary Carpenter heard her father preach. A month later, on 21st June 1839, he broke down in a renewed attack of melancholia, this time with a 'violence of symptoms' which frightened his family. Mary and her mother took him to the coast, where he made little progress. He complained of giddiness, faintness, headache, sleepness nights, and overwhelming misery. All his painful delusions of unworthiness, of being cut off from God by the weight of his sins, returned.[2] To Mary it was mournful to see him, 'once so full of life and energy, now bowing under the stroke'. When they attempted to comfort him, he insisted that 'no one knew his secret faults'. On 22nd July, he went to London to consult a specialist, who advised a repetition of the tour on the Continent, which had cheered him so much ten years before. Lant Carpenter at first refused, 'from an unwillingness to incur expense'. It later emerged that he had adequate capital, but his morbid anxiety attached itself, as often in such cases, to money matters. His friends and congregation, with their usual generosity, promptly subscribed more than enough to pay for a six months' tour abroad. Russell Carpenter had just graduated in theology, and came home to act as locum tenens for his father, 'a loving son and brother', wrote Mary, 'in all our home troubles'. Russell was to take the lead in all the decisions which followed, for their father was incapable of active choice. Mary, of course, would have loved to travel with her father, believing that her devotion could nurse him back to health; but his doctors strongly advised against any member of his family, 'whose presence would constantly recall trains of thought desirable to avoid'. Although they hesitated to say so publicly, many physicians regarded 'erroneous views of religion', especially 'conceptions respecting the awful concerns of futurity', as a cause of insanity.[3] Lant Carpenter was ill enough, moreover, to need medical attention constantly at hand. Finally a young doctor, John Freeman, was engaged to accompany him. Freeman, who had qualified three years earlier, was about the same age as Russell Carpenter; he later returned to England, and spent the rest of his life in general practice in the East End of London, where he became Medical Officer of Health for Mile End. There is good evidence from people who met

---

[1] The Secretary (Mary Carpenter) *Report on the Lewin's Mead Schools.*

[2] These were particularly distressing to his family, because they ran directly counter to his reasoned religious convictions when in health. Carpenter, R. L. *Memoir of Lant Carpenter,* 303–4.

[3] Hunter, R. and MacAlpine, I. *Three Hundred Years of Psychiatry,* 822.

them together that he was kind and devoted to Lant Carpenter, though he had no special qualification for such a case. The two men sailed direct from London on 18th August. For the next seven months Mary lived for her father's letters. He wrote at enormous length, journal letters full of description, which reveal the breadth of his interests. In the Netherlands he delighted in cathedral music, in Germany he approved of public engineering works and public education, at Schaffhausen he was charmed into momentary self-forgetfulness by the Rhine falls, on the Lake of Wallenstadt he appreciated the scenery, and at Zurich he instructed Dr Freeman in the doctrines of the reformer Zwingli.[4] They went on to spend the winter in Rome, where Lant taught his young doctor chess, and they spent the evenings playing together. Freeman was hopeful; he reported how his patient 'delighted in the occupations and amusements of children and would talk to the parties of boys coming back with their satchels from school'.

At home, hopes ran high; family and congregation believed their beloved minister would soon be restored to them; but in March 1840 Dr Freeman wrote that Lant Carpenter had been depressed by a month of the sluicing rain an Italian winter can produce, and seriously distressed by a belated, hostile review of his *Apostolical Harmony*, which he picked up by chance, in a copy of the London *Standard* at Naples. Dr Freeman, who had become devoted, as everyone did, to Lant, bitterly regretted 'the injurious effect of this critique on his mind', and proposed as a diversion that they should travel back from Naples to Rome by sea. This was the last news the family had for the time being. So leisurely was the pace of travel and indeed of illness in those days, that they had not seen their father for eight months, since he left Bristol for London the previous July. They could only remind one another of the touching gentleness of his manner to them then. On the day before Good Friday, they heard that their father was missing, believed dead.

There were few facts to go on. Dr Carpenter, constantly and devotedly attended by Dr Freeman who never left his patient alone, embarked at four o'clock in the afternoon of Sunday, 4th April 1840, on board a French steamer, the *Sully*. Once in open water, they ran into rough weather; Dr Freeman was overcome by seasickness and took helplessly to his bunk. The night grew dark and increasingly stormy, but Lant Carpenter walked on the deck for fresh air until about ten, when violent rain drove everybody, except the officer on watch, down to the cabin. Lant was last seen sheltering in the hatch of the cabin companion-way. Next morning he was missing. Dr Freeman was in despair; the entire ship's company searched, but not a trace of him could be found. What followed may be discovered in a despatch from John Freeborn, banker and British Consular agent at Rome, to Lord Palmerston at the Foreign Office, London.[5] He begged to report 'that a British subject named Lant Carpenter had disappeared during the night of the 4th April from on board the French mercantile steamer Sully, on passage from

---

[4] Carpenter, R. L. *Memoir of Lant Carpenter*, 434–9, gives a selection from this correspondence.

[5] Public Record Office, Foreign Office, class 43, piece 32.

Naples to Civita Vecchia, and it was not known whether the said Lant Carpenter had fallen overboard or had thrown himself into the sea. Subsequently I have received a letter from his Eminence the Cardinal Secretary of State[6] communicating to me that the body of a drowned person which from passports found in the pocket appeared to be Lant Carpenter had been washed on shore near Porto d'Anzio, 50 miles S.S.E. of Rome, and which according to the sanitary laws existing was burnt on the shore together with the clothes. The property found in the pockets however was preserved and has been handed to me. It consists of an English silver watch, a promissory note for three hundred pounds, and two small portfolios with memoranda.' Three months had passed before the recovery of the body, and Freeborn was still at a loss to know where to send these possessions, until Dr John Conquest, lecturer in midwifery at St Batholomew's Hospital, called at the bank. He was a well-known Puritan; while most obstetricians affected a style of conversation said to be 'more indecent than the dramas of the Restoration', he interlarded his remarks with Bible texts; indeed some contemporaries complained of his 'sickly style'. He knew William Carpenter and offered to take the property with him when he returned to England. At the end of August the small parcel with all its poignant associations reached the family in Bristol.

At home, Russell Carpenter had taken charge. In this crisis the young minister, who was only 24, and just out of college, showed remarkable firmness and determination. While admitting that 'the manner of departure was distressing to many' he insisted that his father's lonely death *must* have been an accident. He must, Russell said, have been attacked by sickness, lost his balance and been washed overboard. He told the minister who was to 'improve the event' with a memorial sermon, that his father had 'during his latter illness a morbid fear of death', and that the sudden accident was merciful, since it had saved the sick man 'many months of languishing'. Probably he did not appreciate that, as a classical Greek physician put it, 'Many fear death and yet in a contrary mood do away with themselves.' Moreover recovery from depression, with returning will-power, is often said to be a danger point for suicide attempts. Russell was equally firm with the family. He gathered them in their mother's room that Easter Sunday morning, urging them to 'trust where they could not trace'. The April weather that year was particularly beautiful; the brothers and sisters took long walks into the country, returning home with armfuls of flowers for their mother. 'I never felt more grateful', wrote 20-year old Philip, 'for the beauty of the spring.' All were wrought up to a high pitch of spirituality, until Mrs Carpenter, with her usual sober realism, reminded them of possible troubles to come. 'She saw', wrote Philip, 'how clearly the visioned glories all appeared to us, and warned us that if we were on the Delectable Mountains, we might yet have to traverse the Valley of Humiliation.'[7] It was her only recorded comment on the tragedy of her husband's death. Evidently she was not satisfied in her

[6] Civita Vecchia was in the Papal States.
[7] Carpenter, R. L. *Memoir of Philip Pearsall Carpenter*, 27.

own mind, for after the discovery of the body, she asked one of the executors to write to the Foreign Office for any further information from the consul's report. The draft reply has been preserved among the consular papers, and is a curious document. It began; 'I am to acquaint you that Lord Palmerston will comply with your request,' but this has been crossed out, on second thoughts, and she was given instead 'an extract from a despatch received from Mr. Freeborn relative to this subject'.[8] The time, place and true manner of Lant Carpenter's death remained ever after a total mystery. It was comforting to the widow who had fought so long to save her husband's peace of mind, to feel her mourning shared by the whole Unitarian Church. Scores of letters and official addresses came to the house; a memorial service drew an immense congregation, and she was touched to see poor people in Bristol, who could ill afford it, wearing black in Lant Carpenter's memory.[9] The work of answering letters occupied the whole family for weeks.

In all the circumstantial detail of these various accounts there is no mention of Mary. She was stunned by grief. Of all the family she had felt herself nearest to their father, most like him in looks and temperament; she had ruled her daily life by his guidance and attempted to share all his interests. For years she had dreamed of a time when he would support and direct her work among neglected children. Now that time would never come. 'The blank', she later admitted, 'was appalling.' What Mary really believed about the manner of her father's death was never put into words, certainly not to the outside world and probably not even to herself; but the thought of it continued to haunt her. As though to confirm the loss of Mary's hopes, she heard the news, that same autumn, that Dr Tuckerman had died, also in the course of a sea voyage for his health. She had not seen him for six years, but had always looked to his letters for practical advice. He was gone, she wrote, 'but he will live in my thoughts as long as I am here'. In this double bereavement, Mary clung to her religious duty, which was to hope. On the last day of 1840, she wrote a long entry in her journal. 'In outward sorrow, but in inward peace, having lost him whom most we loved on earth, yet possessing him in purer love, in filial memory and in pure hope . . . would I close a year to be forever loved and hallowed.' The conventional phrases of piety and resignation were for her factually true. She took up her duties, though her feelings were centred far outside everyday life. Outwardly she was calm, but for a long time she would be closer to the dead than to the living. The only event which seemed to give her pleasure in these years of appalling emptiness was the unveiling of the monument to her father, which is still to be seen in Lewin's Mead Meeting. A white marble tablet shows in relief the draped sarcophagus bearing a profile medallion of Lant Carpenter, as his sorrowing congregation remembered him. A long inscription records how, 'by sanctity of life as well as force of reason', he led men to the truth.

The family and congregation had originally composed a rather fulsome inscription, dwelling on Lant's piety, but James Martineau criticized this

---

[8] Public Record Office, Foreign Office, Class 43, piece 32.
[9] *The Christian Reformer*, vii, 551–6.

sharply as 'narrowing the view of his life', and they consented to redraft it. The letters which passed between Martineau and the Carpenters during 1841 show how totally Mary was dedicated to her father's memory, and how determined to impose her own version of it on the world. Martineau wrote, 'I have not forgotten nor do I regret my promise to contribute a few recollections of my schooldays to Russell's memoir of your father.' Patiently, he assured her that he recalled all the incidents of which she reminded him, and that delay was caused by pressure of work. When she objected to what he wrote, he was courteous but firm. 'I can only sketch the portrait from my own point of view. That which your more privileged position allowed you to discern, though hidden from others, the memoir must supply.' She sent him proofs, demanding alterations; he returned them unchanged. 'I have left the points without modification because it seemed to me important to put down my impressions faithfully and honestly.'[10] Meanwhile Mary was demanding copies of all her father's letters from his American correspondents. William Ellery Channing, who perhaps had not kept them, but did not like to admit this to a sorrowing daughter, replied in some embarrassment that 'a lamentable want of order among my papers prevents me from finding them.'[11] When the memoir by Russell, unconsciously a most revealing document, was finally complete, Mary demanded subscriptions for it. Poor James Martineau apologized that in spite of appeals from the pulpit he had only been able to dispose of eight copies, although Mrs Gaskell had promised to take one. Early in 1842, Mary was offering him portrait busts of her idol. 'I fear we will hardly sell many here,' he replied, 'the likeness not appearing to strike those who remember your father.' Evidently, in the depths of her grief, Mary could not help resenting her dead father's co-minister and successor. She sent a copy of a report on some parish activity, in which she inserted what James considered '*a rap*' at Mr Armstrong, and which at last drove him to criticize her openly. 'I think this should not have been,' he wrote, quietly but firmly. 'It left a painful impression of the state of feeling between you.' At the same time, however, he wrote that he was grieved to hear of her continuing ill-health; her obvious misery was enough to excuse any sharpness of temper. Moreover, the world of her childhood, hallowed by her father's presence, was breaking up around her.

With the death of Lant Carpenter the life of the family changed. One by one the brothers and sisters left home to take up new work and new relationships, until Mary was left alone with their ageing mother. One year, she lamented, they celebrated Christmas in six separate towns. First to go was her favourite brother Philip, whom she had nursed as a baby. He went to serve as minister at Stand near Manchester, taking with him Susan, the youngest sister, to keep house. Susan, like their mother, was both capable and quick; 'she does everything so fast that I cannot keep up with her at all,' wrote Philip. Vague and unworldly, he was bemused by the whole business of being a householder. 'It seems so funny', he wrote to Mary, 'having a house

[10] Manchester College, Oxford, Library, A3, Box B.
[11] *Ibid.*, Letterbook D.

of one's own and driving in nails just where one likes, and seeing one's own name on the kitchen towels!'[12] Susan organized him firmly, and remained as his housekeeper until 1850, when she married Robert Gaskell, also a minister, and brother-in-law of Elizabeth Gaskell the novelist. Next went Russell, his duties as locum tenens over when Dr Carpenter's successor was appointed. Both Russell and Philip had been among the first candidates for the new University of London B.A. 'It was curious,' Russell wrote after their shared finals, 'we Units, being examined in theology by two clergymen.' The clergymen, to their credit, awarded first class honours to both studious young Dissenters. Russell became minister successively at Bridgwater, Birkenhead and Halifax, where he made his mark, attacking slums and municipal corruption, and teaching kindness to children and animals. He married happily a girl named Mary Brown, and was particularly loved as 'a gentle and sensible visitor of the sick and of all those in trouble.'[13] Anna remained at home, for the time being, to help Mary with the continuing duties of the boarding school, which they moved in 1842 to a new villa, Thanet House, in the Whiteladies Road.[14]

William married in the year of his father's death, and took his young wife Louisa Powell to Edinburgh. There a hard knock awaited them. In 1843 the then rigidly Calvinist Senate of Edinburgh University, scandalized that William not only refused to believe in the Trinity, but also disputed the essential sinfulness of mankind, refused him a Professorship although he was an outstanding candidate. William moved to London where he was for seven years lecturer and examiner in anatomy at the London Hospital. His two text books on physiology became standard works running into many editions, and establishing the subject as an essential science. His appetite for knowledge was vast; he remembered everything he read, and it is said that 'it proved hazardous to disagree with him in any point of detail'. William and Louisa had five lively, intelligent boys, among them Mary Carpenter's first biographer, Estlin Carpenter. William taught his sons for half an hour before breakfast every morning, but it is something of a relief to learn that they were not the model children their elders had been; Philip, the youngest, in particular was famous for his angry bellow, and went by the family nickname 'square mouth'. In the evenings, William would go to his wife's sitting-room. There Louisa made tea, while he played to her on a chamber-organ he had built himself, thoughtfully casing in the swell box, so that the sound would not be loud enough to wake the sleeping children. He described his marriage, in old age, as 'forty-five years of unbroken love and trust'. In this full, satisfying life, William was sometimes uneasily conscious of Mary's loneliness, and the emotional chains which bound her to the past. He wrote to her with great kindness and sympathy on the anniversary of their father's death, which he realized was 'never long absent from your imagination. Yet the memory of our dear father should not be to any of us associated with painful feelings.

[12] Carpenter, R. L. *Memoir of Philip Pearsall Carpenter*, 44.
[13] Carpenter, R. L. *Personal and Social Christianity*, 34.
[14] Matthews' *Annual Bristol Directory*, 1843.

I no more think of his love as lost to us, than I do that of my wife or children when they are asleep.'[15]

Mary was left by her father's death completely dependent on her mother for money, and even when the school moved, continued to live with her in the old family house. Lant Carpenter had left house, land, stables and property to his wife, with a long preamble to his will, 'believing that my children will readily accede to this decision, considering the tried affection and long continued exertion of my beloved wife, the way in which she has been a helpmate to me and a wise and faithful mother to our children and the judgment and steadfastness with which she has maintained the welfare of my family during my long absence.'[16] Thanks to his careful habits, she was left comfortably off; the Great Western Railway shares helped to bring in an income of £300, then worth at least ten times as much as now. In addition, habitual anxiety had led Lant Carpenter to insure his life with three separate insurance companies. Because he had died at sea, in such mysterious circumstances, there was some doubt whether the companies were liable, but after negotiation they paid, one in full, the others, a moiety of the sum originally insured.[17] The habit of rigid self-denial was too engrained for Mrs Carpenter to change her way of life; she continued the school, but friends noticed how much, 'with ampler means of gratifying generous impulses', she enjoyed giving to those in need.[18] She had certainly earned this ease, and none of the family questioned for a moment the justice of their father's will. Nevertheless, Mary, a hard-working woman of 33, was left in the position of a child to whom pocket-money is given.

Lant Carpenter and Mary herself become more comprehensible when one looks at their family history. The Carpenters had a well-marked family constitutional temperament, as well as strong physical resemblances. They were, almost without exception, people of remarkable ability. Among the men of the family it was the rule rather than the exception, to take first class academic honours or gold medals; Lant himself, his three sons William, Russell and Philip, and at least two grandsons were all prizemen at university. Mary Carpenter, robbed by the accident of sex of any opportunity to win academic distinction, showed all the intellectual qualities of her family, plus a driving, obsessional determination, in voluntary work. Moreover the Carpenters, although refusing to compromise with the world, had the power to command love. Russell and William's son Estlin as ministers were both beloved by their congregations. Lant, as we have seen, was adored, not merely by the pious members of Lewin's Mead Meeting, but even by the boys at his school, not usually an impressionable class. Mary, though formidable in public controversy, was increasingly loved as people knew her more closely, for her transparent goodness of heart. 'Miss Carpenter has a long, red, solemn face and is not in the least handsome,' wrote a visitor in the 1840s frankly, 'but

[15] Carpenter, W. B. *Essays and Memoir*, 47.
[16] Will of Lant Carpenter, Public Record Office, Prob. 11: 1929: 401.
[17] Carpenter, R. L. *Memoir of Lant Carpenter*, 442, n.
[18] *The Christian Reformer*, XII, 448.

she gives you the feeling of great goodness, dutifulness and matter-of-fact sincerity.[19] Children always loved her.

The Carpenters, then, had exceptional powers, but there is evidence that they paid heavily for them. Their work was liable to be interrupted by mysterious physical illnesses which appeared whenever they were subjected to extra stress. At the same time, they manufactured such stress by seizing, with morbid conscientiousness, on duties which went against the grain, but to which they persuaded themselves they were morally bound. Thus Lant, with a natural leaning towards medicine, became a minister in deference to his guardian's supposed wishes. William, clearly loving the abstract sciences of mathematics and engineering, became a physician to please his father. He qualified brilliantly, but was intensely unhappy in general practice, since he could not endure the human responsibility of his sick patients. 'They haunted me painfully,' he wrote, 'and I could not put them aside.'[20] In 1840, threatened with breakdown at the age of 27, he finally abandoned medicine for university teaching. Philip, with a passion for his own particular subject, which happened to be the classification of shells, would have spent his life in an optical factory rather than complain, if Russell had not come to his rescue. The two sisters, Anna and Susan, both affectionate and domesticated, delayed marriage until they were almost middle-aged themselves from a sense of duty to their own family. Mary, with the strongest possible vocation to serve deprived children, ate out her heart for more than fifteen years in a young ladies' boarding school, while filling notebooks with bitter denunciations of her own 'self-will'.

Lant in 1807 and his grandson Estlin in 1875, both suffered 'a troublesome affliction of the voice', the clergyman's sore throat of Victorian medical literature, which compelled them to give up preaching, in Estlin's case for nine years. Lant, at his student crisis of faith, and Mary repeatedly, suffered attacks of rheumatic fever, which disabled them for months, and in Mary's case, permanently affected her heart. Sometimes, as with Lant, the illness took the form of acute depression, which crippled mind and body alike; the suffering which this caused, in the absence of any effective treatment, is almost beyond imagining. In 1864 both Mary's brothers William and Russell suffered attacks within a few months of each other. Russell, a hard-working and devoted minister, was forced to take six months' complete rest. William, then Registrar of University College, London, was ill for more than a year, with 'a listless torpor of mind and body'. Although a physician, he had no insight into his own condition; his doctors almost gave up hope of saving him, saying, 'his days were numbered, since he had totally lost the will to live.' Very slowly his pleasure in science and music revived, but fatigue or worry always threatened to bring back the dangerous depression. Perhaps the most striking example of the family temperament was William's youngest son, and Mary's much loved nephew, Philip. As a schoolboy Philip was totally happy, accompanying his father on cruises for deep-sea research

[19] Boston Public Library, MS A.9.2, Vol. 25, No. 15.
[20] Carpenter, W. B. *Essays and Memoir*, 29.

in the Faroe Islands and the Mediterranean; at Cambridge he took first class honours in natural science and continued original work in zoology. He became a popular, energetic and highly successful science master at Eton, married happily and had five sons, to whom he was devoted. He had 'buoyant spirits and a vigorous constitution', but at the age of 39 he had a severe attack of influenza, which left him tired and depressed; nevertheless from a sense of duty he insisted on teaching again at the earliest possible date. A few weeks later, in October 1891, apparently without any further warning, he took his own life. It is against this background of too-severe conscience, too-sensitive feelings, and perhaps some innate, familial depression, that one must consider Lant Carpenter's end, and his daughter's continuing inheritance.

A year, two years passed since the death of Lant Carpenter, and still Mary appeared numb from the shock of grief and loss. She could not hide her depression. All her old pleasures had lost their charm. She had no interest in excursions into the countryside to collect fossils or wild flowers. She put away her sketching pad, 'for Nature could not give her back what she had lost'. She read the two-volume edition of 1842, containing the finest of Tennyson's early lyrics, but laid it down 'disgusted with most of what I have read'. Friends of the family invited her during the school holidays for that Victorian panacea 'a change of air'. She accepted, at her mother's urging, with weary civility, but took no pleasure in the visits. The hospitable Fordhams made her welcome at Odsey, and took her to London to see the pictures at the Royal Academy. A London family took her to see 'a most beautiful collection of Turner's water-colours, in the possession of Mr. Ruskin, who had written a work on modern art. . . . I have not however yet arrived at such a point as to admire what I cannot, by a strong effort of imagination, imagine to be like Nature.' Yet even nature itself, the age-old solace, had lost its power over her. When Russell, worried like all the family by her apathy, wrote in the spring of 1842, urging her to go out into 'this most lovely season', she replied, 'To me, the bright opening leaves will always be associated with our irreparable loss.' In the dark shadow of grief she refused to admit anything but 'the beauty which will be made perfect in another world'. This unseen world, because her father was in it, became infinitely more real to her than the dull surroundings of everyday life. In this deliberate withdrawal, she later said her father 'seemed to be close at hand, whispering to her at every step'. Mechanically, she went through her set duties, shrunken, shrivelled and old beyond her time. All she wanted was to continue her father's work and identify herself with him. 'All the poor think of her as her father's representative,' wrote Mrs Carpenter anxiously to her sister. 'She, like him, has all their troubles and sorrows to share. *I am continually fearing for her*.'[21] This fear was clearly not merely the fancy of an anxious mother. Mary's persistent grieving for her father, like her obsessional devotion to him from childhood upwards, had a neurotic quality, rooted in the depths

[21] *Life and Work*, 55–7.

of her personality. There was a real risk, which her mother recognized, that Mary might follow her father into total breakdown and death.

She had however inherited more than anyone realized of her mother's purposeful character. This, and a sense of vocation, were to be her salvation. Moreover, Mrs Carpenter, seeing Mary after two years still sunk in depression, acted with decision and understanding. She used her comfortable means to send Mary for the long summer vacation of 1842 touring on the Continent with two cheerful young companions. It was the first real holiday of this kind Mary had ever had and even now she insisted on making it a pilgrimage to the places her father had visited on his last journey. She was not left to grieve, however. She travelled with Lucy Sanford, who had been one of her favourite pupils at school. Lucy's young brother Langton, an 18-year old undergraduate at University College, would act as their escort, since ladies, of course, could not travel alone. The Sanfords proved an excellent choice as companions. They were devoted to each other, which Mary approved; indeed they were to remain unmarried and share a home all their lives. Both became writers, Lucy, who spoke good French and German, a translator, and Langton a popular historian and editor of the Unitarian journal *The Inquirer*. They were well-read, they were interested in everything; above all they were young and lively. They set out to interest and amuse their sad companion, as they travelled along the skirts of the Black Forest, to Baden, to Strassburg Cathedral, to the falls on the Rhine at Schaffhausen, to Heidelberg and to the Swiss lakes. Slowly warmth and feeling crept back into Mary's letters. On 2nd August they were travelling by steamer on the lake of Wallenstadt as the sun went down. 'We could hardly tear ourselves away from that lovely sunset lake, until Jupiter warned us to go in,' she wrote to her mother. 'We returned next day, feeling we had indeed stored up treasure. I love the mountains more than I can tell; no one but Wordsworth can do so.'[22]

Nature was the key which unlocked her numbed feelings. Her interest in history and literature revived; she loved the very stones of the old buildings, and the wild flowers in the grass beside the road. She was affectionate with the young people and even learnt to joke about her own timidity and shyness with foreigners. 'Judge of my alarm when I found my next neighbour a black-whiskered and mustachioed gentleman speaking French!' When a waiter at Coblenz addressed her as the mother of the two young Sanfords, she took it in good part and addressed them as 'mes enfants'. Privately, she might have felt this rather a wry joke, for although middle-aged and care-worn in appearance, she was only 35. Going home after these happy wanderings, to duty in the boarding school was not easy. Mary confessed to Lucy that she had been tempted 'to indulge in a few quiet tears upstairs, but a summons to dinner obliged me to refrain'. She wrote a fortnight later, when the school had reassembled, 'My head is perplexed between home affairs, hearing lessons and intrusive thoughts of the Rhine. I have as yet no fancy for reading

[22] *Life and Work*, 59

and have dreamt only of setting off by steamboats and railways.'[23] Never-theless, she had turned a corner. Slowly and belatedly Mary Carpenter's character asserted itself. From a depressed, frustrated, neurotic spinster, there evolved a redoubtable woman of affairs, a dangerous opponent and a fearless champion, the Mary Carpenter of history.

[23] *Ibid.*, 60.

PART TWO

MISS CARPENTER'S CHILDREN

1. *Boy prisoners circle the yard for exercise at Tothill Fields Prison in the 1860s*

Lant Carpenter: family, pupils and congregation doted on this celebrated preacher

3. *James Martineau's dark, intense features were as striking as his intellect*

4. (opposite page) Slum tenements in St James' Back

5. (above) The Bristol Rioters set fire to rich merchants' houses in Queen's Square and raided their wine cellars

6. (left) Strangers found Mary Carpenter stiff and 'not at all handsome', engraving from a photograph by T. R. Williams, 1850

7. *Children playing in the street, an engraving by G. Doré*

5
THE MAKING OF A PIONEER
1845-1848

The long-delayed process of Mary Carpenter's development was marked by her first venture, at the age of 38, as an author. In April 1844 a further attack of acute rheumatism forced her to give up part of the teaching in the boarding school, and to take some rest. James Martineau recognized it as the same painful illness he had seen her suffer from as a child. This unaccustomed spare time went into reading, and into choosing and editing a pocket-book of devotional prose and poetry, which she planned as her personal memorial to her father. The memories of him, which had caused such a bitter sense of loss, gradually became, and remained, a source of inspiration. She wrote to James Martineau, now minister of the Octagon Chapel in Liverpool, for his opinion; in spite of their differences about the memoir, she recognized and valued his scholarship. He gave her permission to quote from a Unitarian hymnal he had compiled, with the excellent advice that she should verify the quotations against the authors' original texts, which she conscientiously did. It was not easy to find suitable poems. 'We Unitarians', he wrote, 'are an utterly unpoetical race of people. Depend upon it, my dear Mary, we cannot write poetry for a generation or two yet; at present it requires some effort in us even to bear it!' She asked him 'What we *get* from prayer?' but he found this 'such a question of religious Utilitarianism' that he could not bring himself to consider it. He was sensitive enough to feel that any difference of religious opinion would be deeply wounding to Mary, since her beliefs were so deeply entwined with memories of her father. She asked him to contribute a prayer, and he composed one specially for the book, which she accepted, agreeing that 'the religious sense, like poetry, cannot be defined'.[1]

All through the autumn of 1844 Mary was at work with scissors and paste, developing the method, which she was to use for all her books, and which betrays itself in their repetitive and rambling construction. In March 1845 she sent Martineau the final proofs; he made small tentative corrections and returned them to the impatient author without losing a single post. 'I am glad,' he added, 'that your partial release from teaching the young turns your thoughts to instructing us all.' The whole Carpenter family remained so intensely serious of purpose, so ruled by engrained nonconformist conscience, that even James Martineau, hardly a worldly man himself, could not resist a little gentle teasing of them. He promised to visit Bristol, 'when I hope to find time for convincing Russell that I neither fight nor drink, though not quite up to the mark of his zeal against war and alcohol!' By April 1845, the

[1] Manchester College, Oxford, Library, A3, Box B.

little volume was ready for publication. Mary was far too modest to put her own name on the title-page, and too reserved about her own emotions to reveal the inspiration of the book. Secretly, in her journal, she dedicated it to her father's memory. 'My father,' she wrote on 6th April 1845, 'I have this day made thee a little offering.' *Morning and Evening Meditations*,[2] was Mary Carpenter's first published work, and it was successful beyond her wildest hopes. The first edition sold out in a few months; it was reprinted in Britain and America, and over the years ran through a total of six editions. Today most of it looks stilted and old-fashioned, without being in any satisfying sense traditional. Yet it was of immense value to Mary, transforming her grief for her father into creativity, building up her store of self-confidence, which was still so small, and giving her experience of the practical work of authorship. Much of the book was devoted to family piety, with poems by Lant himself, by her brother Russell, by her mother's two formidably godly sisters, Aunt Fisher and Aunt Bache, or with remarkably prosy prose by Joseph Tuckerman. Yet among these are seventeenth-century passages by Francis Quarles and Jeremy Taylor and a translation by Wordsworth of a Michaelangelo sonnet. Mary had taken particular care to make the choice unsectarian, and success first showed her the extraordinarily wide public she could reach, simply by writing a book. From this modest beginning as an author, there grew a reputation beyond her own or anyone else's imagining.

Mary had always been a catholic reader in various languages. Her letters of the 1840s mention in passing: Strauss's critical *Das Leben Jesu*, which she thought did 'more good than harm', Herder and the poems of Gellert, D'Aubigné's *History of the Reformation*, Mahon's *Essai sur le Grand Condé*, a history of Port Royal, Dante, Tasso and the autobiography of the Italian liberal, Silvio Pellico. In English she preferred history, the *Lives of the Chancellors*, Grote's *History of Greece* and F. W. Newman's *History of the Hebrew Monarchy*. She admitted to Lucy Sanford that she read and re-read all Dickens' tales and novels, clearly feeling that this was rather self-indulgent on her part. When she came to write her polemical books, it was from the resources of a well-stocked mind. For the present, she attempted to set down her thoughts in a series of poems, fluent, correct, but totally lacking the spark of individual talent which lit her modest water-colour sketches. Only a stanza here and there suggests the depths of her rigidly controlled emotions.

> I was so filled with holy awe,
> I nothing felt and nothing saw;
> Yet every power and thought
> Was bent on that excess of light,
> Absorbed, in fullness of delight
> In him whose face I sought.

By a piece of literary irony, these laboured poems led to one of the most influential friendships of her life, with the widow of Lord Byron. Annabella, Lady Noel Byron, as she preferred to be called, arrived at Clifton, Bristol,

[2] Anon: *Morning and Evening Meditations*, 1845.

in the summer of 1844, when she was 52. She took possession of one of the series of drab furnished houses, in which she chose to live far below her natural station in life, in order to preserve her large personal fortune for charitable or educational projects. Earnest, moralizing and determined, she travelled restlessly, with her vast accumulation of papers, from one seaside or health resort to the next. It was hard to imagine this redoubtable, yet somehow pathetic, figure in the rakish Regency setting of a married past already receding into history. Small, pale, regally dignified in sober gown and widow's cap, with firmly folded hands and firmly compressed lips, she was a figure of commanding authority. As she stood on the hearth-rug with her back to the fire, discoursing about the formation of youthful character, about schemes for juvenile communities, about industrial or agricultural schools, about the improvement of the poor, she seemed to one observer the embodiment of power and force of will.[3] Lady Byron had known of the Carpenter family for more than ten years, since, as might be expected, she had been a fellow devotee of Dr Tuckerman and his good works. In 1843, when William Carpenter failed to gain his Professorship at Edinburgh because of being a Unitarian, she offered him a post at Ripley, Surrey, as tutor to her two small grandsons. She had a fixed belief that school-life at Harrow had fatally corrupted Byron, and imposed on her grandsons, whose parents, Lord and Lady Lovelace, seemed chillingly indifferent to their happiness, a dreary succession of tutors, and an education entirely solitary and bookish. William was one of the few tutors remembered as kind and understanding, since he had small boys himself. He moved on to his London Hospital lectureship early in 1845, but was still in charge of the little Lovelaces when Mary Carpenter first went to call on Lady Byron.[4]

The two women thus had a good deal in common. Moreover they had natural temperamental affinities. The older woman, boundlessly kind, filled with universal reforming zeal and firmly convinced of her personal infallibility, was very much what the younger would eventually grow into. Mary listened with admiration and sympathy to accounts of the school for vagrant boys which Lady Byron had opened, at her own expense, in Ealing Grove. It was conducted upon the most approved system which, however, made no provision for play; the boys were supposed to be reformed by working in the garden. The small ones grew bored. 'No sooner are they left together, without a superintendent, than they begin to fight. They are little better than brutes,'[5] said their benefactress sadly. To Mary Carpenter these accounts were of absorbing interest. On her side, Lady Byron seems sincerely to have admired Mary's pedestrian poems, and was always urging her to write more. Perhaps she found it reassuring to meet a poet so undeniably respectable. With all her ceaseless activity and restless moving from place to place, Annabella was lonely and starved of affection. A long, highly-charged series of relationships with women all ended more or less unhappily. She was increasingly estranged from

---

[3] Cobbe, F. P. *Autobiography*, 375.
[4] Boston Public Library, MS A.9.2, Vol. 20, No. 70.
[5] Mayne, E. C. *Life of Lady Byron*, 330–1.

her daughter and son-in-law by the gradual discovery of the couple's appalling gambling debts. Her attempts to protect Medora Leigh, daughter of Byron by his half-sister Augusta, ended in disillusionment when the girl abused and blackmailed her. Yet her friendship with Mary Carpenter remained steadfast; in spite of the difference in their social positions, Mary never lost her independence. Nor, from the first earnest discussion over the tea-cups at Clifton to the last, did she allow the emotional situation to get out of hand. The two women's conversation remained firmly fixed on practical philanthropy, or on higher things, known to them as 'soul communion'. Thanks to Mary's deeply thought-out principles, Lady Byron was for once able to use her money as she sincerely wished, in work of real value to society. Almost alone among her friends, Mary was never arraigned at the bar of Annabella's implacable judgments. It was a remarkable feat of character. All this lay hidden in the future at their early meetings, but Mary had the satisfaction of knowing that someone knew and understood her call to service.

Even in the darkest days after her father's death, Mary had never given up her work for the Lewin's Mead schools or the Visiting Society. Now she took her part in a Domestic Mission, on the Tuckerman pattern, which her father had intended to start before his death, and which was finally established in the early 1840s. The missioner appointed was, she judged, 'a worthy man', useful for working among the respectable poor of the district, but without the vision or energy to reach 'the outcasts of society',[6] who were the centre of her own thoughts. When the districts for visiting were drawn up, she chose the savage and desolate area stretching between Lewin's Mead meeting-house and the docks. This area was notorious as being among the worst slums in Britain. The old houses, once the home of ship-owners and merchants, were let out as tenements and lodgings; sixty common lodging-houses were to be condemned in Bristol under the Common Lodging Houses Act of 1851. They were inhabited by a drifting population of sailors in port, prostitutes, street-traders, tramps, beggars and gangs of children who lived by scavenging. There were a number of negroes, some who had jumped ship from West Indies trading vessels, and some escaped slaves from the New World. Of the working population, most were employed in gangs as stevedores. The work was hard, dirty and dangerous; moreover they were often thrown out of employment, which forced their wives and children into the streets as beggars, the only alternative being the union workhouse. Of the street traders, it was thought, only about one couple in ten was legally married; the district swarmed with children, but it was often impossible to discover their true parentage. One thing certain in this shifting population was the prevalence of rum. Distilling from West Indian sugar had been a Bristol industry since the seventeenth century, and crude spirits were plentiful and cheap.[7] Drinking bouts ended in wife-beating, brutality to children and savage street-fights. Mary Carpenter later described to a Parliamentary Committee of inquiry, how she had made her way through a large crowd watching a knife fight in

[6] *Life and Work*, 95.
[7] Barrett, W. H. *History and Antiquities of Bristol.* 1789, 185.

Lewin's Mead. 'I was not afraid, for I had never been in any way molested,' she said. She sent for help, and it eventually took nine policemen to break up the crowd.[8]

Mary Carpenter's imagination was too sensitive, her senses too fastidious for this work. Memories of black courtyards, of crammed and stinking houses, haunted her sleep in terrifying dreams. Again and again, she had to force herself to take the walk down the hill, which led into another world. 'I do not possess your gaiety', she wrote to Lucy Sanford in February 1845, 'to remove the painfulness of the feeling; but I believe it was intended we should suffer sympathetic pain to teach us to make efforts for our fellow creatures.' Already she was learning that it was society itself which rejected and oppressed these outcasts. The task of helping them was immense: 'the removal of the heavy bonds which oppress our nation, and which are so inwrought into our social fabric that no government measures, however good, can produce more than a partial effect'.[8] At first she tried the natural course of giving money to families huddled ten to a room, without fire, food or clothing. Repeatedly one or other parent, desperate for a brief oblivion, drank it away, while the children remained as before. 'The whole family', wrote Mary, 'is ruined for the vice of one. No one who has not come into immediate contact as I have, with such cases can realize the horror of them.' She wrote for advice to James Martineau, but received little help. 'I can discover no satisfactory guiding principle', he replied, 'to determine the conflict between Christian *compassion* and Christian *economy*, so that I never give, and never withhold without compunction. I fear it is quite impossible to disentangle the mischief of charity from its good.'[9]

Mary was therefore thrown back on her own resources; but gradually she found the work, begun with such desperate resolve, was continuing in affection. A whole series of new human relationships was opening up, which, if they brought sorrows, also brought fulfilment. 'I feel I seem to *love* a family in which I feel I have been of some spiritual good,' she wrote to Russell. The swarms of boys and girls who roamed the streets and pilfered on the quays recognized her as she passed. A docker father, who had always drunk his wages away, actually stayed sober for three months. 'Now a little money will be a help, which it would not before,' she reported to the Committee of the Mission, 'and this is a remedy easy to apply.' A widow who had worked to support her four children fell ill, and asked to see Mary as she lay dying. Mary wrote to tell Lucy what followed. 'She confided to me her little savings, twenty-nine pounds for her two sons and daughters, begging me to watch over them. I think I must have strong natural instincts, for now they seem to have a relationship to me and I quite love them. I feel as if they were my own children.'[10] The shyness, the morbid self-reproaches, the self-conscious reserve of years, began to crumble and vanish. The exact plan of Mary Carpenter's work was still unformed, but she resolved it should have a double

[8] *Life and Work*, 86.
[9] Manchester College, Oxford, Library, A3, Box B.
[10] *Life and Work*, 68.

dedication, in methods to Joseph Tuckerman, in spirit to her father. She approached it with a devotion, which refused to admit the slightest opposition; criticism she regarded as a sort of blasphemy against her father's sacrosanct principles. She was not arrogant, although to mystified or maddened fellow-workers she was sometimes to appear so. Simply, she felt herself chosen, set apart, to rescue children from the abyss. 'The desire of my heart for these twelve years,' she wrote in 1845, 'has been brought near to its accomplishment; and this has given me unspeakable joy.'

The district and Bristol itself threatened to founder under the flood of Irish immigrants, fleeing from the potato famine at home. The press reported in November of 1847 that Bath and the West Country were swamped by armies of Irish beggars arriving via Bristol.[11] The first sight of these emaciated, ragged men, women and children staggering from the holds of the ships became one of the folk memories of Bristol. Many of the children were walking skeletons, skin white as muslin, voice and hair almost gone, dull eyes sunk back into the head. Mary fed starving Irish boys, and collected a fund from the Unitarian congregation to provide hot 'farthing dinners'. Irish families were driven into cellars and bolt-holes where even the lowest of the English refused to live. The Irish settlements figured in the reports of Bristol's first Inspector of Nuisances as the worst slums in the city. In a house in Lewin's Mead he found nine men, women and children sharing one bed for warmth. The grimy alleyways were 'honeycombed with human cells', and blind courts, with no light or air except at the entrance, were crammed against the hill. In Back Street and Host Street five courts held a hundred houses where a shifting population of four hundred and fifty shared the communal pumps and privies in the yard. Behind the houses ran the polluted little River Frome, for centuries a common sewer. In Gun Yard during a cholera outbreak in the 1840s, eighty people died in two days. The Irish lived ten to each room, all rooms opening like crazy cupboards off the dark stairwell. An old sack stuffed with rags served for a bed, an orange box for a table; the whole family ate directly from its one cooking pot. The inspector noted stagnant water, broken windows, black dust and buckets of slops. 'Sure, it's not fit for pigs to live in,' said an Irishwoman to him wearily. From this hideous world the only escape was to drink; whisky dulled the hopelessness and pain.[12]

It was among these families and their children that Mary Carpenter chose to work. She described them vividly, how they lived in clans and would go, all together, street by street, into the country for hopping or fruit-picking, how policemen dare not approach two Irishmen fighting with a crowd around them, how they formed a little Alsatia of dishonesty and dirt, 'a city within a city'. They are 'the very lowest class of population which can be found anywhere,' she said. 'The bulk of the families are known thieves; they keep in a gang together and in fact they rule the city, for the police dare not meddle with them. . . . They are thoroughly uncivilized; they do not care how low and vile and ignorant they are.' Everything about them was calculated to shock

---

[11] C. Woodham-Smith, *The Great Hunger*, 282.

[12] *Homes of the Bristol Poor*—reports collected and published by the *Bristol Mercury*, 1884.

and antagonize this middle-aged woman of sheltered and fastidious habits, yet something in her bound her deeply to them. 'There are great capabilities in that class,' she maintained, 'some of the finest boys I know are Anglo-Irish.'[13]

This strange predilection of her daughter's frankly appalled Mrs Carpenter. She had always been charitable towards what she called 'the decent poor', but she was not hopeful of Mary's new friends, whom she described in a letter as gambling and fighting in the streets, 'with no shirt and no home, sleeping in casks on the quays or on steps and living, I suppose, by petty depredations.' Her real objections were on Mary's account. Mary now taught in the boarding-school, hurrying down the steep hill at midday to help in the soup kitchen and returning for her afternoon classes. Three evenings a week she taught evening classes of rowdy young working men and girls, and all Sunday in different branches of her Sunday School. On other evenings she managed the business of the mission, or visited families in need. She came home at ten in the evening, so exhausted that a friend saw her fall asleep with the spoon half-way between her mouth and the cup of gruel which was all she could take for supper.[14] Her enthusiasm swept protests aside, but failure, especially in young people for whom she cared deeply, reduced her to bitter tears. Mrs Carpenter was inevitably reminded of her husband. 'I am continually fearing for Mary', she wrote once again, 'for the poor think of her as her father's representative, and she, like him, has all their troubles and sorrows to share.' Later, Mary admitted that this had not been unreasonable. 'My mother', she said, 'used to be anxious, seeing me like my father, lest I should break down as he did.' Yet she refused to admit that her mother had the slightest right to interfere; where for years she had bent in obedience to her father's least wish, she now rejected her mother's fears. 'Direct intellectual effort,' she said, 'always does me good, if free from worrying.' Her doctor brother William was urged to point out the dangers to health, Anna the charms of painting and Russell the claims of friendship. 'Some time must I know be sacrificed to what are called the claims of society,' replied his sister tartly, 'but it is not my intention to conform to them in the waste of time and energy usually passing under that name. There is no reason why one should be robbed of one's time and thought, any more than of one's money.' Attempts to make her rest were, she said, a hindrance rather than a help, and the family was forced to admit to conflicts between mother and daughter, which lasted for some years and only ended gradually as Mrs Carpenter discovered that her fears were groundless.[15] For, as Mary wrote to sympathetic Lucy Sanford, 'It is a blessed work and it does me great good, calling me out of myself, stimulating my intellectual activity, leading me to see and correct my faults, and giving me the most undeserved rewards in the smiles of the poor children. She was right in the belief that activity was good for her, just as morbid religious introspection was harmful; the haunting fears for the soul's health,

---

[13] Select Committee on the Education of Destitute Children, *Parliamentary Papers*, 1861, VII, 95ff.
[14] Cobbe, F. P. *Autobiography*, 277.   [15] *Life and Work*, 106–7.

which play such a part in early nineteenth-century literature, were often common self-centredness in a respectable disguise. Her usual meticulous examination of conscience on the last day of 1846 failed to depress her, as it had so often done in the past. She listed her new duties, cheerfully and hopefully carried out: 'I felt as if my existence were increased, that I had more powers than I thought, that my individual being was more prized by others than I had thought,'[16] she wrote. She followed public affairs in Britain, Ireland and Europe, she took an active part in the abolitionist struggle in the U.S.A., and found immense satisfaction in giving hospitality to visitors from overseas. Reading Mary Carpenter's visitors' book, and her letters in the great Anti-Slavery collection at the Boston Public Library, Massachusetts, one sees that this household of provincial schoolmistresses, an elderly widow, and two middle-aged spinster daughters, by no means lived out of the world.

Mary, ever since her father's lessons in childhood, had taken an intense interest in the struggle to free the slaves. On her daily visits to the streets round the docks, she looked at every passing negro, 'as a man and a brother, regarded with particular interest and sympathy'. She had shared her father's pride when slavery was abolished throughout the British Empire in 1834, and now a series of American visitors drew on her support for Abolition in the United States. The first to arrive was Samuel May,[17] a Unitarian minister, christened by his friends with disarming innocence 'the Lord's choirboy', and uncle, in real life, to the heroines of *Little Women*. Like his brother-in-law, Bronson Alcott, May was a high-souled reformer; he was secretary of the Anti-Slavery Society and a supporter of pacifism, temperance and women's rights. His house at Syracuse, N.Y., was a station on the Underground Railroad organization for escaping slaves, and he had taken part in the public rescue of a runaway negro. He fired Mary Carpenter's enthusiasm, and since she was eager to do something active for the cause, invited her to send contributions to his fund-raising Abolition Fair. This was organized every Christmas in the historic Faneuil Hall at Boston, by an energetic member of his committee, Maria Weston Chapman, editor of his abolitionist paper *The Liberty Bell* and an early example of the complete, capable American organization woman. She and Mary Carpenter became friends by post, and soon instituted 'the Box', which became a feature of the Carpenters' lives. This annual box, growing larger and larger with the years, held a collection of gifts and handwork for the Christmas fair, made by the Carpenter ladies, their pupils and friends. '*Even Mrs. Carpenter's housemaids*,' as their contemporaries put it, knitted and crocheted 'for the poor slaves', generously accepting their own slavery to coal-buckets and black-leading as freedom. Each year, even when the box had finally been nailed down and carried to the ship, the girls still talked of it. 'Our box,' wrote Mary, 'is perhaps just arriving in Boston,' adding with a spark of humour, 'What a difference, I hope, from those chests of tea!'[18]

16 *Life and Work*, 84.
17 Bristol Archives, 12693, No. 20.
18 Boston Public Library, MS A.9.2, Vol. 23, No. 170.

In return, Mary's earnest New England friends sent sermons, speeches, newspapers and reports of public institutions. The American abolitionist movement, seen necessarily at second-hand and from afar, played an important part in Mary Carpenter's political education. She learnt how easily disagreement can shatter a reforming movement; this was brought home to her when in September 1846 she heard William Lloyd Garrison and the escaped slave Frederick Douglass address a densely packed meeting in Bristol. Douglass, six feet tall, with leonine head, deep voice and magnificent presence, always had a terrific effect on audiences. Mary took with her a boy who had not slept under a roof for many months, and who had been in prison and whipped; he said, 'he understood what Mr. Douglass meant because *he had felt it himself*'. Mary was deeply moved by the meeting and the boy's response, though she shrewdly noted the effect which the magnificent Frederick Douglass had on the girls of her school and the Bristol ladies: 'We saw one or two who seemed rather absurd in their over-attention.' Douglass, however, Southern-bred, was careful not to respond. 'He could not have avoided more entirely,' Mary reported privately to Mrs Chapman, 'any of those confidential conversations which some persons like to have with young ladies, when the latter are willing.'[19] She herself admired Garrison, but she was alarmed by the violence of his language and his torrents of invective against slave-owners. Garrison was a radical of a now familiar type, driven to violence by hatred of the evils he opposed. His newspaper *The Liberator*, produced since 1831 on a hand-press with borrowed type, denounced not only slavery, but the theatre, 'a deep and powerful source of evil', drink and tobacco and all the orthodox churches as 'augean stables of pollution'. 'Sometimes fatiguing' was the charitable description of this universal denouncer of abuses. He had already provoked the hostility of a mob in Boston, where he was dragged through the streets with a rope round his neck: later he was to burn a copy of the United States Constitution in public as 'an agreement with hell', because it linked together slave-owning and non-slave-owning states. These scenes split the American Anti-Slavery Society right down the middle: abolitionist meetings broke up in shouting and mob violence. Though she respected Garrison's sincerity, this was not at all Miss Carpenter's style. 'I much regret that there are so many divisions among the Abolitionists and especially that this question about the Constitution so interferes with their unanimity,' she wrote to her friend in Boston. Moreover, her sense of propriety was outraged when Garrison attempted to reprint her private letters of sympathy in *The Liberator*; she would only agree to extracts appearing over the signature 'an English lady'. 'I cannot approve', she told her brother Russell privately, 'of the *censoring* tone they adopt towards those who differ from them in any way.' Later she was persuaded to send contributions to Samuel May's milder journal *The Liberty Bell*. She explained, with a truly Victorian nuance, that she offered her name to the anti-slavery cause, in the hope that 'our position in society may help to raise it from the slur of *Vulgarity* which is thrown on it. This course we

[19] *Ibid.*, No. 17.

also pursue in reference to teetotalism, which is thought rather vulgar here, except of course among Quakers. Do not imagine that we shrink from avowing your cause: far otherwise, we glory in it as far as is consistent with our notions of female propriety here in England.'[20] It is interesting to remember that the writer of that letter was already capable of passing through crowd fights where the police hung back. Mary Carpenter, observing the propaganda, the infighting and the factions among abolitionists, learnt a great deal about the generalship of good causes. She continued to show friendship and hospitality towards all sections of the anti-slavery movement. William Lloyd Garrison became a life-long friend; indeed it was to him she wrote her last letter on the day of her death. Many leaders of the movement enjoyed the hospitality of Great George Street, and Caroline Kirkland wrote appreciatively of her visit: 'a day of Italian sky on English landscape, of wandering through cathedral aisles and cloisters, and among cottages such as poetry dreams of'.[21]

Mary Carpenter felt strongly that anti-slavery enthusiasm should not be used, as sometimes in the past, to muffle social injustice at home. Her faith reached out to the whole of society, whether apparently deserving or not. 'The Unitarians do not shut the Lord's table against *any*,' she wrote to Garrison. 'Whether they are sincere or not, I consider a matter between God and their own consciences.' She told a New England minister, 'In some towns the congregations are almost exclusively among the educated classes; our own was, before my father's ministry, the richest and most aristocratic in Bristol, perhaps in England. Now it presents a happy mixture of all classes and continues steadily growing in number.'[22] She believed that faith should 'be the means of awakening a spirit of freedom throughout Christendom, of bringing the spirit of Christ to influence the ordinary affairs of life.' In these she included the great social and political questions of the day, for 'where there is the spirit of Christ, there is freedom'.[23] In this hopeful spirit she attended a Chartist meeting on Brandon Hill in 1847, a sedate, shawled figure among the crowds of labourers and dockers. In 1848, the year of revolutions, she was an enthusiastic reader of the press; Hungary, Italy, France, even distant Russia aroused her curiosity and hope. 'The world is beginning to awake to its true life; I firmly believe it,' she told another friend in the same exciting year. 'One true, strong spirit, with the armour of faith, will destroy a whole army of Goliaths.'[24] In spite of hard experience, she never gave up this hope.

Although still quite unknown in England, Mary Carpenter became a recognized figure in American liberal circles. Samuel May arranged the publication in Boston of her *Meditations*, which came out, somewhat to her dismay, under her own name, and it sold so well that he encouraged her to complete another short anonymous book, this time a memoir of Dr Tuckerman. It was published almost simultaneously in Britain and America, in 1848,

[20] Boston Public Library, MS A.9.2, Vol. 23, No. 17.
[21] Bristol Archives, 12693, No. 20.
[22] *Life and Work*, 75.
[23] Boston Public Library, MS A.9.2, Vol. 22, No. 107.
[24] *Ibid.*, Vol. 24, No. 5.

and for decades remained the only biography of its subject. With these two books, the *Meditations* and the *Memoir*, Mary fulfilled her debt to her two mentors in the past and made ready to look to the future. Their success added to the growing self-confidence which was so strangely to transform a church mouse into a lioness defending her young. R. W. Emerson, when he visited England, wrote warmly attempting to arrange a meeting with her, offering to carry letters and parcels to America and hoping one day to 'read with interest the record of your *own* thoughts in a book.'[25] In the warmth of appreciation, she lost her old, desolating sense of being disliked, 'that there must be something in me that repelled instead of attracting.' She had an intensely happy holiday in the Lake District, when all the brothers and sisters except William stayed together at Ambleside, the last family holiday in their busy lives. Mary walked, explored and painted. She was too shy to approach Wordsworth directly, but 'bribed Miss Martineau' with a sketch of her own cottage, to present him with a sketch of Rydal Water. 'I did not put my name', she added hastily, 'for fear of disgracing the family.' In this poetic landscape, the memory of the past rose before her. She reminded Philip of their child-hood, 'when I used to nurse you, and when I wrote a Latin letter describing you, and when I took my pet china box with a glass in the lid and a picture on the outside to catch your first tears and keep them as a relic—and you had none!'[26] She forgot all her times of loneliness and disappointment, remember-ing only the ideal of family love and happiness, which she wanted to recreate for every child in her care. Writing up her journal as usual at the year's end, she recorded 'greater independence of sympathy, greater consciousness of my own existence and powers'. In this new confidence, a feeling crushed and stifled for nearly twenty years stirred for the last time into life. 'Yet still there seems a want of my nature unsatisfied. . . . I have of late dwelt with much interest on a character exhibiting a most beautiful combination of rare intellectual powers with much gentleness and benevolence. But if my God knew that it would be good for me to have such a companion, to whom I could pour out my inmost thoughts, he would not withhold the blessing.'[27] Wistfully, she put aside the thought and once again took up her work alone. It is hard to see how any mere husband, with mundane demands for roast mutton and clean shirts, could compete with the exalted shade of Lant Carpenter, and perhaps it was as well that Mary never married. Though sometimes lonely, she was consoled, according to her nephew, by friendships of unusal tenderness and ardour. Her fastidious reticence conceals, now as then, exactly what these were.

In the spring of 1848, a new stage in her life began. For some time the boarding-school had been dwindling in numbers; Mary, though she kept some friends among the young ladies, saw them go without regret. Her time was increasingly given to the ragged-school boys and their families. Now her sister Anna, closest companion and confidante, married at the late age of 38. Her husband, Herbert Thomas, was the son of one of Bristol's leading

[25] Manchester College, Oxford, Library, C2 Letter-book D.
[26] *Life and Work*, 80–81.   [27] *Ibid.*, 84.

citizens, Christopher Thomas, who served successively as councillor, magistrate and mayor of the city. The Thomases owned a large chemical works at Broad Plain, and like many leading Unitarian families were solidly, un-ostentatiously rich. There was no question of Anna continuing to earn her living, and indomitable Mrs Carpenter was beginning to grow old. At Easter 1848 the boarding-school was given up. Anna and her husband prepared to move into the large house at 2 Great George Street while Mary and her mother retired to the adjoining wing. On 3rd April 1848, a few days after the last pupil had gone, Mary sat down in one of the empty schoolrooms to write to Russell. It was her 40th birthday. 'As for me,' she wrote, 'I look forward with calm hope to the future. I feel as if I had within me powers which have never had leisure to expand themselves. I desire to work out my own individuality, and to be free from the shackles which I have always felt in various ways imposed upon me.'[28] This was the nearest she ever came to complaining over her lost years. Meanwhile she had no need to search for her life's work; the children of the streets were already waiting for her.

[28] *Life and Work*, 106.

6

A RAGGED SCHOOL 1846-1850

For many years Mary Carpenter had been haunted by the Lewin's Mead children. They swarmed in the streets and alleys, as much at home as the wharf rats and living, like the rats, by scavenging. In hard times she saw them creep barefoot along the pavement's edge, tattered, filthy, stunted in growth, deformed by rickets, pursuing the passer-by with a shrill, persistent beggar's whine. During spells of good luck she saw the same children camping on water-steps or in dark entries, with the casual adaptability of street arabs. They shared raw food snatched from warehouses, passed round a purloined cigarette[1] or beer bottle, laid bets on cockfights, gambled with dice, or, if all else failed, amused themselves by throwing stones at the street lanterns. The boys, when they worked at all, were crossing-sweepers, donkey drivers, scavengers of coal from the river at low tide, breakers of crates and hawkers of firewood, dodgers about cargo-ships and railway stations, holders of horses in the street. The girls were sellers of oranges or watercress-bunches, ballad singers, match sellers, flower-girls, growing up to back-alley prostitution. All drifted aimlessly on the surface of life, like the sea birds scrambling for flotsam in the harbour; like the birds, too, they were sociable, motley-coloured shrill and without knowledge of good or evil.

In France or Germany, such children would have been in compulsory day schools. The reasons why they were left to run wild in the streets of British towns were deeply rooted in national tradition and prejudice. At the beginning of the nineteenth century two charitable societies had been founded: The National Society for Promoting the Education of the Poor in the Principles of the Established Church, which taught the Church of England liturgy and catechism in its schools, and the British and Foreign School Society, largely for the service of Dissenters. Financed by voluntary contributions, both were limited to huge classes, dreary, mechanical teaching and cheapness at any cost. Yet, so intense was the suspicion and hostility between Church and Dissent, that any attempt by the state to provide a common public education caused bitter conflict. A series of proposed Education Bills in 1807, 1818, 1820 and 1843, had all foundered in storms of acrimonious dispute. The idea that all children, apart from sectarian considerations, deserved education for its own sake, aroused little official enthusiasm. In 1834, when the first government grant of £30,000 was grudgingly made for school building, Parliament voted over twice as much for the future Queen Victoria's

---

[1] Cigarettes of West Indian tobacco were introduced in 1842; their manufacture became a leading Bristol industry.

81

new stables. A typically botched-up compromise allotted government grants in proportion to private subscriptions: an advantage to the wealthy Church Establishment, and a considerable hardship to the fewer and generally poorer Dissenters. From 1844 militant Dissenters, led by the Congregationalists, mounted a fierce attack on Church privileges, claiming the right to refuse Church rates, to perform their own marriages and funerals, to enter Oxford and Cambridge and to conduct their own sectarian schools. Both Church and Dissent repeatedly blocked secular education.[2] In this deadlock, improvements could only be made through a series of administrative Minutes, issued by the Committee of Council on Education. Matthew Arnold, who became, in 1851, one of the most sensitive and sympathetic of Her Majesty's Inspectors of Schools, described the whole system as a chaos of conflict and mismanagement, in which narrow-minded sectarian self-righteousness was 'retarding and vulgarizing'. Moreover, the schools were compelled, from the smallness of their grants, to charge fees of up to sixpence a week; many people could not, and more would not pay these, since no law compelled them. 'I am far from imagining,' wrote the young Inspector Arnold, 'that a lower school fee or even a free admission would induce the poor to send their children to school . . . it is my firm conviction that education will never become universal in this country until it is made compulsory'.[3] Meanwhile, the poorest children ran wild. It is against this background of conflict and neglect that Mary Carpenter's achievement must be judged.

She was not the first in the field. John Pounds, a Unitarian, son of a sawyer in the naval dockyard at Portsmouth, was crippled by an accident at the age of 15 and supported himself by shoe-mending. In 1818 he began to teach a small nephew and a boy who roamed the streets all day while his mother was out at work. Gradually he persuaded other children to share the lessons with a promise of free food; he was seen hobbling along Portsmouth Hard, holding a hot baked potato enticingly under a boy's nose. In the end, forty children roosted on benches, old boxes and ladders round his small workshop, while John Pounds taught them to read, count and copy on slates as he hammered and sewed at his cobbler's bench. He taught the girls simple cookery, collected old woollen clothes for the children in winter, nursed the ailing and made toys for the smallest. John Pounds took no salary, but his work was supported and extended after his death by the Portsmouth Unitarian Congregation.[4] By 1844, when the Ragged School Union was founded, to give 'permanence, regularity and vigour' to the movement, there were similar schools in London and many large cities, to which children could come 'in filth and rags'. The schools were in barns, old warehouses, under railway arches; the children were those too noisy, dirty and wild to be acceptable in National or British schools, even in the unlikely event of their parents finding the few pence for fees. Lord Shaftesbury, addressing Parliament in 1848, said, 'Of 1600 children in fifteen ragged schools, 162 had been in prison, 116 had

[2] Crowther, M. A. *Church Embattled*, 17.
[3] Walcott, F. G. *Origins of Culture and Anarchy*, 27.
[4] Young, A. F. and Ashton, E. T. *British Social Work in the Nineteenth Century*, 243.

run away from home because of ill-treatment, 170 slept in common lodging houses, 253 lived by begging, 216 had no shoes or stockings, 101 had no underlinen, 68 children were children of convicts, 219 never slept in a bed, 306 had lost one or both parents.'[5] 'These children', wrote an Inspector, 'live in *holes* not *homes*.' They had to be taught, said Kay Shuttleworth, to stand upright, to sit without crouching like a sheepdog, to practise some decency; they had never seen a book, had no habits of attention, while the 'effort of abstraction required to connect a sound with a letter is impossible to them'. The standard of teaching generally in ragged schools was as low as could be imagined. They were repeatedly criticized in inspectors' reports, but per-sisted until the end of the century, because they filled a social need. Some, as at Aberdeen, provided a penny meal of stew or hot porridge; others, as at Edinburgh, provided a night shelter, for children huddled in the icy winds of the Old Town.[6] Mary Carpenter was the first to see that, with govern-ment support, these barrel-scraping schools could give a civilized education to the most needy children.

As a Unitarian, Mary Carpenter was familiar with the work of John Pounds and she read the reports of the Ragged School Union, with particular interest in Sheriff Watson's school meals at Aberdeen. She felt bitterly how little the general church- and chapel-going public knew or cared about the lost children in their midst. 'The mass of society', she wrote a few years later, 'are better acquainted with the actual condition of remote savage nations than with the real life of these children swarming in the bye-streets; they are less visible to the public eye . . . than the little heathen children exhibited in the reports of missionaries'.[7] Yet, as she saw from everyday observation, 'these children are fashioned as we are, have mental and bodily powers often of the first order, have immortal souls'. She felt an overwhelming urge 'to make them feel that they are not forgotten, nor beasts; that they too will be men'.[8] Perhaps this was the great duty which she had prayed in lonely, frustrated girlhood might be reserved for her.

In 1846 Mary Carpenter formed plans for a school in the neighbourhood of Lewin's Mead. It was to be a ragged school with a revolutionary difference; instead of an education poor, tattered and third-hand to match the pupils' appearance, she was determined to offer all the richness and variety of interest she had brought to teaching in professional families. 'It is a mistake to im-agine', she wrote, 'that because the children are ragged, the education need be ragged also.' She was clear-sighted about the practical difficulties of the work. A school of this kind, she wrote, 'was as yet unheard-of in Bristol', and the public had 'but a vague idea of what such a thing should be'. The district was a degrading slum; two Bow Street detectives, who came down in pursuit of a criminal, told Mary they considered it as dangerous as their

[5] These figures show how meaningless was the general advice of the middle to the lower classes to practise prudence and postponement of marriage as a means of limiting their fami-lies. See Banks, J. A. *Prosperity and Parenthood*, 198.
[6] Guthrie, Dr T. A. *A Plea for Ragged Schools*. Contemporary pamphlet.
[7] Carpenter, M. *Reformatory Schools*. Introduction.
[8] 'A Worker' [M. Carpenter]. *Ragged Schools* introduction.

'manor' in London. Money would be difficult to raise for this unappealing
cause, since most churches were already supporting their own parochial and
Sunday Schools; yet the continuing expenses of a ragged school must be
heavy if it were to give the quality of education she intended. Altogether, as
Mary summed it up, 'Success was doubtful, for the attempt was a novel one,
and it was quite uncertain whether, if it succeeded, funds could be raised to
carry it on.'[9] Nonetheless, she was determined to try. The Unitarian congregation, which now numbered seven hundred in Bristol, was generous.[10]
Mary rented a room in a tenement house in Lewin's Mead. A schoolmaster
was more difficult to find, since there was not enough money to pay a certificated teacher. In the end a temperance missioner named Phelps volunteered
for the job, and though he had no experience with children, Mary accepted his
offer. Perhaps neither of them realized how difficult the work would prove to
be. Dickens described such a situation in one of his telling metaphors.
'The Ragged School teacher lands in some district rather like a navigator in
new islands, and hoists his flag before an astonished population. Out the boys
buzz, with matted hair, piebald with mud, fluttering in rags, capering in squalor
before the navigator.'[11] The school opened on 1st August 1846, and Mary
wrote in September to W. L. Garrison in Boston, modestly giving all credit
for the idea to 'our much loved Dr. Tuckerman. I went into a school we have
lately commenced here for children deep in misery. It is called in the public
press "a ragged school", but *we* call it a free school.'[12] She strongly objected
to the insulting name, but it stuck, even in the reports of H. M. Inspectors, at
whatever cost to the pupils' struggling self-respect. Mrs Carpenter described
the beginnings of the school in more down-to-earth style. 'On Sunday', she
wrote, 'nearly twenty boys were assembled. The seven Mr Phelps had collected brought a dozen more in the afternoon, which showed they liked it; but,
beginning to be tired, one of them said, "Now let us fight," and in an instant
they were all fighting. . . . It is literally a ragged school; none have shoes or
stockings, some have no shirt and no home.' Mrs Carpenter was never a
woman to withhold practical charity. Characteristically she provided combs,
soap and towels, hoping for 'some sort of approach to cleanliness' and thus
started an important side of the school's work.[13] Mr Phelps' method was to
go into the street, where groups of boys were hanging about in the gutter, and
invite them in. They were as inconsequential and cheeky as city sparrows.
'I say! He's a funny fellow!' he heard them say. 'Wilt 'ee go, mate?' 'Aye.'
'So will I.' 'We'll all go!' Pushing and shouting they elbowed their way into
the dingy room, roving restlessly around, poking at everything with dirty,
inquisitive fingers. Mr Phelps, well-meaning and sincere, had no idea how to
cope with their nomadic habits. 'I could neither teach them nor rule,' he
admitted frankly. Benches were overturned with loud crashing, books torn
apart, pictures ripped from the walls, the floor sprinkled with blood. One

[9] *Parliamentary Papers, 1850*, XLIV, 428–35.
[10] *Christian Reformer*, Vol. 3, 1847, 290–1.
[11] *Household Words*, 30 August 1851.
[12] Boston Public Library, MS. A.9.2, Vol. 16, 83.
[13] *Life and Work*, 82.

boy pushed another's head through the window, shattering the glass and cutting his scalp. Sounds of the fight attracted more and more boys to see the sport, or join in. Mr Phelps, whose only experience had been as a missionary, felt obliged 'to offer up a short prayer', which struck them as irresistibly comic. They rolled over one another with laughter and sang 'Jim Crow'. 'These boys have not been trained like other boys,' wrote Phelps in explanation to the committee, 'living constantly in the open air, having the greatest liberty, under no restraint whatever—boys as high-spirited as blood horses.'[14]

One boy, F., accused the master of hitting him; he flew on Mr Phelps, cursing and kicking his shins, fortunately with bare feet. Later, F. lay in wait outside, and pelted him with what the master decorously called 'soft mud'. 'I never struck this boy once,' added poor Mr Phelps. Considering all he suffered at their hands, his patience and sympathy with the boys was beyond praise. Occasionally, goaded beyond endurance, he laid about him with a cane; 'but I never did so without regret,' he said. After a few days Mary Carpenter began to teach in the school, and he watched in admiration the authority, born of long experience, with which she held the boys' attention. 'They were much pleased', he wrote, 'with Miss C's. visits to the school, and delighted by her explaining to them the mode of making blacklead pencils.'[15]

Mr Phelps visited the parents with unremitting kindness, distributing unheeded temperance tracts as he went. Several times the poor man wanted to resign in despair, but Mary persuaded him to continue. Very gradually, as the autumn of 1846 passed into winter, some faint glimmerings of order began to appear. The neighbours noticed the streets were quieter, and were astonished to see a troop of barefoot boys march two by two down Lewin's Mead with their master, as docile as a Sunday School walk. The Mayor of Bristol, who had said 'nothing was taught in that school but thieving and roguery', called and was pleasantly surprised. Even the Superintendent of Police, 'not a man of melting mood', as Mary dryly observed, visited and was struck to see boys, used to much rough handling, submit to her quiet directions and settle to work. He was to become a valuable ally. 'The boys behaved wonderfully and excited much admiration,' wrote Mary with as much pride as if they were her own. 'Altogether, we thank God and take courage.'[16]

By Christmas the school was so successful that it was time to look for larger premises. More than forty boys were turning up as the fancy took them in the daytime, many more, and many girls, clamoured to come if a night school could be held. Mary found, and rented for an experimental year, a disused mission chapel in 'a filthy lane named St James' Back'. Once the land had been green fields round the still beautiful priory church of St James; Benedictine monks used the waters of the silvery Frome to grind their corn; for centuries it had been the site of a famous fair on St James' Day. By 1840 the district had become a notorious thieves' kitchen and slum. Mrs Carpenter

[14] Carpenter, M. *Ragged Schools*, 13–15.
[15] *Ibid.*, 4. [16] *Life and Work*, 83.

M C—D

was alarmed to think of Mary walking at night, after the long line of lamps in Lewin's Mead was extinguished, through the depths of black archways into a courtyard from which there was no other escape,[17] to the squalid chapel, with rough benches, broken stairway, rickety gallery, and iron roof. Mary herself admitted that she was often disturbed by screaming and fighting; two policemen had been killed attempting to end a midnight fight.[18] The attempt to open a night school nearly ended in disaster.

News that there was a room with lamps and a bright fire spread through the neighbourhood. At first fifty or sixty, later nearly two hundred young men and girls 'of the most vicious appearance' forced their way into the building. One Sunday evening in February 1847 a gang fight broke out with screaming and smashing of furniture, and the police had to be called in. The neighbours were angry, and Mary was threatened and insulted as she passed through the alley. Fortunately the police superintendent was by now a firm friend; he cheerfully agreed to post a constable at the school for protection. Gradually order was restored; the vandals drifted away and the rest settled to work. By late spring the policeman's job was easy, and some local busybody reported him for neglect of duty 'having been two hours in the ragged school setting copies to the boys'.[19] Summer came and numbers dwindled as whole streets migrated en masse to the country, in search of casual labour, hop- and fruit-picking.

Mary had already decided that a trained teacher was essential, and persuaded the managers to let her advertise for one. An advertisement in the Unitarian newspaper *The Inquirer* produced a young Scotsman, Mr Andrews, and his sister. These two took charge in the summer of 1847, and Mary was the first to say that the continuing success of the school owed everything to them. They had both been at the Glasgow Normal School run by the British and Foreign Schools Society for training teachers and had experience of teaching deprived children in workhouse schools; 'they used only plans', wrote Mary, 'that they had tried and approved.' Soon they had reduced the noisy crowds to more or less orderly classes: 100 infants and juniors in the mornings, 40 each of boys and girls for shoemaking and sewing in the afternoons, and 100 young people for general education in the evenings. Miss Andrews was an excellent needlewoman, friendly drapers gave remnants, and Mary saw, with wonder, girls, 'the sweepings of the streets, who could hardly thread a needle, make and wear their own clothes with pride'.

The infants were equally proud when Miss Andrews put up their own paintings to decorate the walls. Mr Andrews began to keep registers, which show how casual attendances were; of 531 children in the school during 1848, only 54 attended regularly for the whole year. From the Andrewses Mary learnt a great deal, especially about discipline. She noticed 'the friendly

---

[17] Cobbe, F. P. *Autobiography*, 279–81. All that now remains of it is an area of worn cobbles in the road and a memorial tablet on the wall of a new office block, to the east of St. James' Church.

[18] Carpenter, M. *Reformatory Schools*, 156–9.

[19] Carpenter, M. *Ragged Schools*, 58–9.

confidence of the boys to their master . . . each one feels that his personal existence is recognized . . . and he knows when to loosen the rein to these wild, uncurbed creatures.'[20] Above all, ignoring their rags and filth, Mr Andrews treated the boys with respect and consideration. An officious visitor wished to know how many boys had been in prison; Mr Andrews replied that he would not humiliate them by asking such a question in public. On the basis of eighteen months' experience, Mary drew up a set of rules, which she considered should apply to all ragged schools. The schools should be restricted to children who cannot attend any other, 'owing to their own want of character or necessary clothing'. The school should teach general knowledge, non-sectarian Christianity, some trade which will give the child a chance to earn his living, and habits of self-respect, which he cannot hope to learn at home. The managers may receive gifts of books or materials for the school, but casual visitors should not be allowed to give the children money. The master and managers should visit the children's homes and try to win the parents' confidence. Above all the children should be approached in a spirit of affection and trust. 'Corporal punishment is not necessary and we believe it hurtful. . . . *No* corporal punishment or holding up to shame or ridicule shall be made use of; discipline must be maintained by the master's own firmness, order and kindness.'[21] These principles, or an extension of them to children convicted of offences, formed the basis of all Mary Carpenter's future work.

Mary had taught since she was 16, first in her father's school, then as governess in private families, last as her mother's assistant. Paradoxically, she used her new freedom to teach again. The difference was that this time her whole heart and soul were in the work. She went to the ragged school every day and to the night school every evening. All accounts agree that she was a brilliant teacher. Her approach was imaginative and startlingly modern. She saw these urchins not as 'the poor', to whom reading, writing and arithmetic should be doled out in grudging rations, but as lively young people whose curiosity demanded to be satisfied with science, current affairs, stories and novels, just as their growing bodies demanded skills, singing and play in the open air. The boys, like all neglected children, had an exceedingly short span of attention, and were too wild to submit to enforced discipline. Mary learnt to tolerate apparent disorder, while she tried to capture their roving interest. The master noticed with professional respect, 'Miss C. can keep the noisiest class quiet by telling them stories.'

'It was a wonderful spectacle', wrote a friend, 'to see Mary Carpenter sitting patiently before the large school gallery, teaching, singing and praying with the wild street boys, in spite of endless interruptions caused by shooting marbles into hats on the table behind her, whistling, stamping, fighting, shrieking out Amen in the middle of the prayer, and sometimes rising and tearing like a troop of bisons in hob-nailed boots down from the gallery, round the great schoolroom, and out into the street. The irrepressible outbreaks she bore with great good humour. . . . The droll things which occurred

---

[20] *Ibid.*, 52–3.
[21] Carpenter, M. *Reformatory Schools,* 62ff.

and the wonderful replies she received from the scholars amused her intensely, and the more unruly were the young scamps, the more I think, in her secret heart, she liked them and gloried in taming them.'[22] Mary Carpenter had never in her life been so happy.

Her lessons ranged far beyond the three Rs of the usual schools' curriculum. She used much imagination to capture the boys' attention, starting always from their interests and their viewpoint. She showed and let them handle an orrery, in spite of gloomy prophecies that they would smash it; instead 'it greatly delighted them and they seemed quite to understand it'. Then she discovered that none of them had ever seen a map, and had the greatest difficulty in imagining it; they were finally convinced when she let them find Bath and Bristol in the atlas for themselves. 'Always begin with the *known*,' she noted, 'carrying them afterwards to the unknown.' She showed them a spirula shell. 'It was striking to see this group of rough boys bending with delight over the delicate shell; they seemed quite to appreciate its beauty and the wonderful skill in its structure.' At first their untrained attention could not be held for long, but as she skilfully conveyed what she called 'the *pleasure* of knowledge for its own sake', she could carry an idea from one week to the next. Thus she showed them some pressed ferns; 'none knew what they were, though W. thought he had seen some growing'. Next week she took a piece of coal shale with the impressions of fossil fern. 'I told them to examine the specimen and then tell me what they thought it was. W. gave so bright a smile that I saw he knew; none of the others could tell. He said they were ferns "like what I showed them last week" but believed they were chiselled on stone. Their surprise and pleasure was great when I explained the matter to them.'[23] There is something intensely human in these records of a teacher and her class. At this date most orthodox church-goers refused even to admit the existence of prehistory and its evidences. History lessons in the average school consisted of reciting the Kings and Queens of England, just as geography consisted in reciting the bays and capes.

Mary followed the same teaching methods in the night school where she kept open house to more than a hundred boys and girls of all ages from 7 to 17. As they grew more orderly, she became more ambitious for them. On one night in 1849, two hundred crammed themselves into the ramshackle building, where they had been promised a science lecture with a demonstration of experiments. These object lessons, derived from Pestalozzi, were a highly progressive teaching method in the 1840s. Mary provided the apparatus, saying 'it gives me deep pleasure when my dear father's things are used in this way'. She also found the lecturer, a close friend, who had been a fellow pupil in her father's school. Samuel Worsley came from a distinguished family of teachers, and though he was now middle-aged, and his sight had failed, he still lectured with freshness and enthusiasm. He could judge his success by the unwonted stillness of his audience. Mary watched them as they edged forwards to follow the experiments. Dull faces brightened into in-

[22] Cobbe, F. P., *Autobiography*, 279–80.
[23] Carpenter, M. *Ragged Schools*, 38.

telligence; even the girls forgot to giggle and whisper. 'The wild-haired F., who three years ago violently kicked the master with his bare feet and covered him with mud, now looked quite transfixed with delighted attention. Of course Z., who has powers as fine as any lad I ever met with, was drinking in everything with eyes and ears, while little George was listening so quietly that one could hardly imagine he had been roving wildly about all summer.' A substance was heated, with great excitement and cries of 'It's roasting!', 'It's boiling!', 'He's busting!' Yet, she said 'they looked at these things with understanding and not as mere conjuring tricks'. Even boys and girls who could not read answered questions so intelligently that Worsley suggested that those who could should try to write down what they had learnt. This new idea rather frightened them; their efforts were untidy and ill-spelt, yet they had clearly understood the purpose of the experiments. 'One boy was so astonished at his own performance', said Mary, 'that he wrote at the end, "Master, you have teached me very well." '[24] Their quick wits continually surprised and delighted her. 'These boys are sharper than I am,' remarked a Cambridge undergraduate, whom she had roped in to help during his vacations. Knowing the animal simplicity of their lives, she tried to give them some idea of the outside world. By an astonishing stroke of imagination she invited an escaped Virginian slave to visit the school and tell the children about his adventures. Their response was immediate and heartening. Here was someone whose troubles they could understand and share. 'Truly indignant was my class of ragged boys and girls,' wrote Mary. ' "Why, I could not work hard if I was a slave," said a very bright, warm-hearted Irish lad, "because I should be in trouble." He felt his spirit would be crushed. They have a strong feeling of sympathy for the oppressed.' To her wonder and admiration the children adopted a homeless negro boy whom they found wandering the streets and brought him to school. He lived chiefly on food they shared with him, and her letters record their kindness and gentleness towards him. 'One boy said he would like to be black, but I said we had all better be content with the colour God has given us!'[25] From the depths of their own poverty, they wanted to give to the anti-slavery fund. The girls made a beautiful patchwork quilt from dressmakers' scraps. Little girls knitted and crocheted edging; a crippled girl in the evening school netted purses and dressed a doll; a little girl got up every morning at five to finish an embroidered handkerchief. 'When it was all finished,' wrote Mary to Samuel May, 'I offered to pay them, but they all exclaimed that they wished to *give* their work.'[26]

This was one of many revelations of goodness and generosity in children who had been dismissed as parasites on society. 'These children have been so despised', Mary wrote later, 'that they hardly know whether there is anything in them to be respected.' It was hard to foster self-respect while they were left not merely tattered but filthy, many with matted verminous heads and skins

[24] *Ibid.*, 64–5.
[25] Boston Public Library, MS. A.9.2, Vol. 23, No. 58.
[26] *Life and Work*, 102.

crusted with impetigo. The first step was 'to make school a happy place' with a bright, welcoming fire. 'School should be almost a second home to them, not squalid or dilapidated, but bright, airy, warm . . . it is an attraction and comfort to these poor children, which those who know little of them can hardly understand.' The risk of infectious diseases was serious, for some of the pupils who had slept in common lodging-houses had to be stripped and their clothes stoved before they could be let in to the class. Mary was determined not to exclude anyone, however filthy. 'No child', she wrote, 'is *ever* made to feel that his miserable tattered condition renders him an object of contempt.' She provided a wash-room with a good supply of hot water, soap and towels. It proved so popular that Mr Andrews reported children were calling in at the school simply to wash. Mary considered that they also needed 'pleasures that are real enjoyments to them'. She introduced games, singing, dancing for the girls, home-made Christmas decorations and a visit to a penny panorama. As the children grew quieter and more orderly it was possible to take them on excursions. They were given free passes to the Clifton Zoo where they behaved well. The young children had a magic lantern show, the elder a trip to the science museum.[27] It is hard to realize now how unheard-of these simple pleasures were in schools for poor children of the mid-nineteenth century. They provoked the hostility of one anonymous pamphleteer, who complained of working-class children learning 'fancy work, geography on the globes and even music. Witness for instance the school in Bristol, where the children of the poor are so luxuriously accommodated and so elaborately instructed . . . this is one cause of the *discontent* which prevails among servants.' This was contrasted with the admirable lessons in 'humility, subordination and deference to their superiors', taught in a Sunday School where little girls were turned away for the crime of wearing flowers on their Sunday bonnets.[28] Mary ignored criticism. 'The senses should be cultivated and not shunned,' she wrote. 'Beauty is never an unnecessary luxury in the schoolroom. Natural beauty, pictures, good music all develop the child, just as bodily exercise, cleanliness and care of physical health show the essential respect due to the child as God's handiwork.'[29]

The burning question for all supporters of ragged schools was of course, religious instruction. This was supposed automatically to 'reform' children, in the same way as the visits of the chaplain would 'reclaim' the convict in his solitary cell. Yet in many ways organized religion added to the problems it was supposed to solve. On the one hand, Irish Catholic parents, understandably suspicious, would not allow their children to attend a school which criticized their faith. On the other hand, the Ragged School Union would not for some years admit a school whose management committee included Unitarians. The only possible policy was for religious teaching to be totally unsectarian. 'It is *no purpose* of the school', wrote Mary firmly, 'to make Episcopalians or Methodists, Independents or Quakers, Unitarians or even

[27] Carpenter, M. *Ragged Schools*, 60–1.
[28] Anon. *Why do the servants of today dress as they do?*
[29] Carpenter, M. *Principles of Education*, 8.

Protestants out of these half-civilized beings.'[30] Scholars, teachers, voluntary helpers and subscribers were drawn from every church. It is difficult now to realize how revolutionary this was. Until late in the century religious differences were regimented and militant, with rival church and dissenting groups working against each other, rather than for Christianity. These absurd yet tragic conflicts robbed the churches in England of a great social opportunity for while they were engaged in cardboard sieges and mock fights, the major problems of the nineteenth century remained unchallenged except by individuals. Organized religion as such never came to grips with society's most urgent needs; sometimes as in the case of free schools, it actively opposed reform. For Mary Carpenter by contrast the work of education was in itself religious. The Andrewses noticed how the wildest children sat enthralled with attention when Mary told them Bible stories. She told them of Joseph and his brothers. 'One boy asked if Egypt was real and if people lived there still; I showed them a pyramid and they were satisfied.' When she came to the cup found in Benjamin's bag, a boy said he knew how the brothers felt, 'because a man was picking a pocket near me and a woman said I did it.'[31]

When she told them the parable of the prodigal son, Mary was struck that they identified themselves with the prodigal and had no use for the righteous elder brother. Z. put the class viewpoint when he said 'I likes t'other brother the best.' By Easter 1849 she felt they were ready to hear the gospel narrative. 'I had to make no effort to control them or keep their attention,' she wrote. 'A year and a half ago there was scarcely one of these boys with whom I could have ventured to read this, so wild were they and untouched by religion; yet now they delight to understand every incident and to realize the whole scene for themselves. By this means I trust the living character of Jesus will take hold of their hearts.'[32]

This approach was too unorthodox for many of the clergy. A few years later Mary invited her racy Irish friend Frances Power Cobbe to tell the children about her travels in the Near East. An impressive young curate entered and sat silent, sternly critical, to note what heresies were being instilled into the minds of his flock. ' "I am giving a lesson on Palestine," I said, "I have just been at Jerusalem." "*In what sense?*" said the awful young man, darkly discerning some mysticism of the Swedenborgian kind, perhaps, beneath the simple statement.'[33] In some quarters Mary Carpenter was still suspect; when a committee was formed to establish schools in Bristol, the Unitarians, like the Roman Catholics, were pointedly excluded from membership. Her feelings were deeply wounded, but she comforted herself in the belief that she was beginning to reach the children at last. 'I feel this work inexpressibly glorious,' she wrote in the spring of 1849, 'nor have I ever felt the inextinguishable greatness of the human soul so much as I have in seeing it rise superior to very degrading circumstances as it does in many of these children.'[34]

---

[30] *Parliamentary Papers*, 1850, XLIV, 428–635.
[31] Carpenter, M. *Ragged Schools*, 23–30.
[33] Cobbe, F. P. *Autobiography*, 280.

[32] *Life and Work*, 92.
[34] *Life and Work*, 100.

From the first Mary had realized that deprived children could not be handled in a mass. 'We must carefully study the individual character.' She was distressed by the enforced uniformity of barrack-like workhouse schools, where hundreds of children with cropped hair, in hideous uniforms and shuffling shoes, moved mechanically at the word of command. Orphanages too, herded infants together without toys or companionship. Many could hardly speak, and a party of children on foot were seen clinging to each other and to the railings; they had never learnt to walk.[35] Mary Carpenter's ideal was precisely the opposite; 'a teacher *must* become personally acquainted with the individual children of a class'. A series of vividly observed individuals emerges like a tattered but indomitable procession from her pages. 'The middle classes,' she wrote, 'know them scarcely by sight.' L.'s mother was dead; his father deserted the family and the small children were carried to the workhouse. L., who was 13, ran away, preferring a wild and predatory life, and sleeping where he could. The school gave him dinner, to prevent his stealing it, and he proved so bright that Mary made him a monitor; she was proud to see him 'intelligently and kindly managing his little class'. B., now a charming and clean little girl, had been found wandering in the streets, dirty beyond description, with a careless, bold manner that left her probable future in no doubt. R. had been whipped by order of the magistrates and had run away; filthy and destitute, he refused to sleep under a roof, and lived in hostility to society, but showed 'great susceptibility of kindness'. He was the boy whom Mary took to hear the escaped slave, Frederick Douglass. Little George was stunted in growth, but a tough character, whose drink-sodden mother left him to fend for himself. He resented injustice 'with dogged sullenness' and would tramp the country for months at a time, but once his confidence was won, he came regularly to school for two years.[36] 'These children are free agents,' wrote Mary, 'it is useless to attempt to force them into mechanical obedience; they must learn to submit *themselves* to the laws of duty.' Great tact as well as patience were needed in handling them. Mary sent H. out of the class because he persistently interrupted during the reading aloud. 'He went very indignantly taking his copy book and declaring he should never come again. On going into the schoolroom, I found H. actually *gnawing* his book to pieces in great vexation. I could not let him go home in this state of mind, so after a little gentle reasoning, I made him acknowledge that I could not in justice to the class have acted otherwise than I did. He went home in a good temper and was never sent out again.'[37] Z., the clever boy, was one of the school's successes. He was full of fun and stole for amusement, 'executing little thefts as ingenious feats'. Mary decided to capitalize his intelligence, and persuaded a bookseller to give Z. a trial in the shop, where he grew so interested in the work that he gave up stealing; eventually he was trusted to take money to the bank every day. X. was filthy, disorderly and quarrelsome. The first sign of any improvement was 'the evening of his coming to school with hair combed. I called on his mother to congratulate her and the visit was

[35] Hill, F. *Children of the State,* 127.
[36] Carpenter, M. *Ragged Schools,* 18–20.　　　　　　　[37] *Ibid.,* 48–9.

kindly taken as a sign of my interest in him. Since that time his conduct has been gradually improving.' After leaving school he was employed by a druggist, who described him as intelligent and trustworthy.[38]

At first, identifying herself with the children's interests, Mary Carpenter condemned their parents. She saw the little ones 'so small and cramped in growth that you can see they have hardly had a full meal in their childhood', and how, shoeless and half-clad, they suffered from winter's cold; 'where there is a properly warmed school they thankfully go in. If you saw the state of these children's homes, you would not wonder at their liking to come.' Her fastidious taste was repelled by the sordidness of the children's background. Prostitutes preyed on returning Bristol sailors until they had stripped them of every penny; children would go home 'to keep an eye on mother,' left dead drunk. Some of the households were bizarre in the extreme. Two young women, with a clutch of illegitimate children between them, possessed only one shawl in the world. Each morning they borrowed a pair of sheets from a neighbour, pawned them and used the money to stock a basket with cheap fruit from the docks. One wore the shawl and hawked fruit round the streets, while the other minded the children at home. Each night they redeemed and returned the sheets, buying food from the minute margin of profit. The children, who ate the leftover fruit, were filthy and noisy but in surprisingly good health. Nothing in Mary Carpenter's upbringing had prepared her for such people. Yet gradually she learnt how family love persisted even on this knife-edge of destitution. With longer experience, she would not have it said that her children had 'no reputable homes'. 'It is not right for us to denigrate them,' she argued. 'I cannot say a home is not reputable because the parents are in the lowest degree of poverty.' The suggestion that children should be removed from slum homes to barrack-type workhouse schools made her really angry. 'It would be a most improper thing to take all these children from their parents; even if it could be done it would be a monstrous action.' Anyway, the mothers would never submit. 'Who has the right to take her children away from her? Would she consent to it! *She would die first !*'[39] The right approach was to work with the parents, for, as the visit to X.'s mother showed 'there are few so degraded that they will not be pleased by interest in their children'.[40] To knit together the school and the surrounding community, Mary organized a party on Christmas Day 1848. The children marched in a body to church, the boys in stout boots made by themselves, the girls in warm frocks and shawls knitted at school. Next Christmas Mary found volunteers to cook a dinner of roast meat and plum pudding for the night school, and gave 'a cheerful New Year's Eve tea party for two hundred parents. One woman said, "I've lived thirty years in Bristol and never enjoyed myself so much before!" '[41]

On 22nd December 1848 and 19th February 1849 the school was visited

[38] *Ibid.*, 72.
[39] *Parliamentary Papers*, 1861, VII, 395.
[40] *Report of St. James' Back Ragged School for 1858.*
[41] *Bristol Mercury*, 5th January 1850.

officially for the first time by one of Her Majesty's Inspectors of Schools, Joseph Fletcher. Fletcher was a barrister-at-law, had served as secretary to the Commissions of Inquiry on hand-loom weavers and children's employment, and had drafted authoritative reports on the health and welfare of children. He was primarily a statistician, editor of the *Statistical Journal*, with a marked gift for reducing miscellaneous facts to purposeful order. He had been an inspector of British Schools for five years. It is not too much to say that this highly professional observer was bowled over by Mary's achievement at St James' Back. He had seen nothing like it in his work before. He prepared a detailed account for his general report, but withdrew it in favour of what he called 'a characteristically vigorous' statement by Mary herself which he reproduced in its entirety, giving it much more space in the report than any other school.[42] He considered she had made 'out of the dregs of a large city a school as good as any paying day school'. He singled out the trained teachers, 'the good order, pleasing manners and gentle tone of the school' and the trusting friendliness of the children, which only wise and good treatment created.[43] The H.M.I.'s praise heartened Mary beyond words, not because she took it as a personal compliment, but because a well-qualified observer had understood and believed in what she was trying to do. For the first time in 40 years of life, she was moving outside the familiar network of family and church connections and testing her ideas in the wider world. To find them accepted made her confidence soar. On the advice of Joseph Fletcher she took a step of historic importance. In May 1849 she became the first ragged-school manager to apply for an annual grant from the Committee of Council on Education, to engage 'teachers of age and firmness of character suited to the arduous work'. She asked the Committee to waive the usual condition of training pupil-teachers, and Fletcher himself proposed that grants should be made 'in double the usual proportion, on the report of an inspector showing the character of the locality to be one of our well-known sinks of all that is degraded and degrading'.[44] Encouraged by this, Mary continued to the very end of her life, to press the claims of ragged schools to government aid. As she continued to point out to an increasingly harassed series of government officials, the schools which needed help most received least, because, in their abject poverty, they were unable to fulfil the official conditions for a grant.[45]

Joseph Fletcher also encouraged Mary to write more fully about her experiences in the school. Her first attempt was a series of anonymous articles in *The Inquirer*. Fletcher said they were the best account of principles and practice he had ever read; she must expand them and publish in book form. The result was one of the most vivid of Mary Carpenter's books, *Ragged Schools, by a Worker*. Though she still could not bring herself to see

---

[42] *Parliamentary Papers*, 1850, XLIV, 428–35.
[43] *Ibid.*, 297–9.
[44] *Ibid.*, 1852, XL, 513.
[45] Carpenter, M. *Claims of Ragged Schools to Pecuniary Educational Aid from the Annual Government grant.*

her name in print, Mary enjoyed writing this book. For the first time she claimed the privilege of a small study in which to work; it may have been now that she took over her father's sermon cupboard, in which all her papers were to be meticulously filed for the next quarter of a century. Conditioned though she had been to self-doubt, she began to feel 'the consciousness of new power'. Her mature character, with its remarkable blend of mysticism and practical ability, self-sacrifice and intolerance of the least opposition, was revealing itself. 'I have had a peculiar pleasure in this book,' she wrote, 'a strange and very unusual feeling of satisfaction in being able thus from my quiet study to tell the world, small and unimportant as it may be, the deep and earnest desire of my soul.' *Ragged Schools* attracted much less attention at the time than the more dramatic books on young delinquents, which Mary was to write in the next few years, and has ever since been overshadowed by them. This has led to a false emphasis on delinquency in her work, and an unduly narrow view of her aims. *Ragged Schools* contains the germ of all her essential ideas. Its concern is not with the offenders, but with all children deprived of home life and upbringing. Mary saw its proposals as the outline of the work for which she was destined. Looking back, she saw 'hindrances put in my way until the fulness of time was come and then removed . . . I believe that I have no self-seeking in anything that I am doing'. Consciousness of power grew in the belief that she had been chosen for a great work.

So Mary Carpenter emerged at last from the guarded seclusion of the Victorian family circle to play a part in public affairs; she would not lay down her work until her death. Intellectually she was well-equipped for public life, with a first class mind, an exceptional education for a woman of her times and apparently boundless powers of work. Personally she could hardly have been less suited to the buffetings of controversy. From exaggerated dependence and devotion to her father, she remained in middle age as painfully shy and morbidly sensitive to criticism as an adolescent girl. She masked these inner shrinkings with a fierce, tenacious aggression in debate. She had never defended her own interests, but she fought for her children like a tigress defending her young. Her profoundly feminine love for them was hidden from the world. Only close friends knew her childlike sense of humour, her romantic love for poetry, painting and landscape; her spiritual life, filled with mystical passion, she preferred to keep, she said, 'as a sealed well'. The love and sorrow of her early life was hidden from the world in the pages of her journal. This was the unlikely figure who became, by sheer force of conviction, a power in the land.

In August 1850 Mary took steps to secure the future of her school. With the help of her well-to-do brother-in-law, Herbert Thomas, she bought the tumbledown mission hall and the whole of the slum court in which it stood. This set the pattern for future enterprises; increasingly, she liked to have personal ownership and complete control. By October the sordid tenements had been converted into 'most comfortable little dwellings', and the buildings painted throughout. 'No fingermark was ever observed on the wet paint,' wrote Mary with reasonable pride, 'though the freshly coloured doors offered a singular temptation to boys.' Against quantities of gloomy advice, she planted climbing plants on the courtyard walls, saying, rightly as it turned out, that the children would take care of them. The yard itself became an outdoor playground, where Mr Andrews played with the boys, while the little ones enjoyed a maypole and swings. The most startling development was a school bathroom, still an unknown luxury in many private houses. All the Carpenters shared a passion for cleanliness; indeed Russell preached a sermon for the opening of a public bath-house, on the text 'Wash and be clean'. 'As God's reasonable creatures', he said, 'we glorify him in our bodies by the grace of cleanliness,'[46] and this reflects the family philosophy. Finally, the casual vagrants, whose brawls had disturbed the school, were evicted, and Mary secured working families, 'thus providing a healthy moral atmosphere for the children'. By 1850 the school had each morning a hundred children aged 4 to 14 for general lessons. In the afternoons, while the infants had games, songs and stories, like any modern nursery school, the older boys and girls made shoes and clothes for themselves, from materials provided by the school. Mary's appeal had produced a government grant of twenty pounds a year towards the cost of these. In the evening 130 boys and girls learnt subjects of general interest, including geography, history and current affairs with lantern lectures on the Bible, from Mary Carpenter and a team of volunteer teachers. The evening ended with singing and the Lord's Prayer. The registers showed that more children were attending regularly; the fact that they came in such numbers proved that they enjoyed school. The teachers were excellent, the buildings in good repair, and Mary had hopes, with Mr Fletcher's support, of a regular Government grant for materials and equipment. It was a remarkable achievement to have created this unique school out of voluntary subscriptions and part-time work in the space of only four years. For many people it would have represented a satisfactory life's work, but Mary Carpenter was already looking ahead. What would be the future life of these boys and girls, especially of those who broke the law?

[46] Carpenter, R. L. *Personal and Social Christianity*, 227.

7

AN EXPERT WITNESS 1850-1852

Mary Carpenter was well aware that many of her pupils were thieves. They worked in gangs, the Lewin's Mead gang, the St James' Back gang, the Milk Street gang, and so on; a favourite pupil was head of a gang and well-known to the police as an expert thief. 'I remember,' she said, 'one evening I looked round my class and saw that more than half of them had been in prison—yet a large proportion have turned out very well.' She refused to consider them as criminals. 'I have a very great objection to calling them even semi-criminal, because the word has a moral meaning. I consider the condition they are in as one of *extreme neglect*.'[1] She had always noticed how generous they were to each other; now it struck her how honest they were towards people they accepted as their friends. 'We never have a theft in the school,' she said. When a boy called J. yielded to temptation and stole a toy cannon, the other boys took it from him and returned it. Sometimes their loyalty went to almost comic lengths. 'I beg your pardon, I did not know it was you, Sir,' said a young sneak-thief, politely returning a handkerchief to Mr Andrews, whose pocket he had picked by mistake. 'Can there be a stronger proof of the power of kindness!'[2] asked Mary. The boys continued to steal everything they could lay their hands on outside the school, regarding themselves as the natural enemies of a society which had been no friend to them. When arrested they were usually sentenced to imprisonment in an adult gaol, where Mary always visited them. Escorted by a puzzled warder, she stood and talked to them through the prison grating: two starving Irish boys, who seemed not to understand what was happening to them, T. with two younger brothers, in hideous prison dress, with cropped hair, little George, 'so young to fight with the powers of darkness'. Q. had escaped from the shop where he had broken in, but his little brother, less experienced, got caught and was serving a sentence at 10 years old. Q. put on a tough front, but when questioned the little boy burst into tears. 'I felt the deepest pity for these poor boys,' wrote Mary, after one such visit, 'feeling sure that in better circumstances they might be very different.'[3] The casual brutality of prison life, in her observation, did these children nothing but harm. They took pride in bearing their punishment like men, and boasted to win an approving nod from some eminent offender. Professional criminals recruited the most likely boys as useful members of gangs, and the same young offenders were sentenced over and over again. The other boys naturally admired them for it. 'I learnt to my

[1] *Parliamentary Papers*, 1861, VII, 395-6.
[2] Carpenter, M. *Ragged Schools*, 72.   [3] *Life and Work*, 91.

surprise and sorrow,' wrote Mary in the school journal, 'that K. who had left prison only the previous week was again confined for stealing bacon, and that Q. had been with him but had escaped.' The effect of prison was most marked on L., the monitor who had been so kind to the little ones. 'When released, within a week he was in prison again for a similar offence. No one would have recognized the same boy. He now looked thoroughly reckless and at school talked carelessly with the boys of his prison adventures.'[4] Whipping, the magistrates' panacea, did most harm of all. A boy would scream under the lash, but as the scars healed, his terror turned to hatred and a vindictive resentment against society. After a whipping and a number of convictions, boys were almost automatically sent for transportation. Mary visited P. and R., the boy who had so often been flogged, while they were awaiting their transport ship. She tried to describe to her class the hardships they would have to face, and the misery of their parents, who hardly expected to see them alive again. 'I spoke seriously and affectionately to them, and I think their hearts seemed touched.'[5] As if to stress the horrors threatening these children, Bristol was convulsed in 1849 by its last public hanging of a woman, at the Cumberland Road gaol. Huge crowds gathered to watch; gruesome ballads and broadsheets circulated in the city and the school. Watching the children, Mary imagined their future; her sleep was haunted by nightmares and the burden of anxiety grew almost too heavy to bear.

She was not alone in her concern. Formerly, persistent offenders had been got rid of by shipping them off, out of sight and out of mind to Australia and Tasmania. This transportation was largely suspended in 1846 and finally abolished in 1852. Now a yearly crop of 70,000 offenders, including at least 16,000 under 18 and many young children, must be provided for at home. A number were confined in hulks for hard labour on public works; 2,000 for work under armed guard on the Portsmouth Dockyard alone. Enthusiastic amateur penologists filled columns of the press with their proposals. Reading them, Mary Carpenter was appalled. A writer in the *Edinburgh Review*, considering the reports of Inspectors of Prisons, was gratified that the new system of separate, solitary confinement provided punishment 'so severe as to reach the point at which the powers of human endurance fail'. The writer found this system satisfactory as 'a means of protecting society against criminals by terror, restrain and removal', while paying tribute, in so many words, to the 'sacredness' of property. He noted with approval that even in the new Boys' Prison at Parkhurst, boys from the age of 10 were locked in separate cells for the first four months, until 'broken in and thoroughly obedient . . . its softening power is irresistible.'[6] Opposition to Parkhurst, based on accounts like this, was to become an obsession with Mary Carpenter. A writer in the *North British Review* dealt specifically with 'Juvenile Criminals'. His enthusiasm for solitary-cell imprisonment for children was so great that he objected to school lessons or morning prayers

---

[4] Carpenter, M. *Ragged Schools*, 88–9.
[5] Ibid., 32.
[6] *Edinburgh Review*, 1849, Vol. 90, 1–39.

in chapel as 'diluting wholesome severity. . . . Imprisonment should be of *unvaried gloom,* without communication with friends, without the distraction of labour, without the exhilaration of exercise. . . . In case of need additional energy ought to be given to the system of Prison Discipline by whipping. It may be,' the writer conceded, 'that in carrying out this great scheme some of the unhappy objects of the discipline may sink beneath it. These are accidents to which we must look in all general systems to regulate the masses of mankind.'[7] Where this worthy writer was thinking of an abstract entity, the juvenile criminal, Mary Carpenter was thinking of real boys whom she knew and loved, of H. who had gnawed his reading book but been sorry for it, of Q. who had cried because he got his brother into trouble, of little G. who had the courage to survive against all the odds. From periodicals, Mary turned to the Inspectors of Prisons' reports and the Blue Book of the House of Lords Committee in 1847 on *The Execution of the Criminal Law respecting Juvenile Offenders.*[8]

She found very little here to reassure her. In 1849, according to the Prison Commissioners' figures, 17,126 young people under 17 were in prison: 2,557 girls and 14,569 boys, two-fifths from London, three-fifths from sea ports and large cities. These represented the annual convictions from an estimated total of 50,000 young thieves. Yet witness after witness had assured the Lords' Committee that prison did them nothing but harm. 'I am prepared to say', Captain W. J. Williams, an ex-army officer and Prison Inspector, had testified 'that whenever a boy goes into prison, he can never come out, in point of feeling, the same individual again.' He agreed with the Recorder of London that it was hypocrisy to pretend reform could be brought about by such degrading punishment. When asked if reform was possible under any circumstances, he replied cautiously, 'A considerable number of prisoners might be reclaimed, *if* you went to the expense of doing so, and *if* you placed the prisoner in a very much better situation in life than before he committed the crime.'[9] This was exactly Mary Carpenter's belief, based on her experience of boys in the ragged school. She found it incredible that 'evidence of the worse than uselessness of prison for juvenile offenders had been before the Lords for nearly four years, without any change being made. A Bristol magistrate told me that for twenty years he had felt unhappy at going on committing these young culprits. And yet he had *done* nothing!' In November 1850 she took a decision that was to change her own and many other lives. The world must be converted to her own views on juvenile delinquency, and she would write a book 'to put forth the subject in the strongest possible manner'.[10]

The enormity of this proposal in 1850 struck her friends and relations with dismay. Books on serious questions were written by people in the qualified professions, by learned clergy or barristers, by graduates of Oxford or

[7] *North British Review,* 1848, Vol. 10, 'Juvenile Criminals'.
[8] *Parliamentary Papers,* 1847, XXIV, 1, 461.
[9] *Ibid.* paras. 2705 and 762.
[10] *Life and Work,* 115.

Cambridge; above all they were written by men. Ladies, if they must write, contributed innocuous stories or decorous verse to keepsake annuals; the first women to storm the citadel of the professions would not appear for another fifteen or twenty years. Even her own family surrounded Mary with fears of a breakdown in health or exposure to ridicule. Mrs Carpenter reminded her with habitual irony, 'how jealous the Lords of creation are of the interference of women'. Mary felt the lack of support keenly. 'Few know,' she confessed, 'what a lamb's heart I have under my coat of armour. I used to think I had a more masculine than a femine nature, but I feel more and more that my essence is womanly to a peculiar degree . . . it is a great pain to me to be brought into any degree of notoriety, but yet *I must speak.*' She had gained confidence from the success of the ragged school and the encouragement of Joseph Fletcher, but, above all, she was driven on by belief in her own mission. 'I was discouraged by those around me who loved me . . . it was intense conviction on my part that determined me to write in spite of obstacles and cold water, to speak the truth without fear.'[11] The difficulties were formidable for a woman without qualifications and debarred by convention from travelling alone. Mary now revealed her administrative talents and her prodigious powers of work; without missing her daily visits to the ragged school, she studied Blue Books, prison inspectors' and chaplains' reports. Like all authors on penal questions, she found vivid material in the narratives of prisoners' lives, which they dictated to the Reverend John Clay at Preston Gaol. In November 1850 she wrote to Clay, outlining the plan of her book. She wrote endless letters, to chaplains and officials, to Sheriff Watson, founder of the Industrial school at Aberdeen, to the Philanthropic Society, and to M. D. Hill, the Recorder of Birmingham, a fellow Unitarian and a family acquaintance of her mother. Their replies, neatly filed and docketed in the manner Lant had taught her, filled up the sermon cupboard. She could document ragged schools from her own experience, and industrial schools from reports published in Scotland and in Boston, Mass. Joseph Fletcher's statistical tables of convictions in England and Wales established the increase in juvenile offences, and the Blue Book of 1847 the contamination of young prisoners in overflowing adult gaols. When discussing more hopeful alternatives, Mary acknowledged her debt to a paper which Joseph Fletcher read to the Statistical Society in February 1851, showing the good results of farm schools on the Continent. These were cottage homes, on Pestalozzian principles, in which convicted boys, sometimes with girls, lived in a family relationship under house-parents and worked on the land. There were examples in Switzerland and Belgium, at least nineteen in different German states and forty-one in France, of which the best known was Mettrai near Tours, a pastoral village in the silver-green landscape of the Loire. The boys lived in eight simple houses with masters, who shared their work and pleasures from a genuine sense of vocation. The life was spartan, but there were no brutal punishments and no wall; the boys were reclaimed by personal influence and made no attempt to abscond. Fletcher considered the essential

[11] *Life and Work*, 116–17.

conditions for success were: 'farm industry rather than workhouse idleness', cottage homes 'on the principles of a *Christian Family* with a genuine domestic spirit', the mixing of boys and girls 'in fraternal daily relations', much healthier than sexual segregation, and properly trained staff. 'The great difficulty', he warned, 'will always be to find the proper persons to manage children on the farm school plan.'[12] Mary might have taken notice of this, which proved only too true; but her ardent idealism responded passionately to the concept of a healing family love. No difficulties or disappointments in the years that lay ahead could ever shake this belief.

In eighteen months of intensive solitary research, Mary Carpenter filled notebook after notebook with a mass of facts, laying the foundations of a vast, detailed knowledge. Florence Nightingale considered her unique in her generation; 'here and there a solitary individual makes a really careful study, as Mary Carpenter of reformatory discipline'.[13] Theoretical knowledge was not enough. She explored every family and church connection to visit prisons for herself. The exception was the Boys' Prison at Parkhurst, an omission which was to prove damaging, both to her and to the movement. Elsewhere she insisted on seeing everything. Thus on 8th August 1850, while on a visit to the Martineaus, she toured the Liverpool Borough Gaol. She followed the warder, with his bunch of jangling keys through endless corridors of cells, where prisoners sat blankly, in prison canvas or red uniforms if awaiting transportation. 'They must be brooding over bad thoughts,' she wrote, imagining herself in their position, 'hopeless of the future, in a sort of living death'. There were 153 child prisoners, one serving his sixteenth sentence, one 'poor little child only seven years of age, committed for trial for stealing $2\frac{1}{2}$d'. 'When a boy once comes in', the warder told her, 'he is almost certain to come again and again until he is transported.' She saw the cold, bleak schoolroom and the girls sitting at their sewing under the charge of a matron, who said 'she knew them well already, for they were old offenders, although so young'. For many, added the woman, not unkindly, 'this seems their only home'. Mary's wakeful nights were to be haunted for months by the memory of two children crying bitterly under solitary confinement in the dark punishment cells. 'Instructive, though painful visit',[14] she noted when she got home. She conscientiously developed all the utilitarian arguments against imprisoning juveniles, on grounds of inefficiency and expense, conscious always of the need for what Lant had called 'a sound intellectual foundation'. But over and above this, she identified herself with these desolate children. Years before, she had told Lucy that she read Silvio Pellico's prison autobiography *I Mei Carcieri*, not once, but five or six times. Something in her character responded deeply to the theme of imprisonment; perhaps it was her own life-sentence to servitude in the Puritan bonds of duty. Perhaps too, having suffered the pain of rejected love in girlhood, she had a fellow feeling for the rejects of

[12] Fletcher, J. *The Farm School system of the Continent and its applicability to the preventive and reformatory education of pauper and criminal children in England and Wales.*
[13] Nightingale, F. *Cassandra*, Part IV.
[14] Carpenter, M. *Reformatory Schools*, 277–81.

society. For whatever reason, just as early training in hard work and method created the factual structure of her book, deep feeling gave it intensity. She knew, if no one else did, why certain children refused to conform, refused even to go to school. 'They *will not* come to be looked down on.'

Once started, she wrote fast. Beginning in November 1850, by May 1851 she was drafting the last chapter, while at the same time correcting early proof sheets. 'I cannot read a proof,' she wrote, 'without feeling my blood boil with indignation and sorrow for these poor children. I hope that the same feeling will be kindled in others.' This sets the tone of *Reformatory Schools* which came out in the summer of 1851.[15]

The book describes the number and condition of children 'perishing' from neglect and destitution, or 'dangerous' because already hostile to society, who are nevertheless 'young beings, susceptible as our own children of privation and suffering'. It states their needs. They need more, not less teaching than other children 'for words, names of places, with which they are totally unacquainted stop them at every line; a book to them is in an unknown tongue'. They need enlightened care for their physical well-being, to be treated with 'respect and true Christian politeness' before they can respect others. Above all, they need love, not weakly sentimental but wise; 'to children it is an absolute necessity of their natures and when it is denied them they are no longer children'. They will respond to discipline only if they know it stems from love. Prison is an 'utterly useless method . . . it neither deters nor reforms them'. On the contrary, it 'renders them almost certainly for life members of the criminal class'.

In place of repeated prison sentences, Mary Carpenter proposed three types of school, for three types of child. First, for the deprived, free day schools like St James' Back, employing good teachers; for 'it is needful to know *how to teach*, how to adapt one's language and manner to these children'. Second, for young vagrants and beggars, industrial schools on the Aberdeen model. By court order children should stay all day and be given their meals, but return home at night to preserve the all-important family tie. A court order was essential, for child beggars earned their parents' keep. Third, for convicted children, who would otherwise be sent to prison, boarding reformatory schools, under voluntary management. These should not be government institutions like Parkhurst, which is 'in name and fact a prison', with escapes, whippings, irons and armed sentinels. Instead they should be family homes, on the Mettrai principle, to allow 'the liberty of action so essential to a true reformation of character'. The book ends with a plea for legislation, to encourage the founding of schools, to enable magistrates to commit to them, and to make parents or parish liable for support of children in care. This was Mary Carpenter's system, which was never altered by one iota. She worked till the last month of her life to see it imposed whole, without compromise.

A great deal can be said against *Reformatory Schools*. It is a collage from

---

[15] Its full title, *Reformatory Schools for the Children of the Perishing and Dangerous Classes and for Juvenile Offenders*, had been suggested by the Boston Unitarian, Theodore Parker.

existing sources, with a highly slanted use of figures and evidence. The prejudices are violent, the arrangement muddled, and Mary Carpenter had heard too many sermons in her young days ever to write in an appealing style. Yet for all that, it is an extraordinarily powerful book. For the first time the child offender appears *as a child*. The accounts of individual children are unforgettable. Every page is marked by deep thought and deeper feeling. Mary was probably right when she wrote modestly to Lucy Sanford, 'It is not that I have talents, but that my soul puts itself forth, and I have no doubt that is the reason people have been so touched by my book.' For the book was an instant success and marked the beginning of the movement which changed national policy towards young offenders. It was widely and excellently reviewed, and not only in the Unitarian press. This was partly due to the determination of Mary, who sent out the review copies herself, with personal letters to each editor. The letter to Dickens's friend, John Forster of *The Examiner*, pointed out that the book dealt with a subject 'of great importance to the well-being of society: I hope you will kindly give to the accompanying work as early and full a notice in your periodical as the circumstances will allow'.[16] The *Edinburgh Review* called it the first book to treat the subject adequately. *The Athenaeum* said, 'In seven brief but terrible chapters she discusses some of the darkest problems that perplex jurists and statesmen of our day.' Probably most influential with the general public was a notice, under the title 'Lambs to be Fed', in Dickens's popular middle-class journal *Household Words* for 30th August 1851. This described the work of 'an earnest, grave, Christian lady, Miss Mary Carpenter' as 'not only of national, but one would think of personal interest to every thoughtful citizen'. It ended 'cordially thanking the good and wise lady . . . we must add how entirely we agree with her'. It rankled to find herself called patronizingly 'the fair reformer'; nevertheless *Reformatory Schools* changed Mary Carpenter's life. From provincial obscurity she emerged as that then almost unimaginable figure, a national expert who was also a woman.

Changes began at once. In the spring of 1851 M. D. Hill, the Recorder of Birmingham, moved to Bristol, and Mary Carpenter formed with him one of those impersonal working relationships with men, unique until Florence Nightingale, which were such a feature of her life. Even by Unitarian standards, Hill came from a remarkable family. One brother was a reforming Inspector of Prisons, another created the Penny Post. Their father founded the most progressive school of its day, visited by educationists from all over the world, and still a model for many similar schools. This school, Hazelwood, claimed to teach 'self-government and self-education'; the school formed a republic in which an elected government of boys drafted the rules, which boy government officials enforced, with the headmaster as self-styled President. Rule-breakers were tried in due form before a boys' jury, but no 'degrading punishments' were allowed; instead offenders offered 'voluntary labour of

---

[16] Victoria and Albert Museum, Forster Collection. In later years if her books were remaindered, Mary Carpenter took over the publisher's entire stock and sold the copies herself. She sent orders by post all over the world, with discount for five books or over.

their own free choice' out of school hours as an act of reparation. This ethic united Hill and Mary Carpenter. Like her, he had early taught in his father's school. 'At twelve years old', wrote his proud mother, 'Matthew was instructing others.'[17] After a successful career at the Bar, he became a reforming M.P. at the 1832 election, and Recorder of Birmingham, where he made a practice of giving juvenile offenders a second chance. A holiday visit to Mettrai in 1848 struck him, so he said, with all the force of a pilgrimage to Mecca. He and Mary Carpenter found themselves totally in sympathy, and he coined the phrase, often attributed to her, that prison should be 'a moral hospital'.[18] Their temperaments were as similar as their interests, not always with the happiest results. Some people wondered why such an outstandingly able lawyer should have stuck at a provincial Recordership, but as the memoir by his adoring daughter makes artlessly plain, Hill was both dogmatic and opinionated. He was out to reform everything in sight; 'his ambitions', as a *Times* leader put it tactfully, 'may possibly be too sanguine and his zeal occasionally too fervid'. He was unremittingly serious. 'I cannot draw,' he said, 'nor practise music, nor garden nor agricult, nor play with dogs or cats or canary birds. I cannot talk to children, although very fond of them.' His only recreation was serious reading, and even his daughters admitted his photograph to be of 'austere and gloomy aspect'.[19] He considered the least compromise or even open-minded discussion on matters of principle, as a betrayal and he encouraged Mary Carpenter, all too easily, to be as rigid as himself.

The feeling that a public servant of such weight and authority agreed with her satisfied Mary's twin needs for a father figure and for a secure intellectual foundation. She felt ready to take the step of convening a public conference on juvenile delinquency, an unbelievably daring undertaking for a woman at that date. She began to travel in search of supporters. Staying with William's family in London, and Philip in the north, to satisfy the proprieties, she went from M.P. to magistrate and from magistrate to gaol chaplain, suggesting that something ought to be done. Lord Ashley was gracious, six newspapers took up the question and 'I was much pleased to find in all quarters a warm feeling in favour of such plans as I suggest'. The whole experience was dreamlike for the former schoolmistress of Great George Street. 'It is a very curious feeling to me when I think about it,' she confided to Lucy Sanford, 'to give out my opinion with a certain degree of confidence and have it received as worthy of consideration. As I have written a book, it seems to be supposed that I know something about the matter.'[20] Mr Hill left her to draft the agenda of the conference, issue the invitations and make all the practical arrangements, which occupied the autumn of 1851. She was secretly afraid she would be 'too terrified to speak', but Lady Byron helped with the endless letter-writing and gave encouragement. As replies began to come in, Mary noted significantly, 'all the people whose opinion I value approve'; the others she

[17] Hill, R. and F. *Matthew Davenport Hill*, 5–7.
[18] Hill, M. D. *Draft Report on the Principles of Punishment to the Law Amendment Society*, contemporary pamphlet.
[19] Hill, R. and F. *Matthew Davenport Hill*, 97.
[20] *Life and Work*, 122.

hardened herself to ignore. She confessed to being 'excessively timid underneath my armour', but allowed no sign of it to show. Lucy asked if she did not miss the books, painting and music they had shared, Mary replied without hesitation, '*all* other objects appear to me insignificant in comparison with the rescuing of these poor children. . . . I have been a sort of centre of communications in the Conference matter, which has caused me to write multitudes of letters, and so I must go on till the machinery is fairly at work. Sometimes I almost ask myself with wonder if I be I.'[21] In the pressure of work everything else, except the daily and nightly visits to St James' Back, was abandoned. Mrs Carpenter, with her old-fashioned sense of the proprieties, was acutely distressed by the state of her daughter's clothes; Mr Hill met the now frail and elderly lady one bitter winter's day, looking in shop windows in College Green, Bristol, for something for Mary to wear, 'for she would never buy anything for herself and had really nothing to put on'. The ragged school children blessedly took her as they found her. 'Miss Carpenter give away all 'er pennies to the naughty boys,' explained an obliging urchin to a visitor, 'an' only keep enough to make 'erself clean and decent.'[22] Mary cheerfully accepted her clothes as a family joke and turned to more important things.

The conference met at Birmingham on 10th December 1851, a thin sprinkling of earnest reformers, 'shivering in the cold of December and not half numerous enough to fill the table.' There was not much enthusiasm at first, but Mary marshalled the Conference through the agenda with discreet generalship. She declined to speak in a gathering of men, on the grounds that it would be 'tantamount to unsexing herself', but the final resolution of the conference, demanding an Act of Parliament in favour of ragged, industrial and reformatory schools, was clearly drawn up by her. A standing committee of the conference drafted a Bill to present to the Home Secretary, but received the answer 'public opinion was not yet ripe'.[23] Instead, if they would collect evidence, they were promised a Parliamentary Committee of Inquiry at an early date.[24] Mary went home, fretting and restless with inactivity. 'It is easy for those to be philosophic', she wrote bitterly, 'who have not these children weighing on their hearts.'

For already, in the drafting of the trial Bill, a gulf had opened within the newly founded reformatory movement, which was finally to be fatal to it. Mary, brought up in the social isolation which is the common experience of progressive intellectuals in England, innocently expected everyone to agree with her that juvenile delinquents could only be reclaimed in the trusting, affectionate atmosphere of a substitute family. She was appalled to hear not opponents but colleagues declare that 'a crime committed involved *sin*, which must be expiated by suffering, deliberately inflicted as retribution, before reformation could even begin'. They insisted on a period of preliminary imprisonment. 'Some have disclosed themselves in a very unpleasing light,'

[21] *Ibid.*, 125. [22] *Ibid.*, 177.
[23] *Report of Conference on Preventive and Reformatory Schools of 1852.*
[24] Clay, W. L. *The Prison Chaplain*, 375.

lamented Mary to Russell. 'The vindictive principle of punishment, which is based on popular theology, has taken firm possession of the minds of many.'

John Clay himself, patron saint of prison chaplains, thought fourteen days' preliminary imprisonment *'far too short* a term'. He was a strong believer in the 'softening effect of solitary confinement, when the chaplain's visit is greeted with tears of repentance' and suggested 'three months' discipline in a separate cell would make a lad attach a proper value to the more active life and advantages of a school'. He also thought the expense of school-training could only be justified where three or four ordinary prison-sentences had failed.[25] As sacred to many as the dogma of retribution itself was its secular counterpart, the New Poor Law principle of less eligibility. 'Every penny bestowed that tends to render the condition of the pauper more eligible than that of the labourer is a bounty on indolence and vice.' All early social work was influenced by the spirit of the Poor Law and, when this was applied to children, the result was a startling callousness on the part of the educated classes. Even Sydney Turner, the enlightened Chaplain of the Philanthropic Society's farm at Redhill, and future Inspector of Reformatories, proposed 'exposure to weather and cold . . . diet studiously plain . . . no hot slops, cocoa, soup or gruel . . . no attractive dress, but plain rough clothing. Let there be no high education with "lectures on chemistry illustrated by experiments", no formation of bands and glee-singing classes, but only plain, useful instruction'.[26] Poor Miss Carpenter; the chemistry lecture at St James' Back, of which she had been so naively proud, was clearly to be held against her. These proposals, where she had expected unquestioning support, drove Mary Carpenter almost frantic. 'It will lead to a multiplication of Parkhursts instead of Mettrais and Red Hills,' she objected. She pleaded, wrote, argued with the members of the Committee, one by one; many of them were clearly very disagreeably surprised by her persistence and determination. 'It may seem rather presumptuous', she wrote apologetically to Lady Byron, who was following every stage of the struggle, 'but in a matter of principle, I often feel rather courageous.' She persuaded herself that she had carried her point, but she had reckoned without the strength of 'vindictive theology' and the English punitive obsession. From the first, the English reformatory schools were committed to contradictory and irreconcilable aims. They were to make the children better, but they were to make them suffer at the same time. As this proved impossible, they eventually lost the confidence of the public. Mary Carpenter's tragedy was that her whole life was devoted to the creation of a system, which in eventual practice by others ran counter to her true beliefs. Meanwhile, she stifled any doubts, as her father had done before her, in ceaseless activity. 'Where do you think Mary is now?' wrote Mrs Carpenter to her son Philip, in frank disbelief, during January 1852. 'On her way to London . . . to a meeting of the Committee held to settle the draft of a Bill to be submitted to Sir George Grey before the meeting of Parliament.' She had

[25] Clay, W. L. *The Prison Chaplain*, 464–5.
[26] *Edinburgh Review*, Vol. 94, October 1851 (identified in Wellesley Index as Sydney Turner).

previously corrected the drafts, 'all of which have been submitted to her inspection'.[27] Increasingly, work was to be her drug against doubts and fears.

A Select Committee of the House of Commons, under the chairmanship of the Rt. Hon. M. T. Baines, was appointed to inquire into the question of Criminal and Destitute Children. On 21st May 1852, Mary Carpenter was summoned to give evidence before them, her first appearance in public life. She was a strange figure in these official surroundings. At this time she was 45 years old, although her angular, stooping figure appeared to belong to an earlier generation, in dark, dowdy mantles bought for her by her aged mother. Stout boots, an umbrella and a portfolio bulging with papers completed her working gear. On either side of her long solemn red face bobbed incongruous grey curls, in the manner approved by her father in her girlhood. Even kindly Miss Louisa Twining described her appearance as 'somewhat singular', and a sharp-tongued acquaintance said she looked like 'one of those spinsters whose life was devoted to sentimental novels and the education and nurture of a parrot'.[28] Her notions of propriety were extreme.

Yet, seeing her now, no one would have guessed the effort it cost her to hide personal timidity and deep passion behind her self-possessed manner. Joseph Fletcher kindly came to the House of Commons to give her 'an hour's encouraging conversation' before the ordeal of this first public appearance. She had overcome her fear of public speaking and answered the opening questions composedly. She was, she said, the author of *Reformatory Schools for the Children of the Perishing and Dangerous Classes*, published in 1851. Her voice was low and pleasant but very clear and she spoke with the fluency of long practice as a teacher. She continued to explain that she had visited industrial schools in Liverpool and Manchester, and gaols at Bath, Bristol, Liverpool, Preston and London. She had 'minutely, enquired into the principle' of institutions for young offenders in France, Germany and America.[29] When questioned about her day school for poor boys, she rejected the term Ragged School with some spirit. 'I use this term merely because it is one that is understood, but I decidedly object to it, nor would I continue it except for that reason.' A strange childlike smile played round her lips at times and though everyone's first impression was that Miss Carpenter was exceedingly plain, many people afterwards noted her fine grey eyes, so intelligent, expressive and kind. She went on to analyse the state of mind of the slum boys in her school, whom she had come to know well. 'When they are out of school', she explained, 'they are in a state of antagonism with society, and consider everything is lawful prey to them if they can get it. When they are in school, they know and feel they are under a bond of union with those who are trying to do them good.' She added that, to show her confidence in the boys, nothing in the ragged school was ever locked up—though at this

[27] *Life and Work*, 129.
[28] Boston Public Library, MS A.9.2, Vol. 25, No. 15.
[29] Report of Select Committee on Criminal and Destitute Children. Parliamentary Papers 1852 (515) VII 1ff.

date in middle-class households sugar and tea were locked away from the maids. 'We *never* have a theft in the school,' she concluded.

When she was asked on what principle a school should treat children convicted of serious offences, her reply went straight to the heart of the matter, as she understood it. 'I would enlist the will of the child in the work, and without this I do not think that any true reformation can be effected. I would next consider the nature of the child, *as a child*. We must not', she said, 'treat him as a man.' She added further, 'I think there should be that degree of confidence shown to the children, which will make them feel that they are workers together with their teachers.' One of the Commissioners objected that this was hardly a punishment 'for the correction of juvenile crime', and Mary Carpenter admitted that many people felt this strongly. 'But', she insisted, 'we ought in the first place to consider the position of these children in regard to society. I consider society owes retribution to them, just as much as they owe it to society or in fact more.' Mary Carpenter insisted that it was not the children who were the true culprits. 'If society leaves them knowingly in the state of utter degradation in which they are, I think it abolutely owes them reparation, far more than they can be said to owe reparation to it.' In 1851 this was a revolutionary statement. It clearly scandalized one of her hearers, who asked if she did not find something 'extravagant and absurd' in that statement? She replied shortly, 'I do not.'

Very many people found this central idea of Mary Carpenter's philosophy not merely extravagant and absurd, but a positively sinful flouting of the will of providence. How revolutionary it was can be seen if one compares it with the writing of another famous Bristol school-mistress and philanthropist of the previous generation, Cobbett's 'Old Bishop in Petticoats', Hannah More. Her *Cheap Repository Tracts* were planned as 'safe' reading for the inferior orders, to counteract the 'poison' of Paine's *Rights of Man*. They recommended the blessings of poverty to agricultural labourers, of chastity to dairymaids and frugality with sweets to small boys. Her Mendip schools taught poor children 'such coarse work as may fit them for servants. I allow no writing.' She was shocked to find at Nailsea glass works, 'The wages high, the eating and drinking luxurious, the body scarcely covered, but fed with dainties of a shameful description.' The famine of 1801 was ordained 'by an all wise and gracious Providence', she thought, 'to show the poor how immediately they are dependent on the rich'. The sufferings of the poor in the postwar depression were easily explained

> Of God's displeasure they're the token
> Because His holy laws we've broken.

As her biographer justly says, Hannah More 'lived in a static world on which the idea of social responsibility had not yet dawned'.[30] In 1851, most conventional believers still followed her and accepted social and economic inequality as the will of God. It was this which caused such long-drawn, entrenched and bitter opposition to all reforms involving state aid to the poor.

[30] Jones, M. G. *Hannah More*, 236.

Mary Carpenter showed no sign of being aware that she had said anything shocking. She went on at considerable length to describe the changes she thought necessary, and presented a coherent scheme. This repeated the proposals of *Reformatory Schools*. She proposed three types of school, all under voluntary management, but open to Government inspection. The first type was free day schools, aided by parliamentary grant, to receive the vast mass of neglected and deprived children. The second type was industrial schools, with simple food and work training, to which magistrates could send homeless, destitute or vagrant children in danger of falling into crime. The third type was reformatory schools, as a last resort, for children who had been convicted by the courts. They should never be used for children who were merely rough and wild.

The average magistrate felt it not merely his right, but his duty to punish the wrong-doer, but Mary Carpenter insisted that the schools should not exist to punish. There should not be too much rigid, mechanical discipline. 'Some persons judge of the excellence of a school and the condition of the children by the degree of mechanical order which is observable. Others may judge in a very different manner and believe that too great a degree of order may be injurious.' The school should try to create a family for the child who had lost his own. Of course the sexes should be mixed. 'As nearly as possible the home features should be introduced; school cannot be made at all like home unless there is a mixture of boys and girls. No stigma should attach to the reformatory pupil. . . . When he comes reformed out of the school, he should be in as good position as formerly.'

'You would entirely abolish punishment in case of juvenile offenders,' asked a member, 'substituting for that punishment a reformatory system?' Mary Carpenter answered, 'The term punishment is defined in many different ways by different persons. I would in the case of the child merely refer to the spirit of the English law, that a child is to be *treated as a child*.' The Marquess of Blandford, one of the Committee members, was concerned that the schools might lack 'penal character', and the children fail to realize that they were being punished. Miss Carpenter solemnly reassured him that 'confinement and hard work would be felt by them to be a considerable punishment'; this was certainly no more than the truth in many reformatories as they turned out to be in practice.

So far Mary Carpenter had made her usual impression of matter-of-fact goodness, combined with an unusually clear grasp of principles. It was only as she was questioned on debatable points, or when her suggestions were queried, that she began to show the intense, suppressed passion below her quiet manner, and give some indication how formidable she was to prove in controversy. She was asked if the training for boy prisoners at Parkhurst would not fulfil her aims. At this, she bristled with disapproval and dislike. When questioned, she was forced to admit that she had never visited Parkhurst for herself. This admission was clearly damaging to her credibility as a witness. Nor had she studied recent developments there; her impressions derived solely from out-of-date reports. Nevertheless, her objection was on principle. 'I consider the radical defect of Parkhurst is that it is in fact a *prison*, not a school; and that it acts on the principle of compulsion and restraint, which is entirely fatal.' When agitated, Mary Carpenter was said to show the whites of her eyes, like a shying horse; Jowett of Balliol, seeing her photograph, said, 'That is the portrait of a person who lives under *high moral excitement.*' Now she became vehement. She told the Committee she had an absolute objection to any public or government institution. 'If I had the power', she said, 'of establishing Parliamentary or purely Government Reformatory Institutions over the kingdom, I would not do it. I should fear I was doing harm to the cause.' When pressed further on this point, she became annoyed, and answered sharply, 'Let Government do what it feels most conducive to the child's good, and to effect the ends of justice. If the Government thinks it can best effect these ends by establishing purely government schools, which *must* deteriorate into juvenile prisons, let it do so.' Some of the questions reflected a general anxiety in the public mind that crime might seem to pay. 'Does it not strike you that having given moral and industrial training to these criminal children, you would place them in a very much better position than the children in the workhouse school?' This represented the classic 'principle of less eligibility' in the Poor Law. The same anxiety applied still more strongly to 'sinking in condition the child of the honest labourer, while you raised the condition of the criminal children'. Miss Carpenter replied tartly that competition would lead to a much needed improvement in the workhouse and free schools, which were bad from 'what I might almost term the narrow-minded selfishness of the rate-payers'. In fact, largely as a result of her determination, schools for convicted children preceded free public elementary education in Britain by more than fifteen years.

Later, alone in her room at her brother William's house, where she was staying for her London visit, Mary Carpenter wrote in her journal, 'I feel my mind greatly relieved, for though I have not said nearly so much, nor that so powerfully as I desired, yet I have been enabled to speak some words of truth.' She asked to be recalled before the Committee, in order to 'enlarge on some details she had left incomplete' and on 25th May gave evidence again. Looking at her evidence as a whole one is struck forcibly by the distance between her ideas and the public opinion of her time, still more forcibly by the fact that she was determined to override it. Before being dismissed she was asked, 'Do you think that this subject is now ripe for legislation, or would you propose further individual efforts to give us more experience?' Her reply was decided and emphatic. 'Power should be given to the Government to certify schools which appear to be carrying out the object; aid should be given in supporting such schools, and magistrates should have the power to commit children to them.'

Mary went home, satisfied that her words would remain in the Blue Book. She returned to a sharp conflict, which no amount of family loyalty could hide from the outside world. Her relations urged 'home duties', the life of a middle-aged spinster with an aged mother and a decorous modicum of good works;

but Mary, at 45, stood out for 'larger claims'. 'I feel,' she wrote in her journal, 'that I have a work which *I must do* . . . an idea to develop in acts; I *must* try to do it.'[31] The work would be harder than writing books, harder than giving evidence. Her purpose was to prove the truth of her ideas by founding her own reformatory school.

[31] *Life and Work*, 135.

8

THE CHILDREN AT KINGSWOOD 1852-1854

The Committee of Inquiry had left Mary Carpenter with the feeling that the public was sceptical, if not hostile, towards her ideas. She set to work at once on another book packed with facts and ideas to convince them, but she was increasingly obsessed with the need to give the world a practical demonstration. She could think and talk about nothing else. 'People don't understand the first principles of the matter,' she wrote to the always sympathetic Lady Byron. 'These must be dinned again and again, in every shape and way, into their ears. The thing must be shown to them to be *practical*, far more practical than their present system.' Yet the idea of founding a reformatory school seemed a hopeless dream; the law was doubtful on the point, she had neither time nor money to spare, and her family, seeing her increasingly overwrought, was determined to shield her from further responsibilities. 'I have been more trained to bear disappointment', she told Lady Byron wryly, 'than the prospect of ever accomplishing my plans.' In her private journals she wrote of 'conflicts within and without. I have had sore ones lately.'[1] It was appalling to her to be in conflict with her family; for herself she could never have faced it, but for the children she would face anything. Then, suddenly and quite unexpectedly, help came from a place she hardly knew.

Kingswood was a straggling industrial village in the centre of the four-mile belt which formed the great Bristol coalfield. Coal had been mined there since the thirteenth century, and the giant hollies and oaks of Kingswood forest were gradually hacked down to make pit props. By the time John Wesley first preached there in 1739, there were twenty thousand miners in the district, squatting in huts and shanties among the spoil-tips which covered the ravaged land. They were a fierce, brutal race, given to hard drinking, prize-fighting, machine-breaking and riots. Here Wesley made many converts and established in 1739 a boarding-school for the sons of Methodist ministers who were forced to be much away from home, preaching. The school building and its rules were austere. 'I will have one or other, a Christian school or none,' said the founder. Yet he laid out an approach avenue of trees, and an enclosed garden with small individual plots for the boys. On a window pane in his study he scratched the words 'God is here.'

In 1852 the school moved to its present site at Lansdown, Bath, and the old buildings, with chapel, stables, farm and gardens stood empty. Russell Scott, a wealthy resident of Bath, had visited the famous Rauhen Haus at Hamburg on a continental journey and been much impressed; he

[1] *Life and Work*, 134–7.

now bought the whole property for £1000, and invited Mary Carpenter to join him and 'try an experiment' of a reformatory school. To Mary this seemed an answer to prayer; she accepted impulsively, confident that she could solve all the problems in store. Her first visit to Kingswood was like a dream: the children's garden, the lofty, whitewashed schoolroom and dormitories. Sitting in the quiet of Wesley's empty study, she felt how she would love to live there if she were free. Meanwhile, there was work to be done. Lady Byron at once offered to give all the furniture from her former charity school at Ealing Grove, and Mary hurried to London to collect it. 'It will be *sure* to be useful,' she wrote in gratitude. 'I learnt from my dear father to adapt things to purposes.' The school had no fixed income and she turned again to the drudgery of letter-writing for subscriptions; to her surprise and pleasure, she had collected more than three hundred pounds by the end of July. The days passed in a whirl of accounts, plans and builders. The whole venture being private, no official recognition, inspection or support was either asked or given. To Nonconformists who had met such opposition from the Establishment over schools this seemed a triumph of 'the great voluntary principle'. Only gradually did the grave drawbacks appear. Mary was confident. 'I have now an idea to be worked out, to develop in *acts*,' she wrote.

Her happiness was shadowed in August by the sudden death of Joseph Fletcher, H.M.I., at the age of only 39. 'I feel this a very near loss,' she wrote, 'though personally, or in any other way than publicly, we scarcely knew him.' She remembered his early visits to the ragged school. 'He first made me feel my work was understood and appreciated . . . it was he who encouraged me to write and gave me confidence by his approval.' There had just been time to tell him of the plans at Kingswood. She felt the loss, not for herself but for the work, 'no one around really understanding and most showing misconstruction'. Later students may mourn Joseph Fletcher with equal sincerity, for he seems to have been the only member of the reformatory movement with any real grasp of statistics; he would never have accepted the fudged figures which some enthusiasts felt were lawful in a good cause. Mary took up work on her book again 'as his last legacy to the children', laboriously assembling notes from many sources with scissors and paste. She privately dedicated the growing book 'in love and gratitude to my three helpers in Heaven, my dear father, Dr Tuckerman and Mr Fletcher'. She worked on characteristically, with a mystical sense of a world unseen though near, and a firm grasp of practical detail in the everyday world around her.[2]

In the autumn came a brief, charming interlude. Mr Andrews, master of the St James' Back school, had long been engaged to Harriet Martineau's faithful maid Martha, and all the middle-aged ladies of the circle took a great interest in their romance. One of these was the novelist Mrs Gaskell, now a family connection, since her brother-in-law Robert Gaskell had recently married Susan Carpenter. 'I saw your future assistant the other day and a very nice person she is,' wrote Elizabeth Gaskell to Mary. The couple were to be married from Harriet Martineau's pretty cottage at Ambleside, and

[2] *Ibid.*, 138, 146.

Mary made a long, slow Sunday journey with many changes of train to take part in their wedding. Her brother Philip conducted the marriage service, with Mary herself as bridesmaid and Martha's brother, who was Miss Martineau's gardener, as best man. This friendly arrangement was rare in those class-conscious days, but came naturally to the Carpenters.

Philip's vague, unworldly character was becoming increasingly eccentric. Only that year, his house at Warrington had been burgled. His response was to print handbills, inviting the burglars to call on him. 'I shall be glad of an opportunity of conversing with them. If they are afraid to meet me now, we shall meet hereafter at the judgment seat.' He appeared disappointed and genuinely surprised that the thieves preferred the later rendezvous. A prison chaplain thought this 'the most singular thing I ever saw', but Mary, in many ways so unworldly herself, understood it perfectly.[3]

She returned to Bristol where her mother now rarely left the house. Mrs Carpenter was now frail and tired, the incessant duties of a lifetime laid aside at last. She kept her habits of rigid self-denial, but her formidable character mellowed with age; she delighted to see old pupils in her immaculate parlour, and was generous to all in trouble.[4] Mrs Carpenter now admitted that she had been wrong to oppose Mary's work 'fearing the effect upon her mental health'. On the contrary, Mary was fulfilled and her mother unselfishly rejoiced for her. 'It is quite a happiness to see Mary, she is so cheerful and interests herself so much more in her friends.'

Early in September came the day for which Mary had waited so impatiently. The buildings were ready, the master and mistress installed. '*Kingswood entered*,' wrote Mary Carpenter on 11th September 1852. It was a golden autumn evening when a cart drove slowly over to Kingswood with the last load of bedding, and the first boy riding on top of it in triumph. Within a few days the family group of which she had so long dreamed was assembled. They were a motley collection. There were, at first, ten boys and five girls, aged 8 to 14 and including several brothers and sisters; most came from Bristol and all were sent by permission of parents or guardians, since magistrates had as yet no legal power to commit them.[5] Some were not in any modern sense of the word delinquent at all, others deeply disturbed. The youngest had received a six-year prison sentence for housebreaking, another had been eight times in the hands of the police for thefts from shop tills before the age of 10. William, aged 13, had been sent by a father and stepmother who disliked him; he was half-starved, frightened, suspicious, and continually ran away;[6] in the end Mary found him lodgings with a homely family. Most of these children worked, out of school, in the garden, under the care of a cheerful, friendly gardener. Within a few months visitors commented on their growth, healthy appetites and red cheeks; but some among them were more difficult to help. A boy of 10 had hanged himself in gaol and been

[3] Carpenter, R. L. *Memoir of Philip Pearsall Carpenter*, 131–4.
[4] *The Christian Reformer*, July 1856, XII, 448.
[5] *Bristol Mercury*, 14th February 1852.
[6] *Bristol Advertiser*, 8th March 1853.

cut down nearly dead; when he cried he was beyond reach of words; Mary found that only kisses and caresses could soothe him. A poor girl called Caroline had been arrested sixty-one times for being drunk and disorderly; when thwarted she became hysterical and attempted suicide. The magistrates and the local doctor who had volunteered to attend the children free of charge feared for her sanity.[7] 'All the evil I find out in these poor girls', wrote Mary to Lucy Sanford, 'only makes me love them more desperately.' From this flotsam and jetsam of misery she hoped to make 'a family and a real home'. The children kept chickens, pigs and pet rabbits; the kindly gardener helped the boys to lay out their plots and taught them to 'take delight in their work'. Mary was perceptive enough to see this working man as the best influence in their lives.[8] She was less happy with the master and matron, whom she considered 'inadequate to the undertaking, though faithful according to their powers'. She was disturbed on an early visit to find a little boy locked in solitary confinement for some piece of naughtiness, 'a most dreadful punishment to these wild creatures'. Eventually she calmed his hysterical sobbing and 'restored him to a sane state; the poor little fellow felt that I loved him and I was grateful for his love'. She determined to keep a close watch on the Kingswood household, without neglecting her other work.

Throughout the winter of 1852–3 her days were filled. She got up while it was still dark and worked by candlelight on her book. The rest of the morning went on housekeeping duties. After an early lunch she set out to walk the four miles to Kingswood, for it was only by rigid personal economy that she could afford to be generous. There she spent some hours with the children and trudged back in time for the night school at St James' Back, where she seldom missed an evening. Rain or snow were no bar to her journeys, on the evidence of Florence and Rosamond Hill, who accompanied her one black winter's afternoon. On the way she disappeared into a police station and emerged with a half-starved-looking urchin called Joe. Snow began to fall heavily; the young ladies suggested a cab, but the roads were so icy that no driver would take them. There was nothing for it but to tramp the whole way on foot, while as they passed through the factory districts of east Bristol, gangs of toughs came out from the alleys and hurled snowballs, which fell with a thump on their umbrellas. Mary Carpenter, pursuing some argument, seemed totally oblivious. She had already acquired the manner of fixing people with her eye, like some amiable Ancient Mariner who only wanted to talk philanthropy; this was later to subdue cabinet ministers.[9] It was quite dark when they arrived, much to the Hills' relief, but Mary seemed unaware of cold or sodden clothes. She reached home at the end of these days too exhausted to swallow the mug of gruel which formed her only supper.

Mary had no complaints, and no regrets. What she felt for these children was not some general, social sentiment, but real love, in all its sorrow and

---

[7] *Bristol Mercury*, 14th February 1852.
[8] *Life and Work*, 154.
[9] Cobbe, F. P. *Autobiography*, 276.

delight. As Christmas approached, she determined to draw in 'friends rich and poor from the neighbourhood of Bath and Bristol. I perceive,' she added with dry humour to Lady Byron, 'that persons who positively *work* with "dangerous" children, insensibly slip out of their evangelicalism, while they think they still have it safely embalmed in their innermost spirits. I *never* undeceive them!' On Christmas Day 1852, she gave a party for the children, their parents and friends. The girls had decorated the schoolroom with holly and ivy, the boys had baked a huge fancy bun; all joined in round games, and singing. The smallest housebreaker confidently challenged Mary to a game of shove-halfpenny.[10] 'A day of deep joy and inexpressible thanksgiving,' wrote Mary in her diary on Christmas night. 'I have had a season this week too full of deep and soul-stirring happiness, ever to give it utterance in words.' Later, among discord and disappointments, over long years of uphill work, she was to remember this as a golden time, 'one of the brightest seasons of my life'. Meanwhile, early in 1853, and still full of confident hopes, she brought out her new book.

Juvenile Delinquents incorporated research material left over from *Reformatory Schools*; as in the earlier book, Mary Carpenter's intention was to make scattered information, known only to experts, readily available to the general reader. She insisted that this was necessary because of 'many objections by those who see the subject in a different light', and particularly because of '*scepticism* as to the possibility of really reforming children'.[11] The early chapters offer brilliant descriptions of delinquent children, their homes and families, collected with the care of a patient's case-history in hospital. The individual vignettes are vivid: the resourceful young thief who recouped his losses after a wet Saturday in Manchester by picking pockets on Sunday in church, the small boy 'with the resolute gait of a man' who made his killing among the crowds at Wombwell's menagerie, the little girl who boasted 'my brother Edward could pick a woman's pocket as she ran along the street'. The parents appear: hawking, tinkering, chair-mending, pilfering from houses and hen-roosts, with their children as nimble assistants. Family love between them is real. Mary Carpenter witnessed the scene at Liverpool Assizes in 1852, when a mother who used her little girl for shop-lifting was sentenced to transportation. She saw 'the agony of parent and child when sentence was pronounced, their despairing grief when they were removed from the dock . . . and the child torn from the mother whose guilt she cannot comprehend'. Considering the early lives of the parents themselves, 'deep pity should move us for their own sake as well as for their children'. Later chapters of the book contrast good and bad environments for reclaiming juvenile delinquents. Among the bad are all Mary Carpenter's familiar bêtes noires, prisons, workhouses, prison schools, and, of course, Parkhurst, which is singled out for gratuitous attack. This is based on the evidence of a visitor, who began his account with the ingenuous remark, '*what I saw was just what I anticipated*', good material conditions, flourishing crops but armed guards in the fields,

---

[10] Bristol Archives, 12693, No. 23.
[11] Carpenter, M. *Juvenile Delinquents, their condition and treatment,* 14.

8. Children sleeping in the street, an engraving by G. Doré

9. (above) Useful work and improving texts at a boys' ragged school of 1846

10. A photographic study of a ragged boy, by O. G. Reylander

and 'almost all the boys working under fear instead of kindness'.[12] Reformation, he concluded, was impossible under these conditions. Among good institutions, by contrast, she describes the Massachusetts Farm School, the colonies agricoles of France and the RauhenHaus at Hamburg. This offered no deaths, no illness, no walls, free home visits and no escapes. It claimed only five failures out of 207 children in twenty years' work. This is surely one of the statistics which would never have passed Joseph Fletcher's scrutiny. From these admittedly invidious comparisons Mary Carpenter deduced her essential principles of treatment. 'The child must be placed where he will gradually be restored to the true position of childhood . . . he must in short be placed in a *family*. Love must lead the way; faith and obedience will follow. . . . This is the fundamental principle of all true reformatory action with the young.' Mary Carpenter is often seen solely as a propagandist for reformatory schools, and one of her most interesting suggestions is overlooked. This was, 'a discretionary power to magistrates to restore the child to his or her parents on the first offence, provided they give satisfactory security for future conduct'. This, one of the first proposals for probation, was perhaps too far in advance of its time and apparently passed unnoticed. *Juvenile Delinquents*, like its predecessor, was well reviewed, although the *Athenaeum* struck a condescending note, eloquent of sexual attitudes in the 1850s. 'When Miss Carpenter trusts to her sentiments and her womanly emotions she is admirable—we would counsel her in all kindness to leave speculation and philosophy to those who may stand in more need of it than she is likely to do.'[13]

Mary Carpenter's reputation and continuing influence as a worker for children rests on these three books, *Ragged Schools*, *Reformatory Schools* and *Juvenile Delinquents*. Her contemporaries found a somewhat macabre, Gothic fascination in the idea of reformatory schools, and their enthusiasm has tended to distort later views of her work. Mary Carpenter should not be regarded solely as the originator of a now largely discredited penal experiment. Her writings, taken as a whole, show a passionate concern for all children, whether delinquent, disturbed or deprived by extreme neglect. Where other writers saw delinquents as a race of ugly changelings, cut off from common humanity, she pleaded and argued for their rights *as children*. 'Most people imagine', she said, 'when they see or hear of bad boys that they are a worse *kind* of boy than others. In my experience *it is not so*.' Modern critics, even where they disagree with her practice, pay tribute to Mary Carpenter as a pioneer in the theory of child care. 'Few people', writes Carlebach, 'have thought more deeply or expressed more forcibly and clearly the theoretical principles on which an institution for children should be run.'[14] Dr Hunter and Dr Macalpine place her among the pioneers of social psychiatry; 'she made juvenile delinquency her cause, the problems of which touch on sociology, criminology; medicine and foremost psychological

[12] *Ibid.*, 193ff.
[13] *The Athenaeum*, 19th March 1853.
[14] Carlebach, J. *Caring for Children in Trouble*, 54.

medicine. . . . The growth of social services for disturbed or delinquent children shows how very necessary Mary Carpenter's pioneering work was.'[15] Bridgeland sees her as 'the most significant and "pioneering" worker for deprived children. . . . That there is so much which is startlingly modern about Mary Carpenter's work is above all a tribute to her understanding of essential child nature.' He notes as particularly modern, foreshadowing psychotherapy, her insistence on the essential importance of love in the child's development.[16] These principles are as valid today as when she wrote, more than a century ago. The tragedy for Mary Carpenter, and for deprived children, is that they proved so difficult to put into practice.

At the height of her confidence, after the successful publication of *Juvenile Delinquents*, Mary Carpenter received several shocks. The first came in the form of a personal letter, written to her on 2nd March 1853 by the Director of Convict Prisons, Joshua Jebb.[17] Every line of his letter showed how Mary Carpenter's repeated public attacks on Parkhurst had outraged his sense of justice. In fairness to his officers, and above all to the boys themselves, he felt bound to point out the harm she had done 'in branding a Parkhurst boy before the face of the whole world'. The boys would find it much harder to get work because she insisted they could not have reformed, and might be driven 'from sheer want and necessity into a criminal career'. This was not all. Jebb, who felt sincere sympathy for his boys, had hoped to keep them out of common gaols and create government training-establishments for them; but reports, put about by Mary Carpenter, that 'Parkhurst had been an entire failure . . . have shaken the confidence of the public in any such institution and it will not be easy to win it back.'

Mary Carpenter, who truthfully admitted 'unwillingness to own herself in the wrong', was shattered by this just reproach. It threatened not merely her *amour propre*, but the conviction that she was doing God's work, which lay at the very heart of her emotional life. She rushed to Recorder Hill who urged her to 'show fight' and suggested 'your natural protector is your brother'. Fortunately the pacific, and myopic William refused to start a public quarrel, which could only have damaged Mary and the reformatory movement. Captain Hall, the governor of Parkhurst, sent her a pressing invitation, and in August 1854 she at last saw Parkhurst for herself. In a two days' tour she found open-air work, craft-training, reasonable care for health and rewards for good conduct. On 13th August 1854 she wrote a belated, and, it must be said, grudging apology to Colonel Jebb, acknowledging the changes for the better, which 'I shall make a point of stating whenever opportunity occurs'. In fact she persisted with many of her criticisms. Mary Carpenter never quite got over this forcible helping of humble pie. Her father's liberal indoctrination had made her naturally suspicious of 'government'. Government passed laws against Unitarians, imprisoned her father's kinsman Gilbert Wakefield, throttled free speech in the Six Acts, sent mounted dragoons to

[15] Hunter, R. and Macalpine, I. *Three Hundred Years of Psychiatry*, 995-7.
[16] Bridgeland, M. *Pioneer Work with Maladjusted Children*, 55-65.
[17] Carlebach, J. *Caring for Children in Trouble*, 51-2, quotes this letter in full.

cut down innocent citizens after the Bristol Riots; Government or the Established Church kept Dissenters out of universities, and starved their schools of funds. By family tradition and training Mary had always been a convinced voluntaryist, but from now on there was a note of paranoia in her hostility to government institutions. So obsessed was she, and so strong the influence of this once obscure provincial lady, that state schools for young offenders were not seriously considered until the Gladstone Committee of 1895. The problems of finance and differing standards among so many struggling voluntary institutions naturally proved immense, as time would show, but for the moment, wrote Mary to Lady Byron, 'the voluntary principle was carried most triumphantly.'[18]

Disagreeable as it had been to receive Colonel Jebb's letter, the shock which followed ten days later was infinitely worse. On 12th March at eleven in the morning, as Mary was sitting at her desk, a policeman came to tell her that six girls from Kingswood were locked up at the station. The matron had forcibly cut their hair, and they had absconded next morning as soon as the gates were open, making straight for their old haunts among the wharves and taverns of Bristol. The mother of one had warned the police and the six were dragged screaming and struggling to the police station. With the help of the Andrewses, Mary Carpenter hurried to fetch them. 'Instead of finding them in a room waiting for me, I was told they were all locked up. The Superintendent was most indignant with them: he said he had never seen such girls.' He led her to the cell corridor, where even from the entrance she could hear the girls shouting, singing and screaming. 'The cells had doors made of strong iron bars so that we could see and hear what passed within. He then accompanied me to the door of each cell, calling each little girl to the door as one would call a wild beast to the front of the den.' When she spoke gently to the girls, they hung their heads; one took her hand through the bars. Mary asked for the children to be released and said she would walk with them to the nearest cab stand. The Superintendent warned her there were 'bad people about . . . who might insult us or even try to rescue them. I found the girls had come without bonnets and shawls, so I sent Mr A. for two flies. They had eaten nothing since morning, and having with me two biscuits I divided them among the girls; they ate the few mouthfuls with avidity and said, "How kind," so I sent for two loaves for them.' When they had eaten she suggested they apologize to the Superintendent, who seemed 'surprised and pleased', as well he might be, comparing these hungry little schoolgirls with the screaming furies of the morning. Mary shepherded the girls out through a rough and inquisitive crowd, trying to hide their faces from recognition. They drove quietly back to Kingswood. 'Within an hour after our arrival Catherine had actually run away again, but she was captured and brought back.'

Three days later, Mary received another urgent summons. 'I hastened over, Kingswood school was nearly deserted. The entire school had rioted after two boys were sent out for misbehaving in prayers. The infection rapidly

[18] *Life and Work*, 147.

spread. The other children rushed out and the greater part both of boys and girls ran into the fields beyond bounds, where they danced about in perfect defiance.' The staff in panic shouted to the neighbours for help, and burly quarrymen and miners, on their way to work, seized the frightened children, tied them hand and foot and locked them in the cellars. There they lay, listening for the sound of Mary Carpenter's cab, 'as they were sure I should come'. Mary Carpenter hurried to unbind the girls and bring them home from the various cottage cellars where they were imprisoned, while the invaluable Mr Andrews took charge of the boys. 'The morning's work was most painful and harassing.' A month later, on 16th April, the older girls ran away again, and this time committed various offences in Bristol. 'My poor girls and I wept together,' wrote Mary sadly, 'while I told them they had now compelled us . . . to give them up to the magistrates that they might be controlled as we could not control them; that I would visit them in prison if I could, or that, if not, my thoughts would be with them, and that I begged them as a token of love for me to go quietly.' The girls, very subdued, were taken away to Bristol next morning.

Mary Carpenter was so shocked by the events of these weeks that she never quite regained her old unquestioning optimism. When the boys at Parkhurst had rioted and set fire to their dormitories in 1850, she had been so sure that this was caused by ill-treatment and could never happen in any school of hers. She had confidently expected the same trusting friendly relations with the Kingswood children that she had known with the ragged-school boys; but this was not to be while the children were homesick and resentful at being taken away from familiar homes and families. In the lofty, cold class-rooms, and dormitories large enough for a hundred children, they surrendered to the hysteria of all closed institutions. 'Thankful I am', wrote Mary to Lady Byron, 'that the commencement of the last year did not reveal all I should have to go through.' She comforted herself with the work at St James' Back, which she attended regularly as usual. 'My great refreshment is to be at St James' Back . . . where there is an inexhaustible charm and excitement in watching the development of the young natural beings around me.' It restored her bruised self-confidence and she could write, 'I have been gaining immense experience; I know now what before I believed, but my faith is not shaken. . . . As long as I feel that, I am courageous.'

The boys gradually settled down; eventually they could be trusted to work out of doors unsupervised and to take money on errands to the village shops. They formed a drum-and-fife band, which played 'The Dashing White Sergeant' to visitors. Mary even invited them to tea with her slightly bewildered old mother. 'I seem almost to *live* at Kingswood, for I seem cut off from the rest of the world,' observed the old lady, but Mary was satisfied the boys had done themselves 'much credit'. The thirteen girls, on the other hand, led by Margaret, a bold Irish tinker-lass of 15, refused to settle. Mary, like many earnest educators, could never bring herself to understand that girls prefer streets, shops and people to any quantity of improving scenery. It distressed her that little parties of girls, under some bold ringleader, were continually slipping out of the gates and off to Bristol to enjoy a taste of their old life. The school had still no legal authority to detain them; Mary had the task of finding them in the maze of wharves and alleys and persuading them to come home. Her friend the Superintendent of Police warned her this was dangerous work, but Mary replied 'the only time I have been spoken to was when I was taking back three girls and a very low-looking woman as I passed said "God bless you!" '[19]

Nevertheless the riots and abscondings at Kingswood had seriously shaken the confidence of the founder, Russell Scott, and the staff who had borne the brunt of the trouble. Mary identified so closely with the children that she was liable to overlook their teachers' equally human problems, and to demand sacrificial devotion for very small reward. All now insisted, over Mary's anguished protests, that the system must change. In 1854 a Committee of Management was formed from members of all churches, some of whom distrusted her unorthodox beliefs and felt her influence must be kept in check. There must be no more disorder, or subscriptions would fall off and the public grow hostile.

Already there had been criticisms. At the second Birmingham Conference on Juvenile Delinquency, a clergyman had asked how the children at Kingswood spent Sunday; he feared they were allowed to play games. Miss Carpenter solemnly assured him they only went for walks. Privately she tried to find quiet amusements for the children, which would not offend the tyranny of the British Sabbath. 'We must give them a love of the day,' she said, 'or we shall give them a distaste for religion.' Every humane consideration seemed to offend someone.[20] Mary wrote bitterly of 'the distrust, the misconceptions of those around me.' The way the new committee finally took to meet the school's need for a steady income, she believed totally destructive to the children.[21]

The immediate argument was about punishment. The staff, harassed and distracted by continual disorder, insisted on 'physical force as the only means of quelling these appalling outbursts', and a majority of the Committee supported them. Mary protested angrily at 'the fatal principle', and even said she would rather give up the school; but the teachers seem to have been permitted to use corporal punishment and separate cells. Staff came and went at an alarming rate; each change put more responsibility on Mary's shoulders, and she was forced, strongly against her will, to compromise.

Everyone agreed that the elder girls were the source of most of the trouble, and Mary was forced to admit that even at St James' Back, they had been much harder than the boys to interest or influence for good. 'There is much more difficulty in interesting these girls in their lessons than the boys.' They needed imagination and sympathy. 'Low tastes and desires cannot be rooted out except by the introduction of agreeable ones; intellectual powers cannot be cultivated unless the doing so is made pleasant.'[22] Above all they needed

[19] *Life and Work*, 149, 150.
[20] *The Inquirer*, 1st January 1853, and *Prize Essay of Reformatory and Refuge Union, 1857*.
[21] See p. 167 below.   [22] Carpenter, M. *Juvenile Delinquents*, 110.

a home; but the committee considered that the experiment of a family group had failed. They were unwilling to keep fifteen rebellious girls any longer. Mary wanted to take them into her own house, but Anna and Herbert Thomas protested in horror at the threat to old Mrs Carpenter's peace and quiet. Mary was left, in the summer of 1854, to worry over her girls' future.

The conflict of principles at Kingswood which caused Mary Carpenter such distress was merely the reflection of national disagreement on the subject of 'criminal children'. It is clear now that the believers in punishment and austerity were in a comfortable majority. In December 1854 the Conference on Juvenile Delinquency, which had become an annual event, met once again. An evening meeting at Birmingham, with Lord Shaftesbury in the chair, filled the Town Hall. It was suggested from the floor that the reformatory movement must be willing to adapt in deference to public opinion. This 'ignorant and cruel proposal' alarmed Mary Carpenter, but Hill urged her 'to stand firmly on the rock of principle. . . . Are we to be told that we must bend to public opinion? No! We must *reform* public opinion! It requires even more reformation than the children of whom we have been speaking.' In public lectures he boomed from the platform 'that the three great lessons to be taught are religious convictions, industry and self-control. If prosecuted with perseverance, success is *certain*.' This browbeating style probably gained as many opponents as supporters. Mary Carpenter's family claimed that she was universally beloved, but though she was certainly respected, it is clear that love, or even liking, for her overpowering zeal did not always follow. Indeed a religious test was proposed for the conference committee 'to get rid of Unitarians and Roman Catholics, in other words of Demetz and Mary Carpenter'.[23]

In this atmosphere of disagreement on first principles, it was not easy to draft the Youthful Offenders Act, nor did it have an easy passage through Parliament. That it survived at all was a tribute to the skill and popularity of its original proposer, Charles Adderley.[24] Adderley was a stout Tory squire, devoted to horse-riding and tobacco, who had inherited vast estates round Birmingham, in which he created the model town of Saltley, and gave Adderley Park to the city. He held his seat as Tory M.P. for North Staffordshire for thirty-seven years and is believed to have invented the term Local Government. He made a study of convict transportation and in 1849 persuaded the Home Secretary not to send Irish political prisoners to the Cape Colony, where the relieved inhabitants named Adderley Street, Cape Town, after him. Gradually he became interested in young offenders. Adderley, a stern evangelical, was a perfect example of Mary's belief that eternal damnation was quickly forgotten by those who actually worked with the children. Like Cobbett he was moved by a sort of radical Tory commonsense; he believed the best way to make bad boys good was to find them happy foster-homes and good day-schools, a suggestion so sensible that it raised pious horror on all sides. In default of this, Adderley persuaded Palmerston to

---

23 Hill, R. and F. *Matthew Davenport Hill*, 189. M. Demetz was the founder of Mettrai.
24 Later Lord Norton.

accept a Bill, drafted by himself on the advice of the Conference and Mary Carpenter who stayed at his mansion, Hams Hall, for consultation. From one of these visits she returned, remarking with great simplicity that 'the ladies and gentlemen came down dressed for dinner and evidently thought the meal quite a pleasant part of the day'.[25] Adderley laboured through parliamentary debates and committees for his Bill, but failed on a second reading. A government Bill was substituted and became law on 10th August 1854.[26]

Very briefly this, commonly called the Reformatory Schools Act, allowed the courts to impose fourteen days' imprisonment and two to five years in a reformatory school on convicted offenders under 16. Absconders were liable to three months' imprisonment, and by an amending Act in 1855, parents to a weekly payment up to five shillings in support of their children. The schools were to be under voluntary management, with government grants and inspection. Recorder Hill rejoiced that the Act brought out 'the *great voluntary principle* on which above all other John Bull wants instruction'. Mary, by contrast, grieved over the fourteen days' imprisonment, against which she had argued passionately but in vain. She imagined the bewilderment, resentment and fright of a child locked in a cell as a beginning to school life, and the difficulty of regaining his confidence. What must strike anyone now is the extraordinary achievement of rousing public opinion, drafting a Bill and carrying it, all in the space of four years, especially when this is contrasted with the deadlock which paralysed state education until 1870. Convicted children were assured of an education more than fifteen years before children whose crime was merely to be poor. For all Mary Carpenter's prickly prejudice, her books had brought society face to face with its own lower depths.

[25] Cobbe, F. P. *Autobiography*, 278.
[26] 17 and 18 Vict. C.86.

9

PROBLEMS AT RED LODGE
1854-1860

Mary Carpenter's next step was to found the first girls' reformatory school in England; she acted as Lady Superintendent from 1854 when the school opened until her death in 1877. The years at Red Lodge were always represented by her family and the band of reformatory enthusiasts as a time of unbroken triumph and success. It should come as no surprise to anyone that the reality was more difficult and much more interesting. All the problems which beset communal life with disturbed young people arose at Red Lodge. Mary Carpenter, for all her theoretical grasp, was forced to meet them like other child-care workers, as best she could. Her efforts are still revealing today. She had to make a home for the rowdy and rebellious girls whom the committee refused to keep at Kingswood. Very much against her will, she agreed that she could not house them with her frail and aged mother, though she complained of 'want of sympathy'[1] among her relations. In this mood she went off during August 1854 to stay with Lady Byron. They talked about Mary's father and the inspiration of his ideals. 'I desire to be with my children and so let him still live,' she explained. Her father remained her one touchstone for every principle or plan.

One of the unexpected and refreshing things about Mary Carpenter was that any friend of the children became a friend of hers. She had welcomed the High Tory Adderley, and the—by her standards—Bohemian Dickens. Now she formed an unlikely but lasting friendship with the Conservative M.P. for Pontefract whom she had met at the Birmingham conferences. Richard Monckton Milnes was a dilettante, bon vivant and host of breakfast parties, from which no one famous was likely to escape. 'What would happen if Jesus Christ returned to earth?' asked a rhetorical questioner. 'Monckton Milnes would ask Him to breakfast,' was the reply. Among Milnes' many interests, literary copyright, his biography of Keats, connoisseurship, was a Reformatory Bill, which he had unsuccessfully sponsored in 1844. His dissenting ancestors had made their money in the cloth trade, and he knew the problems of industrial society. Mary Carpenter accepted his invitations to stay at Fryston Hall near Wakefield. There she wrote of her deep thankfulness for kindly sympathy after struggling alone through many dark days. She admired Milnes' celebrated library, though she can hardly have been shown the collection of erotica which was its owner's pride.[2] Milnes

---

[1] *Life and Work*, 156.

[2] Pope-Hennessy, J. *Monckton Milnes, The Flight of Youth*, 134, describes him 'genially

wrote from Paris offering her a personal introduction to his political patron Lord Palmerston; and it was to this unlikely confidant that she revealed her new plans, in a letter of 12th October 1854.

'The Bill now passed', she wrote, 'is just what was wanting in the present state of the question, although of course we will eventually hope to give up the imprisonment clause. . . . Perhaps the first fruits of the new Bill will be the establishment of a school for girls only. We have not wished to receive any fresh girls at Kingswood, and shall soon probably discontinue them, although I have continually received many urgent applications for girls, which I could not assent to. Mr Perry H.M. Inspector applied to us to receive under the new Bill a little boy of 13 and a girl of 9 who were to be tried next month for Horse Stealing!' This is the first mention of Kitty, who caused Mary Carpenter to break all her own strictest resolutions against having favourites among the children. More will be heard of her later. For the present, the Kingswood committee refused to admit her, and Mary was desperately unhappy at the thought of the little girl's fate.

'In these circumstances,' she told Milnes, 'and feeling that I have acquired considerable experience, I have been wishing to begin a Girls' Reformatory, particularly now, in consequence of a change in our staff, which sets a valuable Matron at liberty.' Just at that time an old Elizabethan house, admirably fitted for a school of fifty to sixty girls, was to be sold. 'Lady Noel Byron has now bought it for the purpose and will let it to the school at a very low rental. After a time, when we have chiefly government scholars, I hope that the school will nearly support itself, but there must be at first of course considerable outlay. I begin in faith and hope that I shall receive support, for indeed the condition of these poor girls is lamentable, and preparing them for a life most hurtful to themselves and to society.

'I think I remember hearing you make some remark on the subject of a Reformatory for Girls and therefore I trouble you now on the subject. . . . Should you, or any of your friends feel disposed to help us, I should feel honoured and thankful.'[3]

Mary sat at her father's desk far into the night, writing around to family friends for subscriptions and furniture. She expected no difficulty about staff, but wrote confidently to James Martineau in Liverpool, asking him to recommend a matron of the highest principles and experience. He replied with understandable caution that he could not think of any one at all likely to meet her particular requirements;[4] this, as it turned out, was an understatement. For the present a Mrs Philips, 'a respectable widow of an energetic spirit,' was engaged, though in the end she proved not energetic enough for Mary. By contrast the house, Red Lodge[5] in Park Row, where once the gardens and

---

pointing out the choicest corners of the erotic library to his guests', before setting out for church with his wife on a Sunday morning.
[3] Trinity College Library, Cambridge.
[4] Manchester College, Oxford, Library, A3, Box B.
[5] Red Lodge is now a Bristol City Museum.

'prospect house' of a Carmelite Priory had stretched, appeared perfect. Mary, unwilling to waste a day, took possession on 10th October 1854.

The great old house, built in the reign of Elizabeth I, clung to the side of a steep hill. The windows on the garden front looked over a wide sweep of towers, spires and smoking chimneys in the old city, the river with ships rocking on the tide, the line of the Somerset hills beyond. The terrace and walled garden in the heart of the city were, wrote Mary, 'secluded as in all schools for girls of whatever rank . . . yet it allows as great a sense of freedom as in ordinary schools.'[6] Mary had known the house since she was a girl, when it was the home of the celebrated physician and pioneer ethnologist James Prichard, M.D. She had often attended his evening lectures, and Prichard's concept of 'moral insanity' as 'a morbid perversion of the feelings, affections and active powers . . . with an apparently unimpaired state of the intellectual faculties',[7] was to influence her thought. Now, as she turned the massive key in the lock and began to climb the wide staircase of carved oak, 'remembrances crowded thick upon me; yet a new era in my life had for the last few years opened upon me.' She could not feel the joyous hopes of the first days at Kingswood, two years before, yet still she prayed that Red Lodge might be 'holy to the Lord'. The mansion had stood empty for months; it was dusty and desolate, the lofty rooms trailing cobwebs. Yet the magnificent oak hall of 1590 still kept its ancient glory of coffered ceiling, garlanded panels and chimney-piece rich with shells, sheaves, climbing monkeys, bearded athletes and jovial oaken lions. Here her mind saw the schoolroom with its long tables and benches; at Christmas the girls should wreathe it in holly and ivy. Smaller oak-panelled rooms would form library and study. Above, the bedrooms were large, light and airy; so far as means allowed, she meant the girls to have 'their rooms as pretty as possible'. At first no window in the house would open, no door had a key, the kitchen was dark at noonday and the walled garden a wilderness. Mary found a relic of Dr Prichard's researches, a human foot, in an outhouse and removed it hastily, 'in case it should raise ghosts in the minds of the children'. She engaged masons, carpenters and plumbers. All through the autumn of 1854, she hurried these workmen on by telling them that 'several young children in prison were waiting to come'.

The first girl, Annie Woolham, and the new matron arrived on the day Mary took possession of the house; they set to work and scrubbed out two rooms in which to camp for the time being. Six more girls, aged from 9 to 16, arrived in a few days, to be followed later by the girls from Kingswood. The managers transferred these in a body; some arrived fighting and rebellious, others crying at the parting from their brothers. For Mary, who had planned a Pestalozzian family home,[8] these partings were a betrayal of the children; she had still to learn how hard it would be in reality to create the happy community of which she had written so glowingly on paper. There was nothing

---

[6] Bristol Archives, 12693, No. 1. All quotations in this chapter are from this source unless otherwise identified.

[7] Hunter, R. and Macalpine, I. *Three Hundred Years of Psychiatry*, 836–42.

[8] Carpenter, M. *Juvenile Delinquents*, 246, 252.

about these girls to appeal to the conventional child-lover. Visitors 'observed a painful difference between these poor girls and those in ordinary schools'. Some even recoiled in distress at the sight of their flattened, misshapen heads, their rotting teeth, their blear-eyed, scrofulous faces. Indeed the pseudo-science of the next generation was to see, in these pitiful marks of neglect, the stigmata of inherited criminality. Many of the girls carried heavy burdens of trouble on their young shoulders. Some were furtive and withdrawn, others noisily clamorous for attention. Some came from huge, teeming families, others after months of solitary wandering. Some were orphans or illegitimate, others lived in fear or hatred of a step-parent. The girls spoke in beggar's cant, or with casual meaningless blasphemy; the big girls gossiped with 'gross indecency' among themselves, or before the little ones. They snatched and fought over their food like wild beasts. Of the first twenty-seven, of all ages, only seven could read, all slept in their clothes, none had ever taken a bath and most were covered with impetigo. One had not slept in a bed for two years and had lived by what she could pick up, another was so 'thoroughly diseased' that Mary feared for her life. One girl had never been fed by her mother, and had been driven to steal by starvation, another had been locked in a dark cupboard, because no one at home could control her violent rages. A group of older girls had travelled the country with organized gangs of thieves, moving from place to place, as they became too well-known to the police for safety; some of them had been given or sold to master thieves very early and could remember no other life. Most of these adolescents had already served six or eight prison sentences. It was Mary Carpenter's special gift, said James Martineau, to love these children 'while still unlovely' to the casual eye.

Two closely written manuscript books in worn blue-marbled bindings, the Red Lodge Journals, record the first six years of the school. They were little quoted by Estlin Carpenter in his official biography, for in their pages an unfamiliar Mary Carpenter appears, a harassed Superintendent, beset with everyday problems, more fallible and infinitely more human than the sibyl of the conference platform. In public, she denied difficulties and argued away problems with crusading zeal; but in the privacy of her journal she dwelt anxiously on difficult cases and failures. The autumn passed in an attempt to assess the new girls and staff. Between sixty and seventy per cent she considered, beneath their neglected exterior, to be 'good, gentle girls'; it was the remainder who agitated her so unceasingly. Already her too-critical eye had found fault with the matron for 'wanting order and method' and the teacher for being 'inefficient and narrow-minded'. At the same time, she pursued dilatory builders' men, until after weeks of herculean labour, the whole house was converted, scrubbed, polished and aired. It was duly examined by an Inspector of Prisons, and on 9th December 1854 Lord Palmerston, as Secretary of State, signed a certificate that it was 'useful and efficient for its purpose and fit to be a Reformatory School under the provisions of the Statute 17th and 18th Victoria Cap 86'.[9] Mary proudly had the

[9] Red Lodge Museum, Bristol.

certificate framed and hung in her study. Hers was a position of unusual power, for the management of Red Lodge lay entirely in her hands, without any committee and free from any control except the annual Home Office inspection. This had dangers, both for her and for the school. Where ordinary human weaknesses are ruthlessly weeded out, as Mary Carpenter's had been from earliest childhood, the love of authority grows unchecked; many difficulties at Red Lodge arose from her determination to regulate the smallest details of everyday life. Moreover many regarded her as 'outside the pale of Christianity', and so would not associate with her in voluntary work.[10] Unitarianism was still suspect in some quarters. Therefore when the Somersetshire magistrates proposed to make Red Lodge the official girls reformatory for the west of England, the Diocesan Board stepped in with a veto. Mary continued to accept girls and teachers of all denominations, and slowly religious prejudice dwindled.

Christmas 1854 approached; this year it would be celebrated in three schools. St James' Back would give a Christmas dinner to two hundred hungry children; for Kingswood and Red Lodge Mary planned a magic lantern show each, and a Christmas tree 'with a little present for each child from me'. Arms filled with parcels, she hurried up and down the steep hill between Park Row and St James' Back or out along the bleak road to Kingswood. 'Mary goes on her usual course,' wrote Mrs Carpenter to Philip. 'Yesterday after writing all the morning, she got her dinner at half-past twelve, and set off to walk to Kingswood, four miles, busied herself there between three and four hours and then walked back.' She had hardly taken a day off in the past two years. Christmas came, but Mary Carpenter was not to be seen. She had collapsed with a severe attack of her childhood's illness, acute rheumatic fever. The familial and social pattern of this disease is well known; cold, wet, fatigue and inner mental tensions all appear to play a part. Bristol's tall, damp old houses, steep hills, waterways and the silvery Bristol rain which comes down in stair-rods, all form a natural setting for the streptococcal sore throats which initiate, though they do not cause, an attack.[11] Mary Carpenter, thin, tense, anxious and driven by some inner compulsion to carry a crippling burden of work, was, like her father before her, a classic subject for repeated attacks.

For three months her life was considered in danger; she almost gave up. 'Life has been for me a fearful inner struggle,' she confessed to Lucy Sanford, 'and it is only in the doing of my work that I have any happiness I care to live for . . . I feel much being such a burden to others as it seems I must be for some time.' Yet the thought of the children drew her back to life: 'I *know* my poor children want me.' She accepted the fact that her recovery depended on perfect rest, and followed the treatment as conscientiously as any other self-imposed duty. Her mother sat beside her bed for hours; the two stubborn-willed women were closer now than they had ever been. 'The interest which

[10] *The Times*, 17th June 1877.
[11] Coombs, C. F. *Rheumatic Heart Disease, passim.* It is no accident that this standard work should have been written by a Bristol physician and published in Bristol.

the children at the different schools take is very touching,' wrote Mrs Carpenter to her daughter Susan. 'They seem quite afraid of doing any wrong, lest she should hear of it, and it should give her pain.' At last Mrs Carpenter came to accept the reality of her eldest daughter's unaccountable vocation. Once Mary had set her formidable will to recover, slowly, in spite of several relapses, she struggled back to life. By April 1855 she was able to write lying on a sofa; by May she was planning 'to resume a portion of the labours that are so dear to me'. She had already begun by drafting what became the printed *Principles, Rules and Regulations of Red Lodge.*[12] These show Mary Carpenter at her most obstinately doctrinaire; if rules could make good conduct, the inhabitants of Red Lodge would have been model children. In fact, they had probably the opposite effect; minute regulations made the staff constantly correct the children, a bane and an annoyance to both sides.

The rules were to be read to each new arrival; the essence of them was that she should make a new start in life. 'Every girl on entering the school is to begin with a new character. She must as far as possible forget the evil of her past life,' and there would be no outward sign that this was not an ordinary girls' boarding-school. Girls were not to go out or to receive money or mail without permission. Books were to be read aloud during meals or sewing. 'Irreverent use of God's name and low language' were forbidden; diligence, neatness, politeness and kind consideration to companions were required. In theory new arrivals were kept apart until they had shown they could mix with the others without injury,[13] though in practice this does not seem to have happened in the period of the journals. The rules for the girls were not unlike those of any boarding-school of the period. The rules for the teachers, however, were open to serious criticism. They were required to do their very poorly paid work 'from their hearts as a sacred duty'. They were not trusted to 'converse with the girls about their past history, which is to be confided to the Superintendent *only*, and they must carefully avoid any expression or mode of treatment calculated to arouse resentful feelings in the girls or make them feel themselves members of a degraded class.' This well-meant rule was surely calculated to 'arouse resentful feelings' in any teacher worth her salt. The staff must be religious—this went without saying in the 1850s— but they were also required to be strictly non-sectarian. Religious and moral principles must be 'indirectly but powerfully taught by the daily life of the teachers'. A staff of angels could hardly have carried out Miss Carpenter's rules.

By May 1855 Mary Carpenter was able to go out of doors. The first sight of her shocked many people; she had never seemed young, but now looked really aged. She looked shrunken, sharp-nosed and anxious with the stoop of a woman of 70; her pinched lips were bluish, and her speech broken by occasional gasps for breath. William Carpenter, always a pessimistic physician, warned his sister that she must resign herself to the careful life of a cardiac

---

[12] Bristol City Archives, 12693, No. 3.
[13] Carpenter, M. *Red Lodge Girls' Reformatory School: its History, Principles and Working*, p. 3.

invalid. Yet, as so often, personal courage played an incalculable part. Mary had something vital to do, and for its sake she put up a fight. Dogged, self-disciplined in habits, determined in this as in everything Mary Carpenter took up her work again. Many people of both sexes in this period took to invalid sofas with far less reason. In spite of several further attacks, one serious, Mary still had more than twenty years of useful work ahead of her.

In June she returned to Red Lodge and the need to begin all over again. The routine had hardly been established before her illness, and now her critical eye found everything in disorder. The matron, against strict instructions, had gossiped 'about evil doings' with the washerwoman and the older girls; the teacher had allowed the younger girls' sewing afternoons to pass in rowdy idleness. Of the girls: Agnes had set fire to the house 'supposing they should all be sent home', Margaret Peters, released too soon to employment, had burgled her employer's house and been sentenced to two years' imprisonment, while Eliza Collins 'under the mask of peculiar sweetness of disposition' had encouraged the little girls to prostitution in most immodest language. After a searing interview with Mary, the matron resigned, while the teacher, 'unable to grapple with the girls', and no wonder, left too. In November two girls climbed the garden wall and ran away. One was never seen again, but the other, Eliza Collins, was brought back from Cardiff fighting. She smashed the windows at Red Lodge shouting 'she would rather be in bed with the man she loved than anywhere else.' Against police advice, Mary Carpenter took her back. This was followed by the case of Michael and Margaret Lynch, two children of a drunken mother in Liverpool with relations scattered through prisons and workhouses over half the world. Michael was released from Parkhurst Boys Prison with five pounds to emigrate to America, and Mary had him to stay for a fortnight to say good-bye to his sister at Red Lodge. She wrote in rapturous terms to Lady Byron of their 'pure, innocent love for each other'. He left, promising to make a home where Margaret could join him, and they saw him off on the coasting vessel to Liverpool, where he was to take ship for Boston. Two weeks later Mary, collecting some girls, found him in the Liverpool Borough Gaol, convicted of theft.[14] Margaret who was 'weak and easy' begged to stay at Red Lodge; she was afraid of her violent mother. Although she had already absconded and picked six pockets in a few hours, Mary agreed to keep her. This difficult decision was justified. Margaret became a skilful dressmaker and left three years later 'able and willing to earn her own living and with a good character', for a post in New York.

It soon became clear that many older girls, big, lusty young women, used to living with men in the rough freedom of life on the road, would never settle into the all-female, child-centred world of Red Lodge. Mary Carpenter was forced to admit in 1856 that two girls had been discharged to relatives, as incorrigible, and another two were extremely difficult to manage.[15] Yet Lant Carpenter's principles of education were as sacred to his daughter as the Ark

14 *The Bristol Mercury*, 5th January 1856.
15 Bristol City Archives, 12693, No. 3.

of the Covenant; it would need five years of serious problems before she could bring herself to admit that they could not be applied invariably. They proved inadequate with her first seriously disturbed case. Rose Ackroyd arrived in January 1856, with a history of continual petty thefts; she had stolen as long as she could remember. She was a thin, sharp-featured girl, irritable and perpetually fidgeting.[16] On the night of her arrival she broke open the matron's work-box and pathetically distributed the contents as presents from herself to the other children. She crept and pried into every corner of the house, 'gliding into places in an inconceivable manner'. In February a bunch of household keys was missing for weeks; Rose at last admitted that she had taken them and buried them in the garden. 'Poor girl, I did not give her any additional punishment,' wrote Mary Carpenter, who had noticed that separation from the other girls did her harm. It was punishment enough that when the others went out for excursions Rose had to be left behind, since she stole anything she could lay hands on. In March Mary noted 'Rose Ackroyd goes on stealing to a remarkable degree'; at the end of May she was still 'pilfering foolishly, daringly and shamelessly'. In October articles were missing from all over the house, and Rose was caught out of bed in the middle of the night, stealing balls of cotton from her room-mates' work baskets. Dr Prichard, the former owner of Red Lodge had written 'A propensity to theft is often a feature of moral insanity, and sometimes its leading, if not the sole characteristic.' Mary was forced to conclude, 'I consider this *absolute mania*.' Rose's family decided to emigrate to Australia and applied to take her with them; between relief and regret Mary discharged her. The girls from whom she had stolen loaded her with parting gifts and good wishes. 'I *cannot* but have hopes of her,' wrote Mary.

The general health of the school was good for the period; in twenty years there was no outbreak of infectious disease, or the skin and eye conditions so common in nineteenth-century institutions. Yet in June 1857 two girls died within ten days of each other. Sarah Mail, a lively noisy girl of 13 was ill for only a few days, and died quite unexpectedly in her sleep. Elizabeth Adams, 'our dear Elizabeth', was ill when she arrived; Mary admitted her because her mother was in prison and she had no other home. Elizabeth was nursed for some weeks, but was slowly failing, and wanted her mother. In this crisis, Mary Carpenter showed her true quality. She wrote to the Home Secretary, not suggesting, but demanding the release of Mrs Adams to nurse her child. The mother came and was with Elizabeth to her death; the girl was just 14. Later Mary was very anxious about another girl, Emily Cams, who suffered like herself from rheumatic heart disease; she was too ill to be moved and was nursed in her dormitory. Mary noticed how quiet and considerate the usually rowdy girls were during Emily's illness, and that 'her neighbour Annie Crooks, is a very kind little nurse'. To her great relief Emily grew slowly better, and could sit by the kitchen fire, or out on the terrace in the sunshine.

---

[16] The description sounds as though she may have suffered from chorea, popularly known as St Vitus' dance, which was frequently reported among slum-dwelling children in the nineteenth century.

She had no family, but Mary was touched that the policeman who had brought the girl to the reformatory came to visit her and was very kind. Two local physicians attended Red Lodge, apparently free of charge, but the cost of special foods and medicines weighed heavily on the budget. The problem of sick children who had no home was insoluble. In practice Mary kept them at school and cared for them as well as possible, since she refused to send them to the workhouse.[17] The two girls who died were mourned with true Victorian piety, their graves, planted with flowers, and their anniversaries remembered like those of members of the family.

On 15th August 1857 the newly appointed Inspector of Reformatories, the Rev. Sydney Turner made his first official visit to Red Lodge. He was far from the conventional clerical enthusiast; his father was the distinguished pioneer of Anglo-Saxon studies, Sharon Turner, and he had himself been a Wrangler at Cambridge. He possessed what most reformatory managers lacked, professional experience, having been for sixteen years resident warden of the Philanthropic Society's farm school at Red Hill. No one could call him a soft character after reading his suggestions for refractory cases. Yet Turner was just, if severe, and his reports show him alert for any neglect or serious ill-treatment of his charges. Essentially a practical man, he was by no means an uncritical admirer of Mary Carpenter's theories, and from this date onwards his reports form an interesting commentary on her work. He found sixty girls at Red Lodge, with a matron, two schoolmistresses, a laundress and a seamstress. He considered 'Miss Carpenter has not been as successful as she wished in engaging really efficient assistants.... However she does a good deal herself, and the improved temper and character of the majority of the girls affords good evidence of the influence she has exercised over them. Their answers to questions on general and religious subjects were remarkably satisfactory.' His chief criticism was 'the discipline errs perhaps too much on the side of kindness and indulgence'.[18] This was a serious matter for Mary Carpenter, who was anxious to win his support.

In autumn 1857 Mary went to Liverpool to escort some girls and took the opportunity of visiting some of their homes. The picture of their family background was pitiful. 'Aunt wants to *get rid* of Annie Lewis . . . Mary Crooks' mother a very drunken woman with wretched children . . . the Barkers miserably poor . . . Mrs Williams very poor and ill-used by her husband.' She looked for the family of Michael and Margaret Lynch and found a sister serving four years' hard labour, with the alcoholic mother in the Liverpool workhouse. It was hardly surprising to find that one of the Red Lodge children, crowding round her to say goodbye at her departure, had skilfully stolen a shilling from her reticule. After this beginning, the winter of 1857–8 went from bad to worse; it was the darkest period in the school's history, and one of the worst in Mary Carpenter's life. All the girls had been fond of their kind, cheerful young teacher, Miss Williams: 'Miss Williams is

[17] Later she was able to send chest cases to the Hampstead Hospital, probably through her brother William, who served as organist at Hampstead Unitarian Church.
[18] Report of the Inspector of Reformatories, *Parliamentary Papers*, 1857, XXIX.

an *angle*!' wrote one enthusiast. When she left to marry, they behaved as badly as they could to her unpopular successor, Miss Robertson. They were so difficult that in October 1857, at the insistence of the staff, 'cells' were constructed for violent and refractory girls. 'I believe', wrote Mary earnestly, 'that their *existence* will check the necessity of their *use*.' Like many pious hopes, this proved an illusion. On Saturday 1st November, while Mary was visiting Kingswood, three girls broke open one of the teachers' boxes, dressed themselves in her best silk frocks and escaped over the wall. They were brought back late at night by two policemen, 'not at all penitent'. They were put in the new cells, where they screamed and shouted incessantly; the kind, rather weak matron, Miss Stewart, sat up all night with them and Mary spent all Sunday with them, attempting to reason with them and hoping 'that we could somehow bring them round without external aid'. When they were let out to use the washroom and lavatory, four teachers were needed to put each girl back in the cell. On Monday they began to smash up the furniture and Mary reluctantly fetched three policemen, who removed them bodily. They were charged before the magistrates and sentenced to three months in the Bridewell. Mary, overwhelmed with shame and distress at the manhandling of these hysterical girls, collapsed and was ill for the rest of the week.

Hysteria, in this closed institution, proved catching. Emily Jones, wrote Mary, 'flew into a violent passion when she wanted to sit by me and another girl took her place;' put into her bedroom alone, she smashed all the crockery. Susanna Flanagan broke a window and screamed to passers by in the street with splendid Irish logic that she would never come out alive, 'and when I am dead I shall tell everyone that Red Lodge killed me!' 'She was quite mad,' wrote Mary, anxiously. Nothing in her experience with normal children, however naughty, had prepared her for this. Ellen Robinson stole the matron's housekeeping keys from the kitchen table and ransacked the house, secreting the teachers' brooches, rings and silk handkerchiefs; she even stole the supply of well-sharpened red pencils from the Superintendent's tidy desk. A smaller girl stole Mary Carpenter's gloves from the table, while she was distributing picture cards as a reward for good conduct. She passed them with professional skill to an accomplice to hide. 'I asked her why, and she replied hypocritically, "Please, ma'am, it was to *take care of it*." Thus do these poor children exhibit their propensities. I told them they should all begin quite fresh without any allusion to the past.' Christmas was subdued, and the year 1857, wrote Mary, 'closes somewhat under clouds'. These were trifles, however, to the troubles 1858 was to bring.

On 2nd February, Mary went to the Bridewell to collect the three absconders, Jane Crawford, Martha Coley and Eliza (or Elizabeth) Barry, at the end of their sentences. She was disturbed by the jocular, familiar manner in which the Governor of the Bridewell said goodbye to his charges, and promised Eliza a tip 'if she continued to be a good girl'. Within a few hours of their return, the school was in the state known by the Victorians as 'high excitement'; the girls were noisy, restless, dishevelled and neglectful of work.

They whispered in corners, and Miss Stewart, the harassed matron, 'could not bring herself to repeat what they said; she seems paralysed,' wrote Mary.

She soon discovered the cause of the disturbance. Eliza, a big, bold girl, who looked 19 or 20, declared herself pregnant by the Governor of the Bridewell, who, she said, had visited her secretly in her cell. Mary sent for the school doctor, who confirmed the pregnancy, and the prison chaplain, who to her horror seemed to accept the story as quite probable. Meanwhile discipline at Red Lodge was almost breaking down. It was no longer a question of a difficult minority, but of the whole school getting out of control. Jane and Martha ran away again and were missing for several days; they were found working in the house of a prostitute they had met in prison. Eliza's mother arrived, loudly weeping at her daughter's disgrace; even in this crisis, Mary found time to pity the poor woman. The girls were in an uproar. There was no hope now of concealing the situation; Mary was forced to pocket her pride and appeal to Sydney Turner for help. He came at once and conducted a searching investigation, until Eliza broke down under his questioning and admitted that she had lived with several men when on the run the previous autumn. Turner considered that for the sake of the younger children the three runaways ought to be removed as soon as possible. At his insistence three magistrates came on 4th February and held a Petty Sessions privately at Red Lodge. This was a wise precaution; of five local newspapers, not one carried a report of the proceedings. The three girls promised Mary to 'behave modestly, but when they were brought before the Magistrates, they were as daring and low in their behaviour as any girl of the town'. Yet she was still concerned for them; she pleaded that they should not be sent back to the corruptions of the Bridewell. The presiding justice spoke kindly to them, but sentenced Eliza to six months' hard labour, and the other two to three months each. The police removed them at once, and the true paternity of Eliza's child will never be known. The Governor of the Bridewell had been at best indiscreet and neglectful of duty. A public scandal had been averted by Turner's presence of mind, but Mary Carpenter feared, with good reason, that she had lost his confidence. The sordidness of the whole affair revolted her fastidious nature. It had been the negation of all her hopes and beliefs, a bitter admission of failure.

For weeks afterwards there was 'constant difficulty in maintaining steady discipline'. On 7th March six girls ran away from a walk on Clifton Down. In April 'disorder begins as soon as I leave the room,' and on 13th May three more absconders were brought back by the police. Mary Carpenter was away, and for the first time in the history of Red Lodge, the friend who was acting as her deputy, ordered them to be punished by the staff, who caned the girls and cropped their hair; the younger girls were 'much affected by it'. It is a measure of Mary's depression that she allowed this without protest; she was worn out and disheartened. A few months later eight more girls scattered and ran away, while at play on Durdham Down. Mary passed a sleepless night, 'in which I could only pray that our fugitives might be kept from the worst of evils. How thankful I was to have my poor girls back!'

The police rounded them up, hungry and dirty but unharmed, at the railway station. The one comfort in this wretched time was that the ordinary constables, who knew her problems at first hand, were invariably kind and helpful; some even went out of their way to be kind to the girls. The Inspector's annual report for 1859 was naturally frankly critical. 'Miss Carpenter's exertions were very greatly hindered at the beginning of the year by the gross misconduct of some very vicious girls, who were in the first instance committed to prison for desertion and insubordination and afterwards discharged. I found the school in a more satisfactory and encouraging state on my second visit in June. A more efficient schoolmistress had been engaged and a stricter discipline enforced, to the manifest advantage of the girls,' though he censured the close-cropping of girls' hair as punishment. He admitted that the school children 'answered my questions very intelligently, on scriptural subjects especially', but his chief criticism was unanswerable. 'On comparing this school with other female reformatories, I feel satisfied that the great desideratum in it is a really efficient matron. The present matron is kind and well-meaning, but hardly sufficiently firm.'[19] The criticism of 'kindness and indulgence' in his first report is implicit; discipline at Red Lodge later came under serious attack.

The failures and troubles of this year had a profound effect on Mary Carpenter. Slowly and reluctantly she was forced to admit that seriously disturbed girls, or almost full-grown young women with a string of convictions behind them, might be beyond the reach of even her father's hallowed principles. She sincerely pitied the older girls, but she never really understood or liked them as she liked small children or her ragged-school boys. She had not cared overmuch for the young ladies of her mother's boarding-school; how was she to understand the Red House girls she described in an entry on 1st July 1858? 'Sims a sulky look, she is kept in order only by fear in the background, Gough, inexpressibly coarse and dirty in her ways, Forbes very vulgar and with an entirely unawakened mind. All their kitchen and housework very slatternly done. At present I am obliged to exercise repression over them, which *ought* not to be.'[20] She would never openly admit defeat on any point however small, or withdraw her opposition to 'Juvenile Prisons'. Yet writing in 1861, she was forced into an admission she would not have made five years earlier. This was that 'unruly or dangerous cases' might need for their own protection and the safety of other children, 'schools conducted on a somewhat stricter plan, with the possibility of continued separate confinement where necessary . . . though now called *incorrigible* they are not necessarily so'. At present they terrorized reformatories, were hastily discharged and usually reconvicted at once.

Almost more serious than the problem of difficult older girls were the continual staffing difficulties at Red Lodge. Mary Carpenter's attitude to her staff was all too human; like many people she wanted two contradictory

[19] Report of the Inspector of Reformatory and Industrial Schools, *Parliamentary Papers* 1859, Session 2, XIII, Vol. 2.
[20] Carpenter, M. *Supplementary Measures needed for Reformatories*, 1861.

things at once. The staff were to be totally subordinate to her as superintendent, since 'I must be free to develop my principles.' Recognizing that
they were untrained and usually ill-educated, she expected them to conform
to standards and methods drawn up by herself. Yet at the same time she
expected these underlings to exercise a strong personal influence over the
characters of the pupils. Caught between the Utopian demands of their
superintendent and the constant company of sixty difficult girls, these
unfortunate women led a hard life. They lacked independent authority. 'The
tone always seems to go back when I am away,' lamented Mary Carpenter to
her private journal. 'There is a noisy, bold manner which they ought not to
have.' Girls were even heard to say 'I shan't!' It is a sidelight on Victorian
upbringing that she had never heard this before. The first matron and teacher
left Red Lodge in less than a year. The next two kept up a running fight
between themselves, with tedious lists of grievances and repeated threats to
resign. 'Mrs B.,' as Mary wrote, 'evidently trying to undermine Miss W.
with me'. This internecine warfare continued for six months, until among
angry scenes the housekeeper gave notice. 'Mrs. B. throws off the mask she
has worn and shows violent jealousy of Miss W.,' wrote the harassed superintendent. Abandoning work, the matron took to her bed and went after a
week, leaving a Trojan horse, apparently a massive one, in the person of the
cook. Mary Carpenter was not easily frightened, even by a cook in full
panoply. 'I informed her of my intention to be obeyed in *all* things, by *all* in
this house." The cook retaliated by breaking the strictest rule of the house,
and gossiping with the girls about each other's previous offences. Reproved,
she too gave notice, leaving Mary to check the stores and write, 'I fear she
certainly drank both brandy and porter.' A new matron and cook were at last
found, but Mary felt she must add to her exhausting list of duties a weekly
checking of household accounts and stores; this in turn undermined the
matron's authority.

   The next three years saw a bewildering series of comings and goings at
Red Lodge. Miss Stewart, the new matron, was kind and good to the girls,
but too easy-going. She allowed meals and laundry to be late, and stockings
to go unmended, evidently a serious crime in Mary Carpenter's scheme of
things. 'I am beginning to fear that she is unequal in mind or body to the
engagement,' she wrote after a few months; 'she is really incapable of carrying
on the house as it ought to be done'. Confronted with near rioting in the
troubled winter of 1857-8, the poor woman became 'completely bewildered'.
She resigned, but an attempt to replace her was disastrous, and she had to be
asked to return. Mary had wanted to replace her with an experienced matron
from Exeter Penitentiary, but this shrewd woman, having met Mary
Carpenter, 'declined upon reflection, thinking it not sufficiently *superior*,
too much like a housekeeper's place'. In fact, no matron of the right calibre
would come, unless her independence was guaranteed. Good certificated
teachers were equally hard to come by. The sewing-mistress was dismissed
in October 1857, as 'quite destitute of power of controlling the girls', and the
laundry-mistress after complaints about the washing. But the new sewing-

mistress left after a fortnight saying she did not like children and never had, while a stout and kindly new washerwoman 'never having met with such girls before is quite in despair'. In November, Mary, much to her chagrin, was forced to ask the original pair to come back again. A young assistant mistress called Miss Gamble came in 1858; she was kind and intelligent, but in Mary's opinion 'wants *force*'. Luckily she was learning caution and did not dismiss her, for Miss Gamble grew to be an excellent teacher.

More serious than all this was the lack of a good head teacher. Miss Robertson from the Glasgow Normal College taught 'in the driest and most uninteresting way'; the children were bored and restless during her lessons, their copybooks blotted and badly spelt. On 31st October 1857 J. C. Symons, H.M.I., came to inspect the school work of Red Lodge. He was a barrister and had been a Commissioner of Inquiry into the conditions of hand-loom weavers and child factory-workers in the north, and he was an intelligent supporter of reformatory schools. Mary was mortified by the bad impression her classes made on him. 'Mr Symons formed a very unsatisfactory idea. . . . I begged him to make every allowance for the backwardness of the girls . . . he kindly offered not to report but to come again.' After this unsatisfactory inspection, Miss Robertson left in a huff, saying 'she *could* not make such girls improve'. In December Miss Milne came on probation to succeed her, and as usual Mary Carpenter started with high hopes: 'unaffected and fair as well as kind. I have great hopes of her.' Miss Milne was unlucky. Her probation coincided with the scandal of the Bridewell girls and the near-breakdown in discipline. By March 1858, 'both she and the girls had evidently come to a tacit agreement that they were stronger than she'; she permitted 'disorderly conduct and low, gross habits in the dormitories.' When dismissed, she was not surprisingly glad to leave Red Lodge.

It is a measure of Mary Carpenter's discouragement at this time that she actually welcomed her successor, a virago named Miss Swanbourne, who professed to be 'strict and very firm with the highest religious principles', She at once demanded the right to corporal punishment. On 20th April 1858 Mary wrote, 'After serious reflection I determined to place a cane in her hands, which I did publicly.' She had serious misgivings. A few days later 'I told the girls how much I disliked the cane being used or even seen; I offered them to try whether they could not be managed without it.' But of course by then Miss Swanbourne was well into her stride. She taught with the cane lying conspicuously on the desk. By December 1858 there could be no doubt that Miss Swanbourne's iron hand had restored the school to order after the chaos of the previous winter, yet Mary was not happy. 'It cannot be doubted', she wrote, 'that the children have *never* before been under such control. Even the older girls obedient with Miss Swanbourne, but frequently unmanageable at other times. I feel a great want of *real* improvement.' No one was sorry when choleric Miss Swanbourne complained of headaches and left in July 1859. 'Her going was received by the girls with less sorrow than I have ever before seen on such an occasion. No one cried; some smiled. . . . She has certainly done them harm by using the cane.' Probably still more harmful were five years of continual changes and bewildering swings between softness and severity. It was impossible for the girls to rely on the adults around them, or to know what to expect at any given time.

Nothing is easier than to blame Mary Carpenter for this tragi-comic series of misadventures and she has been severely criticized by at least one recent writer.[21] The situation called for tact, adaptability and a good-humoured sense of proportion, not a set of fixed principles which made no allowance for circumstances. Yet the problems of caring for disturbed children were real, and remain as real now as in the early days at Red Lodge. In his very first report as Inspector of Reformatories, Sydney Turner had written 'much depends on the moral condition of the school and therefore on the influence of the master or mistress in charge of it'. He regretted the supply of good teachers was so inadequate. Reformatory work was physically and emotionally exhausting, badly paid and unjustly low in social status. It offered no professional future, and for many years no financial security. Qualified masters and mistresses were so hard to find that managers were sometimes forced to take anyone who would come. These unknown characters then took entire charge of children living in isolation from normal society. The Royal Commissions of 1884 and 1896 criticized reformatory and industrial schools on these grounds and urgently demanded 'improvements in the quality of senior staff'. This is the background to the series of reformatory scandals which shocked the public in the last years of the nineteenth century. The problem of staffing institutions for children still haunts the twentieth. A government survey reports low incidence of trained staff, heavy dependence on single women and a high rate of turnover.[22] British approved schools showed 'enormous difficulty in providing staff and devising methods merely to contain the most disturbed and recalcitrant'.[23] The problem is international. Welfare schools in Sweden, complaining of old buildings, add, 'even more difficult is the problem of staff'.[24] The U.S. Children's Bureau, in a humane attempt to provide something approaching family life for young delinquents, found 'in reality, very few houseparents meet the standards of personality and maturity demanded'.[25]

The problem of caring for difficult and disturbed adolescents, especially girls, appears if anything worse now than a hundred years ago. They are a great trial to schools or homes and sometimes a source of dread and danger to young children. A third of the pupils, it was estimated, absconded from senior girls' approved schools. 'We must face the fact,' concluded a researcher in 1969, 'that they cannot be cured under the conditions that existed in approved schools at the time of this research. Often the damage on doubtful constitutions seems irreparable.'[26] The Children and Young Persons Act of 1969 has brought this problem into the open, as never before. 'For the time

[21] Carlebach, J. *Caring for Children in Trouble*, 39–46.
[22] H.M.S.O. *Staffing of Local Authority Residential Homes for Children*, 1961/2.
[23] Conrad, J. P. *Crime and its Correction*, 95.
[24] Ibid., 125.   [25] Ibid., 33.
[26] Richardson, H. J. *Adolescent Girls in Approved Schools*, 277.

being approved schools have a discretion—which they will lose next year when they become absorbed within the community home system—as to whether they will take a particular child, and many of them are exercising this to refuse the more troublesome cases.'[27] Social Services Committees report an urgent need for specialized institutions, however expensive, for the most difficult cases. Seriously disturbed adolescent girls, perhaps the most difficult of all, may be impossible to place or to care for properly. This is still the problem which faced Mary Carpenter at Red Lodge in the 1850s.

Having seen the failures at Red Lodge, we must now look at the achievements, which were real. The majority of the children promised hope for the future. As Mary had always maintained, most of them were not delinquent in any real sense, but rather grossly neglected. Given a secure framework, a healthy regular life and ordinary affection, most of them developed as normal children. Twice a week Mary taught them herself, and like most children they enjoyed her skilful lessons. She put the young ones to bed, with the nursery routine of warm baths and stories read aloud; she as well as they needed these interludes of affection. 'I indulge them in those warm embraces so necessary to young children,' she wrote. 'S. begged me to kiss them as they have not had a kiss for so long. *Poor children!*' They wanted her to come and live with them, but accepted that she must care for her other schools and her aged mother. On her side, Mary appreciated their sincerity. She trusted these derelict waifs as she trusted few adults. 'When harbouring bad feelings', she noticed, 'they never venture to kiss me. There is a wonderful truth of nature about these children.' Sundays were by convention sedate, but in summer they went into the country, while in winter she read stories aloud. At evening prayers they took turns to choose their favourite hymns. Thursdays were visiting days, but Mary did not want sensation-seeking strangers. 'The school is not to become a show place'. At Christmas she was happy to see the young ones play, like any normal children, enjoying round games, cutting a huge Christmas cake and receiving the individual presents she had wrapped for the tree. She brought them long-cherished toys from her own childhood, and was touched to see 'little Ellen nursing my wax baby like a mother'.

The standards of immaculate order, cleanliness and punctuality, bred in the bone of the Carpenters, came hard to these wild children. They made a fuss over the spartan ritual of the daily cold bath in summer, though Mary hopefully insisted they 'came to enjoy it'. They tore illuminated texts from the walls, not from malice but because they wanted paper to light the schoolroom fire. Forbidden to sleep in their clothes or three in a bed as they had been accustomed, they dressed in bed under the blankets, until Mary put a stop to this 'most unwholesome, dirty and self-indulgent habit'. Like almost all nineteenth-century institutions, Red Lodge provided only bread and milk for supper, varied by coffee and unlimited bread and butter at weekends;[28] it is to be feared these growing children were often hungry. They made secret

[27] *New Society*, 21st December 1972, Smith, G. 'The Children's Act'.
[28] Carpenter, M. *Food, Work and Rest for Boys and Girls in Reformatories*, 1857, pamphlet.

pockets in their petticoats in which they concealed slices of bread, lumps of sugar, cheese or anything their nimble fingers could pick up in the kitchen. They also refused to eat 'wholesome oatmeal porridge', snatched one another's bread and butter, slapped one another, and burst paper bags in class, a not very serious crime sheet which could be matched in most preparatory schools. Once they yielded to temptation and stole money from the sewing-teacher's purse; this they used while out on an errand to buy 'quantities of liquorice' for a dormitory feast. They owned up of their own free will and collected pennies from their pocket money to replace the sum. 'Culprits very affectionate,' wrote Mary, 'and seem really penitent.' To encourage good behaviour, she distributed picture cards or coloured hair ribbons to all children who passed a month without a bad conduct mark. She gave to each child a box for her own private 'treasures'; 'children should have possessions of their own and learn to respect those of their school-fellows,' she argued. The treasure boxes were very seldom stolen.

Where accounts of the eldest girls were discouraging, Mary Carpenter was able to record progress among the younger children, both in the general tone and in individual cases. In March 1856 she took twenty-seven girls to a Diorama, where they paid their own entrance money and 'behaved perfectly well'. On another occasion, at a charity bazaar, a child stole a little brass kettle, evidently a tempting object; she hid it successfully in the fowl-house, where she went to play with it, but later returned it of her own free will. The school children gave a party to their relatives and friends in the great Oak Room, where they sang songs and served tea 'very nicely indeed'. A detective from Liverpool, escorting a new pupil to Red Lodge, declared 'he would not have recognized any of the Liverpool girls, they were so changed in looks and manner.' He obligingly carried home the first pair of socks one girl had ever knitted, as a present for her father, surely a unique errand for a member of the C.I.D. As Christmas came round again, Mary noticed the children's 'great delight in making presents to each other; very striking—more of their money is spent in this way than on sweets'. When three big girls received permission from the Secretary of State to emigrate to America, all the children subscribed to buy each a writing case, while Mary gave them warm cloaks for the journey. The children saw them off 'with many tears on both sides, as they left what had been their home. I rejoice to see what warm feeling has grown among my girls!'

All this progress was threatened by the scandals and upheavals of 1857 and the strict rule of Miss Swanbourne which followed. It was months before Mary could report that 'the younger ones seem reverting to their natural condition, orderly, affectionate and increasingly gay and lively at play. They are also more susceptible of affection; however sternly I may have been speaking in public, when I go among them I am greeted most lovingly by the younger ones.' When subscribers visited Red Lodge, she always said it was most important for the children to play. She built up a collection of dolls, toys, puzzles and picture books. Believing that 'the care of animals awakes kindly sympathies', she brought the youngest children pet rabbits.

'They were received with the greatest delight; one said lovingly "Bless you" to her pet.' To the great grief of their owners, some of the rabbits died of over-feeding; the children showed Mary their graves, tastefully arranged in a corner of the garden.

Individual children come and go in the closely written pages of the journal. Kitty, one of a family of tramps, was brought to Red Lodge by a policeman at the age of 10. She and her 8-year-old brother had scrambled on the back of an old grey mare in a field and ridden away. This constituted horse stealing; they appeared in court, where their heads hardly reached the top of the dock, and were duly sentenced. Kitty herself was rather like a pony, a stocky, shaggy little creature, with a mane of rough hair. Whenever some piece of mischief was discovered in the school, Kitty's hand went up. 'Sure, ma'am, I did it!' She was everyone's favourite and Mary Carpenter admitted, 'I had a hand in spoiling her too.' By bending the law a little, she kept Kitty until she was 16, when her mother called for her. Kitty went off, loaded with kisses and presents by the girls, half-laughing, half-crying to be gone. Within a few months she was dead of a fever caught on the road.[29] Mary Carpenter, when she heard the news, laid her head on her crowded desk and wept bitterly.

The deprivation of many children was heart-breaking, as with the pathetic 'little girl Sims', who seems to have lacked even that humblest human possession, a name. Brought up as an orphan in Plymouth workhouse, she was placed at 11 years old as a farm servant. She was so unhappy that she set fire to a bed one afternoon; before coming to Red Lodge she had endured nine months' solitary confinement. This child seemed frozen. 'She has never known what love is,' wrote Mary. At last she began to speak, almost to smile. *'For the first time,'* noted Mary in the journal, 'I felt a real opening of this child's heart towards me, and of mine to her.'[30]

One serious problem remained, mentioned by the Inspector in all his reports; there was still no one at Red Lodge capable of taking effective charge during Mary Carpenter's absence on her other multifarious concerns. This was solved in August 1859, with the arrival of Mrs Johnson as matron. Mrs Johnson must have been a remarkable woman; she deserves to be remembered, if only as one of the very few people of either sex who successfully stood up to Mary Carpenter on her own ground. She arrived and asked Mary Carpenter not to introduce her, 'as she wished to take possession of the girls alone'. When Mary protested that she would need guiding 'as things were unfortunately in great disorder in many parts of the school', she calmly said that she would soon rearrange them to her own satisfaction. Warned that some of the older girls might be extremely difficult, she confidently 'expressed her intention of doing without punishment'. As Mary expected, the children proceeded to the ritual trial of strength with authority, which is common to all institutions. They refused to eat their meals and complained loudly about the food, in hopes that Mrs Johnson would resign, and easy-going, popular

[29] Cobbe, F. P. *Autobiography*, 290–1.
[30] Bristol Archives, 12693, No. 1.

Miss Stewart return. Mrs Johnson merely remarked that if she left, Miss
Swanbourne was still seeking a situation. 'At this,' wrote Mary, 'they gave
an involuntary shudder and were evidently most anxious to retain Mrs
Johnson! . . . I soon perceived that she had great power and tact with the
children. She is a woman of considerable energy, experience, courage and
feeling. She devoted the rest of the evening to bringing the girls under her
influence and certainly succeeded.' On 15th September Sydney Turner
called for his annual inspection, and was struck by the improvement in the
children. 'A change in the chief matron,' he reported, 'has been followed, I
think, by a considerable advance in the conduct and manner of the girls.'
Turner praised the experiment of placing the older girls 'under the conditions
of free domestic service',[31] then almost the only job open to them. At the
1871 census, of girls between 15 and 20 years of age, no less than one in three
was a domestic servant; a workhouse slavey could be hired for two shillings a
week.[32] The alternatives except in textile towns were the sweated, in every
sense, trades of seamstress or laundress, or rough gang labour on the land.
Turner commented on the intelligent teaching of mild young Miss Gamble,
who was now promoted to be head teacher and seemed very well liked by the
children. On this visit Mrs Johnson talked independently with the Inspector,
in a manner which Mary Carpenter privately thought 'most assuming and
unwarrantable'; but Turner was evidently satisfied that Red Lodge was
efficiently staffed at last, after five years of trial and error.

During the next three months Mrs Johnson calmly gathered the reins into
her capable hands. She was quite unencumbered by theories and chose to
disregard the Superintendent's hallowed rules where necessary. She had one
difficult case to handle in the person of an Irish girl, Mary McNally, whose
mother had sent her voluntarily to Red Lodge because she was beyond
control at home; the parents were even willing to pay five shillings a week to
be relieved of their troublesome daughter. Mary was affectionate and lively,
but given to violent rages in which she snatched a flat-iron and smashed all
the china within reach, tore out other children's hair in handfuls and bit a
teacher. She was a particular favourite with Miss Carpenter, who required
to be called whenever Mary became unmanageable, 'to bring her to a better
frame of mind'. Faced with one of Mary's tantrums, Mrs Johnson calmly
borrowed a pair of handcuffs from the police-station as a precaution, but
meanwhile poulticed a boil in the girl's ear. It burst, and Mary soon became
calm. Miss Carpenter returned at the end of November to find 'perfect order
in the dormitories, no bad spirit appearing anywhere; all the teachers are in
good heart and I believe things are getting straight'. Mary McNally was
docile and taking an interest in her lessons, but on December 15th she had
another fit of rage. Miss Carpenter had expressly asked to be called, but the
matron had already coped with the situation. She put Mary to bed, applied a
blister, then the standard treatment for inflammation, and asked the other

---

[31] Report of the Inspector of Reformatories and Industrial Schools, *Parliamentary Papers*,
1860, XXXV.
[32] Best, G. *Mid-Victorian Britain*, 87 and 104.

children and teachers to avoid exciting her. They were very forbearing, and with the inevitable ups and downs this difficult child slowly grew out of her difficulties. Mary Carpenter had achieved the ambition of every administrator and worked herself out of a job. At Christmas 1859 she found the general order and spirit of the house better than ever before. Families and friends were invited to a Christmas tea and carol-singing in the great Oak Room. 'I went in to prayers, when I was deeply gratified to see this large assembled family, all serious and happy. . . . The girls voted it their best Christmas yet.'

Of course it was not in Mary Carpenter's nature to surrender authority gracefully, or to give up the work to which she had sacrificed her entire personal life. She did not hand over the reins to her new matron without a sharp struggle, revealed in the pages of the diary. 'Mrs J. recklessly alters arrangements,' she wrote after the Inspector's visit, 'and then complains of want of order in the establishment, throwing imputations of inefficiency everywhere . . . it is evident that having been praised by Mr Turner she is determined to exalt her own merits.' By October Mrs Johnson boasted of her 'strong moral influence claiming that results show the superiority of her plans. . . . She evidently wishes to take the position of independent manager, with myself as a sort of sleeping committee or necessary incumbrance, which must be kept from hindering her.' Yet the only alternative, as Mary lamented to her journal 'is Miss Swanbourne's stern sway. I have no wish to change'. At the end of November she interviewed her matron, in the manner which had crushed parliamentary committees. 'The whole responsibility is mine,' she said, 'and I *must* feel that officials will faithfully carry out my plans and principles.' For answer, Mrs Johnson wrote directly to the Inspector of Reformatories, saying that she would resign unless she were given more independence in her work. Sydney Turner was alarmed that all the gains of recent months might be lost through Miss Carpenter's intransigence; he knew her formidable tongue and pen from first-hand experience. Early in February 1860 he arrived at Red Lodge for a special visit of inspection.

It was a mortifying day for Mary Carpenter, alone, no longer young, and recently ill. A three-cornered interview took place, so painful that she could not even bring herself to write it down until the following Good Friday. 'Mr T. came. He said he regretted always to find things going badly at R.L., that Mrs J. was exceedingly uncomfortable, that I *shackled* her improperly etc. etc. . . . He seemed to support her in everything against me, and she spoke to me in an overbearing way, which I am sure she would *not* have done to a gentleman.' This is one of the very few times Mary Carpenter complained of the disadvantages of being a woman. Morbidly sensitive to criticism, and unwilling, as she herself said, ever to admit to being in the wrong, she passed a wretched sleepless night. In the morning she produced her ultimatum. 'I *must* be free to develop my principles.' She would write to the Secretary of State and resign the Red Lodge certificate; but Turner, having made the essential point, went out of his way to be conciliatory. He asked both women to forget the past for the sake of the children. Mrs Johnson assured Mary 'that we should never have a repetition of the same unpleasantness' and she was as good as her word. Mary reported a year later 'nothing but co-operation' from the entire staff. The incident was closed; but so was her close personal involvement with the Red Lodge children, though she remained honorary superintendent to her death.

It is a tribute to Mary Carpenter's essential goodness of heart that she overcame her smouldering resentment at this humiliation, when she saw the new arrangement was for the good of her girls. Gradually during 1860, she withdrew from everyday management at Red Lodge, and busied herself with urgent questions of public education and penal reform. 'I have found', she wrote towards the end of the journal, 'other things more necessary to do at this particular time.' In May 1860 she was asked to receive extra cases and with sixty girls the house was full. Yet 'the staff works comfortably together and there is a general improvement in the tone of the school. I perceive much may be checked which was thought unavoidable.' This was an honest and generous admission. 'I was a fortnight from home during the month (April–May) and was pleased to find that all went on well during my absence.' The girls were given new blue Sunday frocks, each with a skirt pocket as a sign of trust. At the annual Charity Schools service, 'all conducted themselves with perfect propriety and looked very neat. They sang sweetly and it was a happiness to hear them.' Soon after this the Red Lodge Journal ends. Mary Carpenter had a new and overwhelming emotional interest at home.

10

FRIENDS AND RELATIONS
1856-1860

For some years Mrs Carpenter had been slowly failing, until at the age of 74 she seemed to her children to be living 'on the confines of two worlds'. At last she was free from incessant duties and the one great sorrow of her married life. In her soft, autumnal days she mellowed; 'her character', wrote a friend, 'seemed not to lose its force, but to be marked by increasing beauty and serenity.' All past conflicts with her eldest daughter were forgotten. She sat by the front window each day, watching Great George Street for Mary's safe return, always welcoming her with a loving kiss, ready to be cared for and to care. She developed bronchitis, the order of release for the old, and on 19th June 1856 her life ebbed gently away.[1] The entire family, of whom she had been so proud, met for the last time at her burial. 'Her passing from our living sight seems but a slight remove,' wrote James Martineau. Russell replied that he was anxious for Mary, who 'felt the loneliness acutely'. The family circle which had bound her affections from childhood was broken at last, leaving her alone in the world.

Anna and her husband, Herbert Thomas, were generous. At their invitation, Mary moved out of her rooms in the wing and into the main house next door with them, but here she found herself cramped and bowed by thronging memories from the past. She took her usual escape route into work, though they pleaded with her to rest. 'People don't like me to tire myself,' she said. 'But it is better to come home ready to drop, and go to bed and sleep at once, than to feel the loneliness of this large house once so peopled.' On her fiftieth birthday she wrote down her real longing, in a pathetically humble prayer. 'In most entire submission I pray, but still I do pray, that Thou wilt give me the means of having *a home of my own*.'[2]

In January 1857 Mary went to stay for a few days at East Sheen with Lady Byron, who was now forced by a failing heart to live an invalid's existence. She was a purposeful invalid, on the model of Florence Nightingale, directing an empire of high-minded good works from her fireside sofa. Here was someone who could understand the difficulties of starting independent existence at the age of 50, as so many Victorian daughters were compelled to do. 'I feel old memories forming too large a part of my inner life,' confessed Mary. With her usual generosity, Lady Byron responded by buying two more houses to round off the Red Lodge estate.[3] One, Red Lodge Cottage, now

---

[1] *The Christian Reformer*, July 1856, XII, 448.
[2] *Life and Work*, 183.
[3] Manchester College, Oxford, Library, Letterbook D.

demolished, became the family home for nine of the older girls, where they were trusted to go out shopping, or stay unsupervised at work. Mary hoped it would prepare her girls for marriage. She loved to see them lay the tables neatly, clear away quietly and wash up without breaking the tea things. 'When I hear one of them talk of "*My* kitchen" I know it is all right!' she said. Her greatest reward was to see them happily married.[4]

The second property bought by Lady Byron was Red Lodge House, which still stands on the corner of Lodge Street and Lower Park Row. It is a tall narrow street house, with a flight of steps leading up to a wrought iron porch, and a walled garden sloping away to the rear. The upper windows looked over the same prospect of spars and spires and drifting smoke as Red Lodge itself; the side windows looked into the school garden. By February 1858 Mary Carpenter had left her home of forty years and moved into this house. She had inherited her mother's furniture, linen and plate, also 'a small independence for my very moderate wants'.[5] Among the packing cases of china and chests of books, she felt herself beginning a new, happier and freer life. By 5th July she was writing to Lucy Sanford an extraordinary unconscious commentary on her life. 'I cannot tell you,' she wrote, 'how thankful I am for this house and for the sense of freedom which I now have. I have lived in so very cramped a condition that in many ways I feel as if—now past fifty—I were only emerging from childhood. This rather sets me back at times; yet I feel more myself and nobody else, or rather that I shall soon be so.'[6] The kind and reliable cook, Mary Ann, moved in with Mary, becoming in many ways her closest companion. She was happy, working in her little garden and planting scented flowers in the window boxes. She welcomed 'old Children', a brisk young sailor or a young wife with a baby in arms. Yet she had never given up her girlhood's longing for 'natural ties'. Poor, plain and solitary, she was too proud to ask for pity, or even to pity herself; but reading Mrs Gaskell's *Life of Charlotte Bronte* brought back 'agonies which I could well comprehend'. Charlotte's marriage, belated pregnancy and death moved her deeply. As she wrote to Lucy in May 1857, 'It was very touching for her to go as soon as she desired to stay. But I am glad there was that sunshine at the end.'[7] For herself, prematurely aged by illness, there could be no more hope of love; yet the longing for children persisted. In September 1858 her family were startled by the news that Mary had adopted a child.

This child's story can be gradually pieced together from a variety of sources; nothing could show more vividly the fearful precariousness of life for the poor in the Victorian Golden Age. In 1853 the town missionary of Plymouth, a man named Foxon, was called to the common lodging-house to a woman named Margaret Powell, or sometimes Sharpe. Her husband had taken his own life, leaving her destitute with a baby girl, six weeks old, named Rosanna. The woman put her baby in the care of Foxon's wife at a charge of one shilling and sixpence a week, and herself found work as a washerwoman.

[4] Bristol Archives 12693, No. 1 Red Lodge Journal, 1858.
[5] Public Record Office: Prob. 11, 1156, 583.
[6] *Life and Work*, 196.   [7] Ibid., 183.

Later she went to Jersey as a servant and after a time the payments ceased. Foxon put the little girl into the workhouse, where she was soon said to be 'declining in health'. In 1858 he applied for her admission to the famous Muller Orphanages, a showplace of evangelical philanthropy in Bristol.

Pastor Muller refused to take Rosanna, because, at 5 years old, she could not produce evidence that she had been born in wedlock. The missionary then wrote to Mary Carpenter, who agreed to admit the girl to the reformatory, in the belief that she was an orphan. In September 1858 Foxon travelled to Bristol and arrived, leading the small bewildered child by the hand, at the door of Red Lodge.[8] Mary Carpenter was quite frank about what followed. She had intended Rosanna to grow up in the reformatory but when she saw the little creature—'regarding her extreme infancy, her freedom from criminal taint, and the sad position in which from no fault of her own she was placed'— the whole idea seemed suddenly unthinkable. 'God put it into my mind,' said Mary ingenuously, 'that I ought to be a mother to the little thing.' She took Rosanna's hand and led her into her own house next door. 'Do you think you could live with me in this house and love me, and be happy?' she asked. Rosanna, fresh from the workhouse, looked up at this strange lady and said simply 'Yes.'[8]

Mary Carpenter, usually so guarded in her emotions, was in the seventh heaven of happiness. She resolved to provide for Rosanna 'as my very own'. 'Just think of me', she wrote to a disconcerted relative, 'with a little girl of *my own*, about five years old! Ready made to hand and nicely trained, without the trouble of marrying, etc. a darling little thing, an orphan. I feel already a *mère de famille*, happy in buying little hats and socks and a little bed to stand in my own room, out of *my own* money. It is a wonderful feeling!'[9] Rosanna accompanied her adopted mother on visits to the different schools. At Red Lodge 'she sits very still at lessons and is a great darling at all times with the girls.' In May 1859, Mary took her to the annual Charity Schools Service at Lewin's Mead, proud to have the little bonneted, booted creature beside her in the family pew. Once again, Rosanna was very good.[10] Nature, for thirty years repressed by duty, overwhelmed Mary like a tidal wave. Perhaps her brothers and sisters were alarmed to think what Mary might do next. With one voice they urged her to take a 'nice friend' to live with her. Anna hoped it might 'draw her off' from her obsession with needy children. A Miss Bathurst had already come briefly but soon broke down in health under the regime of austere living and incessant work which came naturally to her hostess. Mary was frankly unwilling to accept another house-mate. All she wanted was one or two efficient women to work at Red Lodge under her direction. 'I am not at all adapted', she wrote firmly to Lady Byron, 'to be a Lady Abbess or Superior of a Protestant Sisterhood, or anything but the sole manager and superintendent of Red Lodge—that position I must *absolutely* maintain.' Lady Byron proposed one of her aristocratic friends, but Mary was sceptical of lady amateurs. 'The work is not of an attractive kind,' she replied. 'People cannot

---

[8] Bristol Archives, 12693, No. 23.
[9] *Life and Work*, 198–9.
[10] Bristol Archives, 12693, No. 23.

at once plunge into it and feel they are doing great things.' She did not care what the religious opinions of colleagues were, so long as they worked hard and were 'independent of my society. I should hardly think your friend would care to come on these terms.'[11] Nevertheless Lady Byron persisted and, in November 1858, the masterful figure of Frances Power Cobbe burst on the scene.

She was a vast, bluff personage of gentlemanly aspect and bearing, which once caused an acquaintance to exclaim in admiration, 'You are your father's *son*!' From this father, a large landowner of the Anglo-Irish Ascendancy, she had inherited a fiery temper and a despotic will, but also great warmth of heart and generosity. Together they had stayed on their demesne and provided food for their Irish tenants all through the calamitous potato famine. Attempts to train Frances in ladylike accomplishments had failed dismally. At a fashionable boarding-school she was bored, and had educated herself by leisurely and omnivorous reading. At 20, to the scandal of her rigidly Low Church family, she ceased to attend services or family prayers, declaring herself 'creedless'. At 36, she was passing through a phase of liberal Unitarianism, to become a high-minded theist, a state of mind which she most mistakenly expected Mary Carpenter to share. She habitually wore something resembling a riding habit, with skirt of 'sensible length' which caused strangers to remark 'How odd!' Though combative, she was genial and vastly hospitable, keeping open house to thirty guests at the groaning table. 'Greediness, alas,' she said with disarming frankness, 'has been a besetting sin of mine all my life!' She was already hugely stout, with multiple chins and a booming, jolly laugh. After her father's death she had travelled in the near East, on a series of hard-pressed mules, camping alone in the desert. She was in fact the 'new woman' of 1880, prematurely arrived some twenty years before her time. This was the person who now squeezed herself, followed by her equally stout Pomeranian bitch, up the narrow staircase of Red Lodge House to meet her new landlady.

'The first glimpse in the doorway set my mind at rest!' wrote Miss Power Cobbe enthusiastically. 'The plain and careworn face . . . the figure which at fifty-two was angular and stooping, were yet all alive with feeling and power.'[12] She could hardly have known that from the first they were to be at unspoken cross-purposes. Lady Byron, so well-meaning, so at sea with turbulent human nature, had typically failed to grasp the difference between her friends. Mary Carpenter was looking for a competent subordinate not for a woman friend, still less a lesbian lover. Her ideal had always been conventional marriage. Denied this, she was content to exchange letters with intelligent male colleagues 'whom I reckon among my particular friends, without knowing them personally'. Frances Power Cobbe, whose passionate love for her own sex had never yet found fulfilment, was seeking a soul mate. In this hope she valiantly accepted a life unlike anything she had ever known. She suffered much from 'hideous Bristol and the sordid surroundings of Miss Carpenter's

11 Huntington Library, Carpenter Letters, CB 67–8.
12 Cobbe, F. P. *Autobiography*, 276.

11. Mary Carpenter brought her first boys and girls to Wesley's old school at Kingswood in 1852

12. *Mary Carpenter believed in play in the garden, but it looks rather sedate*

13. *A beggar girl becomes 'a useful little maid', the only job open to her in Britain; girls who emigrated had much more freedom*

house'. She had never lived in a street before; the pocket handkerchief of lawn and the window boxes, which were Mary's pride, seemed intolerably cramping after the vast demesne of her beloved home. She endured the oil-cloth on the floor, the gas-lit breakfasts in the basement dining-room, the hard horse-hair chairs and the company of two senior convicted girls from Red Lodge. Mary's distress when one of these two absconded with some household belongings was pitiful to watch; yet Frances noticed she grieved with vicarious repentence for the girl, not for her own disappointment.

The work was relentless. 'There were classes at the different schools, endless arrangements and organizations, the looking up of little truants from the ragged school, writing reports and so on. Every hour of the day and week was pretty well mapped out, leaving only space for brief dinner and tea. At nine o'clock or ten at night when we at last met, Miss Carpenter was often so exhausted that I have seen her fall asleep with the spoon half way between her mouth and the cup of gruel which she ate for supper.'[13] Every meal was snatched like the Passover, with Mary's umbrella at hand 'ready to rush off to Red Lodge if not the Red Sea'. Frances had never taught before. Yet she struggled on in the 'horrid slums' of St James' Back, setting her teeth to endure the smell of unwashed children and the horrors of the tripe-and-trotters shop next door. At Red Lodge she sat in the Oak Room trying not to be repelled by the 'poor faces scarred by disease and the mis-shapen heads' of the fifty girls from 7 to 15 lined up on the benches opposite, while 'I ploughed along trying to get *any* idea into their heads'. Unused to children or poor people, she talked over their heads, too fast, in words they could not understand. The street gangs of the St James' Back Street pursued her, shouting '*Cob*web!' after her stout figure. 'I'm tougher than a cobweb!' she replied, brandishing her umbrella at them. 'And fatter too!' yelled her unregenerate pupils. They enjoyed her lessons, she said, 'rather like fireworks than instruction'.[14] Yet still she struggled on.

For Frances was one of the few people with heart and mind to accept Mary Carpenter, with all her acrimonious prejudices, and love her for herself alone. She had vision enough to see beyond the lined face, the bent figure and the gasping, breathless voice, to the spirit within. She understood Mary's love of beauty, her true artist's mind, so much at odds with hobnailed boots and sordid schoolrooms. She appreciated Mary's sardonic humour and her contempt for cant. She was among the very few people who understood what Mary was trying to do. It was not hand work nor brain work alone, she said, but soul work, 'the very depths of her nature stirred and flowing out to these poor children. . . . Her interest was in the children *themselves*, in their souls, and not, as philanthropy too often becomes, an interest in her own institution.' This essential distinction has seldom been better made. Mary was always grateful for intelligent sympathy in her work; but she made it clear that her interest in the younger woman was only as a fellow-worker. Frances made endless attempts to 'draw her off'; to get her to talk as she could do very well about literature, politics or the affairs of the day.

---

[13] *Modern Review*, April 1880. [14] Cobbe, F. P. *Autobiography*, 281.

The celebrated Carpenter monologues always wound their way back to her children. This had its funny side. Samuel May came to stay from America, and two or three times attempted to talk to Frances about the forthcoming struggle for Abolition. Mary relentlessly led the conversation back to her schools. Then all three, returning from meeting, had to climb the steep stone flight of Bristol's famous Christmas Steps. 'Now,' said Mary Carpenter benevolently, 'you may have your little talk!' Carefully, she husbanded her own scanty breath up the steep flight; but as soon as they reached the top, she launched on the needs of deprived children again. 'It was the *sole* subject of her discourse,' wrote poor Frances with feeling.[15]

The delicious exchange of spiritual confidence for which she longed was not forthcoming. Mary Carpenter stated flatly that her religious opinions could be read in her *Meditations*, in her uncle's sermons, and of course in her father's *Collected Works*. Attempts to probe further met a blank wall of distaste. 'I believe it is unsafe to attempt to look into the mysteries of the soul's sanctuary—so *please let it alone*,' she wrote in a note on 17th March 1859. Her contempt for Unitarians who 'turned Church' for social or careerist reasons was fathomless, yet she had no use for modernist views. Once Frances attempted to discuss Biblical scholarship and the new higher criticism. Mary Carpenter interrupted her. 'Oh, but my father settled all that!' she said sharply. Confessions of doubt and appeals for sympathy made no impression on her. 'I always told you that I could not sympathize on religious matters,' she wrote finally. '*Please* let us say no more.' Protestations of undying love and demands for affection irked her. Her replies to little notes thrust under the door, or long screeds poured out on holiday, were uniformly damping. 'My work and my cause require and must have the devotion of all my heart, soul and strength,' she wrote. 'I know you think much better of me than I deserve ... I feel increasingly that I never can be a companion to any one, nor give that inner sympathy which might be expected.'[16]

The enormous, masterful young woman was not accustomed to be gainsaid. Her demands became more pressing, her manner more emotional. It had not the slightest effect. One evening they both came home late and very tired from the night school. They sat in the dusky drawing-room, while Frances, yielding to an impulse, talked with longing of her old home, the enchanting spectacle of dogs, cats, horses, grooms, milkmaids and the old tame peacock. 'She listened, as I fondly imagined and smiled, though rather absently, then suddenly said, "I don't think those boys in the school will ever attend to Mr Higginbotham!" I could hardly answer her, so awful was the sudden return from my dreams to the ugly school and dirty boys.'[17] There were angry scenes. Mary, with maddening superiority, assured Frances that she never took any notice of anything she might say in a temper, as of course she did not mean it. Frances became ill: she suffered in splendid eighteenth-century style from gout. On her doctor's advice, she went away for the summer,

---

[15] *Modern Review*, April 1880.
[16] Huntington Library, Carpenter Letters, CB 70–89.
[17] *Modern Review*, April 1880.

thinking, 'I could be of no real comfort or service as an inmate of her house; she cannot bear the idea that anyone might expect companionship from her. She would have liked me better if I had been a delinquent.' While she was away, Mary wrote not unkind, but brief and decidedly cool replies to a series of letters. She was fully occupied with the power struggle between herself and Mrs Johnson, who had just arrived at Red Lodge. Frances returned in September and began to see at last that the *tête-à-tête* of years, for which she had so longed, would never be forthcoming. Both women were determined to behave with dignity, but life was not easy at Red Lodge House. Frances, who loved a hospitable house and well-decked table, begged for more leisurely and more appetizing meals than Mary's eternal cold salt beef. She had been used to dinners of many courses with 'sherry and milk punch, hock and chablis, champagne and claret, with a little *gaiety* of a well-bred sort towards the end of the long meal'. Next day Mary greeted her with a complacent smile as she entered the basement dining-room. 'You see', she said, 'I have not forgotten your wish for a dish of vegetables.' There, surely enough, on a cheese plate stood six little round radishes. Frances complained of the noisy, restless presence of Rosanna; she was generally kind and jolly, and one cannot help feeling she was a little jealous of this particular child. Mary, on her side, disapproved of the pampered Pomeranian. This dog liked to lie on her stout back on the hearthrug, monopolizing the fire. Mary was seen to inspect her, then turn solemnly away, remarking in tones of deep moral disapproval, 'self-indulgent dog!'[18]

A flurry of notes passed between the two ladies. 'You are your own mistress,' wrote Mary in December 1859, evidently answering a letter full of reproaches. 'I have long perceived and thought you did too, that your particular talents have not their development in the work of these schools.' Frances was welcome to live in the house. 'If you cared to remain, the cook would do her best to provide dinner in the evening,' she wrote; she herself would of course not be present. She added next day: 'the only hindrance to your comfort which I *cannot* prevent is my poor child. I feel bound to her as brought to me by a higher power; I do *not* feel that it would be right to send her away from me at all and I am trying to bring her under more control.' She concluded plainly, 'I do not see that I can alter my own plans without deranging my work.' Poor Frances raged and stormed, then pleaded ill-health. 'I do not like fainting fits,' replied Mary firmly. 'I never had them. . . . The injury which my mode of living does to your health is a definite reason why you should feel it necessary to remove from my house.'[19] After this, inevitably, Frances packed her rational dresses and her chest of advanced books and departed shortly before Christmas to comfortable lodgings. In the end it was a relief to be gone. 'It is rather an awful thing,' she wrote, 'to live with a person whose standard is so exalted.' Mary wrote a letter of farewell. 'I am truly grieved to be the cause of disappointment to you,' she wrote, 'but, dear friend, I cannot find that anything is my fault about it . . . I shall

[18] Cobbe, F. P. *Autobiography*, 278–9.
[19] Huntington Library, Carpenter Letters, CB 70–89.

not seek another fellow worker and I shall always be grateful for your love.'
In time Frances's generous nature forgot the pain and remembered only the
good. The two women became lasting but distant friends. So this grotesque
comedy ended; yet it was sad too, for the love offered and rejected had been
warm and sincere.

The later history of Frances Power Cobbe is quickly told. In 1860 she met
an aspiring sculptress and fellow animal-lover, Mary Lloyd; the two women
bought a house in South Kensington and settled down to thirty years of
what was in all but name a marriage. Frances addressed her partner in
sentimental poems and brought up an adored substitute-family of pet dogs.
She earned a living by free-lance journalism. 'What my poor father would
have said if he had known that his daughter wrote articles for a halfpenny
newspaper, I cannot guess!' she said with evident relish. She both attended
and conducted Unitarian services, and engaged in combative but genial
controversy which included an attack on ritualism, under the rousing title
'Backward Ho!' A ritualist vicar, with unconscious aptness, once invited her
to settle their differences 'over a glass of sherry and a cigar'.[20] She became a
feature of the London scene. In June 1886, the diarist Munby records, 'I was
introduced to Miss Cobbe, who chatted in a cheery, jovial fashion and talked
of her *gout*.' On other occasions he saw her 'fat and beaming as usual' or
holding forth, Turkish fashion, to a harem of admiring ladies. She continued
to serve jolly luncheons of six or eight entrées, exclaiming as she lowered her
vast bulk into her chair, 'I could always entertain myself with my knife and
fork!' She crusaded naturally for feminist causes, but later devoted most of
her enormous energy to anti-vivisection; in 1898 she founded the British
Union for the Abolition of Vivisection, while remaining an ardent meat-
eater. Her *Autobiography* is a racy classic, in which various eminent Victorians
appear in unusual guises: Matthew Arnold mourning a dead dachshund and
grave Lord Shaftesbury disporting himself with a Siamese cat. Mr Gladstone
proved as unsound on pets as on Home Rule. Frances died in 1904 at her
devoted friend's country house in Wales. Altogether hers was a brave and
honest life, lived in the face of conventional prejudice.

The future history of little Rosanna was not so unclouded. Mary devoted
every spare minute to the child, and all went blissfully until April 1860 when
Mary suffered a devastating shock. The missionary Foxon forwarded a letter
from Rosanna's real mother, demanding the child whom she had not seen for
seven years. All the happiness of Red Lodge House, all the security of
Rosanna's future seemed threatened. Mary yielded to temptation. She wrote
to Foxon that if the mother was 'an unfortunate' who might use the little girl
for begging, she hoped that she would never learn her child's whereabouts.
It was an appalling action for such a scrupulous woman, which can only be
understood as an overwhelming impulse of primitive, possessive mother-love.
Disastrously for her this letter was read in court, when Rosanna's mother
brought an action against Foxon for child stealing. The mother could not
prove malicious possession, but the missionary was hissed and the bystanders

[20] Cobbe, F. P. *Autobiography*, 434–8.

took up a collection for her. Armed with Rosanna's address, she took train for Bristol the same day, arrived at the door of Red Lodge and demanded to see Mary Carpenter. The two women, real mother and foster-mother, met face to face. Mary, frail, care-worn and bent, her inmost happiness threatened, displayed all her iron strength of will. Boldly she accused the mother of abandoning her child, whom she had adopted in good faith as an orphan. The poor woman was overwhelmed by the flood of accusations. At the news that Miss Carpenter was 'bringing up the child as her own', she burst into tears. She is reported to have said 'her prayers had been answered, Miss Carpenter was a true friend, and little Rosanna would be better cared for than ever she could manage. She went away,' concluded the Bristol newspaper account, 'with a resolve to leave the girl in the excellent hands into which she had so fortunately fallen.'[21]

After this extraordinary scene a long silence falls on the subject of Rosanna. She went to school, conveniently out of reach if her mother should appear at Red Lodge again. When she returned to Red Lodge it was generally supposed that she was an orphan, some thought the daughter of missionaries who had conveniently died abroad. It is not known if she ever learnt of her mother's visit or her own true identity. Certainly Mary always remained devoted to her, writing of her as 'my own dear R', keeping her at home at Red Lodge House to the end of her own life, and providing for her in her will. The real mother was never heard of again, and the Carpenter family was impenetrably silent on the whole subject. The ways of high-minded philanthropy were strange indeed.

In May 1860 Lady Byron died and Mary Carpenter lost one of her few intimate friends. The news came early in the morning, filling the day with a dull sense of desolation. Yet Mary worked steadily through it, teaching classes and writing reports without interrupting her routine. She had agreed to undertake the duty of trustee of the Byron literary estate, but after various delvings into trunks full of papers gave up in despair. They included the separation proceedings, evidence of the poet's 'gross indecency in language and conduct.' Letters of the most trivial or compromising kind, poems and tradesmen's bills were mixed together in hopeless disorder and dirt. Gossip said that the famous 'Fare thee well, and if for ever' was written on the back of a butcher's bill, unpaid like most of the rest. Whatever she may have found about her friend's calamitous marriage, Mary Carpenter had seen enough to refuse Harriet Martineau access to the papers; she finally decided to seal up the trunks with their load of literary scandal for several decades.[22] She put up a memorial tablet to Lady Byron at Red Lodge and always celebrated the anniversary of her death as Founder's Day for the whole school. Otherwise she went on steadily with her work.

The work continued uninterrupted by any changes in her personal life. There was so much to be done. The public persisted in associating Mary Carpenter only with reformatories, but she never ceased to stress the needs

[21] Bristol Archives, 12693, No. 23. Album of press cuttings.
[22] Cobbe, F. P. *Autobiography*, 476.

of all deprived children. She never gave up her original demand for three types of school: Ragged for the neglected child, Industrial for the vagrant, and Reformatory only as a last resort for the child convicted of a serious offence. She was incensed by the Minute of the Committee of Council on Education in 1856 which extended capitation grants to voluntary schools, but excluded Ragged Schools because they failed to meet the required educational standard. In practice four-fifths of the grants went to Church Schools of the Established Church. A year later Mary was the only woman member of a deputation to the Committee on Education, which included her brother William, now the Warden of University Hall, London, and Lord Shaftesbury. They asked for the grant to be given to ragged schools, even though they failed to meet the H.M.I.s' standards, because they fulfilled such an urgent social need. Mary explained the need to civilize the children: to persuade them to wash hands and face, to comb their hair, to stop fighting, to sit reasonably still on a bench and listen to her, to sit at table and eat instead of snatching rotting food from garbage dumps. Without this first training, the three Rs would be forever out of their reach. 'If all Ragged Schools were to have you as manager,' replied Lord Granville, the President, diplomatically acknowledging a printed memorial, 'then there would be no difficulty.'[23] Mary was not placated by flattery. She returned to the attack next year, and each succeeding year until the last year of her life.

The outlook for Industrial Schools was more hopeful. Mary Carpenter called the Industrial Schools Bill of 1857 'the great cause of the age'. Her old ally Charles Adderley carried it through Parliament the same year. Vagrant children aged from 7 to 14 could now be sent by magistrates or Boards of Guardians to Industrial Schools for training. As at Reformatory Schools the parents were liable for maintenance of up to five shillings a week. Government help, denied to Ragged Schools, was given to provide half the rent, teachers' salaries and school meals. Thus the second part of her great plan was achieved. Mary raged at magistrates who were still unwilling to commit children. As a forcible demonstration she collected money from her usual long-suffering friends; only fifteen pounds had come in when she was sent two hundred pounds by a total stranger, Mrs Evans. Frederick Chapple, a Liverpool friend, bought a large house and garden in Park Row and established an Industrial School for the 'street Arabs' of Bristol.

This became one of Mary Carpenter's happiest and most successful ventures. At first she managed it herself, but in 1862 handed it over to a committee of management headed by her brother-in-law, Herbert Thomas. A certificated teacher and his wife moved into the roomy, old-fashioned house with fifteen wild, ragged 'pilfering boys' in danger, so the police said, of being recruited by professional gangs on the quays of Bristol. It was the first home many of these boys had known, and for many of them a happy one. The school was, said Mary, 'as far as possible a family' with the master and his wife as house parents. All ate good hot dinners round the big kitchen table. The boys spent half the day in craft work; a woodwork teacher, Mr

[23] *Life and Work*, 195.

Langabeer, proved to have a craftsman's patience with children, as well as with wood. An oak box made by them had pride of place in Mary's house. Mary bought an extension to the garden for outdoor games, and two cottages for the staff. 'I like producing order and beauty out of disorder and chaos,' she said. The boys shared fruit from the orchard, which was never stolen. The honorary physician, Dr Lansdown, reported the improvement in their health and growth as wonderful, and the Inspector, Mr Turner, was well satisfied with their cheerful looks. Mary urged the committee never to use their boys in mechanical labour for profit, even when funds were low. 'In all respects', she wrote, 'the welfare of the boys and their own individual development, physical, mental and spiritual, should be the primary concern . . . the object is not to save money, but to save *the child*.' The boys received individual pocket money, and handled the school's petty cash from selling firewood 'with strictest honesty'.[24] Like the St James' Back boys, they went out for picnics, to the zoo and the circus. By 1870 Mary was able to report that there were seventy-eight boys at school, and that old boys were doing very well in Canada as pioneer farmers. Most remarkable of all perhaps, in the first ten years 'no attempt to abscond has ever been known'. The school was genuinely offering the boys a better life than they could have scavenged in the streets, and so winning their willing co-operation.

Mary was now responsible, wholly or in part, for four different schools: St James', Kingswood, Red Lodge and Park Row. The founding of the Association for the Promotion of Social Science in 1857 gave her a new platform. This earnest body held annual conferences all over Great Britain. 'It presents an opportunity for doing some knitting,' explained the lively red-headed medical student, Elizabeth Garrett. 'The meetings go on incessantly, with relays of fresh subjects, and speakers (and audiences too it may be hoped) for nine days.'[25] Mary Carpenter scorned anything so frivolous as knitting. She sat out every conference and read one or two always forceful, sometimes swingeing, papers each year. She was equally powerful in the newly formed Reformatory and Refuge Union which met for the first time in Bristol, also in 1857. At the same time she kept up a correspondence as vast as Florence Nightingale's, bombarding Ministers with pamphlets and good advice, drumming up subscribers, lobbying managers. She wrote to Lord John Russell, to Matthew Arnold, who was sympathetic to Ragged Schools, to Robert Lowe, who 'could not concur' in her views, to Arthur Hugh Clough. Charles Dickens politely regretted that he would be unable to escort her round Miss Coutts' home for young prostitutes 'and tell you the private history of the different cases', with the tactful excuse that the story of their ruin could 'hardly be said to apply to juvenile delinquency'.[26] With so much high-powered correspondence, Mary yet found time to write kindly personal letters to her old boys and girls. When her sister Susan asked how she did so many things at once, she replied, 'When I am in each, I throw myself

[24] Report of the Park Row Industrial School. Bristol Archives, 12693, No. 23.
[25] Manton, J. *Elizabeth Garrett Anderson*, 127.
[26] Manchester College, Oxford, Library, Letterbook D.

entirely into it.' 'For me, as for Napoleon,' she once said, 'the impossible does not exist.'[27] Matthew Hill once said she was like a boy running down Greenwich Hill, who cannot stop until he gets to the bottom. Family and old friends at last gave up trying to persuade her. '*I will not*', she wrote, 'be made to rest while justice is not done to my poor children.'

By 1860 Mary Carpenter was a power in the land; the shy, plain, painfully sensitive girl had become a formidable woman, with, as she said 'no use for cant'. She inherited her father's ideals, but also her mother's caustic humour. She visited the famous Muller Orphanage, which had refused to accept Rosanna and which claimed to be miraculously supported by prayer alone. She was shown round the five large houses with beds for two thousand children, and told how faith had been severely tried: 'the inmates have risen in the morning penniless and without food or fuel for the day'. However, prayer had been answered to the tune of six hundred thousand pounds over the first thirty years. 'Indeed!' inquired Mary Carpenter. 'Do you receive annual subscriptions?' 'Oh no, Madam! We are supported entirely by prayer.' 'But perhaps friends, once moved, continue to send money regularly?' 'Yes, they do.' 'And perhaps at the beginning of the year?' 'Yes, as it happens they do.' 'Ah well,' said Miss Carpenter, 'when people send *me* money in that way, I enter them in my report as *Annual Subscriptions*.' Such encounters made her respected, if not universally liked. Officialdom had no terrors for her. 'There never yet was man so clever,' she confided, probably *à propos* of Mr Turner's admiration for Mrs Johnson, 'but the Matron of an institution could bamboozle him about every department of her business.' Sometimes her humour was kindly. 'He came back resembling the Prodigal,' she said of a returned absconder from Kingswood, 'in everything of course except repentance.' Pious subscribers, keen to see wicked children repenting their sins, were disconcerted that this made so little appeal to Mary Carpenter. 'I would far rather,' she said, 'have Annie Crooks in the cell for outrageous conduct, acknowledge "I know it was wrong but I am *not* sorry" than any hypocritical and heartless acknowledgements.' For 'sham reformations' and those deceived by them, she had a fathomless contempt.[28]

The seal was set on Mary Carpenter's position in June 1860, when she was invited to address a meeting of the Statistical Section of the British Association at Oxford, opened on 27th June by the Prince Consort as retiring President. She remembered wryly how she had not been allowed in to hear the papers at the Bristol meeting of 1836 because she was a woman. She chose to treat her subject in the widest possible way, under the title 'Educational help from the Government grants to destitute and neglected children'. If she was nervous, she did not show it, though a large crowd gathered to hear her speak in the Sheldonian Theatre. Both as a woman and a Unitarian she was an object of intense curiosity in an Oxford more devoted to port than puritanism. Her brother Philip, who went to support her, found people kept trying 'to pump me about Unitarianism. Mary must be a great puzzle to those people

[27] *Life and Work*, 236.
[28] Cobbe, F. P. *Modern Review*, April 1880, 283–9.

who think it some horrid form of infidelity.' Mary resented comments on her costume, 'as though I were a queen going to her coronation, or a murderer going to her execution.' Nevertheless she took pains to be neat: tidy grey hair bound up with a black velvet ribbon, black satin dress, luckily inherited from her mother, and her father's gold watch on a chain round her neck. Listeners noticed the kindness and character of her worn face, and her voice, low and gentle, yet full of authority.[29] 'I suppose it was the first time', wrote Philip to a friend in the United States,' that a woman's voice had ever read a lecture there, before dignitaries of learning and the church.'[30]

Mary's paper followed her invariable line, that the most deprived children in the country were excluded by the regulations from Government help, and that their desperate need could never be met by voluntary charity alone. Both on grounds of social justice and utility there was an unanswerable claim for 'educational help through the government grant to the destitute and neglected children of Great Britain'. Only civilized education could 'make the child feel the worth of his own soul and perceive that he is a member of society'.

Afterwards Mary was mildly lionized, 'sought after by Lord This and Professor That'. It may seem inconsistent with Philip Carpenter's Socialist principles to notice this, but it was a new experience for Nonconformists. Compare the attitude, also in 1860, of the diarist A. J. Munby, connoisseur of working girls, who was distressed to hear of a shopkeeper at Tooting 'whose maidservant was actually the daughter of a clergyman!' but 'found to my relief that the "clergyman" was only a dissenting preacher'. Mary was inwardly shy, and as usual it made her aggressive. 'She looked more the old woman than she used to do but still had the same determined energy.' Philip added with brotherly frankness that she 'gave them stick' to drive her ideas into their heads.

Soon after the Oxford meeting, Mary lost the company of this favourite youngest brother. Philip had been at odds for some time with his rich, conservative congregation in Lancashire. All his sympathies were with the cotton operatives against the mill-owners. He put up a large noticeboard: 'Men and women who do not think their clothes good enough to appear in Chapel are particularly invited to attend and to sit where they like.' Three years later he declared himself no longer a Unitarian and resigned his charge. 'I can feel no fellowship with those who only want so much of Christianity preached as they themselves can see.'[31] He emigrated to Canada where he made a precarious living by lectures on natural history, and by cataloguing a collection of over 100,000 shells. Mary was grieved to lose him, but of course thought him in the right. Not everyone agreed. James Martineau, who knew the Carpenter family as intimately and long as anyone knew them, summed up Philip's character in words which applied equally well to his sister Mary. With the occasional disconcerting shrewdness of the saintly, Martineau wrote

---

[29] *The Times,* 28th June 1870.
[30] Carpenter, R. L. *Memoir of Philip Pearsall Carpenter,* 246.
[31] *Ibid.,* 235.

to Russell, 'I do not for a moment doubt Philip's self-sacrificing love to persons, providing it may be upon his *own terms* for doing good. But his sympathy with the ideas and types of character prevailing among others appears to me exceedingly narrow, and balanced by a proneness to intense, unjust antipathy. . . . I cannot help feeling much for the older families in his congregation.'[32] Luckless officials, smarting after an encounter with Mary Carpenter, might well have qualified for a share of this feeling.

Frances Power Cobbe compared Mary to a plough, steadily pushing everything out of the way of its lonely furrow; she might equally well have compared her to a steam-roller. She was now at the height of her powers, demonstrating the extraordinary influence which a private individual, prepared to sacrifice everything to one chosen cause, can exercise in a democracy. At every conference and convention she was there, on platforms and deputations, pouring out lectures, books and memoranda, filling page after weary page with her sharp copperplate handwriting. Bound to her self-imposed mission, she pursued Members of Parliament with memoranda, browbeat apologetic officials, wore down opposition by total dedication to her children's needs. Inwardly, if we may believe her family; she was still the same hypersensitive woman, shrinking 'with inexpressible pain' from conflict or lack of sympathy with her ideas. Outwardly she was sharp of tongue and sharper of pen, an adversary to be respected, if not liked. Between meetings and deputations at Whitehall, she snatched half-hours of delight in the National Gallery. Sometimes she even took out her water-colour box again, appeasing her more than Nonconformist conscience by selling the paintings, and scrupulously devoting the proceeds to charity.[33] In 1860 after reading two papers to the Social Science Association at Glasgow, she slipped away to the Highlands. Two surviving sketches show how deft her touch still was and how delicate her colour sense. The tawny trees of a still, autumn morning still shimmer upside-down in the water of Loch Katrine. In another view of the same scene, a fresh wind sends clouds scudding through the mountain tops and drives a little boat across sharp steel-blue waves.[34] 'I seem my old self in these places,' she confessed to Lucy Sanford, 'and rush to my sketch book, absorbed in my colours and in love with every bit of beauty as much as ever'.[35] Somewhere within the embattled reformer of 53 still lived the romantic young girl who had learnt that happiness was not for her, her heart still fresh. Vanished colleagues, Fletcher, Tuckerman, old loves, her mother, and overwhelmingly her father, still lived in her thoughts. Her reticent but deeply personal faith gave her comfort. 'It seems', she wrote on Easter Eve 1860, 'as if I increasingly feel our Saviour to be our tenderly beloved friend.' She accepted the burden of continual work and loneliness, keeping only a small corner of existence for herself. 'My own private life', she told an inquirer, 'is chiefly in the past.'

[32] Manchester College, Oxford, Library, A3 Box B.
[33] Dorset County Record Office, D43/C59.
[34] Red Lodge Museum, Bristol.   [35] *Life and Work*, 216.

II

CHILDREN IN NEED
1860-1865

Mary Carpenter admitted privately to Anna Thomas that her speeches and writings were 'wrung from my heart'. In public she was careful to argue on rational grounds. This was the keynote of her campaign in the first half of the 1860s, for free education for all children in need. She started from what she called 'the great principle that *society is bound*, by every principle, economic, political, moral and religious, to undertake the care of children who are spiritually orphans'. If young people went to prison from hostility to the law, or to the workhouse from ignorance of a trade, the fault lay with a society which had let them grow up, ignorant and uncared for, 'passed by, as it were, on the other side of the world's highway'. Her campaign was not merely for delinquents but for all children in need of help. It began in the autumn of 1860 with a long letter to the *Daily News*, which was reprinted in newspapers all over the country. It continued in January 1861 at a third Birmingham Conference on Neglected and Destitute Children. In 1869 she was still arguing against waiting until a child had been convicted before offering him practical help. Fifteen years' experience of Reformatory and Industrial Schools, she wrote, had convinced her of the 'necessity of an agency which should be extended to *all* destitute and neglected children, entering on the difficulties of life.'[1]

Mary Carpenter claimed government grants for ragged schools which alone reached these children. She has sometimes been accused of wanting to remove children from their parents. She argued exactly the opposite case: that institutions were enormously expensive and unnatural places for a growing child. 'Who would desire,' she asked, 'that children should become diseased so that they may have the benefit of being placed in a good infirmary? . . . A real good home is infinitely better than any school for the education of girls, even a second rate or third rate one is preferable.'[2] Justice and common-sense alike demanded free schools where children could be fed and educated daily without leaving home. 'Religion and true political economy are not at variance . . . if a great duty is neglected retribution is sure to follow. It rests as a blight on our country and is felt in the enormous expenditure of public money in gaols and workhouses.'[3] She described 'the fearful odds with which these poor children were compelled to fight the battle of

[1] *Reformatory and Refuge Journal*, December 1869, Carpenter, M. 'Reformatory Schools'.
[2] Carpenter, M. *Supplementary Measures for Reformatories*: Paper read to the National Association for the Promotion of Social Science 1861.
[3] Bristol Archives, 12693, No. 23.

life'. Their offences were often thoughtless: scrumping apples or throwing stones at a passing train. 'Do we hear of young gentlemen in public schools being punished by imprisonment for such offences?' Yet the children of the poor, sometimes as young as 8 years were regularly committed for them. Penitentiaries were set up to reclaim adult prostitutes, yet at the same time little girls, most in need of care and protection, were left cold and hungry on the streets, an easy prey to anyone who would offer them shelter.

She was also concerned with the quality of education deprived children should receive. She feared it might be a meagre doling-out of the three Rs and 'useful information'. 'Useful information is *useless*', she argued forcefully, 'if it is simply crammed into the mind.' Equally, so-called religious education, which consists of mechanical repetition of catechism or Bible texts learnt by heart, is powerless to awaken spiritual life. The only way to educate is to accept each unique individual. 'Of such wonderful and complicated nature is each little child we see before us in the crowded gallery of a large school!' The teacher must educate the affections, love the loveless, train, but not attempt to crush, the will, cultivate and not shun the senses of each child; 'beauty is *never* an unnecessary luxury in the schoolroom.' The body should be educated as well as the mind; 'bodily exercise and a care of physical health are an essential part of respect for a child as God's handiwork'.[4] Mary Carpenter was speaking as a teacher with a lifetime's experience; yet it is clear that to the vast majority of her contemporaries these seemed merely the sentimental maunderings of an eccentric spinster.

In March 1861, Stafford Northcote, M.P., moved for a Parliamentary Committee of Inquiry on the *Education of Destitute and Neglected Children*. In June Mary Carpenter was summoned to give evidence. She was now a very different person from the provincial lady who had answered questions in such a low voice before the Baines Committee in 1852. Now an established author, lecturer and seasoned veteran of controversy, Mary put her arguments in no uncertain terms. 'A child born into a civilized country has certain rights, something to expect from such a country. The country should not leave him without education . . . education is as necessary to a child as food is.' 'You have stated', asked a member, Mr Black, 'that education is as necessary to a child as food is—that a child is as much wronged by being left uneducated as by being left unfed? You give your assent to these propositions?' 'I do.' 'You do not see', here he evidently hesitated, 'anything extravagant or absurd in them?' '*I do not*,' said Miss Carpenter, firmly.[5]

She was equally combative at another Parliamentary Committee of Inquiry later the same year, this time on *Poor Relief*. She boldly advised that it should be made illegal to take children into workhouses. 'It is the nature of children', she said, 'to be in a *home* and to feel around them a family attachment and sympathy. I believe this is especially essential to the nature of girls;

---

[4] Carpenter, M. *On the Principles of Education*: Paper read to the National Association for the Promotion of Social Science, 1860.

[5] Select Committee on the Education of Destitute and Neglected Children: *Parliamentary Papers*, 1861, VII.

it is important for boys, but it is particularly necessary for girls. But Boards of Guardians have as their chief aim a desire to keep down the rates.'[6] To prove this point, she attacked the workhouse schools of the Bristol Guardians, on evidence gathered from her brother-in-law, who was a member of the Board. Little girls in thin cotton frocks were turned out from bare draughty wards into a high-walled sunless yard for exercise. Children were punished by being forced to eat out of a trough like pigs. With crusading zeal, she failed to add that this had taken place ten years previously. Naturally the present workhouse officials denied it, and an angry war of pamphlets and letters broke out. Even Mary's own family were surprised at the intense and lasting resentment with which she pursued the luckless Bristol Guardians, holding them up to execration in the national press. As one of them, Mr Hunt, said glumly, Miss Carpenter stood very high in the estimation of some, and there was more consideration paid to her statements than if they had been made by any other person.[7] With no official position, Mary Carpenter had made herself a power in the land. Harassed officials found it increasingly risky to differ from her.

Personalities apart, Mary Carpenter was right about the vast, barrack-like workhouse schools. Visitors were horrified to see a thousand mechanically drilled, uniformed children, moving and answering as one. Large metropolitan schools, as at Sutton or Hanwell, contained fifteen hundred to two thousand children. At Stepney, visits from parents were allowed only once in three months, and then in the presence of an official. Children were degraded by hideous uniform, shuffling boots and prison-cropped hair. With overcrowding, vermin and skin diseases spread like wildfire; purulent opthalmia was so common that it was proposed to open schools for eye cases only. No child had ever handled money; some had never eaten with a knife and fork. Workhouse children grew up permanently unfitted for normal life.[8]

Mary Carpenter's own ideas on the subject were set out in a lecture to the Social Science Association, which she afterwards sent to Edwin Chadwick at the Local Government Board. She applied the same principles to workhouse children as to street arabs or pick-pockets. 'They are *our* pauper children! They are our pauper children and if we neglect our duty to them we shall suffer for it. . . . ' 'The pauper stamp is impressed on young children who ought to be rising freely in life. They have a sense of bondage; they are cut off from it, and their ignorance makes them enter it unprepared. . . . Crushed and degraded themselves, they will rear up children to be the same.' Her proposal was that it should be illegal to send children under 16 to any institution within three miles of a workhouse. Instead the ratepayers should elect a School Committee in every district, and the Guardians contribute five shillings a week for the schooling of every destitute child. Every school committee should have some women members, and an office or refuge, always open, to which needy children could come. Any school should be

---

[6] Carpenter, M. Letter on the Charges of the Bristol Guardians, *Western Daily Press*, 10th October 1861.

[7] Bristol Archives, 12693, No. 23.   [8] Hill, F. *Children of the State*, 70–72.

inspected yearly, and children might well be supported by the Guardians at existing industrial schools.[9] The one great essential was an education which would 'make the child feel the worth of his own soul and perceive that he is a member of society.' After the revelations of this inquiry, the Pauper Education Act of 1862 empowered the government to make grants to voluntary homes for destitute children. Within the next few years, the cottage homes for little boys at Farningham, Princess Mary's Village Homes, and the first of Dr Barnardo's homes for boys and girls were founded. From 1869 the National Children's Homes trained Home Sisters in child care. From 1874 Poor Law authorities admitted women members and themselves began to provide cottage homes, on the advice of their first woman inspector. They also boarded out children under the supervision of Miss Mason, an inspector of legendary efficiency, who, however, concluded each visit by giving the child a sugar mouse.[10] This might stand as the modest symbol of a new humanity towards children in need.

The war over pauper children had hardly died away when Mary Carpenter roused herself to do battle once again for the Ragged Schools. In August 1862 all previous minutes on education were cancelled, and the notorious Revised Code was introduced by Robert Lowe, launching the system of 'Payment by Results'. Henceforward there would be a single grant, entirely dependent on the results of an examination each year for each child over 6, in reading, writing and arithmetic.[11] The luckless examiner would be the H.M.I.; Matthew Arnold described the 'difficulty of resisting, without feeling oneself inhuman, the appealing looks of master or scholars'. The teachers' job depended on the results of the same examination, and from all over the country came protests that it 'gives a mechanical turn to the school teaching' or 'fosters teaching by rote'. Matthew Arnold concluded it was 'a remedy worse than the disease it was supposed to cure'.[12] To Mary Carpenter, 'Payment by Results' represented total disaster. Ragged Schools were automatically deprived of the meagre grants they always received, since they had no hope of reaching the 'Standards'. In further determined economies, the grants for books and pupil teachers were withdrawn. Mary Carpenter called this 'the most perplexing and difficult battle I have had to fight. I am obliged to write the same thing backwards and forwards and crossways and every way possible, to get things, or rather one simple thing into people's heads.' The one simple thing was that every child needed an education. Like an old war-horse scenting battle, Mary Carpenter returned to the attack. 'We tried not to come to open war with the Council, but Mr Lowe has *compelled* us,' she wrote to Stafford Northcote. 'My present business is of the unseen order, viz. working up an attack on the Council and supporting the claims of the children in Parliament.' Once again she rallied the influential support of Monckton Milnes. 'Being aware of your wish to benefit the portion of the community

[9] Carpenter, M. *What Shall We Do With Our Pauper Children?*, 1861.
[10] *Social and Economic Administration*, October 1967, 55.
[11] McClure, J. S. *Educational Documents 1816–1933*, 112.
[12] Arnold, M. (H.M.I.) *General Report for 1863*.

which most requires aid, I venture to beg your influence on the following points.' These were, briefly, to alter the Revised Code, so that any assistant teacher 'over sixteen and equal to Standard VI' who proved good and efficient in a ragged or workhouse school, might apply to be examined for a teacher's certificate. 'If you and a few other *influential* people approve,' wrote Mary persuasively, 'Mr. L. may be willing to make the alterations.'[13] It is impossible not to feel that she enjoyed a good fight in a good cause. Free and compulsory education for all children was still many years away, but she was determined to live to see it. She ended 1862 by writing in her journal, 'Each month, each day as it passes, seems richer than the last, and I feel life more precious.' She greeted her birthday in 1863 as putting her 'six years on the sunny side of fifty'.

She needed all her iron strength of will, for 1863 brought her face to face with crippling conflicts in the reformatory movement, generally considered the most successful part of her work. Its success was the source of the trouble. After the passing of the Young Offenders Act of 1854, a number of enthusiastic amateurs rushed to open reformatory schools. The managers tended to be benevolent clergymen and local ladies, with a sprinkling of Bible-punching ex-naval or army officers. With the best intentions, they had no experience of the work. They were continually harassed by shortage of money for the children's everyday needs. Above all, they were divided in their own minds whether to reform the children or punish them; inevitably and disastrously they tried to do both at once. By 1858, when Sydney Turner as Inspector of Reformatories, issued his first report, there were forty-five reformatories, housing 1953 boys and 370 girls, committed by the courts. The new Inspector in his first report found it necessary to point out that ordinary physical provisions, warm beds, well-cooked meals, fresh-air and exercise are 'rather medicines than comforts'. There was no fear that they would prove 'seductive to the children', who would always prefer the roughest liberty. Turner found the schools Spartan in the extreme. He saw some schools with one unheated room for work, dining, lessons and recreation, barred windows, unpaved muddy yards for exercise, children washing in winter at outdoor troughs, earth closets without doors, dark punishment cells, children at work by six a.m. in order to cram eight hours' manual work and three hours' lessons into their crushing day. The crop-headed boys and girls looked dirty and rough. 'Many have said to me,' he reported, 'I would rather be in prison than here.'[14] Children kept for years under 'excessively strict and regular discipline' were quite unfitted for ordinary living, unless they were allowed progressive freedom from restraint. 'Many disappointments are due to a neglect of this simple precaution.[15]

Mary Carpenter of course must have been aware of these dangers. She read all Turner's reports and had many conversations with him. Yet she

[13] Trinity College Cambridge Library.
[14] Report of the Inspector of Reformatories and Industrial Schools: *Parliamentary Papers,* 1857, XXIX.
[15] *Ibid.,* 1860, XXXV.

remained obstinately optimistic. Like her brother Philip, she expected others to do good on her own terms. Now, on the basis of twelve years' experience, she restated her own principles, blindly confident that they would be accepted by all. She had always argued, and believed she had convinced others that 'a vindictive element in chastizement excites in the mind of him who receives it, especially of the child, a rebellious and vindictive feeling in return . . . such punishment defeats its object'. The only way to cure an antisocial child was to restore to him his lost birthright of true childhood, active, affectionate, healthy, thoughtful and gay. Reformatory children should live 'as in a well-ordered family of the working class', welcomed into society and mixing freely with the outside world. 'The love of their own families must not be repressed and natural ties must be cherished.' The head, helped by a 'motherly matron', should have a parental influence; 'the care of animals awakens kindly sympathies in the children themselves'. Freedom from restraint should not mean empty boredom. 'The activity and love of amusement natural to children should be cultivated in an innocent and healthy manner,' with swings and games for boys, fancy-work or individual gardens for girls, dolls and toys for the youngest children; all together could share excursions, nutting, blackberrying, half-holiday picnics or swimming where possible. Good food, attractively presented, and eight to ten hours' sound sleep would often stabilize a difficult child's behaviour; rewards and punishments should be administered with the greatest caution, and food should never be withheld to punish a child. 'The best teachers will secure obedience and good conduct with the least punishment.' Above all 'the children *must* be able to look back on the school as "our happy home." '[16] Mary Carpenter was obstinately confident that magistrates, managers and public would be convinced by the logic of these arguments, an extraordinary illusion in a woman otherwise so clever. It can only be explained by the innocence of her upbringing and early life, in the circle of her father's adoring Utopian admirers. Until nearly forty, in her prolonged childhood, she had hardly met anyone else. Many progressive hopes have been dashed by such illusions.

Slowly, Mary Carpenter was forced to realize that most reformatory enthusiasts had ideas very different from her own. In 1861 she was the sole woman guest at a house-party of twenty-one magistrates, prison governors and managers from all over the country. They met at Hardwicke Court near Gloucester, the mansion of Thomas Barwick Baker, a vigorous, fox-hunting squire of High Church and High Tory convictions. As J.P. and High Sheriff of Gloucestershire he had been appalled by the repeated convictions of young offenders, and founded a reformatory, which he hastened to reassure county neighbours, 'need not be an objectionable looking building to have on one's estate'. Only his own words, collected under the crusading title *War with Crime* can do justice to the squire's enthusiasm. His cure for juvenile delinquency was simple. 'I know of no employment which will allay excitement and tranquilize the mind . . . like steady hard digging on stiff clay.' School at

---

[16] Carpenter, M. *Suggestions on the Management of Reformatories and Industrial Schools.* Pamphlet issued by the Reformatory and Refuge Union, 1864.

Hardwicke was confined to the evening when the boys were satisfactorily 'exhausted by the bodily labours of the day'. The treatment of a refractory boy was by 'limiting him to bread and water and not too much of it'. Now Barwick Baker was able to announce to his guests the triumphant success of this regime. 'There is *no* punishment', he said with simple pride, 'that boys dread so much as a reformatory, and certainly none that their parents dread so much.'[17] This was greeted with rumbles of approval in Tory beards.

Baker was convinced that punishment was essential 'to impress on a boy's mind that he has done *wrong*'; otherwise his character would continue to resemble 'a doubtful half-sovereign or a slightly unsound horse'. A reformatory, he said, should be a place of strict stern discipline and hard work, because everyone who has done wrong *ought* to suffer some pain. His friends and colleagues agreed. All were enthusiastically in favour of a preliminary term of imprisonment, against which Mary Carpenter had argued so bitterly, in vain, in 1854. In fact, by 1884, when the judges, the inspectors and a Royal Commission had rejected previous imprisonment, it was the reformatory managers who insisted upon retaining it.[18]

At every stage the same basic clash of philosophy appeared between punishment and cure, each with sincere, well-meaning and earnest supporters. A hundred years' confusion in aims and methods has followed which is far from being resolved today. Those working with children have always been aware of it; the Children and Young Persons Act of 1969 has brought home to the general public the difference of attitude between magistrates, social workers and the approved schools. 'Justly or unjustly, social workers feel that approved schools represent a punitive tradition'[19] and are therefore unwilling to trust children to them; on the other hand some magistrates feel like Barwick Baker, that punishment itself forms an effective part of treatment.

Sydney Turner as a leading authority was of course present at the Hardwicke conference. His experience, and his devotion to the children was unquestionable; he showed it by the labours of thirty-five years, retiring only when his health could no longer stand a life of continual travel. He had already stated the methods in which he believed. The 'tone of discipline, dietary, industrial occupation, lodging, habits of recreation etc. etc. must have something of the hardness which Saint Paul prescribes as an essential element in the Christian's training. . . . A manly training to obedience, regularity, industry and self-control is the needful remedy.'[20] This was the muscular Christianity of the English public school, in which most magistrates had themselves been brought up; they could give it their heart-felt assent. Perhaps only a woman could see how repressive it was to the natural instincts of girls or young children. The resolutions drawn up by the conference filled Mary Carpenter with dismay, but she was completely outnumbered. The conference concluded that reformatories should be reserved for the 'worst

[17] Baker, T. B. H. *War with Crime*, 167–9.
[18] Carlebach, J. *Caring for Children in Trouble*, 73.
[19] *New Society*, 21st December 1972. Smith, G. 'The Children's Act'.
[20] General Report of the Inspector of Reformatories and Industrial Schools, *Parliamentary Papers*, 1859, Second Session XIII, 2.

juvenile criminals' and that the regime must never 'give them superior advantages and so make them an object of envy to the innocent'. First offenders should always receive the 'lighter and easier remedy' of prison; 'if *that* fail, try the more costly expedient'. 'Our work is to *stop crime*, whenever and however we can,' concluded Baker, announcing that he would accept in his reformatory only 'bad boys—the worse the better!' With unconscious irony he added that these hardened criminals must, of course, be sound Churchmen; 'I receive none who do not assent to Church of England doctrines.'[21]

Mary Carpenter's feelings as she listened to all of this can only be imagined, though it is recorded that a member of the conference objected from the floor. She pleaded the cause of girls, exposed to moral danger through no fault of their own, and here Sydney Turner supported her. He considered that even many young prostitutes would be suitable for treatment. Yet he too was against accepting first offenders on grounds of the heavy expense to the public. Mary could only offer to take little boys at Park Row Industrial School, rather than see them go to prison at a tender age.

The resolutions of the conference were in due course published in *The Times* and Mary was determined not to let them go unchallenged. As usual, she did not mind how unpopular she made herself, or how much extra work she undertook. With the help of Recorder Hill she drafted a set of counter-resolutions, which she personally sent out to a long list of influential people. Among the people she wrote to, was her old reformatory ally Richard Monckton Milnes. 'You have doubtless seen,' ran a letter of 26th November 1861, 'the Hardwicke resolutions in *The Times*, and will I am sure not be surprised to find that we in Bristol do not at all agree with the manner or the matter of some of them. The enclosed resolutions of the Kingswood Committee will show you Mr Hill's views, with which I am sure you will accord. This enclosure will be sent to *all* Reformatory Committees and *all* Chairmen of Quarter Sessions.'[22] Exhaustive tactics like these made Mary Carpenter understandably unpopular in many quarters, but they also made her in the long run very difficult to defeat. The secret of her extraordinary influence, which has puzzled so many people, lay in iron determination with an endless capacity for detailed work. She maintained a constant watch on public bodies, and used every ounce of personal influence she possessed to bend them to her own views. 'The Magistrates', she informed Frances Power Cobbe, 'have been lapsing into their usual apathy about the Industrial, so I got a piece of artillery to help me in the shape of Mr M. D. Hill. He asked Mr Williams the Clerk, to call, who looked frightened and promised to do all in his power. He also advised my writing a letter to the Bench who have a Quarterly Meeting today. This I have written and sent, having been advised by Mr Hill. *Nous verrons!* They have learnt by painful experience that I cannot be made to rest while justice is not done to these poor children.'[23] No wonder the unfortunate Magistrate's Clerk looked frightened.

[21] Baker, T. B. H. *War with Crime*, 166–91.
[22] Trinity College Cambridge Library.
[23] Huntington Library, Carpenter Letters CB 70–89.

Mary Carpenter still assumed that any boy or girl sent to a reformatory would, as a matter of course, find a kindly and happy home. An undated cutting in her album describes a harvest home at Kingswood, the boys with red cheeks playing football in the paddock, the drum-and-fife band playing 'The Girl I left behind Me', the dinner of beef with a mountain of roast potatoes, and plum pudding to follow. Mary gave each boy a present to mark the occasion, to the little ones a picture book, to each big boy a pocket knife, as a token of trust in his good conduct. 'The Committee acknowledge with good reason the kindness of Miss Carpenter in continuing to visit the school regularly at much personal inconvenience, to assist the instruction of the boys,' noted Turner in 1861. In fact she walked four miles each way through all weathers to teach them. Boys worked in the gardens that year; they tended horses, cows and pigs; no boys were put in the cells, and there was not a single attempt to abscond.[24]

A year later the superintendent had changed, several members of staff resigned, and there were strong charges of harshness and illtreatment towards the children. Turner found these exaggerated, but warned that with the younger boys 'no excuse exists for even occasional severity'.[25] At about the same time the managers invested in a steam press for brick-making, hoping this would put their struggling institution on a sound economic footing. This was a common trend at the time. Soon the ninety-six boys were producing four thousand bricks a day. The work in the brickyard involved heavy digging, carrying hods of raw clay, working to the mechanical speed of the press, and breathing the fumes from the kiln. Turner, at his next visit, commented on their rough appearance, which he intelligently said had a tendency to degrade their self-respect. He also thought they would be too tired after a day's brick-making to be taught in the evening and warned that their general education would suffer. The managers pleaded economic necessity, and persisted with the brick-making. In June 1862 Mary Carpenter resigned as a protest. All her happy memories of the school seemed, she said, 'turned to ghosts'. She grieved at parting from the boys whom she had really loved. Shock and exhaustion laid her open to illness; all through July and August she lay helpless, a prey as always when ill to miserable regrets and self-reproach. Oddly, at exactly the same time, her brother William was prostrated for months with a crippling depression very like their father's. Two years later, her brother Russell suffered a similar illness which forced his retirement to a smaller church at Bridport, Dorset. Both men eventually recovered, as did Mary herself, dragging herself slowly and wearily back to work.

Two years later Mary Carpenter started to visit Kingswood again. 'The boys were so glad to see me,' she wrote, 'and remembered so wonderfully my old lessons, that I determined never to stay away again, unless compelled by illness.' But her influence on the running of the school was at an end.

---

[24] Report of the Inspector of Reformation and Industrial Schools, *Parliamentary Papers*, 1861, XXX.
[25] *Ibid.*, 1862, XXVI.

Sydney Turner as Inspector reported 'a great deal of disciplinary trouble' in 1866, with numerous punishments; he demanded a serious inquiry, leading to improvements in the infirmary after the death of a boy in 1867. In 1869 the boys were 'restless' and three had been flogged; in 1870 the staff were 'unsettled' and the superintendent desponding of progress. The reports of the visiting committee during the 1870s were largely devoted to the progress of the brick industry. The managers refused to receive boys who were not in sound health for heavy work. A new superintendent who complained there was no room in the time-table for the boys' education, was told he must maintain output and fit in the lessons as his predecessor had done. The monthly reports usually recorded two to three boys in the punishment cells and three or four in the infirmary. Later committee members, of the 1890s, under whom the school came to have an excellent reputation, considered the discipline of the brick-making period 'very severe indeed'.[26]

The story of Kingswood was typical of many reformatory schools opened in high hopes and good faith. The managers were well-meaning, perhaps somewhat self-important people, confronted with problems they could neither understand nor control. Brute economic necessity drove them to provide poor education, monotonous drudgery, bleak surroundings, uniforms and food. Their conscious minds were set on reformation, but their unconscious minds demanded punishment; not surprisingly the unconscious usually won. Moreover a committal to a reformatory was a very long sentence. These grimly clean, rigidly disciplined institutions were at the opposite pole from the happy community families Mary Carpenter had planned. Her unease was not shared by the general public, at least until a series of scandals and the report of a departmental Committee of inquiry in 1896.

From the point of view of the public, reformatory schools were a triumphant success. There was such a steep drop in the number of juvenile offenders and in the drifting population of young vagrants during the second half of the 1850s, that, looking back on the period from later years, it has been said, people saw it as 'a great watershed'.[27] Seeing the streets emptied of their gangs of loitering young beggars and thieves, most contemporaries gave credit to the reformatory schools, rather than to any general social change.

Barwick Baker, of course, was triumphant. He argued, with justification, that long reformatory sentences had broken up the gangs, put the ringleaders out of circulation, and destroyed their skills. 'Twelve months' hard work in a reformatory destroyed for ever the delicacy of finger necessary for a pickpocket.' As one might expect, his claims were vigorously stated. After five years' experience he claimed 'an extraordinary result. They received a thousand children per annum, convictions fell by six thousand per annum because the ringleaders were removed, and the professional class of boy thief was put an end to.'[28] There were still critics of the schools on the grounds of

[26] Bristol Archives, 28776, KS/A5/1.
[27] Tobias, J. J. *Crime and Industrial Society in the Nineteenth Century*, 47.
[28] Baker, T. B. L. *War with Crime*, 23, 156.

expense to the public. *The Examiner*, with a policy of playing on its readers' middle-class fears and prejudices, commented on Sydney Turner's report for 1861–2. 'Parents of the kind of which there are too many in the lower classes, will be glad to get their children off their hands, by some offence placing them where they will be well taught . . . and with a greater prospect of getting on in the world. The more successful the reformatories are, the greater will be the temptation to seek their advantages.'[29] The majority, however, would have agreed with the report of the 1884 Royal Commission on Reformatory and Industrial Schools, which said they could be credited 'with having broken up the gangs of young criminals in the larger towns, with putting an end to the training of boys as professional thieves, and with rescuing children fallen into crime from becoming habitual or hardened offenders'.[30]

In the eyes of the country at large, Red Lodge, the first girls' reformatory, appeared a wholly successful institution and a model of its type. In 1860 the girls still came mainly from Bristol and the West Country; by 1862, girls were sent from Sussex, and next year from Essex. By 1867, there were girls from London, Liverpool, Nottingham and Scarborough and by 1872 from thirty-five different counties and boroughs. The school was well known abroad and had a number of foreign visitors. A French Protestant pastor, Monsieur Martin Paschaud, was moved 'avec ravissement' to burst into verse, while a visitor from Louisville, Kentucky, wrote a tribute to the 'spirit which converts Institutions into Homes'. In February 1865, a personal Commissioner of Czar Alexander II of Russia came to inspect Red Lodge and the Boys' Industrial School, as model progressive institutions. 'My warmest wish', he wrote, 'is that they should be transplanted to Russian soil and take root.'[31] The girls' favourite visitors were William and Ellen Craft, two escaped slaves from the Southern States, who came to describe their adventures on the Underground Railroad. The subjects of escape and freedom must have been very near the young listeners' hearts.

What was the quality of life at Red Lodge? It was decidedly austere by present-day standards, for having decided not to undertake industry for profit, Mary was forced into the only alternative, to keep living expenses as low as possible. Red Lodge was the cheapest girls' reformatory, at an annual cost per head of £14.15 against a national average of £18.16.5. This figure could only be achieved through very tight budgeting. At the end of 1864, the balance in hand was precisely eleven shillings and tenpence. In particular, the expenditure on food seems very low,[32] and the school was censured for this after Mary Carpenter's death.[33]

The health of the girls was good, by comparison with the admittedly abysmal standards of many mid-Victorian schools. Schools suffered repeated

[29] *The Examiner*, 27th September 1862.
[30] Quoted in Tobias, J. J. *Crime and Industrial Society in the Nineteenth Century*, 250.
[31] Bristol Archives, 12693, No. 20.
[32] See Appendix I for a specimen year's accounts.
[33] Report of the Inspector of Reformatory and Industrial Schools, *Parliamentary Papers*, 1878, XLII.

outbreaks of 'fever'; epidemics at Winchester in 1846, 1848 and 1861 were traced to faulty drains. Arnos Court, the other girls' reformatory at Bristol, where the Sisters of the Good Shepherd, who never refused a case, struggled devotedly with a hundred wild Irish girls from the slums of Liverpool and Manchester, suffered twenty-three deaths in four years.[34] The mental health of girls was also gravely at risk; at Liverpool in 1859–60, Sydney Turner found that 'violent temper amounting to mania' had led to girls being put in strait-jackets. By contrast, in the first twenty years at Red Lodge, there were only two deaths. Girls often arrived stunted and disfigured with skin diseases, but grew so much that visitors hardly recognized them. Some of the mothers were touchingly pleased and proud.

Discipline demanded a delicate balance. The first years of Red Lodge passed as we have seen in a continuous struggle to establish and keep some sort of order. By 1860 this battle was more or less won; the school now admitted girls under the age of 13, and promoted them as they grew older to the comparative freedom of Red Lodge Cottage. This made it possible to have a full and active school-room, and to cater for the natural interests of growing girls. Sydney Turner noted the improvement on his visit of inspection in 1862. 'Miss Carpenter is fortunate in having a very efficient matron and schoolmistress,' he reported. 'The improvement in the condition of the school and the manner and appearance of the girls is very satisfactory. Girls can write from dictation, do simple sums and make and mend their own clothes.' Visiting in 1863, he noted a decline in the number of punishments, and a decided improvement in looks, school-work, behaviour and manners among the girls. In 1864 he found them 'cheerful, contented and comfortable; their answers to questions showed much intelligence and knowledge'. Most were young; all appeared healthy and there had been no attempt to abscond for two years.

In 1865 Mary Carpenter published an account of a typical day at Red Lodge. This shows the care she took to reconcile public opinion and to forestall criticism. For instance, one of the most vexed questions was religious instruction and the Lord's Day. Sunday church formed an inescapable part of all Victorian schooling. To prove that Red Lodge was genuinely non-sectarian, Mary sent the girls not to her own church, but to the nearest place of worship, where the minister and his wife were very kind to them. Words can hardly convey now what an astonishingly broad-minded gesture this was among all the sectarian in-fighting of the 1860s. It is doubtful though whether the poor children's Sundays were much enlivened by it; the nearest church happened to be the sternly Calvinistic Countess of Huntindon's Connection.

Everywhere, Mary Carpenter kept the same careful balance. Before her eyes she saw always the standard of happiness to which the child offender, *as a child*, was entitled. Yet she knew that to the public she was housing, feeding, clothing and educating convicted children far above the abject poverty in which many labourers dragged out their entire lives. The result

[34] Report of the Inspector of Reformatories and Industrial Schools, *Parliamentary Papers*, 1865, XXV.

was an elaborate system of checks and balances, designed to reassure subscribers without harming the children. There were fifty-four little girls, from the age of 9, with ten seniors in the cottage and two in Mary's own house. They got up each morning as Bristol Cathedral clock chimed six over the old red house.[35] As in all Victorian families, the day began and ended with family prayers, for which they trooped up the old oaken staircase to the grand, carved oak drawing-room. No talking was allowed at meals and strict attention was paid to table manners. Most of the girls had never used fork, spoon or table-cloth, and at first seized their food 'like beasts of Prey'. The food itself, though wholesome, was monotonous and plain. The girls disliked oatmeal porridge or suet dumplings, hated green vegetables and summer salads, and preferred to steal the cat's meat when they could. Meat or bacon came only three days a week; the other days offered dumpling and gravy or pea soup with meat stock, recalling Charles Lamb's famous description of the meals at Christ's Hospital. The girls were required to work hard, with an hour's housework or gardening each day, and sewing or knitting each afternoon in addition to their lessons. They were expected to take a daily cold bath in summer, to brush each other's long hair every morning, to strip and make their beds neatly and to 'admit, pure, fresh, morning air'.

Yet Mary did everything in her power to humanize this strict routine. Meal-times were 'never gloomy'; the matron read to the children or told them stories; afterwards she showed them pictures from the *Illustrated London News*, to interest them in the outside world. At sewing they took turns to read aloud, or sing together. They could earn and draw money from the matron as well as make their own new frocks. Their lessons were interesting, 'not filled with routine copies or crabbed sentences to which they can attach no meaning'. Each girl kept her own school books and an album for her own favourite pictures or poems. There were about twenty-five in a class, but backward girls were coached individually in reading and writing. They enjoyed the morning and afternoon hours in the garden. 'Our little maids', wrote Mary, 'get a brisk run to their hearts' content, while each older girl has her own little plot of ground and takes a delight in raising flowers of her own.' She saw the need to break the monotony for these girls to whom the law allowed no holidays. On fine days, school stopped early; they went to Clifton Down, four hundred acres of open country, high above the city. Every week end there was a 'long ramble' or a picnic in the country or at the seaside. She took them to the Zoo, watching the intense delight with which they fed the bears and monkeys they knew only from picture books. She took them to see every Bristolian's pride, Brunel's new Suspension Bridge, airy as gossamer, spanning the Avon Gorge. Afterwards they sat round with 'huge baskets of cake and fruit' for a picnic on Clifton Down. At Christmas she gave each girl an individual present for the Christmas tree, to enhance a sense of personal worth. Those who had experienced Miss Carpenter as a she-dragon in controversy would have been amazed to see her escort her family, in their new frocks and bonnets, to the annual church service for

[35] Carpenter, M. *A Day in the Red Lodge Reformatory*, 1864.

Bristol schools. 'No one can deny', she observed, with a complacency as ridiculous as any natural mother's, 'that the Red Lodge girls are the neatest, the best behaved and have the pleasantest faces of all.' Nothing pleased her more than to see their pleasure, for instance when they planted a Japanese fir tree in the garden, each spading the earth round the roots in turn. 'It was a touching sight to see them, poor children; here they were again as children should be.'

Mary's estimate of the Red Lodge girls at this time is much more sober and balanced than her earlier theoretical claims. For the years 1860–6, she wrote, there had been an average of sixty girls in the lodge and cottage. Of seventy girls discharged, sixty were thought to be doing reasonably well; some had married and wrote happy letters. The rest had returned to a tramping life, usually with a man or a series of men, and of these two-fifths could not be traced. The girls, being younger, were easier to handle; they were no longer seasoned members of gangs with six or eight convictions behind them. For this reason there were fewer serious faults and punishments than with the big wild girls of early days, and no attempts to abscond for the last two years. Nevertheless, she added, the supply of convicted girls from 'the lowest part of the population' continued unchecked. The depths of society were still quite unplumbed by voluntary education, social work or the organized churches.[36] Moreover, the staff position was always precarious. The excellent, and now very experienced matron, Mrs Johnson, had given notice, because she had been appointed head matron of a large penitentiary; she would not be easy to replace. With good reason Mary had begun to wonder since her last serious illness what would happen after her own death. 'I thought', she wrote in her journal, 'that I must never leave my children. But I cannot be always with them and they must be prepared for the time when I shall be called home. It would be well to test my plans and principles while I may still return to correct errors.'[37] Anxiously, she turned to the next item of work on her crowded schedule.

The results of the boys' Industrial School were consistently encouraging. From 1861, by an amendment to the Industrial Schools Act, the schools were transferred to Home Office control and the Treasury empowered to award them annual grants; their stability was therefore ensured. The Inspector noted several times how remarkably alert and cheerful, as well as healthy, the boys looked. The carpentry, shoemaking and tailoring they learnt provided for their own use and also equipped them with a trade for life. As well as daily lessons in the schoolroom, Mary took them several times a week for 'subjects of general interest' often arising from the news of the day. From 1864, her engineer nephew William Carpenter lived in Bristol, and volunteered to teach the boys practical science and mechanics; the Inspector noticed how intelligently they talked.[38] The school's reputation in Bristol was so good that parents sent wayward boys, not only under court order, but of their

36 Bristol Archives, 12693, No. 12.   37 *Life and Work*, 221.
38 Report of the Inspector of Reformatories and Industrial Schools, *Parliamentary Papers*, 1865, XXV.

own free choice. This success encouraged Mary to open in 1864 an Industrial School for girls. She was now in her 60th year, and had been seriously ill the previous summer; she was honest enough to see that she could not undertake it herself. She invited a number of unsuspecting women to tea, mostly subscribers or voluntary helpers at the ragged school. She related to her nephew, with her curious child-like smile, what followed. 'I said to them, "This must be done and you are to do it." And they did it!'

The most successful of Mary Carpenter's creations, and the one which gave her most pleasure, was still her first, the ragged school and night school at St James' Back. She still taught regularly in the night school. Her angular, rusty-black figure was to be seen, cautiously descending, or painfully climbing the steep stone flight of Christmas Steps, through languid summer evenings or drizzling winter fog. With no help from public funds, she raised the money to extend her little oasis of order and decency in the dockside slums. Now, as well as the school and children's playground, she planned a working man's club, which was opened in March 1865 'in Great State'. The members were her old scholars. 'Why need they go to America,' she asked, 'to have a chance of getting on in life?' They stared at one another when they met again, not recognizing the wild little savages they had been in these respectable young married workmen. Yet their old teacher knew them all. Generations of boys and girls had passed through the school since it opened. In the first year twenty-six of them had gone to prison, but between 1855 and 1861 not one was imprisoned. The money was a continual worry; 'we are reduced to a degree of begging which is most repulsive to our feelings'.[39] Yet the results were more than worthwhile. As Thomas Guthrie wrote in 1860, schools were 'the cheapest police and the surest sanitary process'.[40]

Her fertile brain was as full as ever of schemes, some of them remarkably forward-looking. She had always tried to keep in touch with children who left the schools. 'We have assumed parental care of them and this should continue after they leave us,' she wrote. Yet with five schools this work could no longer be fitted into her crowded days. Some people thought it should be handed over to the police; regular visits from the uniformed law would have the additional advantage of frightening potential backsliders. Mary Carpenter was indignant at this suggestion. A girl in respectable domestic service, once visited by the police, would instantly be told to pack her bags and leave. Something different was needed for aftercare. Boys and girls going to Australia were met by Mrs Caroline Chisholm, the emigrants' friend, who welcomed them on arrival. Those travelling to Canada went with an accredited agent, who found them work and lodgings. At home there was no such person. Boys and girls needed someone to give them help and advice, said Mary Carpenter, above all 'they need *a friend*', whom they know and trust. In 1864, by careful budgeting, Mary Carpenter was able to appoint a full-time 'Children's Agent in Bristol'. He found work and lodgings for newly discharged boys and girls,

[39] Select Committee on Destitute and Neglected Children, *Parliamentary Papers*, 1861, VII.
[40] Collins, P. *Dickens and Education*, 71.

visited them regularly and reported any problems. His reports were filed, as a source of practical information in drafting future plans. Mary Carpenter considered every large city should have such a children's officer.[41]

Several other interesting suggestions were not tried during Mary Carpenter's lifetime. One was for probation, 'a discretionary power to magistrates to restore the child to his or her parents on the first offence'.[42] The second, perhaps suggested by Hazelwood school, was for an experiment in group self-government, where the pupils held a weekly meeting under a boy or girl chairman to form their own rules. A third was for a crèche, attached to each free day-school for girls. Here the small children of working mothers could be cared for in safety, playing, feeding and resting under the care of big girls, who would thus learn 'affectionate consideration' for children's needs.[43] The Victorian age sentimentalized motherhood and the family, while denying the poorest girls any training for this most important part of their lives.

In 1865, Mary Carpenter could look back and see that the creation of Reformatory and Industrial Schools, however far from ideal, represented two-thirds of her programme for children in need. In 1866, it was estimated there were sixty-five reformatory schools in Britain, housing 4,915 children, and fifty Industrial schools housing 2,062 children. A Reformatory and Industrial Schools Bill of 1866 consolidated the experience of the pioneering years, and remained statutory until the Children's Act of 1908. It fixed the age limits of pupils at a minimum of 10 and maximum of 16 years, and codified the dual system of voluntary control and Home Office inspection. In practice the Home Office had authority over buildings and rules and could withdraw its certificate of approval on six months' notice.[44] The early Inspectors carried an enormous load of work and responsibility over a very wide area; it needed a man of the calibre of Sydney Turner to exercise a really effective control. Yet, with all their faults, the schools offered an opportunity to many children who would otherwise have had none.

At 60, Mary Carpenter planned to write a major book, under the title *Our Children*. It would contain the impressions and conclusions of twenty years spent working with children in need, and would define 'the relation and consequent duties of the state towards child citizens'. This book, alas, was never written; it was squeezed out of existence by other pressing problems, children in workhouses and prison, women prisoners, the social disabilities of women and girls in India. From every point of view this was a great loss. The book would have put Mary Carpenter's work for all kinds of deprived children into a truer perspective, correcting for later ages the morbid obsession of her contemporaries with infant sin and sinners. For the historian it would have been a fascinating record of pioneering social work in the lower depths of Victorian society. Mary Carpenter, however, was too busy to regret the book

[41] Carpenter, M. *Supplementary Measures needed for Reformatories.*
[42] Carpenter, M. *Juvenile Delinquents*, 283.
[43] Carpenter, M. *Reformatory Schools*, 190.
[44] *Life and Work*, 244.

she might have written. The children themselves and their future were what mattered to her; the young sailor on watch, the Canadian farmer in his fields, the newly-married wife in her own kitchen, gave meaning to her solitary, drudging days. 'They are the poetry I now delight in,' she had written, 'but it cannot be expressed in words.'[45]

[45] *Ibid.*

PART THREE

MARY CARPENTER'S CONCERNS

12

WOMEN AND CHILDREN IN PRISON 1860-1865

While the country as a whole congratulated itself on a marked drop in juvenile delinquency during the 1850s, and gave the credit to the reformatory schools, Mary Carpenter, characteristically, grieved over individual failures. 'What we have been permitted to do', she wrote in a paper for the Social Science Association, 'only reveals to us what has not been done.' She thought of girls she had known personally, dragged back to the slums by their parents, blindly loyal to criminal lovers, too wild to be taught, too weak to resist easy temptation. What would become of them? 'There are failures,' she wrote; 'there must always be so. Where will a large proportion of these poor girls be sent? Most, we fear, will find their way to the Female Convict Prisons at Brixton and Millbank.'[1] For a long time it was difficult to find out what happened to them there. Inquiries in 1861 to the Chaplain of Liverpool Borough Gaol, who had sent many girls to Red Lodge, produced disturbing answers. He spoke of overcrowding, in which 78 young girls were forced to share cells with older women, often old offenders. Apart from natural deaths, insanity and suicide, he reported an increasing number of re-convictions; of 207 women recently discharged, he could only say that 8 were 'positively doing well'. In 1862, the Inspector of Prisons' report on the vast, unhealthy Millbank Penitentiary revealed 172 recorded punishments to women prisoners, many of them very young. 45 girls under 16 were said to have been put in dark cells on bread and water diet, while 127 were strapped in handcuffs and canvas strait-jackets, after 'breaking out' in violent attacks on other inmates or staff.[2]

Within the next two years the country was enjoyably scandalized by the best-selling *Memoirs of Jane Cameron, a Female Convict* and *Female Life in Prison*, both purporting to be the work of 'A Prison Matron'. These told of 'women harder to tame than creatures of the jungle', whom 'physical restraint transforms into a wild beast rather than a human being'. The books were not, in the Victorian phrase, 'family reading', but, perhaps for this very reason were the more widely read. Some people even thought the books were the work of Mary Carpenter herself, who, alas, never wrote anything half so lively. For many of the characters are haunting: Sarah Baker, who threw her child down a mine-shaft, Mary May, a little weak in the wits and given to fortune-telling as well as petty larceny, Mrs Solomons the receiver, whose grateful

---

[1] Carpenter, M. *On the Treatment of Female Convicts*, read to the National Association for the Promotion of Social Science, 1863.
[2] Carpenter, M. *Our Convicts*, II, 233.

former clients came to visit her in satins and silks, or the pale, quiet murderess who grew slowly insane and was removed to the criminal lunatic asylum. The author described the hair-cropping of new arrivals, with women on their knees, begging to be spared, the swallowing of powdered glass to gain admission to the infirmary, the attempts at suicide by hanging from ventilator grilles, the sudden quarrels with 'scuffling and scratching and fighting and screaming that only Pandemonium might equal'. Books catering so delectably to feelings of prurient curiosity and moral superiority at the same time were sure of a sale; the second ran through three editions in a year. They were, though this did not emerge until long after, not fact but fiction, a commercial venture by a pulp novelist, Frederick William Robinson. He had judged his moment and his readers well; commercially these sensational thrillers were a gratifying success, selling considerably better than his more high-souled titles like *High Church* and *Shy Violet*.

From the public point of view, as Mary Carpenter noted, 'the general impression excited by these volumes is that these women are so incredibly bad that any attempt to reform them must be hopeless'; or, as Harriet Martineau put it, 'the only alternative is being shut up like wild beasts in a cage, or let loose to ravage society like escaped animals'.[3] Mary's own opinion was exactly the opposite. 'It does not appear to me that the women depicted are different in their natures from women who may be met with at large in the world.' Their wild loves and hates, their fantasies and feminine vanities were those she knew in the Red Lodge girls, but 'excited to a frightful intensity' by harsh treatment and an unnatural life. Her conclusion was that 'the present mode of treatment of women in our convict prisons is a complete failure . . . the system adopted must be completely wrong, and can never do what is intended, *reform* female convicts'.[4]

Moreover, children were still being sentenced to prison, in spite of the laws consolidated by the new Reformatory and Industrial Schools Act of 1861. 'We hoped', wrote Mary Carpenter, 'we had gained the cause of the children when the Act was passed, and that henceforth our police courts and gaols would no longer be frequented by children.' By law a young offender 'can be handed over to parental correction, or cautioned and discharged, if his case does not appear a serious one'. Children homeless on the streets could go to industrial school, more serious offenders to reformatory training. 'Notwithstanding all this', concluded Mary Carpenter, 'we find young delinquents still sent to prison. We still find that when they have completed the curriculum of crime thus begun, they help to fill our convict prisons.'[5]

At the Social Science Association meeting in London, in the summer of 1862. Mary read a paper, 'On the Essential Principles of the Reformatory Movement', before a large audience, which included Sydney Turner himself and Sir Joshua Jebb, the Director of Convict Prisons, who had already

---

[3] *Edinburgh Review*, October 1865, 'Life in the Criminal Classes'.
[4] Carpenter, M. *On the Treatment of Female Convicts*, pamphlet.
[5] *Reformatory and Refuge Journal*. November and December 1864. 'On the Non-Imprisonment of Children'.

14. *Mary Carpenter (second from left) with Kitty at Red Lodge; after her serious illness she looked shrunken beside her girls*

15. *These young children were photographed eating and sleeping in a street corner in 1862*

16. *A woman convict at Millbank wears canvas dress, as a punishment for tearing her clothes*

crossed swords with her on the subject of Parkhurst Boys' Prison.[6] Discussion after the paper centred on the problem of the 'hard cases', so difficult to contain in a school. Mary was asked whether they were sent from school back to prison? She replied she had only once done so, in the case of the girls sent to Bristol Bridewell in 1857, and had regretted it. Another speaker asked, casually, whether for problem cases 'a portion of Parkhurst Prison would not be inappropriate'? To this Joshua Jebb replied there could be no difficulty in taking boys into it. 'If the proposal was made he would give it his support.'

Mary Carpenter sprang up, and the startled audience heard her reply in a passionate outburst. In one of her states of 'high moral excitement', she was an alarming sight; her gaunt frame shook, her large, usually mild eyes showed white in her worn face, her speech was broken by gasps as the damaged heart struggled to pump air to the labouring lungs. Afterwards she would collapse in total exhaustion, but for the moment nothing could stop the torrent of words. She said stricter confinement might be needed, 'but this should *not* be a convict prison. . . . She had pointed out what she considered to be radical errors in Parkhurst Prison as a reformatory institution, and she had never met with any youths who had come out from thence reformed.' As an example she told the story of Michael Lynch, now serving fourteen years for house-breaking, and concluded she would not send anyone to Parkhurst.[7]

Mary Carpenter had been seriously criticized both by Turner and Jebb. Her puritan upbringing would not allow her to admit ordinary human resentment by so much as a syllable, yet encouraged her to feel part of a persecuted minority. It is likely she felt for them both that 'intense theological antipathy', which Martineau noticed the Carpenters reserved for anyone who ventured to disagree with them on a question of principle. It burnt so brightly in Mary at this moment that she felt she must expose the entire prison system in a book. 'I perceived that it was necessary for me to write *Our Convicts*,' she explained. 'I saw that the public ought to know certain things, which those who *could* tell them, *would* not.[8] She set to work on a book, which would review the entire prison system. The Penal Servitude Acts of 1853 and 1857 attempted to create a workable substitute for transportation, in the system known as progressive stages. The first stage, of solitary confinement, had to be shortened and elaborate precautions taken to prevent the suicide of prisoners under its stress. The second stage was labour in association on public works at Portland Bill or in the dockyards at Chatham and Portsmouth. The third stage was conditional release for the convict on ticket-of-leave.[9]

During the 1850s, resentment began to grow against criminals, convicts and discharged prisoners as a burden to society. In face of much criticism,

[6] See p. 118 above.
[7] *Proceedings of the National Association for the Promotion of Social Science*, 1862, 517–21.
[8] Huntington Library, Carpenter Letters, CB 67–8: 1870–89.
[9] Adderley, C. *A Century of Experiment with Secondary Punishments*, 1863.

M C—G

Jebb argued that the prisoners must be humanely treated. 'Many a man,' he wrote, 'had been subdued and cordially rendered willing obedience under just and considerate treatment, who would have been brutalized by the reverse. . . . The final reformation of discharged convicts depends on their being treated with confidence.' He was jeered at by leader-writers as the 'Convict's Friend'. With heavy jocularity, the *Examiner* proposed a Fat Convict show, like the Fat Cattle show, to exhibit the results of 'generous jail diet, a tranquil confinement, nothing to make them sulky or cross, but all according to Jebb'.[10] From about 1857 agitation built up against the prison administration, as public opinion made one of its familiar swings from reform to repression.

For every Victorian ill there was a Victorian panacea, and the 'Convict Question' was no exception. Mary Carpenter had been present at the first meeting of the Reformatory and Refuge Union at Bristol in 1856, under the patronage of Lord Shaftesbury. She was not at ease in the prevailing tone of the Union, a 'come to Jesus' Evangelism; but she was intensely struck by one paper. The speaker was the Inspector of Irish Reformatories and newly appointed Director of Irish Convict Prisons, Captain Walter Crofton. He claimed to have found his convicts 'morally and physically prostrate in every way', and yet to have proved that 'a very large percentage of criminals can by a system of *Reformatory Training* introduced towards the termination of their sentences, be restored to the society they have outraged as useful and industrious members.'[11] In 1857, Matthew Davenport Hill visited the Irish prisons and returned to read a paper to the Social Science Association, praising their 'sound reformatory principles' to the skies. So reformed were the Irish convicts, in his opinion, that even their pocket money 'was rarely wasted on tobacco'. Hill, who was now over 65, had for Mary an almost paternal authority. She accepted his judgment that Crofton had practically solved the problem which had so long perplexed government and the legislature: *What shall we do with our convicts?*

'The Reports of the Irish Convict Prisons', she wrote to Frances Power Cobbe, 'I always *devour*, as many people do the last new novel.' She added, with an archness most unusual in her, 'I am jealous that Captain C. has not yet sent me one, and I shall not condescend to read it out of any copy but my own. I discovered his spirit in the first report before I knew of his existence, and wondered among prison directors to meet with such *true reformatory spirit*. . . . I adopt the same principles that he does with my girls and with the Kingswood boys, mutatis mutandis.'[12]

Before long Mary was able to see the vaunted Irish prisons for herself, when in August 1862 the Social Science Association held its annual conference in Dublin, and prison-visiting provided a series of pleasure-trips dear to the members' sober hearts.[13] They began with a lecture, in which Captain Crofton explained how his 'novel convict system' made ticket-of-leave men fit to be

[10] *The Examiner*, 22nd November 1862.
[11] *Life and Work*, 225.
[12] Huntington Library, Carpenter letters, 1857–8: CB 70–89.
[13] *Once a Week* throughout December 1861 and 7th June 1862: reprinted in *Our Convicts*, II.

'absorbed into the population as honest labourers'. A discharged convict—the figure of Uriah Heep, the model prisoner, sidles irresistibly to mind—offered thanks for the 'kindly supervision of the constabulary'. Duly edified, the members of the Association set out in carriages to visit Mountjoy, the long galleries, tier above tier, the deep, unbroken silence in which prisoners endured their first nine months of solitary confinement, each 'made aware that his future condition will entirely depend on his conduct day by day, of which careful records are kept'.

Other expeditions were to the 'Intermediate establishments between prison and the world', where convict artisans followed their trades in open work-shops, and to Captain Crofton's show-piece at Lusk Common. Here, a hundred last-stage prisoners, housed in corrugated iron army huts, worked in field parties, with minimal supervision, on land-drainage. 'They wore no prison uniform, but the ordinary peasant dress and no turnkey was watching them,' wrote Mary Carpenter enthusiastically . . . 'the *moral control* appeared to us astonishing, which should be more powerful than bolts and bars.' Some of the English visitors believed the convicts 'so zealous that they will pursue their toil after the regular hour'.[14] Mary was of course particularly anxious to see the seven hundred women who were released from their cells to be taught for an hour each day at Mountjoy; she watched 'an elderly woman in spectacles spelling out a child's reader' for the first time in her life. Out of school, the women were kept busy with cooking, cleaning, laundry, knitting and sewing, new skills to the majority. Mary watched a stalwart manslaughteress vigorously turning a mangle. The last visit was to the voluntary refuge for last-stage women convicts, run by the Irish Sisters of Mercy at Goldenbridge. She was delighted to see women working in-dependently in the vegetable garden, or among the pigs and poultry; 'the care of animals is generally beneficial, and nature always so'. The women talked to their visitors with winning Irish charm, skilled from long experience in pleasing the Ascendancy. The nuns found work or arranged emigration for every discharged woman.[15]

Mary Carpenter was convinced, with the true doctrinaire enthusiasm of the nineteenth-century reformer, that 'the Crofton system' was founded on 'universal conditions of human nature' which 'if proved true in one place may be readily adapted to another, by men who, like Captain Crofton, com-prehend them, and possess the personal qualities to carry them out'.[16]

It must be said in her defence that she was far from alone in this naïve optimism. Nothing could show more starkly the abyss separating rich and poor than the complacency of this party of well-fed, normally well-informed people about how the Irish actually lived since the great famine. They were told how, behind the elegant façades, half the population of Dublin lived one family to a room, lice, lodgers and all.[17] Yet they seemed not to see the

[14] *Cornhill Magazine*, April 1861, 'The Irish Convict System' unsigned, but by Thornton Hunt.

[15] Carpenter, M. *Our Convicts*, II, 277.   [16] *Ibid.*, 52.

[17] Best, G. *Mid-Victorian Britain*, 184 (7); see *The Times* correspondence August–December 1862, for English views of the Irish system.

poverty which destroyed the peasantry, body and soul. Regular meals, work, above all the hope of emigrating and earning, might save the croft and the few loved acres of bog and turf; in extreme cases it might save the lives of an entire family. 'Some people think it surprising', wrote an anonymous Irish chaplain drily, 'that the prisoners at Lusk do not run away. I should be more surprised if they did.'[18]

Mary succeeded in placing her accounts of this expedition with *Once A Week*. 'I send by the post', she wrote to the editor on 19th April 1862, 'the concluding number of my "Visits to the Irish Convict Prisons". I have thought it out of keeping with the paper to enter into criticisms or comparisons with the English System. Conclusions will naturally follow to anyone who reads them thoughtfully.' Crofton was delighted with the articles, which he called 'the most graphic and faithful account of the system'. Well he might, for they amounted to free advertisement for his claims. After the corrosive correspondence with Sir Joshua, the mortifying scenes with Mr Turner, such flattery, not for herself, which she would have despised, but for her work, was balm to Mary Carpenter. All through 1862 a press campaign built up on the subject of convicts and ticket-of-leave men. At the Social Science Conference in the summer, thirty papers were read on the subject and a special evening meeting at Burlington House overflowed with anxious discussion. Mary Carpenter's clash on child imprisonment was only one of many. Crofton and Jebb each read papers, the latter denying any difference between English and Irish prisons. 'The least investigation', he said, 'will show that the two systems are identical. In England freedom is attained stage by stage up to the ticket-of-leave. . . . The gratuitous assumption that the discipline is conducted on erroneous principles and has been a failure has cruelly added to the difficulties of discharged prisoners in obtaining employment.'[19] It is impossible not to feel the greatest sympathy with Jebb, a public servant, exposed to an irresponsible press campaign. The whole agitation about the so-called 'English and Irish Systems' now appears factitious, for the controversy over convicts was about to enter a new phase.

The dark autumn nights of 1862 brought the famous outbreak of garotting in the streets of London; teams of thieves half-throttled pedestrians, while emptying their pockets. The hysterical outcry which followed revealed the deep sense of insecurity in the heart of Victorian England. For this society, outwardly complacent and secure, lived in dread of tramps and tinkers, gypsies and poachers, beggars and spongers, pick-pockets, horse-thieves and burglars; their shadows darken the pages of Dickens with a sombre intensity of fear. To these was added a new menace, the ticket-of-leave man, turned garotter, hideous, vicious, cruel, lurking, noose in hand, in the dark alleys, ready to throttle his prey. Blame fell on the ticket-of-leave system. Only a solitary realist pointed out that 'to be garotted by a man who has

[18] Scrutator—*Irish Fallacies and English Facts*, pamphlet.
[19] *Proceedings of the National Association for the Promotion of Social Science*, 1862, 402–14. The Webbs in *English Prisons under Local Government*, considered Jebb the originator of progressive stages both in England and Ireland.

served his term is quite as unpleasant as to be garotted by a ticket-of-leave man'.[20]

The theatre cashed in with Tom Taylor's immensely successful melodrama, *The Ticket-of-Leave Man*.[21] Honest Bob the hero, so innocent that he mistakes Hawkshaw the Great Detective for a garotter, is wrongfully convicted. After he comes out of Portland on ticket of leave, 'Everywhere that dreadful word jail-bird seems to be breathed in the air about me—sometimes in a letter, sometimes in a hint, sometimes a copy of the newspaper with my trial, and then it's the same story: "Sorry to part with me—no complaint to make—but can't keep a ticket-of-leave man." ' Bob foils a gang-raid on his employer's safe and leaves the stage creditably littered with 'bleeding villains'. This was a sympathetic view, but public opinion in general had now swung violently over to deterrence and reaction. In response to clamorous demand, the Garotters Act was rushed through to re-introduce the penalty of flogging, and a Select Committee of Inquiry under Lord Carnarvon was set up to examine the workings of the Penal Servitude Acts. In planning a book on *Our Convicts*, Mary Carpenter was assured of public interest and a wide readership; but, as so often, she seems not to have realized how far the general public was from sharing her beliefs.

She summoned a meeting at Red Lodge and formed a Bristol Association for the Amendment of Convict Discipline. On 22nd December Sir Walter Crofton came to Bristol as her guest to address this body. He had resigned on grounds of overwork, and had been knighted by the Lord Lieutenant of Ireland. He spoke at the Philosophic Institution, once the scene of Lant Carpenter's triumphs, and for Mary it was an emotional occasion; she had been dreaming of her father, with 'a grateful, joyful feeling' that his spirit supported her in this new work of reform. In a vote of thanks she explained Sir Walter's resignation because his physical strength could no longer bear up. 'He must rest for a season, but let us hope our Government will appreciate the value of the work he has done and place him where he may most completely develop on a large scale the principle established in the Irish Convict Prisons.' 'Here', wrote one caustic commentator, tracing the stages by which simple Captain Crofton had become Sir Walter, 'we have the excellent Miss Carpenter letting the cat out of the bag!'[22]

Mary began 1863 with a spate of correspondence to collect materials for her new book. Her birthday found her happy and confident, full of 'grateful and joyful feelings' about work old and new. From this height of enthusiasm she fell with a sickening plunge into the troubles at Kingswood. Accusations of cruelty to the boys especially horrified and grieved her, when she remembered how confidently she had condemned prisons and praised reformatories only the previous year. She told her nephew Estlin how suddenly 'all the

[20] T. B. L. Baker, W. F. Clifton, W. L. Clay, the Editor of *The Times* and others, *Pamphlets on the Convict System*, 1861–3. Cambridge University Library.

[21] Tom Taylor (1817–80) was editor of *Punch* and for some years Professor of English at London University.

[22] Scrutator, *Irish Fallacies and English Facts*. The lecture was published by Archer, Mary Carpenter's own Bristol bookseller.

memories of the past turned to gloom'. 'Her physical frame', he wrote, 'lacked the power to sustain the violent conflicts that went on within' and for two months, July and August 1863, she was seriously ill.[23] Later she admitted that she lost heart for writing. 'I meant to write it at once,' she told Frances Power Cobbe, 'but then was hindered by the Kingswood troubles and my consequent illness.' While she was still ill, Joshua Jebb collapsed one morning when travelling on top of a horse-omnibus to his office in Whitehall; he was carried into a chemist's shop at Charing Cross, but died within a few minutes. For the last two years of his life he had been under persistent public attack as 'author of the ticket-of-leave scheme', and friends protested that 'his merits as a prison reformer had been clouded by error and misrepresentation'.[24] His administration was certainly much more humane than that which followed.

The agitation in favour of the so-called 'Irish System' continued. Both William and Russell Carpenter wrote pressingly to James Martineau, inviting him to speak or write, but Martineau, now Professor of Philosophy at University Hall, tactfully refused on grounds of overwork. He even visited Bristol without calling on Mary, one of his oldest friends.[25] He was certainly not unsympathetic to her 'concerns', but his balanced, philosophical mind was troubled by the Carpenter intolerance of any opinion but their own. His gentle but marked withdrawal—letters once addressed to 'my dear Russell' now began 'my dear Sir'—showed how thoughtful people might be alienated by over-zealous campaigning, even from good causes. Mary, forced by her damaged heart to rest, played no further public part in the controversy; it would take all her strength to write *Our Convicts*.

During her convalescence, she indulged a lifelong passion for newsprint and read the papers avidly. In politics, she loved liberty, with single-hearted, simple-minded passion. Garibaldi was her hero; sending off a box of comforts for his troops, she 'felt proud to belong to the same century' as the Liberator. When he passed through Bristol she was almost trampled underfoot in the crowd which greeted him. The American Civil War was a bewilderment and a grief.[26] She saw each month of civil war increasing the hatred between North and South, 'strengthening the worst passions in both', and felt prejudices burn deep into Southern hearts by the bitterness of defeat. When the war was over at last, she sent an annual subscription of five pounds towards teachers for negro freed-men and women, and 'wished it could have been more. The work is not done as long as the equal rights of man, irrespective of colour, are not acknowledged and protected.'[27] To England, the American Civil War brought 'cotton famine', with distress and unemployment in Lancashire, to which charity subscribed an unprecedented million pounds. Yet this was temporary relief. 'I believe the only thing anyone can do', wrote Mary to her brother Philip in Canada, 'is to encourage emigration.' To clothe Lancashire emigrants the Red Lodge girls knitted and sewed, while the

23 *Life and Work*, 234.
24 *The Times*, 27th and 29th July 1863.
25 Manchester College, Oxford, Library, A3 Box B.
26 Boston Public Library, MS a2, Vol. 34, p. 94.
27 *Life and Work*, 243.

ragged school children collected a shilling, all in farthings. Anna seized the chance to distract Mary, who was still very weak, from her obsessional work. She suggested painting to raise money; the two sisters, grey-haired now, took out their drawing boards, and sat side by side, as in distant girlhood, sketching scenes from memory, and spending 'happy hours among woods, lakes and mountains'.[28]

Mary could not be distracted from her work for very long. Soon she was reading again, this time with scissors and gum on the desk beside her, pasting up the extracts which were to swell *Our Convicts* to two volumes. As a preliminary, she drafted an article for *The Reformatory and Refuge Journal*, on 'The Non-Imprisonment of Children'. Even in the local papers, reading the Bristol Police Court news, she found continual prison sentences on 'urchin thieves', sometimes quite young children, used to begging and tumbling in the streets, or scavenging and pilfering on the quays. All the offences were trivial. 'The vagaries of boys in the upper classes are *never* looked on with such a serious eye,' wrote Mary indignantly, pointing out that these diminutive gaol-birds might never be able to get an honest job again. Everything showed, she added, 'how completely neglected these poor boys had been, how impossible it was for them to lead anything but a life of crime, and how useless it was to keep sending them to prison time after time.'[29] Yet they were sent, to be sexually seduced and taught to steal by older prisoners, until at last, their criminal education complete, they graduated to convict prisons. 'As to reformation,' wrote an ex-convict in the same year, 'in a system where the worst characters are brought into close association, it is preposterous.'[30] For girls the danger was even worse. Emma G., a little servant girl of 13 in Bristol, faced a future almost irrevocably blighted, when her stepmother found some of her employers' clothes hidden under her mattress at home and reported her to the police. A sentence of four years' penal servitude 'suddenly transformed a young girl into a convict'. Mary led the petition to the Home Secretary, which won Emma a conditional pardon and a transfer to reformatory school.

The winter of 1863–4 passed in collating material for *Our Convicts* from press-cuttings, reports of the Inspectors of Prisons, the evidence before the Select Committe on penal servitude, and lengthy correspondence with authorities in Europe and America. Like *Juvenile Delinquents* the book was essentially a compilation of scattered writings, and as such served a useful purpose at the time. 'The volumes are everything that could be asked,' wrote a reviewer in the progressive *Westminster Review*. 'There is no branch of the great subject neglected: the information on each is comprehensive, trustworthy and complete.'[31] It would be truer to say, with hindsight, that nineteenth-century writing on crime is usually tendentious, and that, for long passages, *Our Convicts* is no exception.

[28] *Ibid.*, 234.
[29] *Reformatory and Refuge Journal*, November and December, 1864.
[30] *Cornhill Magazine*, December 1864, 'A Convict's View of Prison Discipline'.
[31] *Westminster Review*, N.S. No. 27, 581.

The chapters contrasting the failures of English prisons with the transcendent merits of the 'Irish or Crofton System' show many signs of the press controversy which gave the book its birth. Without perhaps being able to understand what were the faults in the Convict Prisons, the public knew they must be bad because the results were bad and they feared to trust anyone who had been in them.[32] Police supervision of convicts on conditional release, practised everywhere on the continent, was 'so little consonant with the tone of feeling in our country' that 'numbers of person out on license are never identified; they are not recognized when they again commit crimes . . . This leads to the so-called immunity of habitual criminals.'[33] English prisons, concluded Mary Carpenter, were 'a great failure, doing enormous harm to the community'. The Irish prisons, by contrast, were presented as a 'moral triumph' by judiciously selected quotations from Crofton's own reports, M. D. Hill's paper to the Social Science Association, Thornton Hunt's description in the *Cornhill* and Mary's series of articles in *Once a Week*. By much diligent letter-writing, Mary secured praise for the Irish 'libération préparatoire' from MM. de Marsagny and de Pontes in France, M. van der Brugghen in the Low Countries, Professor Mittermaier of Heidelberg, and the impressive Baron von Holzendorff, Professor of Criminal Law at Berlin.[34]

When the purely controversial chapters of *Our Convicts* have been dismissed, much remains in the book which is deeply thought and felt, and still surprisingly to the point. Mary Carpenter's starting point was her title *Our Convicts*. Contemporaries were convinced that criminals formed a separate class, estranged from all the rest of society;[35] she herself had called them 'the dangerous class'. Yet in twenty years' work she had come to know many criminal families as individuals. From experience, as well as religious conviction, she knew that convicts in the quarries or the oakum-shed were 'still men and women, still our fellow citizens. How do men and women arrive at such a depth of wretchedness, and how far is society, directly or indirectly, to blame in the matter?'[36]

Much of the book is an attempt to answer this question; from scattered material Mary Carpenter put together what a reviewer called 'the entire natural history of the lawless classes'. She started with convicts as she knew them best, in childhood. Their physical condition was always bad; they were out begging and thieving in all weathers, barefoot and nearly naked, dirty and wild. They came home at night to be chased away from the fire and knocked into a corner of the crowded room, to sleep on old newspapers or straw. A boy in the ragged school, with close-cropped prison hair 'felt he was an outcast and at war with society, the sport of circumstances over which he had no control'. The quickest escape for the growing boy is, momentarily, through drink, for 'there are the gin shops, and the sales of whisky and gin on the sly, the treating out of black bottles in cellars and garrets and the solitary

[32] Carpenter, M. *Our Convicts*, I, 174.
[33] *Ibid.*, 190–1.					[34] *Ibid.*, II, 123–7.
[35] Tobias, J. J. *Crime and Industrial Society in the Nineteenth Century*, 59.
[36] Carpenter, M. *Our Convicts*, I, 44.

drinking in lodgings'. Girls instinctively turn to the passion of love, for criminal women, like any others, have lovers and children. A street girl loves 'the brutal lad, who to her has a giant's strength; she knows days of abject obedience, nights of terror for his safety, of doubt and jealousy, of wild hate alternating with her love'. The young people 'desire and greedily devour such good things as are within their range, but their pleasures are spoiled by the gnawing, unrelenting fear of the police and of prison. Nothing can make up for the loss of the freedom of the streets.'[37]

Such boys and girls are likely to be sent to prison where 'a child in the higher walks of life is sheltered from the law'. This was Mary Carpenter's opportunity to argue her case against child imprisonment as 'the surest way to raise for our country a large body of hardened convicts. Girls are even more vulnerable than their brothers to criminal exploitation.'[38] She quoted Joshua Jebb's view of his convicts: few of them have anything to lose—any change must be for the better. They are past being frightened into good behaviour, once they have grown up in alienation from society. 'No amount of punishment as such will ever produce a change of heart.' Yet, looking back over their lives, the tragedy is that 'young persons become hardened in guilt *through causes over which they have no control and for which society is directly responsible*'.[39]

A long chapter traces the history of the girls who grow up to become female convicts, not a third of the prison population in the 1860s, but a problem to the authorities out of all proportion to their numbers. 'No one understands them,' observed Harriet Martineau, 'neither judge nor jury, chaplain nor matron, neither doctor nor warder, can enter into the mind and feeling of a being who seems to be made up of the idiot and the intriguer, the infant and the devil, the ferocious animal and the idolator.'[40] The general opinion was that criminal women formed 'a pariah class, even among the poorest of the poor'. A writer described their lying, their dram-drinking, their dirt: 'slovenly, wretched-looking creatures that lounge or squat at the entrance of courts, with dirty faces, hair uncombed and half-exposed bosom'.[41] As late as the 1890s, Lombroso was still to consider criminal women more hopelessly degenerate than the males. Yet to Mary Carpenter, these legendary viragos, dishevelled and screaming, were '*Woman*, no more nor less.' She recognized in the reports of prison inspectors, the neglected girls she had known for many years as a teacher in ragged school and reformatory, impulsive, uncontrolled, rebellious, unawakened in mind, given to romancing, affectionate and jealous, sullen and resentful under injustice, easily bored, quick to anger. The fearful scenes which so shocked the readers of *Female Life in Prison* were 'the very violences and wild acts *provoked* by unwise management'. In support of this, she had only to point to the most recent figures available.

[37] *Edinburgh Review*, October 1865: Harriet Martineau reviewing *Our Convicts*.
[38] Carpenter, M. *Our Convicts*, I, 57–8.
[39] *Ibid.*, 80.
[40] *Edinburgh Review*, October 1865. Harriet Martineau reviewing *Our Convicts*.
[41] *Cornhill Magazine*, August 1866, 'Criminal Women'.

At Millbank in 1863, among 383 female convicts, six were removed to lunatic asylums and twenty died.[42]

Mary Carpenter considered the condition of these women 'an unmistakable sign of extraordinary mismanagement, a dreadful void in nature, produced by want of interesting occupation or natural scope for the affections'.[43] She believed they were denied everything which had proved helpful to delinquent girls of the same background and sometimes the same age. There was no chance of a stable environment, of steady discipline, when prison matrons had to work alternate shifts of twelve and fifteen hours. No wonder chaplain and medical officer reported 'they look very worn out at times'. Theirs was demanding work. 'We must seek for officials who are not mere routinists and discipline officers, but who will at the same time act in sympathy with the prisoners while carrying out the strict requirements of duty.'[44] Staffing, pay and conditions of work needed improving, as a first step. Next the prisoners needed useful work, 'to satisfy mind and body and to let them feel they have achieved something. . . . Unless actively employed they become restless and desponding and brood over the wretchedness their crimes have entailed on husbands and children.' Hysterical women should be placed under medical treatment; merely to lock them up was dangerous, since separate confinement 'augments cases of insanity and suicide'. As well as active work, the women need something to develop the mind. It needs great skill and patience to teach an adult to read, for what is pleasant to a child of 6 is extremely difficult and unpleasant to a girl of 16; yet it is worth the effort, for reading gives new interests and relief to the feelings. This leads to Mary's last point: 'the *Affections*—in a woman they never can be utterly lost'. No external force will change her nature, but personal influence may, especially if volunteers can be found to work with individuals or small groups. She admitted that all this would be difficult to achieve in a convict prison, but what was the alternative? '*No* labour or expense is too great to reform criminal women; anything costs less than the harm they do to society.'[45]

As it happens, there is independent evidence that these suggestions made good sense. An anonymous barrister visited the Convict Lunatic Asylum at Fisherton near Salisbury, for all classes of prisoners, said to have 'gone mad in solitary confinement'. The Superintendent Dr Lush pointed out women patients, who had been violent when admitted, now knitting quietly or walking among the trees and flowers in the grounds. 'I have not a pair of handcuffs or a lock-up cell or any instrument of punishment in the whole place,' he said. The only punishment ever used or needed was exclusion from the weekly dances, at which a band of stalwart male nurses thumped out waltzes and cotillions, while patients of both sexes danced with grave demeanour, 'like a well-regulated dancing academy'.[46]

The book ends with a shrewd criticism of society, as Mary Carpenter had seen it in her work. 'The "respectable classes" have rejoiced that they are

[42] Carpenter, M. *Our Convicts*, II, 239.   [43] *Ibid.*, 238.
[44] *Ibid.*, I, 273.   [45] *Ibid.*, II, 252.
[46] *Cornhill Magazine*, August 1866, 'A Convict Lunatic Asylum'.

not as other men are, thieves, pickpockets, burglars, convicts.' They 'dwell in intellectual refinement, justified in their contempt and repugnance'.[47] Meanwhile there are places where children 'stare at you in astonishment, if you speak a kind word to them in the streets'. Respectable society does not want to search for the roots of crime, or to know 'the meaning which is really hidden under the simple word *ignorance*. Whole districts remain in a state of isolated barbarism . . . nearly untouched by any of the institutions of our country, except the workhouse, the police force and the gaol . . . in ignorance of all that constitutes civilized society.' The House of Lords Committee on Juvenile Offenders had resolved as long ago as 1847 to educate the children of this class, but 'no steps were taken by the Government or ever have been taken since to carry out the intention of that resolution'.[48]

Voluntary movements had struggled to reach the lower depths of society, where the roots of crime grew. Temperance and rescue work have an old-fashioned sound now, but drink and prostitution were killers in the slums. Mary was able to quote the figures of Liverpool convictions in 1864; 2316 for prostitutes, of whom 27 were under 16 years old, and 14,000 for being drunk and disorderly. Reformatory and industrial school attempted to 'remove a child who was in danger of becoming criminal, before he has actually joined the ranks of crime'. . . . Ragged schools 'sought out the very lowest and most neglected children they could find' and tried to civilize them, 'to let them know in practise that they were not regarded as the offscourings of the earth, the refuse of society. If *any* class of the population is to be helped . . . this class should receive, for the welfare of society, as well as for the individual'. The mere giving of money was not enough. Everyone must ask himself, 'What shall *we*—shall *I*—do?' For the fact could not be shrugged off; the prevention of crime rests to a great extent with the community.[49]

Our Convicts was published by Longmans Green, the first of Mary Carpenter's books to appear with a firm of national reputation. The reviews were excellent, and Mary was so delighted by Harriet Martineau's long article in the *Edinburgh Review* that she sent two hundred copies of the review to Boston to be distributed in the United States. She gave a copy of the book to Bishop Colenso who gallantly responded with 'a little volume of my own on the Pentateuch'. 'I do not mind about the Creation being cut up,' Mary assured Philip, 'the light he throws helps one out of difficulties and contradictions which I have felt as well as the Zulus!'[50]

Our Convicts continued to sell so well that it provided for Rosanna's education and allowed Mary, after a lifetime of rigid economy, to enjoy the travel for which she had always longed in secret. Meanwhile a new Prison Act was before the House of Commons. The Select Committee, sadly to Mary Carpenter but agreeably to the general public, 'did not consider that the

[47] Carpenter, M. *Our Convicts*, II, 376–7.
[48] *Ibid.*, 353.   [49] *Ibid.*, 356–9.
[50] *Life and Work*, 243. Bishop Colenso of Natal was excommunicated by the Archbishop, but upheld by the Privy Council for a series of treatises on the Pentateuch, which attempted to answer the 'puzzling questions' put to him by the Zulus.

moral reformation of the offender holds the primary place in prison discipline'. Instead it recommended deterrence by 'hard labour, hard fare, hard bed'. It criticized the huge disparities in discipline, food and labour among the traditional county and borough gaols financed by local rates as allowing 'inequality, uncertainty and inefficiency of punishment'.[51] Punishment was reassuringly certain under the Prison Act of 1865, which created a system so savagely deterrent that it is said to have become legendary even in Russia. Lessons in the prison school, productive work in workshops, even water-closets in the cells, were abolished. Restricted diet was prescribed to subdue 'the low animal natures of too many of the criminal class'. The diet of convicts on public works at Chatham we are told, was 'so deficient in fats that prisoners ate candle-ends, live frogs and worms captured at work, even licked the railway grease from the trucks which carried them, chained in gangs, to their work on the fortifications'.[52] There is no evidence that the treatment of women convicts improved. The Superintendent of the Refuge for last-stage women at Winchester, giving evidence before a Committee of Inquiry spoke of damage to the women's health from hobbles, dark cells and bread and water. Mary Carpenter made a special plea for the removal of the death penalty from cases of infanticide, then a very common offence. Dr Lankester, Coroner for Middlesex, told the Social Science Association in 1868 that he had seen five hundred infants dead in suspicious circumstances. Often the death arose from an attempt to hide an illegitimate birth, but sometimes it was a crude method of family limitation; one young woman in Brixton Prison confessed to having killed five new-born children.[53]

The Prison Act did not, as Mary Carpenter had hoped, prohibit the imprisonment of juveniles, though Sir Joshua Jebb's successors did not share his interest in Parkhurst and closed the boys' prison. Mary had argued passionately for its closing. She believed it would mark the beginning of the end of child imprisonment in general. If so, it was a very slow beginning. She had failed to allow for the hardening of public opinion against every class of offender. Gradually she was forced to see 'experience shows that without an Act to prevent the imprisonment of children under fourteen', magistrates would continue to sentence them to prison as an easy way out. In his 1878 report, the Chaplain of Clerkenwell protested that children of 6 and 7 had been remanded to his prison. Mary Carpenter might suggest the child should be 'handed over, *as would be the case in the higher classes*, to parental chastisement'.[54] Public opinion remained indifferent or hostile. Dickens, always a sensitive barometer, wrote of the young rough, 'I would have his back scarified often and deep;' for boys who threw stones at passing trains he suggested 'one's own riding whip and walking stick, the police to which I myself appeal on these occasions.' By his own account Dickens, creator of Poor Jo and Nancy, gave a girl of 17 in charge for swearing in the streets. 'The Magistrate

---

[51] Webb, B. and S. *English Prisons under Local Government.*
[52] Playfair, G. *The Punitive Obsession,* 144–6.
[53] *Reformatory and Refuge Journal,* December 1869.
[54] *Proceedings of the National Association for the Promotion of Social Science,* 1866.

asked, "Do you really want this girl to be sent to prison?" To which I grimly answered, "If I didn't, why should I take the trouble to come here?" '[55]

In this climate of opinion, it was useless for Mary Carpenter to argue. She failed to secure an act forbiding child imprisonment; she even failed to get preliminary imprisonment reduced from fourteen to seven days. She could only record her conviction that 'the passing of such an Act would place children in their true position, as those who are to be cared for, protected and controlled'. Imprisonment as preliminary to a reformatory was finally abolished in 1899. Young people under 17 were in general only excluded from prison by the Children and Young Persons Act of 1933. Some are still being sent to prison or remand.

In writing *Our Convicts*, Mary Carpenter had one last urgent point to make, which might easily pass unnoticed now. She proposed 'removing that great blot on our criminal legislature, the punishment of death. It is a hideous remnant of our antiquated draconic code "an eye for an eye and a tooth for a tooth", from which our Saviour came to set us free.' The time, she believed, could not be long, for 'the public mind is beginning to revolt against it . . . all the pleas on which capital punishment has been defended are gradually dropping away'.[56] Belief in human goodness was an essential part of Mary Carpenter's religion, and it was an article of faith with her never to despair of improvement. It is perhaps as well, though, that she did not know this reform would take a hundred years.

[55] Dickens, C. *The Uncommercial Traveller*, XXX, added in 1865.
[56] Carpenter, M. *Our Convicts*, II, 302.

13
INDIA'S DAUGHTERS
1866-1870

Through all the years of Mary Carpenter's crowded combative public life the body of Rajah Ram Mohun Roy had lain quiet in the grave under the elm trees at Stapleton Grove. Thirty years had passed since his death, and the world seemed to have forgotten him, but she did not. Sometimes she took out the atlas and traced the familiar outlines of India in a dream, as long ago in girlhood; 'my vision of India', she called it.[1] With the self-discipline of a lifetime she turned her mind to work near at hand; yet still she followed Indian affairs in the newspapers.

These decades saw the golden autumn of the East India Company, after two hundred years of informal, often friendly, relations between the British 'factories' and their princely Indian clients. Slowly clouds of mistrust darkened between the two races. Conscientious British administrators reformed the age-old splendours and corruptions of royal courts, leaving resentment in their wake. Restless Western inventions, steamships, the railway, the telegraph, disturbed the timeless contemplation of Hinduism, while army service, mixing men from all walks of life, threatened sacred traditions of caste. Christian missionaries and their converts were everywhere despised and disliked. In 1857 the great tropical storm of the Mutiny swept away the old relationship between India and Britain for ever.

By the Government of India Act of 1858, the Crown took direct government of the Company's possessions. The British Raj was now responsible for the two great religious communities, Hindu and Moslem, for other cults, Buddhists, Parsees, Sikhs, Jains, for the fifteen major languages and more than seven hundred dialects, for the crowded bazaars and sun-stricken villages of India. A new society grew up, of British officials isolated in offices and clubs, understanding nothing of Indian home life. Links with Britain were closer; with steamships, the overland route, and the arrival of the dreaded mem-sahib, few Englishmen still regarded India as home in itself. Yet they were conscientious, and slowly they laid the foundations of a modern state: roads, railways, irrigation channels, cotton mills which boomed when the Civil War paralysed American competition, schools, hospitals, mail and telegraph services. An Act of Parliament in 1861 opened the Indian Civil Service to all subjects of the Queen, including those who were Indian-born.[2] By ones and twos the first Indian Civil Service candidates appeared for their special two-years' course at British universities. In this cold, grey, unfriendly

[1] Carpenter, M. *Six Months in India*, I, 176-7.
[2] Majumdar, R. C., Rayachaudhari, H., Datta, K. *An Advanced History of India*, 876.

land, one place was home to them, the grave of their great countryman, Ram Roy. One by one, from 1861, they made the pilgrimage to Bristol.

Among the first was a Christian convert, who attended services at Lewin's Mead Meeting. Mary Carpenter was deeply moved by the sight of the devout young Brahmin, 'among the white-headed ministers and fathers of our church. . . . His visit here has been a sort of romance to me,' she confessed to Lucy Sanford. 'I find that all my old feelings and enthusiasms are as fresh as ever, only lying dormant or bottled up, as in the Arabian Tales, waiting to come forth.' The fine, dark face reminded her of the long-dead Rajah, 'and if I had had time', she said, 'I should have melted to tears with visions of past loveliness'.[3] During the next five years a series of young men found their way to Mary Carpenter's door. All were Bengalis, like Ram Roy, with the mercurial charm and intelligence of their people, and, to her joy, most were members of his reformed Temple, the Brahma Samaj.

Mary Carpenter's ideas of India were based on people of exceptional intelligence and character, for they risked everything by coming to England. 'It not only meant absence from home and those near and dear to one for a number of years,' wrote one of them, 'but there was the grim prospect of ostracism' from orthodox Hindu society. His mother fainted away when she heard the dreadful news that her son intended to cross the seas, for a Brahmin who mixed with foreigners lost caste.[4] In 1864 came Satyendranath Tagore, member of the great family of artists and musicians and brother of the poet Rabindranath Tagore, to make, as he said, a pilgrimage to the body of his spiritual leader. They went to the Rajah's grave, where they stood in silent prayer, while 'a radiant mystery' filled Mary's thoughts. The Tagore family later transferred the Rajah's body to a fantastic dome on pillars of many-coloured marble in the burial ground at Arnos Vale, where he still lies in exotic repose among the solid ranks of bygone Bristolians. Every year on the day of his death, pilgrims from India House sing Vedic hymns and lay a wreath upon his grave.[5] From the first, this was the spirit of the visitors. 'The place where lies Rajah Ram Mohun Roy', wrote one in 1865, in Mary Carpenter's visitors' book, 'is a sacred place for Hindu pilgrims.'[6] For the sake of these intensely appealing young visitors, Mary wrote and published *The Last Days in England of the Rajah Ram Mohun Roy*, an astonishingly vivid and detailed narrative, which revealed poignantly how much the writer lived in the past. Yet she was content it should be so. 'Having them here', she told Lucy, 'has carried me back thirty years to Ram Mohun Roy and my father.'

The young men talked, in their eager lilting speech, of changes in India. The Government had created Departments of Public Instruction in each province; as the Rajah had long ago petitioned, Indian boys could now receive 'a liberal and enlightened system of instruction, embracing mathematics, natural philosophy, chemistry and anatomy with other useful sciences'. By

[3] *Life and Work*, 120–1.
[4] Banerji, Sir, S. N. *A Nation in the Making*, 56–8.
[5] *The Guardian*, 2nd October 1971, Naseem Khan, 'Ram Roy was Here'.
[6] Bristol Archives, 12693, No. 20.

1857 examining universities existed at Bombay, Madras and Calcutta, but where in all this were the women, 'India's daughters', whom the Rajah had saved from death by fire? No funds were allotted to the education of women, and the problem was not even considered;[7] wise providence had evidently created woman to be a domestic ornament in Britain and India alike.

Mary Carpenter's young Indian friends were all married, and had been married since childhood. They explained to her what English officials seldom saw, the importance in Indian life of woman as priestess of the home, watering the sacred plant, keeping the sacred flame, guarding the sacramental purity of food by her prayers and ablutions. Rabindranath Tagore expressed it in *The Home and the World*: 'When my mother arranged the different fruits, carefully peeled by her own loving hands, on the white stone plate . . . her service would lose itself in a beauty which passed beyond all outward forms. Even in my infancy I could feel its power.' If women were not educated, intelligent men were forced to lead a double life, between the outer world of business and the professions, and the real world of home; from this came the atmosphere of unreality, which so many sensitive Western observers felt in Indian public life. These young intellectuals desired to share their thoughts with the women who would bear and bring up their children. Mary Carpenter's romantic nature responded ardently to their suggestions that she might help. In India she could work 'with the spirits of my beloved father and the noble Rajah'. 'I have quite a vision of visiting India,' she confided, as early as 1861. 'I should so delight to carry some help.' She longed to go to India, but had first to persuade her puritan conscience that it was a duty. This process took three years. In January 1864 she wrote in her journal, 'I here record my solemn resolve that henceforth I devote my heart and soul and strength to the elevation of the women of India.'[8]

Everything seemed to favour this still-secret plan. Capital, the fruit of frugal saving, would pay the salary of a superintendent at Red Lodge, where all seemed to be going well. Her books were bringing in enough to meet the cost of her own journey and Rosanna, her adopted daughter, was now 13 years old, and going in any case to boarding-school. In 1866 Mary Carpenter announced that she would sail for India that autumn, 'purely out of friendly sympathy'.

Nothing in Mary Carpenter's life interested her contemporaries so much as her journeys to India. She made four visits between 1866 and her death, each time a little more bent, breathless and frail, but indomitable to the last. Inevitably her ideas brought her into conflict with missionaries and conservative officials, but India brought her national fame. Enough was written about her work there to fill a book; a wry Forsterian comedy, it would be, with a delayed surprise ending.

The first announcement of her plan brought consternation on all sides. She was in her sixtieth year, tired, ill; India was vast, unhealthy, full of unknown dangers. 'My dear Miss Carpenter,' wrote Sir John Pakington,

---

[7] Mayhew, A. *The Education of India*, 96–8.
[8] *Life and Work*, 236–7.

doubtfully, in July 1866, 'I learn with *much* surprise of your intention to make a tour in India.' Monckton Milnes, now Lord Houghton, asked her with sly humour and the notorious indiscretion which had several times cost him political office, 'whether she approved of the harem'.

Mary Carpenter was not to be put down. She replied roundly on 7th August 1866, 'I certainly do *not* accept the polygamous or harem idea, but I am happy to know that such a condition is not now approved of by young Bengal, or at any rate the enlightened part of it.' Houghton was only teasing his formidable old friend. His Dissenting background and Unitarian family connections made him sympathetic to reform. In practice he helped her with useful letters of introduction, and a seat in the Ladies Gallery at the House of Lords whenever she wanted to hear Indian debates. Mary Carpenter thanked him warmly, visited him regularly at his London house in Upper Brook Street to keep him 'au courant of my present work' and gave him a copy of her little book on Ram Mohun Roy.[9] Many people assumed she was going as a missionary. 'Your friend entirely mistakes my object,' she wrote rather tartly to the philanthropic Rathbones, explaining that she had no thought of founding an institution. 'I simply wish to offer friendly sympathy, and any help or suggestions which might be useful. . . . Do not trouble yourself about any further introductions, thank you; I have *six* to the Governor General.'[10] She prepared to leave in September. She had still no sense of 'personal equipment', and her sisters sewed light frocks, having persuaded her with difficulty that she could not travel to the tropics in her usual rusty black. Mary proved quite human about this, though with lingering puritan feelings of guilt. 'I feel some female weakness', she confessed to Russell, 'in my pleasure in looking at my things all getting ready and looking so nice.' Kind, worried brother William provided 'sanitary counsels' and travelled to Paris to see her off. Before the journey she committed herself to God, her prayer a declaration of faith that all men were brothers.

On 1st September 1866 she left, travelling by the overland route, via Marseilles and the Red Sea. Very much to the surprise of the other passengers she had no servant and travelled in multi-racial company, with an Indian Christian girl, a Jewish bride, who was travelling to marry into the great Sassoon family of Bombay, and a young Bengali barrister, Monomohun Ghose. Mary had always loved the sea, 'such a lovely blue, so delicate, so tender'. She was content to stand for long stretches watching the wake 'where the double track of foam marked a pathway in the sea'. The nights in the Red Sea were hot, and the passengers slept on deck: 'how wonderful to look up and see the familiar stars in strange places!' Already she felt fresh and revived; it was her most complete holiday in nearly half a century's work, for, she said without irony or complaint, 'I was taught to be useful when still a little child.' For the next few months, she declared, she was determined 'to remain in the position I have chosen, that of a learner'.[11] Yet already there

---

[9] Trinity College Cambridge Library.
[10] Liverpool University Library.
[11] Carpenter, M. *Six Months in India*, I, 5–26.

were warnings of uphill work ahead. She was angry to hear a passenger call the dignified, white-clad Indian stewards 'niggers'; her friend young Mr Ghose, recently called to the English Bar, 'felt it most painfully'. Mary did not hide her opinion of such 'low-bred and vulgar-minded manners' which made her 'blush for her own country'. It was the first, but not the last time.[12] Englishmen in the Indian Civil Service whom Mary questioned showed themselves divided about Indian life. George Lynch of Bombay hinted darkly at 'superstitions and practices, many of them too gross to be mentioned', in which Indian women entrapped their men. Meadows Taylor, on the other hand, did not believe in 'the general degradation which it has been too much the custom to impute to their women', whom he had found 'pious, virtuous and intelligent wives and mothers'. He thought that 'as educated men arise, they will naturally look for educated women to be the companions of their lives'. Mary, the eternally hopeful reformer, took heart.[13]

On 25th September they docked at Bombay. The governor, Sir Bartle Frere, was away at Poona for a durbar, but he had left official letters of introduction to all government departments, requesting them 'to furnish Miss Carpenter with any statistical or other information your records may supply and afford her every facility to visit and inspect the institutions under your control'.[14] Frere, nephew of Hookham Frere, the witty translator of Aristophanes, was Tory by birth, yet liberal in outlook. He had served India for a lifetime, introducing cotton and sugar-farming to Sattara, reforming the administration of Sind and governing his Province so well that Florence Nightingale said, 'People will be ordered for their health to Bombay.' Frere wrote that he believed Mary's visit likely 'to be of great public benefit by aiding in the solution of many problems . . . in India'. He can hardly have known what a dedicated disturber of official peace he was unleashing upon his colleagues.

There was just time for Mary to receive a first impression of Bombay from the shady verandah of the travellers' bungalow: the islands, the port, inland the distant blue line of the Western Ghats, seaward the lovely palm-fringed bay, and the brief splendour of the moment when the sun plunged like a fiery ball into the sea, before the swift coming of the tropical night. She set out next day by train for Ahmedabad, the ancient Moslem city of Gujerat, where her friend S.N. Tagore had been posted as Assistant Judge. Decorum would only let her hint at the strain of an Indian railway journey, 'the many inconveniences and discomforts, as it is seldom possible for a lady to alight, or to obtain refreshment'.[15] The sadness of much Indian landscape was haunting; forest reduced to thorny scrub by drought and hungry cattle, the brown plain, flecked with the shade of stunted trees, the mud-built villages, the toiling women in the fields, the apathetic children and starving dogs. At Ahmedabad, an elegant carriage with red-turbaned coachman and footman

[12] Carpenter, M. *Six Months in India*, II, 61.
[13] Bristol Archives, 12693, No. 24.
[14] Secretary to Governor, Bombay, to all Departments, 26th September 1866.
[15] Carpenter, M. *Six Months in India*, I, 27.

carried her along a sandy road bordered with cactus hedges, through a wooded park, to rest at last in the Tagores' cool, darkened guest-rooms.

The visit which followed was deeply happy and in many ways the inspiration of Mary's Indian work. 'I was treated as a *friend*,' she wrote, 'though a stranger in a strange land.' She ate and meditated with her Brahmin hosts, the only ecumenical household in the Empire, she believed. The great Tagore family led the renaissance of Indian arts and letters; 'we wrote,' said the poet, 'we sang, we acted, we poured ourselves out on every side.' The young judge and his shy, dark-eyed wife wished to share their lives fully; she spoke English and appeared in public by her husband's side—'though how much moral courage this must have required', wrote Mary later, 'I did not then fully know.'[16] Their love remained to her an ideal of Indian life as it could be. For a time, paint-box in hand, she gave herself over to new experiences. There were picnics among the domes and triple-arched courtyards of the superb Moslem ruins, plaintive music played on the sitar, as she explored crumbling fortifications, mosques, the rain tank where bare-footed Indian ladies, toe-ringed as well as ear-ringed, gazed dreamily into the still water. Mary adored the animals: the acrobatic monkeys, the squirrels which ran into her room to steal nuts, the green parrots in the acacia trees, the chained tigers of the Gaekwar of Baroda, 'though with respect to the insect part of the animal kingdom, the less said the better!'[17]

By 5th October, Mary's puritan conscience reasserted itself. She began a round of visits in which the lines of her future work were sketched out. When she went to a girls' school, armed with toys, beads and picture cards, 'for children in all parts of the world delight in gifts, especially from strangers', she found only little girls from 6 to 11 chanting lessons by rote under the eye of a massive Hindu pundit.[18] Where were the mistresses? she demanded. 'There are no female teachers in the country,' explained a judge. 'The girls leave as soon as they are of marriageable age (at latest between 10 and 11) and forget all they have learnt.' As married women, they could not, of course, be taught by men. 'Why should not women teachers be trained?' I asked. 'The Government does not care as much for girls as for boys,' answered my native friends in a tone of some reproach. 'Everything,' wrote Mary to Anna, 'is very different from what we have an idea of in England. What I came expecting to do, i.e. bring home some young girls, I find *quite* fallacious ... the great want is to train female teachers as there are none to be had. To organize, bring before the Government and get this carried out is now my work.'[19]

Predictably, in less than a month, the idea that Mary was in India simply as an observer had died a natural death. The reforming strain in her character was too strong. Her Indian friends seized on her suggestions with quicksilver enthusiasm. 'The impossible will now be accomplished, thanks to the friendly exertions of Miss Carpenter, the famous philanthropist of Bristol!'[20] wrote the head of the male Normal School, in the inimitable English of the British

[16] *Ibid.*, 33–8. [17] *Ibid.*, 40.
[18] *Ibid.*, 53. [19] *Life and Work*, 257, 282.
[20] Bristol Archives, 12693, No. 24.

Raj. 'They led me to feel', wrote Mary, 'that *all* other plans must be super-
seded by whatever seemed most likely to promote this.' Continuing her tour,
she travelled to Surat, where the scene enchanted her. Again she made a
round of visits to institutions and to households, where graceful Hindu or
Moslem ladies, giggling like schoolgirls from shyness, gently fingered every
part of her dress. 'I felt it as always extremely tantalizing to be unable to
exchange any expression of friendship except by dumbshow, but I went
among them, endeavouring to make my feelings understood.'[21]

Her hosts everywhere knew the British as officials, merchants, missionaries,
always demanding something of them; they were amazed that a woman, so
elderly and frail, should have travelled an immense distance at her own cost,
simply from good will towards them. Their gratitude, and their reverence for
old age, shone round her like the Indian sun, beginning the gentle mellowing
which so many people noticed in Mary Carpenter's last years. Her album
filled with elegant, exotic scripts, Persian, Arabic, Pali, Sanskrit, welcoming
her as 'venerable lady' or, which touched her heart, Mamaji.[22] From Surat
she travelled to the durbar at Poona, to consult Sir Bartle Frere, who warned
her at once that any educational plan involving government spending could
only be authorized by the Viceroy at Calcutta. As a recreation the Freres
took her on elephant-back to Parbati Hill. 'One feels in an elevated position,'
wrote the dauntless old lady, 'and has certainly a good view of the country
round.' Always sensitive to the relationship of humans and animals, she
was charmed by the musical, confiding tone in which her mahout pleaded
with his elephant. 'Go on, my Lord, I entreat you!' The hardest part of Mary's
journey now lay ahead. 'My course was onward, my present goal Calcutta!'
To cross India from west to east, the route was then by steamer from Bombay
to Calicut, and by canoe upriver to Beypore. 'The coast bordered with thick
groves of coconut-palms, Indian huts under the trees, beautiful clear water.'
Naked brown men carried palm leaf umbrellas; the rice-fields in clearings
were a brilliant green. 'It is a refreshment to my spirit to see these new
scenes,' she wrote to Anna.[23] From Beypore the railway ran cross-country
to Madras, which she reached abouth 5th November. Here she stayed a few
days with the Director of Public Instruction and his wife. Missions had con-
gregated round Madras, the East India Company's original Fort St George,
and she visited mission schools of various sects, which received grants-in-aid
on the British pattern from the Government of India. Mary appreciated the
devoted work of the rival missions, 'yet,' she noticed, 'they do not make
many converts'. Her host arranged a meeting with 'enlightened gentlemen',
both Hindu and Moslem, who were all emphatic: 'We do not want our ladies
made humble Christians.'[24] She noted that 'the great dread they have of
conversion prevents their availing themselves generally of the help the missionaries might have given'. Interfering English ladies were particularly suspect;

[21] Carpenter, M. *Six Months in India*, I, 85–99.
[22] Bristol Archives, 12693, No. 24.
[23] *Life and Work*, 259.
[24] Carpenter, M. *Six Months in India*, I, 138–49.

Mary was often asked if she really intended not to proselytize. She replied with a declaration of faith most unusual at the time, and honourable at any time. 'Christianity must be accepted freely by each individual, from the conviction of his own inner spirit . . . Respecting the individual freedom of every immortal being as I do my own, I would not, if I could, obtrude my own religion upon them.'[25]

On 20th November, weak and rather miserable from four days' seasickness in the Bay of Bengal, she arrived at Calcutta. It was, she felt, a pilgrimage to the place she had so often gazed at wistfully on the map, the home of 'the noble Rajah Rammohun Roy'. Even her enthusiasm could not help finding 'much that is distressing in the city of Calcutta', as her dismayed eyes surveyed the acres of shanties, the cesspools, the sweat-shops, the black jute mills along the polluted river, the swarming, garbage-choked bazaars; 'open sewers run on each side of the street,' she wrote, 'and the stench is intolerable.' 'Calcutta's situation is so bad by nature', wrote a traveller in the 1880s, 'that there is little man can do to make it worse, but that little has been faithfully and assiduously done.'[26] Searching for traces of the Rajah, Mary found neither his house, nor the printing-press he founded, nor any public monument. Instead, there was 'determined opposition to progress and blind submission to the tyranny of custom'.[27] The Brahma Samaj which the Rajah had founded, appeared to have fossilized under its silver-haired Maharishi, the head of the Tagore family. Mary was not staying with Europeans, but in the house of a Bengali professor at the Medical College, the convert whose daughter she had chaperoned on the journey out. One day the doctor's servants showed in a caller, a young man not yet 30, in plain black gown, but with commanding presence, and magnificent orator's voice.[28] He was K. C. Sen, the Acharya, or Chief Minister, of the Brama Samaj, who was already leading a revolt of the progressive younger members against the Hindu traditionalism of the older generation.

Sen proposed radical social reforms: inter-caste marriages, civil marriage, the remarriage of widows, the higher education of women, public health legislation, the reform of the constitution. In 1866, the year of Mary's visit, he was dismissed from the parent society and founded the new Brama Samaj of India, or One God Society, the first all-India movement.[29] Here, she felt, at last, was the spiritual successor to Ram Roy. Sen gave wholehearted support to schools and training colleges for women, but warned this innocent old English lady not to expect too much. 'You will probably find the people loud to talk, but inclined to do very little as soon as you turn your back on India.' A few days later Mary attended a service of the society, devoted to 'the glory of God in creation'. She sat serenely among the white-

[25] *Ibid.*, II, 79.
[26] Spate, O. H. K. and Learmonth, A. T. A. *Advanced Geography of India and Pakistan*, 593.
[27] Carpenter, M. *Six Months in India*, I, 176–7, 195.
[28] *Ibid.*, II, 168.
[29] Majumdar, R. C. (ed.) *History and Culture of the Indian People*, X, 97–106. The important Civil Marriage Act of 1872 was passed at Sen's request.

robed listeners. while others read aloud or chanted Vedic hymns. 'I could not of course understand anything,' she wrote to Anna, 'but it was very interesting to be in the place of worship of the One God which Rammohun Roy established.' She was happy to find her fellow-worshippers 'did not object to Christianity as Christ taught it, but only to the creeds attached'. The seeker after the wisdom of the East is now a stock figure, but was then unknown. Mary, innocently sleeping on a string bed, eating vegetable curry and unleavened bread and listening to mantras, was committing two of the worst crimes of Victorian England, blasphemy and letting the side down. No one approved, especially as the Viceroy was a staunch Low-Churchman and supporter of the Church Missionary Society. 'Many of the missionaries look askance at me,' reported Mary to her family at home. 'Very few English ladies came to call, probably because they were afraid of my heterodoxy. I hear a whole sermon was preached against me in one of their churches. I have perceived many symptoms of latent horror, but that does not matter. I am used to it.'[30] She felt her father near her in spirit, and with the naive vanity of one brought up in an enlightened minority, failed to consider how much support she might alienate from the women's cause.

The Government of India used public funds only for the 'promotion of European literature and science' and, working upon the official 'filtration theory', limited education to the upper classes, in the vague hope that it would somehow trickle downwards. In fact, the use of English acted as a massive dam which held back education from the illiterate masses.[31] 'They affect to believe', remarked Mary Carpenter, 'that the education of the highest classes will affect the lowest.' Noticing the contrast between stately marble college buildings and mud-and-thatch elementary schools, she doubted this. 'I could not but feel that the lower classes have not in any way shared the benefits,' and she regretted the tradition which held intellectuals 'aloof from the inferior castes'.[32] Even in these exotic surroundings, she kept her sense of common humanity with the poorest, especially with children. In the crowded, sweltering prison compound at Calcutta, she saw a baby boy lying in a woman prisoner's lap, stretched in the sun 'with evident delight, a ray striking its dark eye so that it shone like a diamond'. She felt a spontaneous rush of tenderness towards him, and a profound, maternal fear. 'What is to be the future of that little child?'

Official visits done, Mary planned a mixed evening party of Hindu ladies and gentlemen, 'probably the first ever held'. Even by Carpenter standards, it must have been an exhausting evening. She felt sorry for the young women, not because of the 'degradation' which so excited prurient British imaginations, but because 'the seclusion of the female apartments is so *very dull* and devoid of any interest'. She found 'the entertainment of the ladies was a difficulty'; she provided albums and scrap books, but saw a bemused lady gazing at one upside down. 'I therefore explained a portfolio of prints to the

[30] *Life and Work*, 261–2, 268.
[31] Mayhew, A. *The Education of India*, 91–2.
[32] Carpenter, M. *Six Months in India*, I, 206.

gentlemen and requested them to do the same to the ladies.'[33] Not all husbands welcomed the idea of education; as one explained, with disarming frankness, 'I do not believe in Hinduism, nor does any educated man, but my ladies do and it makes them virtuous and obedient to me. If they were instructed, they would soon see the folly of it and so I do not want them taught.'[34] Give or take a point of theology, many Christian husbands would probably have shared this comfortable philosophy, but Mary was outraged. 'I have *no* sympathy with them,' she wrote indignantly to Anna, 'for it is not from any religious prejudice, but a selfish wish to keep their wives perfectly in thraldom that they object to education.' Orthodox Hindu opposition was stirring, and her mixed party was sharply criticized in the press. This was to provide an excuse for the Government's lukewarmness towards girls' schools or colleges.

In December the Viceroy, Sir John Lawrence, returned from Simla to Calcutta and Mary was invited to Government House. The great airy halls and rooms were splendid, with a constant soft-footed coming and going of servants in red livery. Mary attended a Drawing Room, among Indian princes, gorgeous as peacocks in jewelled cloth of gold, while unseen hands played soft music. 'I could almost fancy myself,' said Mary characteristically to the Viceroy, 'at one of the delightful soirées of the Social Science Association.' Fortunately, Sir John took this comment on viceregal hospitality in the spirit in which it was offered, and thanked Miss Carpenter for the compliment.[35]

A few days later she presented her findings and proposals, including the album in which she had collected testimonials as she went. 'Secular education,' said a writer in Ahmedabad, 'makes no progress, because we have no female teachers.' 'Girls who reach ten or eleven and marry have to leave,' wrote a Surat schoolmaster, 'because they cannot be taught by men.' A group of Brahmins in Calcutta pointed out that 'Education is hindered *for men*, unless that of women is brought up to a proportionately high level.' All stressed the need for a training college for women teachers and emphasized that this must be a Government institution, like the Normal Schools for male teachers. Mission schools were wholly unacceptable; 'the Government principle of non-interference with religion is essential to success'.[36] Mary had drafted a memorandum, which she placed respectfully but firmly on Sir John's desk. This memorandum went to the heart of her argument. 'Why *should* the Government do less for girls than boys?'[37]

Sir John Lawrence listened, with keen glances from under craggy, grey brows, and promised to consider the document with the five members of the Viceregal Executive Council, but remained non-committal. As the saviour of Delhi during the mutiny, his prestige was immense; his manner was brusque and his temper fiery, controlled only by stern upbringing and iron

[33] *Ibid.*, 183.
[34] *Ibid.*, 213.
[35] *Ibid.*, 370.
[36] Bristol Archives, 12693, No. 24.
[37] Carpenter, M. *Six Months in India*, II, 142–5, 159–60.

sense of duty. Like his father and brothers he had served a lifetime in India, and his knowledge of the country, especially of its seamy side, was unrivalled. His passion for good administration was almost religious, but he had no taste for increased government expenditure or sweeping reforms. The India he knew, and in his undemonstrative way loved, was the home of the country landowner. Like a sagacious old bloodhound, Lawrence scented trouble for the future from the urban intellectuals, poised between East and West, who were Mary Carpenter's supporters and friends. He was courteous, however, and Mary Carpenter set out on her homeward journey in March 1867, feeling confident that her work in India was successfully done.[38]

A welcoming telegram from the Governor invited her to break her journey at Madras. She was landed, somewhat alarmed, in a surf-boat at the primitive old port, and driven through straggling suburbs and palm groves to Government House. Here she found a very different type of Indian official, 'the one man in India', she wrote enthusiastically to M. D. Hill, 'to carry out my reforms'. Sir Robert Napier was a gentle, cultured, wholly delightful professional soldier, who swiftly disarmed all the Carpenter pacifist prejudices. Nature and fortune had smiled on his career. On lonely hill stations he collected flowers or geological specimens, making exquisite drawings of his collections. He learnt poetry by heart and won over Mary by appreciating Wordsworth and picking for her 'a lovely brilliant white Victoria Regia' [water-lily] from his lake.[39] He painted in water-colours with exceptional taste and skill, having taken lessons from Copley Fielding's brother, and continued to experiment with new techniques to the end of his life. Mary, of course, poured out her hopes and ambitions for India to this sympathetic new friend, in a long philanthropic discourse, which lasted until exhaustion overcame her. 'It's a remarkable thing,' the Governor was heard to say, with great good humour. 'I listened to all Miss Carpenter had to tell me about India, but when I began to tell her what *I* knew of the country, she fell asleep!' These dignified, brief dormitions played an increasing part in Mary's social life as she grew older.[40]

Robert Napier himself was particularly fond of children, and anxious to provide schools for all, but he tried to warn Mary gently that the Government of India might be less than enthusiastic. 'I feel confident', he wrote in a private note, 'that the Home Govt. would say Yes, if Sir J. L. does not say No. But the Indian Minister naturally shrinks from overturning the opinion of the Viceroy.'[41] It is doubtful if she listened; she was too buoyed up by the heady excitement of travel and freedom at last. 'Only think!' she wrote triumphantly to her brothers, 'of two voyages of four days each and two days rail, to get to Calcutta, and the same back, *all alone!*' Yet the lapses into sleep showed how tired she was. With typical tact and kindness, Sir Robert found a rare Unitarian convert among his Indian household, whom he sent to act as courier on her return journey.

[38] Carpenter, M. *Six Months in India*, I, 280–90.
[39] *Life and Work*, 269–72.
[40] Cobbe, F. P. *Autobiography*, 282.   [41] Bristol Archives, 12093, No. 16.

Once again Mary crossed overland to Calicut and by coastal steamer to Bombay, arriving just in time for the festivities of Sir Bartle Frere's retirement. With a sense of duty done, she gave herself over for once to pure enjoyment. In this great mercantile city physically and psychologically nearest to Europe, with its diverse Hindu, Moslem, Parsee and Jewish communities, she saw hope for India's daughters of tomorrow. Her last excursion was a water picnic with the Freres to Elephanta Island. They explored the great temples carved in the rock, and ate an open-air banquet, while sunset flooded across the water. At night Mary woke, as full of romantic excitement as in her distant girlhood. She opened the shutters and looked out on one of Bombay's magnificent moonlit nights, the long silver fronds of palm trees floating in the light breeze, and a flood of glory on the dark silent waves. She felt her sympathy and enjoyment 'as vivid as ever . . . My last Sunday in India!' she wrote on 17th March 1867. 'That now I have reached so advanced an age, in the midst of many trials and difficulties and so much illness, I should find my youth renewed, and strength to do my work, greater than it has ever been before!'[42] Three days later she sailed for England.

Mary reached home in time for Easter, to find herself a celebrity. It is an interesting sidelight on Victorian priorities, that thirty years of devoted service to the youngest and most defenceless of the Queen's subjects at home had received no public thanks or recognition; yet now, after one trip to India, Miss Carpenter was famous. When she spoke on India at the Social Science Association, the hall could have been filled twice over. Mary, once so painfully shy, blossomed under appreciation. For the first time, she spoke without notes; her voice, low but very clear, held her audience with complete authority. She spoke of India as 'a dream-land of which we had long no certain knowledge . . . though we had from time to time nightmares, for instance of women treated with great cruelty'. Now she had visited and seen for herself how 'India is the brightest jewel in the British Crown; yet surely we have not done as much as we ought to have done for the two hundred million Indian subjects of our beloved Queen.' Her old stiffness and shyness vanished. Lord Dufferin, the chairman, paid tribute to her 'unrivalled eloquence and grace'.[43] She founded an Indian National Association, on the model of the Social Science Association, to build up an enlightened public opinion, both in India and at home.[44] At its first meeting in Westminster, Sir Bartle Frere presented her with a tea service of Benares silver, the gift of Indian friends.

Everyone demanded a full account of her travels, and during the summer of 1867, she wrote the two volumes of *Six Months in India*, which Longmans brought out early in 1868. The book sold well and deserved its success. The happy idea of separating the propaganda for woman's education into the second volume made the first a rather breathless narrative, filled with transparent goodwill and an almost childlike enjoyment. It would need a very

---

[42] *Life and Work*, 267.
[43] *Proceedings of the National Association for the Promotion of Social Science*, 1867.
[44] Majumdar, R. C. (ed.) *History and Culture of the Indian People*, X, 521.

hard heart not to sympathize with pleasures for which the writer had waited fifty hard-worked years.

Though her first concern had been with schools, her sharp eye and sharper pen had not been idle on other occasions during her visit. She read another paper to the Social Science Association, on *Gaols of India from Official Reports*, quoting the opinion of Dr Mouatt, Inspector General of Prisons in Bengal, that the state of prisons was 'a scandal and a reproach that would not be tolerated in Britain for a day'.[45] At Mary Carpenter's suggestion, the Social Science Association, to the discomfiture of the Government of India, memorialized the India Office in Whitehall about the state of Indian prisons. The imprisonment of children in India, of course, troubled her deeply. India had only one reformatory school, founded in memory of the great Jewish merchant David Sassoon of Bombay by his sons. Not a year passed without protests from Miss Carpenter to the Government of India and the India Office against the pretext that 'some juvenile departments of prisons are called reformatories . . . there must be free, open houses where they can feel themselves in a home. They should learn trades . . . not for the sake of gaining funds but for the good of the boys. Besides this, care should be taken to watch over them when put out in the world.' She wore them down by sheer persistence, and the year before her death the Council of India passed the Act of 1876, directing convicted children into schools not prisons. Nor was this all. She continued to lobby the government about the slave labour of women and children in Indian cotton-mills, demanding at least half-time schooling for children who worked on the factory floor from the age of 5. An Indian Factory Act was passed after her death.[46]

The government of India might have preferred to ignore this elderly English gentlewoman, with her eccentric urge to reform everything which had so long been left comfortably alone. Unfortunately for them this was no longer possible, for Mary Carpenter, born an obscure provincial Dissenter, now had friends in high places.

India was the key to unlock the most closely guarded doors. 'My dear Miss Carpenter,' wrote Florence Nightingale from her fortress bedroom at 35 South Street, 'I am so very busy and ill that nothing but the pleasure of seeing you and of hearing of your great Indian doings would strengthen me to do anything but urgent business.' She invited Mary to call and added the supreme accolade, 'would you kindly name your own hours'. The two moral amazons met, and took each other's measure with mutual respect.[47]

A still higher honour was at hand. Mary had sent a copy of *Six Months in India* to the Queen, still, after seven years, shrouded in resolute widowhood at Windsor. In March 1868, the Queen commanded the Secretary for India, Sir Stafford Northcote, to present Miss Carpenter for a private inter-

---

[45] *Proceedings of the National Association for the Promotion of Social Science*, 1869.
[46] *Life and Work*, 370–1.
[47] There is nothing earlier than this about Florence Nightingale in the Carpenter papers, and no mention of the Crimean War, when Mary had been fully occupied with early struggles at Red Lodge.

view. Mary's manuscript account of this is a classic Victorian document.[48]
Her dress combined personal economy with sense of occasion. 'Miss Eliz.
Knight provided me a simple and elegant claret-coloured silk on which
Mother's black lace mantle looked very nice. Aunt S's. black bonnet freshly
trimmed, Anna's collar and cuffs from her wedding veil, Aunt B's brooch . . .
Aunt S's handsome shawl covered all properly for a railway journey.' At
the last moment vanity won over thrift, even with Miss Carpenter. 'New
white gloves I considered *essential* to the occasion.' They arrived at Windsor
Castle: 'no guards, soldiers, or liveried footmen to be seen, but the quiet
simplicity of a beloved Sovereign, living among her people'. They were
shown to a Luncheon Room, where Mary took a glass of wine, but was afraid
to eat, for fear of spoiling the pristine freshness of the new gloves. They were
then ushered up a wide staircase, into a gilded corridor, where the Queen,
swathed in deep black crêpe, appeared at the far end.

'Her countenance beamed with intellect, sweetness and animation: yet
she was so full of quiet dignity, that she instantly inspired me with the
feeling that I was in the presence of my *Sovereign*. "We are pleased that you
have been to India," ' said the Queen. Mary showed her various objects:
drawings and illuminations, notes written in English and inscriptions by
Hindu and Moslem ladies in her album. Sir Stafford Northcote, feeling perhaps that the Queen had a professional interest in widowhood, explained
that Miss Carpenter hoped to train widows as teachers. 'When I mentioned
the cruel treatment imposed on those who already had the *deepest affliction*,
the Queen's countenance expressed profound commiseration.' A servant
handed them a parcel, containing *Leaves of a Journal from our Life in the
Highlands*, inscribed 'To Miss Carpenter from Victoria R., Windsor Castle,
March 13 1868.' The Queen said the Hindus wished to have it translated.
'Sir S. said this was being done by an English professor.' Even in these august
surroundings, Mary spoke up for her Indian friends. 'I ventured to suggest
that native gentlemen would be able to render it more satisfactorily in their
own vernacular than an Englishman would.'

They took their leave, the Queen shaking hands most cordially. Safely back
at her brother's house, and free at last from those worrying white gloves, the
elderly lady sat down to write a word-for-word account of her adventure. 'I
did no business on *that* day!' she concluded in triumph. The emphatic royal
style must have been catching.

Meanwhile in India the Viceroy's Council was considering Miss Carpenter's proposals for women's education. Sir John Lawrence had no wish
to offend Christian missionaries on one hand, or ultra-orthodox Hindus and
Moslems on the other, about a matter which seemed to him of very minor
importance. He finally ruled that 'there are many reasons why it would be
inexpedient for the Government to assume entire responsibility . . . an
earnest and genuine effort by the native community must be insisted upon'.
If they would subscribe half the money, the Government would make a

---

[48] Bristol Archives 12693, No. 18.

grant-in-aid of £1500 for the Presidency Provinces though princely states must shift for themselves.[49] From long experience, he relied on the Byzantine laws of caste, and the suffocating lassitude of the hot weather to shelve the whole awkward question. Lord Napier,[50] another old India hand, understood this at once. 'I doubt whether the money will be got,' he warned Mary in a letter. 'The truth is the community is lukewarm if not adverse, and not disposed to be generous. Personally,' he added with surprising frankness, 'I think it was a mistake to demand native co-operation at all. The government might have done it all, but I was over-ruled.'[51]

As he had warned, months passed and nothing happened, except some rather metaphysical discussions in Bombay and Calcutta. Mary Carpenter began to worry. '*Begin at once,*' she wrote to a Parsee physician, early in 1868. 'Only begin, *without talking about it,* as I have done with every one of my undertakings.' Still nothing happened, and in April 1868 she wrote again. 'You say and do nothing . . . I consider this continued delay most injurious.'[52] She argued at the India Office that her supporters were young intellectuals, with very little money. 'They have already done all in their power; more they cannot do.' Thirty Parsee and Hindu visitors signed a memorial regretting that the Viceroy had not supported Miss Carpenter's proposals on the grounds that the natives had not met half the expense. This was hardly calculated to endear her to Government House, Calcutta. Meanwhile, her book sold well, and when she asked for subscriptions for Indian girls' schools, money flowed in from rich, enlightened Unitarian congregations. By August 1868 she had decided to return to India and take a hand herself.

This news was enough to make the dauntless heroes of the Indian Mutiny quail. 'Your energy and devotion to the cause are admirable, but I confess I regard your withdrawal from England with regret and apprehension for yourself,'[53] wrote Lord Napier, with understandable alarm at the prospect of conflict ahead. 'I expect of course many difficulties,' replied Mary stoutly, 'but I can hardly have greater than I had at Kingswood and Red Lodge. I am accustomed to troubles. Then I shall be rewarded by the affection and gratitude of a people; this is very dear to me.' 'As for me,' she wrote in answer to an inquiry from her brother Philip in Canada, 'I have not wavered a moment about returning to India.'[54] On 7th November 1868, she arrived for a second winter in Bombay. Within four days of landing she had persuaded a rich Hindu to lend a house, offered her own services free of charge to the Government as Lady Superintendent of a training college, and begun to collect her first students. The news, causing dismay and perhaps resentment, had barely arrived at Government House, before Mary fell ill in February 1869 with one of her sudden, alarming collapses. She was moved to a house in the hills, where British neighbours nursed her with great kind-

[49] Carpenter, M. *Six Months in India*, II, 154.
[50] Sir Robert Napier became Lord Napier after a brilliantly skilful and successful expedition to Abyssinia in 1868.
[51] Bristol Archives, 12693, No. 16.
[52] *Life and Work,* 278-9.
[53] Bristol Archives, 12693, No. 16.
[54] *Life and Work,* 284-5.

ness. To the Viceroy and Council, it must have seemed a narrow escape. It sounds as though Lord Napier was commanded to get rid of this determined, intrusive reformer, for he wrote with his usual kindness in February 1869 that 'the Government has respectfully declined your generous offer to take the management of a Normal Training School. . . . I am of the opinion that you could do more for the cause of female education by *staying at home and supporting* those who are interested in it.'[55] It would be psychologically interesting to know whether this tactful yet definite rebuff followed or actually caused her sudden collapse. She was compelled to sail home, and spent the spring resting with her sister Susan and brother-in-law Robert Gaskell, who now lived at Weymouth. As soon as her strength returned in the cool, fresh spring days, she announced her determination to return to India as soon as possible.

'The question of female education is attended with great difficulty . . . its development will be slow,' gloomily warned Lord Halifax, a previous Secretary for India. The current Secretary, Stafford Northcote, sympathetic, but known for being 'eminently cautious', found himself trapped between the Viceroy's reluctance and Miss Carpenter's determination. 'When one looks back on all you have done', he wrote in October, with an involuntary cry from the heart, 'the thought which strikes one is this: *Why cannot she stay home and rest?*'[56] 'I have come to the conclusion,' replied Mary firmly to the luckless Secretary, 'that I had better not be entangled with Government, but just do what I can quite alone.' Her various correspondents might as well have tried to turn back the Light Brigade as a Carpenter in pursuit of a self-imposed duty.

She spent the winter of 1869–70 in Bombay at her own expense. She established girls' schools at Bombay and Ahmedabad on her own initiative, and bore the costs for the first year out of her own funds. At Ahmedabad, with the support of the Tagores, eleven women, some of them Hindu widows, began their training under an English certificated woman teacher. At the Bombay school Mary donated her own personal possessions. 'You would be pleased', she told Anna in February 1870, 'to see how pretty the room has been made, with my study cabinet, looking like itself, and my nice bookcase with my own books. These I shall leave,' she added rather pathetically, 'as a token of my wish to *give anything I can*.' Three years of struggle had achieved heartbreakingly little, and any fair-minded person must wonder whether this was her own fault for making untimely or unreasonable demands. This was not the view of the Hunter Commission, which reported on Indian education in 1882, and calculated the percentage of girls receiving any education in the different provinces. These were: Bombay 1·59%, Madras 1·50%, Bengal 0·80%, Punjab 0·72% and North-West Provinces 0·28%. These figures represented 'the segregating religious and social traditions of ages' which would not be easily overcome and the Commission strongly advised providing

[55] Bristol Archives, 12693, No. 16.
[56] *Ibid.*, No. 24. Underlinings in original. Stafford Northcote had sponsored the Industrial Schools Act and a reformatory school himself.

schools for girls 'as a legitimate charge on municipal funds'. Because this
was left entirely to local initiative, variations were chaotic and progress very
slow. In Bengal in the 1920s, 490 girls were in the upper forms of high
schools out of a female population of twenty-two million.[57] Because there
were so few women teachers, infant and junior education suffered, while the
villages were practically untouched by primary schooling. The verdict, not
of some wild-eyed revolutionary or ferocious feminist, but of a responsible
retired English Director of Public Instruction in the 1920s was 'The Government by its timidity and stumbling at the start, has been largely responsible.
The results have been deplorable.'[58] Mary Carpenter fought with single-
minded determination for Indian reform. She was no respecter of persons,
however highly placed, and as an old friend noticed, 'most English statesmen
yielded to her pressure as she became a power in the land'.[59] Whether she
might have achieved more in India by avoiding direct confrontation with the
Government can, of course, never be known. In March 1870, hot weather and
urgent responsibilities at Bristol drove her home, for the last time, as she
thought. In apparent defeat her fighting qualities showed at their best.
Firmly, and as it turned out rightly, she hoped for the future. 'While the
worldly may scoff and disbelieve,' she wrote, making ready to come home,
'*the work will go on.*'[60]

[57] Mayhew, A. *The Education of India*, 97–8.   [58] *Ibid.*, 98.
[59] *Modern Review*, April 1880.   [60] *Life and Work*, 295.

14

SOCIAL WORK AT HOME AND ABROAD 1870-1873

Mary Carpenter came back to Bristol. As a surprise gift to welcome her home, her family had built a little greenhouse in the back garden at Red Lodge House, a luxury Mary had long and sternly denied herself. Mary was enchanted by this; her favourite nephew, Estlin Carpenter, now in Bristol as a young minister, gives an endearing picture of her pleasure. 'There, as she potted her plants, she loved to think over her great affairs, plan new institutions, prepare the heads of her papers for various congresses, or compose memorials to statesmen.'[1] Her brothers and sisters had always deplored the way Mary 'wasted her talents' on slum children. Philip worried over her loneliness, since Rosanna was now abroad to complete her education, and Mary lived alone. 'People with souls like yours', he wrote, 'get driven in upon themselves, and must wait for sympathetic development till kingdom come.'[2] Yet now that Mary was an international figure, her family were immensely proud of her. 'You, my dear sister,' wrote William, 'have found your work, as I have found mine . . .'[3] Herbert Thomas, Anna's husband, commissioned a bust of Mary by Richard Price[4] which was unveiled by M. D. Hill, in the dilapidated old ragged-school hall at St James' Back. Mary, to whom the whole occasion came as a complete surprise, was, for once, too overcome to speak. Only those standing by her heard her murmur, 'How pleased Dr Tuckerman and my dear father must be!'

The summer of 1870 passed happily. On 20th October Mary spent the afternoon, as so often, with Anna, the one person to whom she told her innermost thoughts and plans. 'We had a pleasant, ordinary chat,' she recalled, 'and parted as usual,' expecting to meet next day. During the night, Anna had a cerebral haemorrhage, and died before dawn.[5] Everyone dreaded the effect of this sudden death upon Mary, 'the lonely one in our family', as Philip called her. In human terms her loss was great. The two sisters had met almost every day, in a 'lifelong, most tender sisterly love'. Mary, surrounding family life with an aureole of romance, wrote of Anna in terms usually reserved for a lover. 'We never told each other how much we loved each other, for no words would have conveyed greater certainty than existed

[1] *Life and Work*, 297.
[2] Carpenter, R. L. *Memoir of Philip Pearsall Carpenter*, 299.
[3] Carpenter, W. B. *Essays and Memoir*, 104.
[4] This bust was included in the New Gallery Victorian Exhibition of 1892, but has since disappeared.
[5] General Registry. Register of deaths.

between us. No other departure can take away, as it were, a part of my life.'
Yet fears for Mary's health and sanity were unfounded. She had at last
come through to the strength and serenity, even sweetness, which after a
stormy life marked her old age. 'This is a gentler parting than we had thirty
years ago,' she wrote to Susan, recalling their father's still unsolved death.
'Then, we had to begin the battle of life alone. Now we have fought it! And
we have fought a good fight!' In some ways, she said, she felt nearer to
Anna than when the body 'divided her spirit from mine'.[6] She was gentle and
unpossessive in grief towards her widowed brother-in-law; their ties of
affection and loyalty lasted all her life. Florence Nightingale and Frances
Power Cobbe both wrote sympathetically. 'What blessed spirits there are in
the other world,' replied Mary. 'All whom I most rejoice to commune with
are there, all who have helped me most in my spiritual life.'[7] She shared the
sense of an unseen world with her nephew Estlin Carpenter who had psychological experiences which he described with touching simplicity. Walking
in the country, he wrote, 'suddenly I became conscious of the presence of
someone else. . . . It came unsought, absolutely unexpectedly. I remember
the wonderful transfiguration of the far-off woods and hills. I had not found
God, for I had never looked for him; but he had found me.'[8] Mary understood; her hidden inner nature vibrated in sympathy with the unseen.

Mary Carpenter was willing to tell this favourite nephew what she had
always kept hidden from the world, that in early life she had longed for the
happiness of being wife and mother, and had suffered deeply though secretly
when this was denied. Now, she said, 'I am content that my affection can
be freely given to those who need it.' She had a fastidious dislike for the
habit of interlarding conversation with biblical texts, and rarely quoted from
the Bible. It meant a great deal when she wrote, again to Estlin: 'There is
a verse in the prophesies, "I have given thee children whom thou hast not
borne." The motherly love of my heart has been given to many who have
never known a mother's love, and I have thanked God for it.'[9] She recognized
that her work made her live alone, in a different world from friends and
neighbours. Yet this had its compensations, for in the 1870s she discovered
a network of friends and fellow workers all over the world.

One sign of international interest in social and penal reform was an International Penal Congress which met during the first two weeks of July 1872,
in the Hall of the Middle Temple. Twenty-two countries sent official delegates to the congress, but the committee also invited unofficial delegates
possessing special knowledge and experience. The somewhat macabre attractions included visits to prisons, penitentiaries and 'Homes' in different parts
of the country. Mary was invited to speak after Sydney Turner on the
'Principles and Results of English Reformatory and Industrial Schools'.

On 11th July Mary Carpenter read her paper. She was applauded, but her

[6] *Life and Work*, 301–3.
[7] Huntington Library, Carpenter Letters, CB 70–89
[8] Herford, C. H. *J. E. Carpenter*, 8–10.
[9] *Life and Work*, 310, n. 1.

17. *Police and attendance officers round up truants in 1871*

18. *A free school dinner in 1872*

19. Children outside a shop in 1910; perhaps they were posed, but their backs are eloquent

conclusion was not at all complacent. She spoke of the heavy expenses and heartbreaking difficulties of reformatory work, which she knew so well from personal experience. The real necessity, she said finally, was for 'measures to help, train and educate neglected and destitute children, *before* they sink into criminality and need special institutions'.[10] This was to form the subject of her last great campaign.

In the discussions which followed, work for 'neglected and misguided children' proved to be a genuinely international movement among industrialized countries. Most of the New England states had had voluntary refuges since the 1820s and state reformatories since the 1840s. Most western European nations had both state 'correctional' schools, and voluntary homes of a more 'paternal' character. Italy used transfer to one of these as a reward for good conduct. Switzerland, small as it was, had four large state institutions and no less than seventy voluntary schools. France had at least twenty reformatories for girls, mostly in the care of religious orders. Saxony and Denmark were more advanced than Britain. Although they maintained state schools for their more difficult cases, most girls and all children under 12 were fostered by voluntary societies in private families.[11]

The meetings ended with a banquet, at which delegates of many nations toasted each other. One toast was greeted with cheers: 'the Ladies, coupled with the name of Miss Mary Carpenter.'[12] Next morning Mary was asked to second the adoption of the congress report. Although only 65, she both looked and felt an aged woman. Looking back many years, she recalled the first time she had given evidence to a Committee of Inquiry on juvenile delinquency. 'It was most difficult to persuade the members and the public even that children ought not to be seriously punished for crime; their reformation was quite a secondary consideration. I was asked, "Do you not consider that children who have broken the law owe retribution to society?" My answer was "*society owes retribution to them*". I am proud of that answer. Its truth and justice have been recognized by this congress.'[13] They cheered her again. At last she felt sure her work was understood, and would be carried on when she was no longer there to fight. Mary was transfigured with happiness; her plain black frock and muslin cap, her stooped shoulders, her worn old face took on, from long and faithful service, a kind of beauty at last.

Mary Carpenter had never realized how widely her work was known on the Continent and in the United States. She was genuinely surprised as, one after another, apparent strangers came up to greet her by name. Before they left England she invited several of them to visit her in Bristol and see her schools. They took her at her word. From Sweden came a judge of the Supreme Court 'for the purpose of studying reformatory and industrial schools', from Holland Dr Van Meter, who wrote that what he saw 'makes

[10] Wines, E. C. *International Penitentiary Congress of 1872*, 163ff.
[11] *Ibid.*, 114–16.
[12] *The Times*, 13th July 1872.
[13] Wines, E. C. *International Penitentiary Congress of 1872*, 179.

me thank God and take courage'. Three Professors of Law and Social Economy from German universities noted that Mary's social work was realistic, 'without the sentimental tincture of philanthropy'. Dr Guillaume, the reforming Director of the cantonal prison at Neûchatel, found many of his own methods anticipated. Perhaps the most interesting guest was Ivan Foynitsky of St Petersburg, who intended to found the first colony of village homes in Russia, for children whose parents had been exiled to Siberia.[14]

Mary welcomed these guests with simple, unpretentious kindness, and took them to see her work. She explained that she had tried to provide a substitute for children without homes, but 'no one knew better than her that it was a very poor second best for children who had no chance at all of the true best in early life'. It was her intense belief in home life which filled her with such profound pity for vagrants and criminals.[15] The schools were small and simple, the buildings often shabby, the children rough and sometimes unruly. Yet to the American visitors they seemed 'the working models of an inventor . . . which may at last revolutionize the conduct of governments and individuals towards the criminal classes'.[16]

Everyone saw the need for international co-operation and a permanent commission for penal reform was founded.[17] Mary was showered with invitations from Europe and America, which, in spite of age and frail health, she was determined to accept, since 'no writing or printing or talking can induce people to take up the subject; it is only determined action'. The last five years of her life included a series of journeys to visit fellow workers all over the world. She revealed to these comparative strangers, feelings which had long been hidden in her heart. 'I do not often like to allude to religion in public or to those whose spirit I do not know,' she wrote to a friend, 'lest it should be misunderstood, but you will gather from my books that this has been the moving spirit in my life.' Another friend marvelled that her idealism could withstand the sordidness of so much she was compelled to see. She replied, 'having naturally an almost intense dislike of everything low and mean, I do not know how I could have lived in such close contact with vice if I had not been able to recognize the divine nature everywhere, however dimmed'.[18]

In autumn 1872, Mary Carpenter received a royal summons. Princess Alice, the second daughter of Queen Victoria, passed most of her short life in an atmosphere of strenuous good works, illness and death-beds. Her family letters form a catalogue of condolences and funerals. Prince Albert encouraged her as a child to 'visit the poor', and she was his most assiduous nurse in his own fatal illness. She put off her own marriage to Prince Louis of Hesse while she attempted to calm her mother's hysterical grief and her accusations that the Prince of Wales, by his wild courses, had caused

[14] Bristol Archives, 12693, No. 20.
[15] Reported in *The Spectator*, June 1877.
[16] *Life and Work*, 377.
[17] Wines, E. C. *International Penitentiary Congress of 1872*, 114–16.
[18] *Life and Work*, 311–19. Letters to Dr Strasburger of Warsaw and Dr Guillaume of Neuchate.

his father's death. Once married, at intervals of bearing seven children, she devoted herself to charitable institutions in Germany, and in 1870 organized a women's union for nursing the sick and wounded of the Franco-Prussian war. She returned to England the following year to nurse the Prince of Wales through typhoid, and two years later saw one of her own little boys fall from a window to his death. She was to die at 35, while nursing her own children through a diphtheria epidemic; the day was the anniversary of the Prince Consort's death, and her last words were 'dear Papa'.

In October 1872 this model Princess was organizing at Darmstadt a conference of charitable societies run by women. The German public called it the Parliament of Women. Alice prudently refused to take the chair herself, because 'it is difficult enough to keep one's own people in order when they disagree. I hope and trust', she added to her mother, 'to prevent *all* exaggerated and unfeminine views being brought up which to me are dreadful!'[19] For this reason she was particularly anxious to secure Miss Carpenter. Mary might have a lifetime's experience of forceful social work behind her: she was unpaid and therefore neither a professional woman nor a feminist.[20] 'I would like all to know', wrote Princess Alice flatteringly, 'and share my admiration for such a benevolent and useful life as yours, which has influence far beyond the limits of the sphere.' Mary, accompanied by the translator Catherine Winkworth,[21] travelled to Germany as a personal guest in the Grand-Ducal palace of Hesse-Darmstadt.

The moated palace had its own court, theatre and armoury, a royal library, museum of antiquities and picture gallery; the southern windows looked over the roof and alleys of the medieval town. Here the conference met each day from nine until two; in the afternoons Princess Alice personally escorted visitors to her schools, orphanages and the Alice Hospital, and the evenings were filled with large formal banquets. Delegates reported on women's work as postal and telegraphic clerks, infant teachers, trained nurses or art and craft workers; Mary stressed the need for practical child-care training for girls of all classes.[22] Everyone was amazed by her energy and her lively mind. 'Only think,' wrote Alice to Queen Victoria, 'old Miss Carpenter spoke on all subjects relating to women's work in England . . . her great experience has been of value to us all.' Moreover, to the royal relief, 'not *one word* of the emancipated political side of the question was touched on by anyone'. She would have been surprised to learn of the quiet revolution which was already taking place in Mary Carpenter's mind on this subject. On her side Mary formed an affection for her hostess, who looked, understandably, 'rather worn. The more I saw of the dear Princess,' wrote Mary to Russell, 'the more did I admire and love her. She feels she owes much to

[19] Sell, K. *Alice: Biographical Sketch and Letters*, 284.
[20] Cf. Manton, J. *Sister Dora*, 262–3, on the controversy over professional versus voluntary nursing.
[21] Catherine Winkworth's *Lyra Germanica* brought some of the finest German Chorale melodies into the English hymnary.
[22] Sell, K. *Alice*, 276. Women clerks were admitted to the British postal services in 1870, a secure and respectable job for girls who had to earn their own livings.

her father, of whom she thinks as we do of *ours*.'[23] This was the highest praise she knew.

From Darmstadt, Mary crossed the Rhine by rail, feeling a pang of sympathy for the great wild river, 'to be thus trampled on'. She spent the next weeks at Neuchatel, in the family of Dr Guillaume, governor of the cantonal prison. From the steamers which plied from end to end of the twenty-three mile lake, she saw Mont Blanc in the distance, and along the shores the little medieval towns, each with its wall and fortified towers. After one attempt to sketch the Alps, she sensibly put away her paint-box, and gave herself up to pure delight. Naturally she inspected the prison, finding the workshops, the adult education, the humane treatment of individual prisoners, and the grounds 'unique and quite excellent'; it deserved, she said, to be called a house rather than a prison. She even very creditably gave a 'little sermon in French, on the text of the Prodigal Son, at the prisoners Sunday chapel service'.[24] Dr Guillaume published an account of Mary Carpenter's work in Bristol, which led to the founding by public subscription of a children's home for the canton of Neuchâtel, and it was a joy to her to know her visit had been of practical use.[25] At Geneva, by contrast, she had an experience which troubled her deeply. She suffered horror at seeing a woman prisoner, who had been in solitary confinement for eighteen years. She sat slumped on her stool in silence, unable 'from the weakness of dejection' to do the sewing which lay before her on the table. 'It was difficult to know what to say to her. After we left I heard her singing in her dreary solitude in a wild maniacal manner.' Mary, intensely distressed, begged that the woman might be transferred to an open ward, but was told this was impossible, as in a manic phase she had attacked the warders. Mary could not put the thought of this woman from her mind. She was convinced that with the spread of education the death penalty must disappear from every civilized code, just as torture had already vanished. Yet 'our whitewashed cells with their dreadful monotony, in which a human being is confined without hope of release *are not really more humane*'.

After three months' thought, she drafted and sent off in January 1873, a paper on the treatment of long-sentence prisoners, for the next Prison Reform Congress at Baltimore. Even where a prisoner must be secluded for the protection of society, she wrote, he must be left 'hope of the possibility of regaining some happiness and even making some restitution'. Without hope a person deteriorates beyond recall. She proposed the usual progressive stages of imprisonment, the final stage corresponding to liberty within a large secure enclosure, remote from any ordinary prison. She added that the same freedom could safely be given to most long-term psychiatric patients.[26]

[23] *Life and Work*, 312–13.   [24] *Ibid.*, 313–18.
[25] *Ibid.*, 310 n. 2. A further biography, by the wife of Judge Olivecrona, was published in Sweden.
[26] Wines, E. C. *National Prison Reform Congress of 1873*, 348–54. These humane proposals could of course be distorted to create a penal colony or concentration camp, though no one at the congress made this comment.

At a meeting of the international Arbitration Association, held at Bristol in 1873, Mary Carpenter was asked to take the chair. 'This of course I decline', wrote the old lady to a friend, 'as I always keep within my womanly sphere.'[27] She was a walking paradox. For the sake of her work, she thought nothing of commanding officials, members of Parliament or Cabinet ministers with martinet generalship. For herself, she observed the full rigour of Victorian propriety. As one of the most influential Englishwomen of her day, Mary Carpenter was courted by the budding women's emancipation movement. The first overtures had come in 1856 through Anna Jameson, a lively red-headed novelist, whose tales of her sufferings in marriage to an unworthy husband had quite swept the impressionable Lady Byron off her feet. Mary, struggling with the early crises of Red Lodge, was not impressed. She sent a printed report of her church, 'for your especial benefit, to show you that in our part of England women's rights are recognized. In our congregation, *every* subscriber, male or female, rich or poor, has an equal vote.'[28] In December 1867, she received a very long letter from J. S. Mill in Avignon, arguing that it was not merely her *right* but her *duty* to demand the vote and use it 'as a means of protecting those who cannot vote, such as infants, the sick, idiots, etc.'[29] This argument was well chosen to appeal to the puritan conscience, but Mary remained non-committal. In the summer of 1868 she was asked to present prizes at the new Clifton Ladies College. Smiling benevolently at the rows of young girls, in the blue serge and holland pinafores of emancipation, 'I feel I have as good a right to the vote as any man,' she said, 'but I have not signed any petition and decline to give my name to it. I wish these things to be left, for they will surely come about in the gradual order of change.'[30] Her own career was proof that a woman without a vote could still be a most effective citizen. 'It is quite striking,' she wrote to Dr Guillaume in Switzerland in 1873, 'how much the useful power and influence of women has developed of late years. . . . Widows and unmarried women have quite ample work to do in the world for the good of others to absorb all their powers. Wives and mothers have a very noble work given them by God and want no other.'[31]

What were the reasons for Mary Carpenter's prolonged coolness towards the women's movement? The immediate reason was tactical. As she told J. S. Mill, her work for children, Indian women and women prisoners would at once suffer if she became associated with such an unpopular cause, and naturally the claims of 'the great work I have been given' must come first. Her private reasons were deeper. The women's movement claimed the vote on a property qualification, which would have limited it to independent women householders; it also meant to open the universities and the professions to well-to-do girls. To Mary, concerned with the life and death struggles of the very poor, these aims seemed trivial and self-regarding. Here many of the early Socialists were later to agree with her.

27 *Life and Work*, 317. 28 *Ibid.*, 159.
29 *Ibid.*, Appendix. 30 *Western Daily Press*, 18th June 1868.
31 *Life and Work*, 317.

Then, naturally, in this as in everything, Mary Carpenter was influenced by her father's early teaching. Had not Dr Carpenter preached forty years earlier, in a May Day sermon to the boarding-school Young Ladies, that 'the sexes have their respective purposes in life assigned them by the Lord; and for these they are adapted by their respective characteristics of body and mind. There is even in the intellectual powers and capabilities a general distinction.' Characteristically, the daughter's part, as seen by Dr Carpenter, lay in 'refreshing the wearied spirit of the Father, worn by the trials of life, irritated by its vexations and depressed by its disappointments'.[32] Mary clung to this, as to all her father's pronouncements, and continued to write, in the middle of pitched battles and long-drawn campaigns, 'you know that I am *essentially* a woman'.[33] She would never have admitted to a change of opinion on her own account.

In the last years of her life, Mary Carpenter's attitude towards the women's movement changed gradually but markedly. She still felt no desire to vote herself. She was more useful as an individual, she said, than 'lost in a crowd of Bristol citizens'. Yet the spectacle of other women helplessly suffering in prison, in purdah, in squalid homes, gradually convinced her that women must stand together in each other's defence. Her concern began with sympathy for the brutalized mothers of her children, and developed through her Indian journeys and prison visits; it kindled into anger on behalf of the girls who, on police accusation alone, might be declared common prostitutes under the Contagious Diseases Acts. These Acts, from 1868 to their repeal in 1886, instituted a continental system of licensed, medically examined prostitutes in certain garrison areas. The women's movement led by Josephine Butler attacked the injustice of the new laws. Here, at last, Mary Carpenter was in full sympathy with them; she knew better than most, the ignorant, helpless girls who were predestined victims. She called the Acts 'a gigantic insult to the female sex', and wrote 'with warm sympathy for your own personal efforts' to Josephine Butler.[34] Like many great Victorians she did not mind plain speaking when the occasion demanded it. 'The question is', she wrote, 'whether the two sexes are entitled to equal rights, or whether one is created *for the use* of the other. This once settled, the rest follows easily. Granting the medical necessity for stamping out disease, then any law to effect this *must affect both sexes equally.*'[35] On this question she forgot all her old caution and openly joined 'those who are standing up for the degraded and oppressed'. When a committee was formed in Bristol for the repeal of the Acts, she became a member and later travelled to London for meetings of the National Association, of which, like Florence Nightingale, she became Vice-President. Finally, she broke the rule of a lifetime, and took the chair herself at a meeting. She did not live to see repeal, though she was always convinced it must come.

[32] Carpenter, L. *Sermons on Practical Subjects*, 261–3.
[33] *Life and Work*, 336.
[34] St Andrews University Library, fragment.
[35] *Life and Work*, 337.

Florence Nightingale had already convinced her of the need for trained nurses and midwives. Her own experience had shown her the desperate shortage of competent women as matrons or teachers in children's homes, or of educated women as prison visitors, or school managers. Gradually she found herself making increasing claims for the right of women to serve others. She put this point squarely to the Penal Congress. 'I am not one of those', she said, 'who desire that women should take the place of man or do man's work, but I want to define what is in my judgment the special work of women. I believe that everything which concerns the reformation of female convicts should be wholly and the reformation of children partly under the care of women. Children requiring reformation should be placed in homes, not in prisons, and there can be no true home without a mother, sister or other woman to control it.' Such women must have an official position; when pressed she admitted many women might be 'incapable of managing business arrangements', but was sure they could learn it with training and experience.[36] In practice women social workers, like any other professionals, would need education. At first she imagined them as volunteers, but travel, especially in India, convinced her of the need for professionals. In the last months of her life she signed a memorial to the Senate at the University of London, asking that degrees, especially medical degrees, should be open to women.[37]

By the end of her life she had come round to the view that women needed political organization to defend other women. To the surprise and delight of her young relatives, Mary Carpenter signed a petition demanding, as one who paid rates and taxes, the right to vote. She even appeared on a feminist platform, the bulging portfolio and trusty umbrella mustered in one last good cause. On 8th March 1877, she spoke at the Victoria Rooms, Clifton, to a crowded meeting of the Bristol and West of England Society for Women's Suffrage. Lady Anna Gore Langton, of the west country Whig connection, guaranteed respectability from the chair; all agreed that opinions held by Miss Martineau and Miss Nightingale 'could not be called either wrong or silly'.[38] Miss Carpenter, though a late convert to the cause, was valued by younger women. After her death, the *Englishwoman's Review* recalled how 'her gentle manners and profound sympathy everywhere procure the gratitude and admiration of those whose welfare she had at heart'.[39]

In the spring of 1873 Mary set out on a three months' visit to America, which she knew so well on paper, yet had never seen. 'I cannot fancy I am going,' she wrote to Philip in Montreal, 'but I tell everyone I am, to make myself believe it!' She landed at Boston in April, and found herself in the New England of Henry James' *The Bostonians*, who 'belonged to every league that had been founded for any purpose whatever' and would have reformed the solar system if they could have got hold of it. Anti-slavery had been succeeded by the Prohibition League, founded in 1869, by crusades for sexual

---

[36] Wines, E. C. *International Penitentiary Congress of 1872*, 160–2.

[37] Banks, J. A. *Prosperity and Parenthood*, 229, lists thirty-four major girls' schools founded in the 1870s and thirty-five in the 1880s.

[38] *The Englishwoman's Review*, Vol. 8, 133.   [39] *Ibid.*, Vol. 8, 295–9.

purity and women's rights. Moreover, in Boston, Unitarians were not the small minority they were in Britain. Though liberals disliked the old sectarian name, as Harriet Beecher Stowe observed, 'All the literary men of Massachusetts were Unitarians. All the élite of wealth and fashion crowded Unitarian churches. The judges on the bench were Unitarian.'[40] In this social climate Mary Carpenter found herself, to her genuine bewilderment, a heroine. Everyone wanted to meet her, hear her speak.

At first, with pathetic diffidence, Mary could only think she was being honoured as her father's child. Finding the church split by radical Biblical criticism, she expounded Dr Carpenter's ill-fated Harmony of the Gospels to a puzzled audience. Even at this date it seemed strange to hear an elderly woman explain, 'The life of Christ was so associated in my mind with my father, that I can no more disbelieve one than the other.'[41] Gradually Mary came to see that she was being offered friendship for her own sake. She felt at home in houses where water-colours, which she and Anna had painted for the Anti-Slavery Christmas Fairs, hung on the walls; the earliest was dated 1829. If only Anna could be there to see them! 'There is no one who cares for me as she did,' she wrote in a moment of loneliness.

Yet there was much to enjoy. In three weeks at Boston she wanted to visit Harvard and to see the scenes of the War of Independence, which so appealed to her love of liberty. She visited schools and prisons, and lectured until she lost her voice from tiredness, on India, Education, Reformatories. One visit she treasured was to the veteran abolitionist William Lloyd Garrison. With the end of the Civil War he had closed *The Liberator* after thirty-five years, and retired to one of the tranquil elm-shaded clapboard houses of Cambridge. There the two old people had 'pleasant chats about the great battle fought and won'. In memory of their long friendship, Mary asked him to send her his photograph. '*I hope you will!*'[42] Her hosts felt she needed personal kindness more than people realized and more than she would admit. Sympathetic Mrs Wells rearranged her housekeeping to suit Mary's tastes and habits, and to conserve her strength. 'She would see friends all the morning, address a meeting in the afternoon and go out to dinner in the evening; but twice between times must come the fifteen minutes' rest and the beef tea. One evening when two or three gentlemen had each an appointment with her, she said to the first, after the business part of his visit was finished, "I think that is all you need of me, sir." Bowing to the puzzled man she went to rest before the arrival of her next visitor.' 'I must do so, or I should accomplish nothing,' explained Mary apologetically.[43] In the family circle she showed her most lovable side. Mrs Wells' brother remembered 'her great grey eyes so slow and wise, yet so kind'. She could be unexpectedly feminine. After an important dinner party, her first words were, 'How elegant was Mrs —'s lace!' With young people she showed her own childlike love of fun. 'She seemed younger and younger every time you saw her,' said one.

[40] Wilbur, E. M. *A History of Unitarianism*, III, 436.
[41] *Life and Work*, 316.   [42] Boston Public Library, MS A2, Vol. 37, p. 83.
[43] *Life and Work*, 330.

Her next stop was New York, which frankly overwhelmed her, while its prisons filled her with horror. She was determined, in spite of the midsummer heat, to visit the South, and see some of the colleges for freed men and women to which she was a faithful subscriber. She sailed for Virginia, 'happy to land on that shore, the scene of such frightful struggles and know the slaves are free'. She was touched by the Commencement ceremony at Hampton College, and at Howard University, Washington, lectured to the students. Here she was welcomed by another old friend, Frederick Douglass, who as a runaway slave had been her guest in Bristol. At Philadelphia she lectured to a large audience on Reformatories for the Young; the heat was sweltering, but, she said, 'I got through pretty well.' Her family worried as usual; yet she was surprised by her own powers of endurance.

In July she had fulfilled her lecture engagements, and was free to travel on to Canada, and to join her brother Philip at Montreal, with his German wife Minna, and the small American waif they had adopted. Even here Mary's work claimed her. Philip was sincerely proud of his famous sister, but he found her visit somewhat exhausting. In ten days she addressed seven meetings and visited three gaols.[44] The prison at Montreal was notorious. Mary found time to write at once to Lord Dufferin, the Governor of Canada. 'It is the very worst I have ever visited;' she pointed out that the cells were less than three feet wide. Lord Dufferin replied apologetically, for Mary Carpenter was now a person to be reckoned with, 'I trust that ere long you will find very great improvements have been effected.'[45] A happier visit was to the Children's Aid Society who had received and settled over two thousand young emigrants from reformatory and industrial schools. Settlers with farms in the virgin lands came, eager to adopt healthy boys and girls. The children faced hard work and rough living, sometimes in log cabins on newly cleared land. Yet they shared the same work and conditions as the settlers' own families; the girls found husbands and many of the boys became independent farmers, or as Mary proudly called them, landed proprietors.[46] Most of these children did very well, proving Mary Carpenter's point that urban society rather than themselves was responsible for their troubles. She also determined to visit the American Indian Reservation of the Six Nations near Lake Ontario, where she saw the ten commandments 'freshly painted in the Mohawk language', and asked pertinent questions about compensation, population growth, work and schooling. The schoolmaster, an Indian, regretted that his school was very seldom visited. Later she would demand recognition for its work from the Aborigines Protection Society of London; 'a few books and presents would be an encouragement to the pupils and gratification to the teacher'. Her three months were now almost up. Philip persuaded her to take a steamer on the St Lawrence, and to visit Niagara Falls, 'very glorious

---

[44] Carpenter, R. L. *Memoir of Philip Pearsall Carpenter*, 278, 321.

[45] *Life and Work*, 325.

[46] *Reformatory and Refuge Journal*, July 1874. Supervision by the Children's Aid Society was essential. A report to the Local Government Board in 1875 criticized mass schemes where children were dumped, untrained and unvisited, in the wilds. See Pinchbeck, I. and Hewitt, M. *Children in English Society*, II 566–74.

scenes of nature', she wrote gratefully, 'which are a treasure for ever to me. Still more the certainty that I have been permitted to sow some seed which may bear fruit.' She was satisfied that, though she would not be there to see it, concern for prisoners, children in need, all the rejects and failures of society, had now taken root in Europe and America. The end of July 1873 came; tired but content, she sailed home to her last great campaign.

15

THE LAST CAMPAIGN
1872-1877

The death of Anna, the breaking of this last link in the life-long family chain, and the travels abroad which followed, gave Mary Carpenter new freedom and detachment in her work. 'I have buried all my troubles under the Christmas holly and am free from them,' she wrote to her sister Susan on New Year's Eve of 1873. She felt in herself 'a sort of unmooring of the heart, except when absolutely engaged in definite objects'.

There was no shortage of definite objects near at hand; the reformatory school, the industrial school and the ragged school, all presented urgent problems. Mary, in her sixties, found herself forced to reconsider her life's work. The reason, of course, was W. E. Forster's famous Act of 1870, the first comprehensive Education Act ever passed by a British Parliament, some fifty years after similar laws in western Europe. Mary Carpenter recognized it at once as 'beginning a totally new era in the educational condition of our country'.[1] It did not, as is commonly thought, provide either free or compulsory education, but it did create a national network of schools and School Boards. These, as Forster said in a House of Commons debate, should 'bring elementary education within the reach of every English home, aye, and within the reach of those children who have no homes'. Some country School Boards were slow to provide schools; and H.M. Inspectors reported one where none of the members could read themselves, and had to take all correspondence to the nearest market town. Yet most cities, with Bristol honourably in the lead, were quick to act; one and a half million new school places were created in the years between 1870 and 1875.[2] Until 1870 children from reformatory or industrial schools were better educated than the rest. From this time onwards, reformatory, industrial or ragged schools could no longer claim to provide automatic advantages denied to needy children in the world outside. Increasingly their bleak and economical world had to meet the rival standards of a child receiving public elementary education and living in a good working-class home. Moreover, in the period of liberal reforms which followed the Reform Bill of 1867, these standards were visibly rising.[3] Town life was already less noisome to body and mind. Taine, in his *Notes on England*, had already reflected an uncertainty which was beginning to grow among all thoughtful people, after twenty years' experience, about the invariable

---

[1] *Proceedings of the National Association for the Promotion of Social Science*: Industrial Schools and School Boards, 1871.
[2] Curtis, S. J. *A History of Education in Great Britain*, 277–9.
[3] Best, G. *Mid-Victorian Britain,* traces this process in absorbing detail.

wisdom of removing children in trouble from their own homes.[4] Sir Charles Adderley, who had sponsored the original Youthful Offenders Act in 1854, now regretted some of its provisions. With refreshing freedom from convention, this Tory fox-hunting squire proposed to wipe out the 'penal stain' by removing reformatory and industrial schools from Home Office control. In a House of Commons debate on 10th May 1871 Adderley argued that '*All* schools for poor children aided by public money should be under one Education Department . . . A child born in crime is not a different animal from an ordinary child as some suppose.'[5]

Mary Carpenter visited Sir Charles to discuss this suggestion, but the person who influenced her most was probably a visitor from New England. On 1st June 1872 Dr Howe of Boston, with his celebrated wife, the authoress of 'The Star-spangled Banner', spent 'most happy days with Miss Carpenter'.[6] Dr Howe was a physician, and director of the institute for blind and handicapped children at Boston. He was famous as the first person to have successfully educated a deaf-mute, and from his school came the future teacher of Helen Keller. Howe was a deeply compassionate man, who gave much thought to the lives of his young charges, not simply as cases, but as children, who suffered when forced to live in 'artificial communities . . . more especially,' he wrote, 'should we avoid them for those who have any natural infirmity or any marked peculiarity of mental organization. Beware how you sever ties of family, of friendship, of neighbourhood during the period of their natural growth, lest you make a homeless man, a wanderer and a stranger.' Like many true prophets, Dr Howe went largely unheard in his own generation. Yet Mary Carpenter, however reluctantly, recognized the truth in his words. She had always dwelt with romantic intensity on the beauty of home ties, which her father had taught her to see as the basis of all ethical conduct, especially in women. 'The girl', she had written, 'is specially adapted by nature for a *home*; the affections have large sway over her whole being and nature has given her scope for them in a true home.' She had believed, with all the passionate and burning intensity of her own frustrated maternal love, that her schools could stand *in loco parentis* to their children. Yet by the end of 1869, after fifteen years' experience at Red Lodge, she admitted, 'We desire to reproduce to our children the home, to place them as nearly as possible in the position of the honest working-class family. *This can never completely be done.*'[7]

The reasons were nor far to seek. Irritatingly, the official Scrooges, who had complained of expense, proved to have fact on their side. As standards of living slowly rose, so did the schools' bills for food, heat and clothing. By 1871, the annual cost per head at Red Lodge was £21.10., though schools which used children for industrial work kept the figure as low as £16.[8] The

[4] Taine, H. *Notes on England* (trans. E. Hyams), 169–71.

[5] *Reformatory and Refuge Journal*, May 1871.

[6] Bristol Archives, 12693, No. 20.

[7] *Reformatory and Refuge Journal*, December 1869.

[8] Report of Inspector of Reformatory and Industrial Schools, *Parliamentary Papers*, 1871, XXVIII.

only alternative to factory labour was strict economy in the housekeeping. In 1876, when Sydney Turner made his last report, after nearly thirty years' service as Inspector, there had been two deaths at Red Lodge in the past twelve months. He found the girls 'fairly comfortable though a little inanimate' and he felt the 'dietary requires a little strengthening'.[9] As his standards were Spartan, the food must have been frightful. Kingswood in 1871 was swept by a typhoid epidemic, in which six boys, and incidentally the superintendent, died. It was no longer true that a child was better housed and fed in a reformatory or industrial school than at home.

The same comparison applied to teaching. As long ago as 1853 Mary Carpenter had written that 'an ill-paid and ill-trained teacher was not calculated to raise the condition of children requiring peculiar knowledge, peculiar skill, peculiar zeal and patience'.[10] The Education Act of 1870 made the relative position of reformatory and industrial schools worse, since it both raised the general educational standards and lowered the supply of teachers. 'There is no doubt that in most Reformatory Schools the teaching power is insufficient,' wrote Sydney Turner in his general report for 1875.[11] Like many Englishmen of his generation, Turner never felt quite at ease with nuns; he felt it would be better if they were 'not distinguished by so peculiar a dress'. Yet, to his frank surprise he found the results of convent reformatory and industrial schools among the best in his experience; although taking girls from 'the worst class of Irish population in big cities', they were able to reclaim seven or eight out of ten. This contrasted with 'unfavourable results of some from which I should have expected far more favourable returns',[12] for example Red Lodge, with about six out of ten successes. Strangely enough, he did not draw the conclusion that the convents were the only schools fully and continuously staffed by experienced women.

Finding teachers, especially for delinquent girls, was hard. Finding a good woman superintendent or warden was almost impossible. In the ten years from 1866 to 1876, there were no fewer than four new superintendents at Red Lodge, often with a change of matron and teacher at the same time. The admirably competent matron Mrs Johnson had left for a better job.[13] Constant change made the older girls defiant, the little ones bewildered and unhappy. In 1867, with Mary Carpenter in India, the next matron and schoolmistress were about to resign; the laundry and needlework teachers had already left. No wonder the girls were 'more talkative and noisy than usual'.[14] In summer 1868 'the complete change of teachers which had occurred during the year had a good deal disturbed the order of the school'. Similarly in 1870, when 'Miss Carpenter has been a good deal away engaged in educational work in India . . . the order and general progress of the girls and their school instruction gave me less satisfaction than usual'.[15] The following April,

[9] *Ibid.*, 1876, XXXIV.
[10] Carpenter, M. *Juvenile Delinquents*, 10–11.
[11] Report of Inspector of Reformatory and Industrial Schools, *Parliamentary Papers*, 1875, XXXVI.
[12] *Ibid.*, 1872, XXX.
[13] *Ibid.*, 1866, XXXVIII.
[14] *Ibid.*, 1867, XXXVI.
[15] *Ibid.*, 1870, XXXVI.

before her return, there was a breakdown in discipline for the first time since the disastrous winter of 1856. 'Some girls were insubordinate to the laundry-mistress . . . and order was seriously disturbed. The police were unadvisedly sent for and some of the ringleaders committed to prison.' On a second visit in August, after Mary's return, 'the girls were their old selves, intelligent and cheerful' and 'all symptoms of disorder had disappeared'. He added, with comical caution, 'the responsibility of these unfortunate incidents does not rest with Miss Carpenter, as she was then abroad'.[16] Mary's powers of retaliation were evidently well known at the Home Office.

A pattern was thus established which was to persist to the end of Mary Carpenter's life and beyond. If she were at home, only a narrow street's breadth away, the girls were 'well, cheerful and well-behaved . . . their school work intelligent'. Each time she went away, she found trouble waiting on her return. 'Owing to Miss Carpenter's unavoidable absence a spirit of disobedience and insubordination has crept in and caused trouble and mischief. But the girls are now going on more quietly and thorough good order has been restored.' She came to dread her returns, and her nephew Estlin found her in tears over it. 'I cannot go on as I am, alone; it is wasting my life's powers.'[17] Yet, if she never left the school, she said unanswerably, what would become of it after her death?

What happened to it, in fact, was a series of sharply critical reports. The 'free discipline' at which she aimed could not work without professional skill of a very high order, and the Home Office, at that date, was hostile to it.[18] Everyone agreed that the reformatory and industrial schools had done excellent work. Yet they were beset by so many practical problems that it was increasingly clear they should only be used as a last resort.

The Education Act of 1870 should have put the ragged schools out of business. As even kindly disposed Dickens said: 'although devoted to their uninviting work, they are so narrow-minded and odd, and the whole thing (which might be so good) is such a scramble'.[19] Mary Carpenter had never been hostile to state aid, which some of the more gloomy, austere and wrathful churchmen considered a weapon in the devil's armoury. One writer considered the Act 'a direct interference with individual liberty and parental authority'. Another warned that 'to make a child independent of its parent is to weaken a sacred tie, and so inflict a moral injury on each of them'.[20] Mary closed the St James' Back school, expecting the new Bristol School Board to provide the universal free day-schooling which she had always demanded for the children. 'As soon as the School Boards were established', she wrote, 'the Ragged Schools should be annihilated.' This was a general expectation. As Sydney Turner wrote: 'I had expected that the establishment

[16] Report of Inspector of Reformatory and Industrial Schools, *Parliamentary Papers*, 1871, XXVIII.

[17] *Life and Work*, 347.

[18] In the early twentieth century the positions were reversed. Skilled professionals at the Home Office introduced reforms which many school managers resisted.

[19] Collins, P. *Dickens and Education*, 87.

[20] *Macmillans Magazine*, February 1873, 'The Children of the Poor'.

of School Boards in our larger towns, and their exercise of the power of enforcing attendance, would have lessened the number of disorderly and neglected children.'[21] Yet the Children's Agent, first appointed by Mary Carpenter in 1864, had a different story to tell. Day after day, week after week, as he made his way round wharfs and alleys or up broken stairs, he found the same barefoot, famished children as before. The 'most depraved and disorderly classes', he reported, 'had no intention of losing their children's casual earnings by sending them to school'.[22] People felt comfortably certain that it was the duty of the new board schools to deal with neglected children. 'In the first place,' remarked the *Quarterly*, 'the new system must soon cover all the neglected spots and succour all the neglected classes of the community. Evidently the area the new schools must cover is very large.' As to means, 'the ragged school system must be taken up by authority'.[23]

Yet those who willed the end, did not always will the means. The education rate was fixed low. 'We can only go to 3d in the pound,' lamented a member of the London School Board. In fact the London rate was frozen at 1d, and by 1874 the Board had not established a single truly free school in the city. 'Whatever some few theorists may say,' commented the *Edinburgh Review*, 'the cause of *free schools* is at present hopeless.'[24] The schools were neither free nor compulsory, for 'the temper of an Englishman revolts at the idea of compulsion' as 'a principle novel to the inhabitants of this country, though familiar enough to the peoples of other lands'. Many people objected strongly to the presence of ragged children in the state-aided schools. Llewelyn Davies, the Christian Socialist rector of Marylebone, sent thirty street boys to his church's National School. Within a week the headmaster had expelled them all. Parents felt even more strongly. 'A respectable artizan earning his two pounds a week will not willingly bring his children into contact with street Arabs,' continued the same *Edinburgh Review* article. A conscience clause protected freedom of belief, but 'is there to be no conscience clause against the contagion of infectious disease, or the worse contagion of bad example, against the extreme dirt, roughness and degradation of the very lowest classes of the poor? . . . Many parents had rather make any sacrifice than plunge their children into such a low social atmosphere.'

The certificated teachers, struggling for a precarious professional toe-hold, had enough problems with those children who did come to school, to cram the dark cavernous dens, smelling by evening like a ferret's cage, which formed their class-rooms. 'The children are so poor and dirty', wrote one, 'that the work is sometimes very dirty.' Girls were seen 'absolutely naked except for an old gown'; a boy who had been absent brought the convincing excuse 'fetching the gin and no boots'. In some places pupils attacked their teachers with sticks and large stones, until they had to get police protection in class.[25]

[21] Report of Inspector of Reformatory and Industrial Schools, *Parliamentary Papers*, 1873, XXXI.   [22] *Life and Work*, 305.

[23] *Quarterly Review*, July 1871, 'The New School Boards'.

[24] *Edinburgh Review*, January 1871, 'Results of the Education Act'.

[25] Curtis, S. J. *History of Education in Great Britain*, 293–4.

The board schoolteachers, aware of the wild, neglected truants, were yet determined not to have them in their own classes. They should not be judged harshly for this. Everyone feared that the newly certified teachers might become conceited; no one seemed to worry that they might be hurt by their self-appointed betters. Thus a vicar's wife objected when 'the young person who teaches the National School' appeared at church in a bonnet which showed her pretty hair. Schoolmasters, observed *The Times*, 'are generally of so inferior a class, that they do not venture to sit down in the presence of the clergyman'; while the *Quarterly Review* advised in 1879 that 'pretensions such as the certificated teacher sometimes puts forth must be crushed and checked without mercy'. It is no wonder that these teachers would not risk their precarious, hard-fought-for respectability by taking in 'the sweepings of the street'. Instead, the first President of the National Union of Elementary Teachers proposed compulsory attendance for 'street arabs and wanderers', but special ragged schools to keep them separate from more presentable scholars.[26]

This was not a new idea. In her early books, Mary had written with admiration of the schools provided in Aberdeen since the 1840s, where children stayed all day, were given food, lessons and craft training, but returned to their parents each night. Now in 1870 she corresponded with Sheriff Watson of Aberdeen, who wrote that his schools, open from 7 a.m. to 7 p.m., were 'not encumbered with dormitories. . . . The idle railing of the rich against the vice and improvidence of the poor never affected us; for we knew that the poverty of the poor was their greatest affliction, that it would be greatly alleviated by feeding their children.' He stoutly denied that it was necessary, right, or indeed possible, to remove every neglected child from its own home.[27] Encouraged by this, for she greatly respected his opinion, Mary Carpenter addressed an open letter to the members of the Bristol School Board in June 1871, urging them to establish 'feeding Industrial Day Schools, with compusory attendance'. These schools would help the poorest family to maintain its integrity and meet an urgent social need.

There was no question of punishment; the child would simply receive meals, lessons, handicraft teaching and play, while being properly cared for from 8 a.m. to 6 p.m. The cost should be met by School Boards or Boards of Guardians, and Mary Carpenter argued that money would be very soundly invested in this preventive social work.[28] She received support from an unexpected quarter, the *Saturday Review*, reactionary but always delighted to expose official hypocrisy in high places. 'Until these little outcasts have been humanized and civilized in some degree,' remarked a contributor on 12th October 1872, 'they are sources of physical and moral contamination. That separate schools will have to be provided for this class is in no doubt.'

Mary and Sydney Turner had not always agreed in the past, but were united in caring deeply for the children. Now they found themselves in

[26] Tropp, A. *The School Teachers*, 111.
[27] *Reformatory and Refuge Journal*, January and February 1869, June 1871.
[28] Carpenter, M. *Industrial Schools and their Relation to School Boards*.

wholehearted agreement, and, to the credit of both, worked closely together in this last campaign. Turner's report in 1870 put the case for day feeding schools for children who were destitute and neglected; going home each night would 'infuse a more free and natural tone into the discipline'.[29] After three years' experience of School Boards, he added, 'I am led unwillingly to the conclusion that the Arab class of children as they are called cannot be reached by the powers and provisions of the Education Act as it now stands, or by the purely instructional machinery which it recognizes.'[30] Meanwhile, Mary, never one to preach what she did not practise, had at the age of 65 opened a new school. On New Year's Day 1872, she opened a Day Industrial School, having converted the old buildings in St James' Back. It received at first no grant either from the School Board, the Board of Guardians, or the Government, but Mary, undaunted, began a personal campaign for official recognition and support.

She was as happy and excited as in the far-off first days of the original ragged school in 1846. 'You see,' she wrote to an old friend, 'we have to begin again where we were 29 years ago. But we shall prevail in the end.'[31] Frances Power Cobbe, who wrote wondering how Mary could carry so many responsibilities, received the reply: 'The reason why I have accomplished my undertakings is not that I am in any way superior to multitudes of others, but that I have never commenced anything but from a distinct and clear consciousness of necessity.' She admitted that an evening's teaching at the new Industrial School, after a day 'harassed by anxieties' with the staff at Red Lodge, was 'sometimes too much for my strength,' but by rigorous planning she evolved a working routine to include everything.[32]

Boys and girls of all ages, 'the wild Arabs of the streets', came flocking to the new school. Many were young brothers and sisters, some perhaps even the children, of her old ragged scholars. They crowded round the playground gates on raw January mornings, wizened and shivering as organ-grinders' monkeys; once inside, they rushed and scuffled for a place near the old iron stove. Mary's plan had been to give them a hot dinner of pea soup and dumplings or potatoes and stew with a red-letter day of suet and treacle pudding once a week. But the teachers reported that many children came to school too cold and hungry for work, or even for play. So a cheap hot breakfast was added, for fifty children, by cooking five pounds of oatmeal porridge, with half a gallon of milk and a pound of sugar, in the big wash-house cauldrons. The children wolfed it down, smacking their lips. 'If a boy will eat oatmeal porage with thankfulness,' said Mary from the authority of a lifetime's experience, 'then he *must* be starving!' She added a third meal of dripping toast or bread and cheese with hot cocoa before the children were turned out into the dark streets at the end of the day. These rough and simple meals were entirely free.

[29] Report of the Inspector of Reformatory and Industrial Schools, *Parliamentary Papers*, 1870, XXXVI.
[30] *Ibid.*, 1873, XXXI.
[31] Dorset County Record Office, D43/C58.
[32] Huntington Library, Carpenter Letters, CB 67-8–CB 70-89.

The cost was two shillings per child each week; Mary raised the money by public subscription, with her nephew William Carpenter acting as treasurer.[33]

A few months of regular meals improved the children's physical condition; they began to grow and even to put on weight. Motherly volunteers washed and combed the young ones, while the school lent smocks and pinafores from a common stock. Mary hoped in time to knit and sew warm clothing from donated materials in class. By summer the children, though still unteachable by normal standards, had rediscovered their childhood enough to play happily in the yard. 'In our school,' she reported the following September, in a speech to the Social Science Association, meeting at Plymouth, 'there have been the very lowest that could be found, in so miserable a condition that they cannot be admitted into ordinary schools. . . . The experiment of eight months showed that even the wildest may be brought under steady kindly discipline. 'Of course,' she admitted, 'not one of these waifs and strays could be taught the three Rs, even to the lowest stand demanded by the Revised Code for an educational grant. We strive to introduce elements, not of mere book learning, but of *civilization*. The school has therefore been debarred from any educational award this year, though making more educational effort than other schools.'[34]

Mary wrote in protest to W. E. Forster, creator of the Education Act, who feared 'encouraging parents to get their children fed out of the rates'. Rebuffed here, she demanded help from the Bristol School Board. This had appointed four School Attendance Officers, who drafted children from two hundred 'low and disorderly families' into the new Board Schools. Within a few weeks, though officially at school, the boys and girls were roaming the streets, noisy, wild and dirty as ever. The chairman of the Board admitted that there were hundreds of children running the Bristol streets 'nearly naked and scarcely fed at all'. It would be better to pay for feeding these children in school than in prison, where they would inevitably find their way. To Mary's intense satisfaction the Bristol School Board therefore agreed to certify the Day Industrial School as 'fit and proper for children who will not attend other schools' and to pay one to one and a half shillings a week for each child.[35] The Inspector of Reformatories commended this in his annual report as a good example to other boards.[36] The Industrial School continued its work for the next two years, with an average of sixty to ninety wild ragged scholars. Yet for lack of recognition by the Education Council, its existence remained precarious. The city authorities took over the playground for a street-widening scheme, and the school was forced to move to a workmen's hall nearby. In the summer of 1874 the certificated master left and a new teacher was engaged. He proved patient, efficient and endlessly kind to the children, but he lacked a certificate; the School Board was there-

[33] *Proceedings of the National Association for the Promotion of Social Science*, 1872. This diet was approved by H.M. Inspector. *Reformatory and Refuge Journal*, October 1878.
[34] *Ibid.*, 1872.
[35] *Refuge and Reformatory Journal*, October 1872.
[36] Report of the Inspector of Reformatory and Industrial Schools, *Parliamentary Papers*, 1873, XXXI.

fore reluctantly forced by the terms of the Code to withdraw its grant. Mary took advice from past friends, Sir Charles Adderley, Sir Stafford Northcote, Lord Houghton, Lord Shaftesbury. All advised her that nothing less than a supplementary Bill to the Education Act could alter the regulations.[37]

Mary set to work with all her old vigour, to discover the experience of other big city School Boards. Manchester, Liverpool and Leeds had all found similar populations of waifs and strays or 'street Arabs'. Birmingham found that the only schools these children could be persuaded to attend were former ragged schools, where they casually dropped in 'if sufficiently near their homes'. In London the problem was most acute, with thousands of wandering Arabs in the streets. The children were far too quick in mind and body for the perspiring attendance officers who pursued them. Everyone reported 'a falling off in voluntary charity, now that education rates have to be paid'. Mary had been fighting for the needs of these children for years, only to be met with bland official complacency in Whitehall. 'The Educational Council,' she said, 'has steadily refused to recognize the wants, or even the existence of these children.' Yet they could not ignore the evidence of their own elected Boards. 'It was left to the School Boards to do the work so long neglected and to discover this region, hitherto unknown to the government.'[38]

The first official reaction was to sweep the problem out of sight. School Boards dealt with truants by sending them away as boarders to existing Industrial Schools, sometimes for years. The London School Board alone had placed 1281 of these cases by March 1874, and all the schools in and around the city were crammed to overflowing. At a conference on the working of Industrial Schools, held in May 1874, Mary argued that it was totally wrong to remove children from their families unless absolutely necessary. The Superintendent at the Middlesex Industrial School at Feltham admitted frankly that many of his boys were not the homeless vagabonds for whom the school was intended. They had homes where 'the father goes out to work and the mother goes out charing. They are simply children who will not go of their own accord to school.' It was cruel and ridiculously expensive, said Mary Carpenter, to send all these children away from home. A clergyman present argued that removal from their 'abominable parents' might be necessary for 'the redemption of these children'. 'They do more good to their parents than their parents do harm to them,' retorted Miss Carpenter cheerfully. 'We must *not* say all parents are wicked. . . . We should not sever the family ties of all these young persons, or place the hand of the policeman on so many thousands of the rising generation. Nor', she concluded, 'should we remove from local School Boards, elected and supported by the people, the responsibility of these children.'[39]

In August 1875 the British Association met in Bristol. Mary, who as a girl had longed in vain to see the exhibits arranged by her father and brothers

---

[37] Carpenter, M. *Day Industrial Schools.*

[38] *Proceedings of the National Association for the Promotion of Social Science*, 1872.

[39] Carpenter, M. *Day Industrial Schools not certified Industrial Schools necessary to complete the work of School Boards.*

for the Bristol meeting of 1836, was now invited as a celebrity to address the statistical section. She took the opportunity to put the case of neglected children before this influential audience. At 68, she had lost none of her lucidity or power to marshal an argument. With dry humour, she remarked that when she began to work, 'many strongly opposed the idea that any parent should have his liberty so curtailed as to be deprived of the privilege of bringing up his children in ignorance'. Now on paper every child was entitled to education, but in practice the street Arabs could not go to normal Board Schools. Mary invited any members of the British Association or the national press to visit the school in St James's Back. 'Let such visitors form their own conclusion whether our children could possibly attend any Board School. *They would not be admitted, even if they presented themselves.*' She laid before the statistical section a short Bill, supplementary to the Education Act of 1870 which she and Sydney Turner had drafted jointly. By the terms of this, School Boards should be empowered to establish Day Industrial Schools or to examine and certify existing voluntary schools, contributing up to two shillings a week for each child. Any person might report neglected children to the School Board, which could then make a compulsory Attendance Order. At school, the children should stay at least ten hours daily, receiving education, craft training, physical care, recreation and food.[40]

She returned to the attack at the meeting of the Social Science Association, for which she travelled to Glasgow. 'I arrived late, was rather tired,' she wrote to Russell, 'but had my field day on Thursday. It was a most satisfactory one. The Day Industrial Paper has converted all!' Now all she needed was a parliamentary sponsor for her Bill and as usual she was refreshingly unprejudiced in her choice. 'I have conferred with many M.P.s and Lords in London, chiefly Tories (they are best in this work),' she wrote to old Sheriff Watson in Aberdeen. 'It is too late to try this session; but I am preparing the way and there will be a regular campaign.' A few months later, she sent a further progress report. 'I went to London in February and saw the Government' (a splendid Carpenterian phrase). 'I have great hopes of getting an Act. If the Government will not take it up, they are still not opposed, so I have hopes. . . . I have no one to rely on and am single-handed. But I shall go on fighting the battle of the children!'[41]

The campaign was interrupted briefly by Mary Carpenter's last visit to India in the winter of 1875. She came home in May 1876 to find Disraeli's government preparing an Education Act to establish a minimum of compulsory education, with penalties for parents who failed to send their children to school.[42] This, usually called, after its sponsor, Lord Sandon's Act, also included a clause on children 'not under any control', which it proposed to send to boarding Industrial Schools for one month and then to release them. Mary at once saw that nothing could be less workable; thousands of

---

[40] Carpenter, M. *Day Industrial Schools.*

[41] *Life and Work*, 339–40.

[42] The leaving age was 10, raised to 11 in 1893, to 12 in 1899, to 14 in 1918. No one could accuse the British of rushing recklessly into national education.

wild children would swamp the schools, while a month's detention would do nothing to civilize their primitive savagery. At the age of 70, she prepared to hurl herself into battle with all her old zest. 'Lord Sandon has been bringing in a Bill on Education which we consider useless and injurious,' she wrote to S. N. Tagore in India. 'I have been very busy writing, getting up memorials, in fact giving my whole mind to get the Government to understand that neglected children ought to be educated in a way *adapted* to their *needs.*' Later she described this way as one 'which would address not only their heads but their hearts'.[43]

Within a few weeks she had assembled a committee, encouraged all the industrial school managers to sign a protest and the major city School Boards to petition for a new clause. With this support behind her, she submitted her own draft proposals to the Committee on Education, with a letter 'which showed clearly what she wanted and *why* she wanted it'.

Lord Sandon, Vice-President of the Committee, was a member of the distinguished Dudley Ryder family; his grandfather had been the younger Pitt's foreign secretary, his father M.P. for Liverpool, and he had been brought up to the cares of office. In the first London School Board, he had been president of the statistical committee, and therefore knew the size of the problem. He was a serious, conscientious man, handicapped, like Mary Carpenter, by poor health; but he was not the fighter she was, and eventually allowed his poor health to drive him out of public life. Meanwhile, he was easy material for her practised hand to work on, though now in old age, she had learnt to deal gently with officialdom.

On 18th July 1876, in deference to her authority, he introduced a clause authorizing School Boards to maintain day industrial schools, handsomely acknowledging the 'indomitable perseverance' of Mary Carpenter, for, as he said he did not wish to take the credit for the scheme himself. In the opinion of a *Times* correspondent, 'it was entirely in deference to her authority, that members on both sides of the House agreed to give her plan a fair trial. . . . She thus had the intense satisfaction of feeling she had at last brought to completion the system of prevention, as well as reformation, which she had gradually been working out for thirty years.'[44]

Mary was pleased, of course, but at 70, she no longer thought it necessary to pretend surprise. She merely remarked, 'I have *never* yet failed in anything I have undertaken to do.' Characteristically, she looked to the future and the support which the Education Committee must give to the schools. Lord Sandon meekly 'hoped to have the advantage of talking it over with her as the Bill came into operation'. The schools were certified by the Government and had the same legal powers of detention as boarding-schools, since children attended under court order; but their quality must depend on generous grants.[45]

Sir George Grey, the former Whig Home Secretary, wrote to Mary

---

[43] *Life and Work*, 373.   [44] *The Times*, 18th June 1877.
[45] *Reformatory and Refuge Journal*, November 1867. The R. and R. Union disapproved of them because they were not boarding-schools.

Carpenter in his own hand to tell her the news. He understood and perhaps even shared her commitment to human need, for his own mother had been a member of the early evangelical group surrounding Wilberforce. He wrote that he hoped the certificate to the Day Industrial School 'will be a considerable help to its funds. But as I see there was a small deficiency at the end of last year,' he added kindly, 'I hope you will accept the enclosed cheque as a contribution towards its support. It will be a pleasure to me to feel I was associated in however small a way with so useful a work.'[46] Mary, who had always felt such a craving for understanding sympathy in her work, believed her ideas had found general acceptance at last, and was happy. The three types of school she had proposed at the Birmingham conference twenty-five years before were now in being: reformatory schools for children with serious convictions, industrial schools for homeless vagrants, and day industrial schools to feed and care for cases of simple neglect. The last, she believed, was the most important. Other people must now carry out the work she had planned and fought for: but she believed to the last that day schools, generously supported, could come to the rescue of the majority of children in need, and save them from life in an institution. Even the poorest of parents cared for their children, and should never be condemned unheard. 'When we consider their own early nurture, the influences under which they grew up, the condition in which they are now living, deep pity should move us for their own sake, as well as for their children.[47] As for the children, especially the girls, home was the best place to 'awaken in them healthy affection and call out their intellectual powers'. With Mary Carpenter, family life was part of religion.

Old age brought Mary Carpenter a golden Indian summer. Nature, which had been an indifferent stepmother to her all her life, bringing ill health and a difficult temperament, now relented at last. Mary, like her formidable mother before her, grew happy and serene. Her rheumatic heart disease was now advanced, and she was living on borrowed time, but the prospect of death did not trouble her. 'I am very grateful', she wrote to her brothers, 'that we are so united a family, both the beloved ones gone before, and those that remain. May we remain so to the end!' She made her will, orderly and competent as ever, neglecting no claim or interest. At the end of a frugal, hardworking life, her property amounted to nearly eight thousand pounds, worth more than eighty thousand at current valuation. She provided an income of fifty pounds to 'my adopted daughter Rosanna Powell', with Herbert Thomas as trustee. Russell and Philip, who were not well off, received similar annuities for their lifetime. All the employees of her institutions and all the Lewin's Mead charities received small bequests. Her nephews and nieces each got a hundred pounds and even her cousins small legacies. The family books and pictures were carefully distributed among them, her own library of books, reports and papers on philanthropic subjects housed at Red Lodge, and her personal manuscripts bequeathed to Estlin, who was to be her biog-

[46] Bristol Archives, 12693, No. 16.
[47] Carpenter, M. *Juvenile Delinquents*, 160.

rapher. Two hundred pounds went to Sasipada Banerji for his work among the Indian peasants. All the residue formed a trust for her various charities, including work for women in India 'on the principle of non-interference in religion'.[48] Every line of this lengthy document revealed the same conscientious attention to detail, which had made an obscure provincial schoolmistress a power in the land.

In 1874 her favourite brother Philip came on a visit to England. Everyone wanted to see him, but he stayed with Mary, for she seemed to him, with all her engagements and committees, 'the lonely one of the family'. Together they talked about old days, success and failure, their work. Philip was struggling to make a living by private teaching; his heart was affected by the family rheumatism, and though only 58, he looked increasingly tired.[49] Mary begged him to give up his school, saying with perfect truth that it would be a pleasure to her to make up his income, since she had more than enough for her own needs. Philip refused; to his credit, he had never forgotten the years of sacrifice and toil by which Mary had paid for his education. He had a happy time with all the family, but returned to Canada, comforting Mary with long, vivid scribbled letters. This impractical, sometimes maddening man, with his unfocused talents, outwardly achieved little enough in life. Yet from his letters one can see why Mary loved him so intensely, for he understood and shared her deepest beliefs. From his earliest days, he confirmed her faith in the goodness of life. 'Contrary to theology,' he had written, 'the natural man has always been the *happy* one, receiving a fulness of delight from study, music, etc.' This beloved eccentric brother took Mary Carpenter back in old age to the hidden springs of her life. As long as she lived, she treasured the memory of his last happy visit.

However bent and breathless her body, Mary Carpenter's mind and will-power remained clear. She could still hold the reins of her work. 'I am truly thankful', she wrote to an old friend, in the last year of her life, 'that though I cannot do much walking, I can get through really as much as ever, in *intensity* if not in *quantity*, though often in the latter.' A life which was not useful would have been no life to her. To the last she could lecture—'I was quite *astonished* at myself in my power of public speaking'—draft minutes and reports, visit London for calls on the Home Office or the Education Committee, with stolen hours of pure pleasure at the National Gallery. Memory sometimes grew a little treacherous; to make sure nothing was forgotten she kept a small notebook in her reticule. 'Day Industrial Schools, Indian National Association, Canada, Prisons and Indians', read her private agenda for a London trip in April 1874. These official calls were no longer the scenes of combat they had so often been in the past. 'The great battles are over,' she wrote thankfully, 'and I have only to carry on the work to its completion.' Francis Power Cobbe, who had known Mary in her moods of freezing dedication, came to visit her, bringing a young niece. 'She insisted on my going with her over all our old haunts, and noting what changes and improvements

---

[48] Principal Probate Register: Will of Mary Carpenter.
[49] Carpenter, R. L. *Memoir of Philip Pearsall Carpenter*, 321.

she had made. I was tenderly touched by her great kindness to my young companion and myself and by the added softness and gentleness which years had brought her. She expressed herself very happy in every way.'[50]

During the 1870s, crowded as they were, Mary Carpenter loved to keep open house for all visitors from India. First to come was the very young great-grandson of Ram Mohun Roy, 'to pour forth my veneration over the grave of my ancestor; to me it is a place of pilgrimage.'[51] In the summer of 1870, K. C. Sen led family prayers in her house, and preached to a huge congregation at Lewin's Mead, where a tablet records his visit. Each day began with his morning invocation to the universal spirit. 'May thy counsel rule my mind, may thy love warm my heart, may thy holy presence go with me as the light of my path.' Mary thanked him for this prayer. 'You, as a stranger and a Hindu, have been able to say things which we can only feel.'[52]

Her feeling for Indian family life was not an abstraction, but warmly human. The opportunity came to share in the innermost circle of Indian family life, when Sasipada Banerji, the Bengal landowner, who had won Mary's respect by trying to ease the life of his labourers, brought his wife to England. Mary introduced him everywhere as 'one who has laboured for his countrymen more than anyone I know'. She remembered Lord Houghton's notorious weakness for social novelties and suggested, 'If Lady Houghton or your daughters are in town, they would I am sure, be pleased to welcome the *first Brahmin lady* who has ever ventured to cross the "black water".'[53] Learning that the wife was pregnant, Mary invited the young couple to share her home until their child was born. The Banerjis lived for six months at Red Lodge House, and their son was born under her roof; in the lucky dip of Victorian naming-ceremonies, he became the future Sir Albion Banerji,[54] while a brother was named Lant.

Another visitor from Bombay, a young graduate called K. M. Shroff, gives a vivid picture of Mary Carpenter at 68. He came on a Friday, and found her writing letters to friends all over the world, which must catch the overseas post. Later, she gave him lunch, and took him to visit her schools, the Museum, the Library, introducing him everywhere as a personal friend. He noticed wherever she went, she was welcomed and loved heartily by people, especially by children. After a week's stay, he went to say goodbye to Miss Carpenter, and found her, to his astonishment and delight, packing up a box full of toys and children's picture books, which he was to give as a home-coming present to his little brothers and sisters in Bombay. She added a carefully wrapped slice of Christmas cake for him to eat in the train. 'What struck me most in the preparation of all this', said the young man, 'was a sort of motherly affection.' He found her tender to everyone, but especially to those in need.[55] She was anxious to know the progress of social reform but he

[50] *Life and Work*, 383.   [51] Bristol Archives, 12693, No. 24.

[52] *Life and Work*, 298–300. These Indian friendships were valuable to Estlin Carpenter who became a leading scholar in the field of comparative religion.

[53] Trinity College Cambridge Library.

[54] Politician and author, in 1935, of *The Indian Tangle*.

[55] *Life and Work*, 342–50.

answered that 'nothing could be done unless she came out to India'. Before he left, she had promised to make the journey. In October 1875, she sailed for her fourth and last visit to India. She was happy to be going, pathetically delighted and grateful to have been asked. 'In India,' she wrote to her Polish friend, 'I am regarded as *The Old Mother* and I am proud of the title.'[56]

In contrast with her earlier visits, everyone approved, the Queen, Princess Alice, even Florence Nightingale, who wished that 'I could come to India too, if it were only for a few months . . . to inspect the premises.' Fortunately for the Viceroy's peace of mind, this alarming dual visitation could not take place. Mary relived old memories on the voyage out. Her long itinerary, Bombay, Hyderabad (where the S. N. Tagores were now stationed), Poona, Madras, Calcutta, Dacca, Baroda, was a triumphal progress. A Gujarati poet wrote 'By special order of God a fairy named Miss Carpenter has come down. . . . Every man will be astonished at seeing such valour *in a woman*.'[57]

Looking back, it seemed as though ten years of effort for the women of India had achieved very little. Yet Mary Carpenter, who earlier in life had been plunged into anguish at the smallest check to her plans, was now hopeful and serene. She believed that the future of India lay with her handful of young friends in K. C. Sen's Brama Samaj of India, although their ethic of self-sacrifice and moral force was so utterly opposed to all worldly wisdom. Yet this group formed the Indian Reform Association to demand social reforms for the poor, education for women, charity even between castes, and civil rights for all. In 1885 they met with other spiritual movements at Calcutta in the first Indian National Congress. Afterwards they met each year to demand local and national self-government, while slowly their principles transformed the life of educated Hindus. From these apparently impractical, other-worldly beginnings came modern India.[58] Mary Carpenter did not live to see this new India; yet, a wise and hopeful godmother, she had foreseen its birth.

At the end of March 1876 Mary Carpenter sailed for home. To her intense joy she was no longer alone. Sasipada Banerji had decided to train two of his sons in Western sciences, to carry on his practical work among the peasants. Their mother had died, so Mary agreed to serve as their foster-mother, and to give them a holiday home during their school days in England. The boys were Satya, who was about 12, and his younger brother Lant, who had been named in honour of her own father. The journey passed swiftly, as Mary won the boys' confidence and answered their questions. At home, loneliness was a thing of the past. Rosanna, who had been abroad to complete her education, came home to help with the housekeeping. Mary's sixty-ninth birthday was one of the happiest in her life. So many presents came from India that she had to have a special cabinet made for them, and when this was full, to convert a china pantry. 'How very many they gave me! I am quite astonished when I look them over,' she wrote, happily. Mary realized that the Indian adventure must be her last journey; walking was increasingly difficult, and any physical

---

[56] *Ibid.*, 310.   [57] Bristol Archives, 12693, Nos. 24 and 25.
[58] Majumdar, R. C., Rayachaudhari, H. and Datta, K. *An Advanced History of India*, 878.

exertion left her out of breath. Yet her mind was as lively and her enthusiasm as youthfully fresh as ever. The Bristol Philosophical Institution, which her father had helped to found fifty years before, had just moved to a new building. The committee asked Mary Carpenter to give a course of six lectures on her work in their new theatre. She delivered these during the winter of 1876–7. Each talk lasted an hour and a quarter, and audiences were amazed to see this worn, bent little figure address them fluently, without notes, in the soft clear voice, which had always been her chief charm. The lectures made her tired, but very happy. She felt that all past differences were forgotten, and that Bristolians now honoured her as a fellow citizen who had served their city well. Moreover the work which had filled her whole life was now 'so shut up in me, I am glad to give out a little'.

Already she was carefully sorting and filing her papers for Estlin, who would write her biography after her death. Her brothers and Susan were anxious about her water-colour sketches. Slowly, dwelling with affection and a little regret on long-vanished scenes, she collected them in a large portfolio for William. They wanted to publish her poems, but this with sensible self-criticism, she would not allow. She compromised by putting together a selection from the earliest to the latest, to be privately printed for close friends.[59] 'You will find my poems as they proceed, form a little autobiography,' she explained. 'I cannot now write any poetry or anything literary, but can only express my experiences in simple language.' She finished the little book, and wrote a few lines of introduction on her seventieth birthday. Her enjoyment of little luxuries was a pleasure to her family. Her tastes were as frugal as ever, cold beef for lunch and a cup of gruel for supper, but, as she wrote to an old friend, 'I am very happy to have enough money to do everything I want! Few people can say that. I am not obliged to stint myself; and I can indulge myself in making my places and things very nice, and binding books, and making presents, and subscribing to good objects and taking journeys! I am only stingy in things which I do not *like* spending money about,' she added with refreshing candour. 'So I am rich.'[60] By chance a letter survives which she wrote to an old lady of her own age. Ellen Wansey had long ago in her girlhood attended Dr Carpenter's Bristol lectures, as a fellow student of Harriet Martineau, and had never forgotten those days. 'On a bright spring day,' she wrote, 'a Bristol feeling comes over me sometimes, and then I see the sunshine flickering through the trees in the square, and yourselves in your pink morning frocks, or dressed for chapel on Sundays. I hear the sound of your voices sometimes and never without longing to hear them again. So much has happened since those days!'[61] Now Mary wrote, with the warmth of old affection, congratulating Miss Wansey on her 70th birthday, some three months before her own. 'We used to think that a very great age and look at those who had attained it as quite old people and yet now I have nearly attained to it, I feel as young in all powers of true enjoyment

[59] Bristol Archives, 12693, No. 40. *Voices of the Spirit and Spirit Pictures*, 1877.
[60] *Life and Work*, 384.
[61] Dorset County Record Office, D43/C58.

and work as ever I did. . . . You have, I hope found the secret of health which keeps me well, to ascertain the measure of your strength and not to go beyond it, but to accept all those little indulgences we did not allow ourselves in earlier life, but which are now lawfully our due.'[62] To the wonder and delight of her young nieces and nephews, who had known her as an austere, awe-inspiring figure, Mary was prepared to be a little spoilt at last. On her 70th birthday, 3rd April 1877, letters, gifts and flowers poured into Red Lodge House. She had not known she had so many friends, or that there were so fond of her. Her letter of thanks to Estlin was filled with serene philosophy. She did not deny her life had often seemed hard, yet 'I do not look back with sorrow on the past. There have been many painful woundings and sad bereavements, and great struggles and dark perplexities, but they have all blended together to make a calm whole of the past, very wonderfully calm when I think of parts alone. There has been one deep moving spirit running through it all.'

This mature philosophy was to be put to its last test, for a few weeks later, a telegram from Montreal told her Philip was dead. Mary wrote firmly to her family that 'we ought not to grieve for him . . . I am so thankful that I went over and saw him, and that he came here in 1874 to see you, and had so happy a time with us all'. But after she herself had died, they found in her private journal an entry recording 'the great grief of the departure of my beloved Philip, whom thou hast called to join those who are gone before, my father, my mother, my Anna. But the parting is very grievous, for I nursed him as a mother in his childhood, and always loved him so, dear brother!'[63] She treasured all the letters about him which she received from friends, but un-selfishly sent them to his widow in Montreal.

Feeling that she must be very lonely, her brother Russell came to stay. They talked of the old days, family history, their work, success and failure. Mary spoke with great gentleness, and without her old dogmatism, yet still with hope. She admitted the difficulties at her schools, the endless problems of money and staff at Red Lodge, the occasional disappointments with children she had loved. Yet she was quite determined to carry on. 'I believe the work is of God and *must* succeed, when freed from all the imperfection and errors, inseparable from every human undertaking. What we have been permitted to do, only reveals to us what has not been done.'[64]

Past and present interwove in her thoughts. On the second Sunday in May there was always a special anniversary service at Lewin's Mead, when all the schools connected with the congregation met together. Mary, as usual, left the family pew, and climbed, breathless but determined, into the gallery with her girls. From the height of the great square room, she looked over row upon row of boys and girls, seated in companies, like the children of Blake's 'Holy Thursday'. There were the Sunday Schools, the Stoke's Croft British Schools, the Day Industrial School, ragged but scrubbed for the occasion, the sturdy

[62] *Ibid.*, D43/C59.
[63] Carpenter, R. L. *Memoir of Philip Pearsall Carpenter*, 355.
[64] Carpenter, M. *On the Treatment of Female Convicts.*

red-cheeked young gardeners from the Boys' Industrial School, the Red Lodge girls in their blue gowns and bonnets. Looking down, she saw the shining pulpit where her father had preached, and the family pew where she had listened to him Sunday by Sunday, hungry for his love and approval. Now her nephew William sat in her place, with his wife and young son 'a small darling standing on the seat between them, encircled by his father's arm. To this day after all these long years, such a sight vividly recalls the feeling of my father's arm around me, either at chapel, or when saying a lesson. . . . It quite drew tears from my eyes when I looked down through the vista of the years.'[65] As early as she could remember, she had wanted 'to be useful', and with all her faults she had done her best.

She continued quite steadily in harness, a lecture at Kingswood, a committee meeting of the Indian National Association at her house, visits to Red Lodge. Happily all remained well there for her lifetime. Inspection in summer 1877 recorded premises 'very clean and well arranged', the 58 girls 'in very good health. I was perfectly satisfied with their general appearance,' education 'satisfactory, reading very good . . . no serious misconduct, no attempt to abscond, order and behaviour in class very good'.[66] On Thursday 14th June, Mary wrote to William and his wife, asking if she might come to stay with them in London. People came to call on her; she corrected the final proofs of her little book of poems; in the evening she went out and, meeting a friend in the street, talked with all her usual clearness and vigour. Coming home, she took her usual frugal cup of arrowroot, and went to her quiet study to write. She had heard that old William Lloyd Garrison was visiting England, and had already written inviting him to stay. 'I shall be very proud to have you as my guest.' Looking back, as so often now, to the past, she added, 'The Anti-Slavery cause was my "first love"; even from earliest childhood my sympathies were enlisted in it. So please be sure to come here *straight* from Liverpool with your son, to my house, where you shall do in every way what you like.' Yet old habits die hard; now she could not resist asking if he felt strong enough to meet 'about a hundred friends for an afternoon tea in Red Lodge Drawing Room'. It was past ten o'clock when she posted the letter, and with an affectionate goodnight to Rosanna, climbed the steep stairs to her room.

On 16th June W. L. Garrison opened the letter at breakfast with his London *Daily News*, and endorsed it. 'It is probably the last letter she ever wrote. Blessed be her memory! W.L.G.'[67] Nature had kept its crowning mercy to the last. On the morning of 15th June Mary Carpenter did not appear downstairs at her usual punctual hour of seven o'clock. At half past seven, Rosanna went to her room for the housekeeping keys and found her still in bed. There was nothing to show when she had made the tranquil passage from sleep into death.

---

[65] *Life and Work*, 381.

[66] Reports of the Inspector of Reformatory and Industrial Schools, *Parliamentary Papers*, 1877, XLII.

[67] Boston Public Library, MS A.1.2, Vol. 39, 27 and 54.

CONCLUSION

CHANGE AND THE
CHILDREN

Mary Carpenter had grown up in the utilitarian age, which was marked by suspicion of public reform, a narrow personal conception of religion and a certain matter-of-fact callousness towards the sufferings of the poor. Even humanitarians like Wilberforce, Hannah More, or later Shaftesbury, remembered the French Revolution and dreaded the mob. Many respectable church-going people interpreted Malthus to mean that the poor, by their nature, must always exist at a level of misery, squalor and vice. Mary Carpenter was one of the first people to rebel against this attitude. The springs of rebellion lay deep in her passionate, intensely repressed nature, her early sorrows, her sense of rejection and her fellow-feeling for the rejected of this world. In part this was a family feeling. The whole family bore the stamp of Dr Lant Carpenter's early teaching. 'In every case of moral conduct there is but *one* right way; *every* other must be wrong.' His children were brought up in a spirit of naïve universal reforming zeal, accustomed from early childhood to see themselves as inhabitants of a small enlightened island in a sea of ignorant and obstinate superstition. When Lant's moral and reforming zeal was joined, as in Mary, to their mother's brilliant organizing ability, the combination was formidable indeed. For all of them perhaps, certainly for Mary, an unspoken, agonizing doubt about their father's death reinforced their loyalty to his ideals. In 1873, when already an old woman, she was still emphatic that her father guided her in everything, and that his teaching 'from the earliest years, did not give any room in my soul . . . for those doubts and difficulties with which so many are troubled'. There is no sign that in a long and active life she ever saw two sides to any question, and however entrenched the opposition, she never doubted her mission to reform.

Sometimes the Carpenter family's compulsion to put the world to rights took on a grotesque or even comical aspect. It seemed to many people disproportionate that Philip, for the sake of a political disagreement with some elderly members of his congregation, should abandon the ministry, emigrate to another continent and, as Mary lamented, 'enslave himself to shells'.[1] James Martineau put it charitably when he said 'even the eccentricities of Philip's thought give originality to his character'; but others took a less kindly view. William's thought shared the same zealous character. As a Fellow of the Royal Society, highly successful medical writer and teacher, and first-class university administrator, he was deservedly one of the most respected and influential scientists in mid-Victorian England. His weakness was his readiness to support any cause, so long as it purported to raise the moral tone of society. A recent critic has shrewdly noted, 'Once his sympathies had been

---

[1] Carpenter, R. L. *Memoir of Philip Pearsall Carpenter*, 278.

fully won to the temperance movement, he had no hesitation in publicly backing its principles with a persuasive medley of moral and scientific arguments.' M. D. Hill described a railway journey, in which he 'talked of temperance matters with Dr Carpenter' all the way from London to Manchester, an improving, if not very enlivening experience for the other occupants of their carriage, who may even have felt driven to take the fatal step to the refreshment buffet. William's obsessions went further. In a prize-winning monograph, *On the Use and Abuse of Alcoholic Liquors in Health and Disease* he put forward the alarming theory that when alcohol was consumed, phosphorus was liberated into the body tissues, producing 'unusual combustibility', and perhaps some connection with the 'extraordinary phenomenon of spontaneous combustion'. The learned physician had thus persuaded himself, at least for the time being, into the belief for which Dickens was so ridiculed, when he introduced it into *Bleak House*.[2]

The family character is clearest perhaps in a less famous member, Mary's brother Russell, going about his duties as minister of the little white chapel with its circular porch, secluded by its long quiet garden from the Dorset town of Bridport, yet feeling himself 'bound to consider the good, not only of his congregation and the community in which he lives, but of his country and of mankind'. Russell felt called to apply Christian principles to public affairs, large or small. In an imperialist age, he attacked ruthless colonial expansion: 'I have allowed no false patriotism to keep me silent on the wars in which we have so frequently engaged in Africa and Asia.' He attacked cruelty to children, especially the common abuse of life insurance for infants: 'What is called the *life* insurance of children is really their *death* insurance . . . cold-blooded cruelty can watch its victim dying for months from starvation.' He argued for public wash-houses to save little children from the danger of scalding at home. He preached movingly on the sufferings of animals in cattle ships, six hundred at a time, penned in three tiers one above the other, legs broken, horns torn off, 'mad with terror and unrest'. He preached the need for funeral reform, and died as he had lived, his burial at his own direction: 'The simplest and cheapest possible.'[3]

In spite of conscientious attempts to broaden its social base, Unitarianism remained almost exclusively the faith of intellectuals and the liberal professions. Its links were overseas, with the New England Transcendentalists or the Brama Samaj in India, rather than with the ordinary, philistine British public. Mary Carpenter drew from religion her great strength, unshakeable faith in the power of human goodwill to overcome evil. Yet because she lived among intellectuals, in England a class apart, she failed to allow for the obstinate prejudices and failings of ordinary human nature. Her life was not the unbroken series of triumphs which her supporters claimed, but rather a running fight, lasting into old age, against hostility, ridicule and social indifference.

[2] *The Dickensian*, Vol. 69, Jan. 1973. Gaskell, E. 'More about Spontaneous Combustion.

[3] Carpenter, R. L. *Personal and Social Christianity, passim.*

It is plain that many contemporaries found the Carpenter family's determination to reform them very irritating indeed. As a remarkably frank obituary notice of Mary put it, 'The concentration of her purposes, and the tenacity of her just self-confidence, concealed from the eye of the world a depth of sentiment, which if it had been as visible as her social aims, would have given her perhaps a greater charm.'[4] Frances Power Cobbe compared her to a plough, driving inexorably forward on its furrow and sweeping every obstacle impersonally out of its path. Such reformers tend to think always in terms of principle, where life demands that they should work with men and women. Mary Carpenter was invariably courteous, in the best traditions of Victorian public life, but she was surely mistaken in believing herself to be tactful. The armour of righteousness, in which she girded herself against doubts, fears or ridicule, made it impossible for her to bend to circumstance, or to yield a point gracefully. Sometimes this did more harm than good. Mary was right to claim that Indian women deserved education, but succeeded in uniting the government and the missionaries against state schools. She was right that prison destroyed women, children and long-sentence convicts, yet any fair-minded person must regret the part she played in the ticket-of-leave agitation and the hounding of Joshua Jebb. She was right that voluntary workers can be friends in need to the homeless, but her distrust of government interference left schools and children's homes with crippling problems of administration and finance. Yet, when all this has been said, her constant compassion, her active concern for the failures and rejects of society, was better than blandly accepting privilege as a mark of divine grace. Without the puritan reformers, strenuous Diggers and Levellers of morality, the Victorian social landscape would have been even bleaker than it was. It is noteworthy that while strangers found Mary Carpenter, at least until her old age, an alarming figure, those who knew her best loved her most. James Martineau, by no means an uncritical admirer of the Carpenters, had known her from childhood, and wrote, 'No human ill escaped her pity, or cast down her trust.'[5] Fifty years after her death, Mary Carpenter's methods appeared distinctly old-fashioned. In the 1860s Herbert Spencer coined the phrase, with all its seductive attractions, 'survival of the fittest'. In the 1870s, the Italian criminologist Lombroso put forward a theory of degeneracy, with obvious physical and mental stigmata, to account for criminal behaviour. In the 1880s the growing eugenics movement suggested that 'every feeble-minded person is a potential criminal'. By 1913 the Mental Deficiency Act identified a class of 'moral defectives' with 'strongly vicious or criminal propensities', requiring segregation and control. The average member of the public, somewhat in awe of modern science, reluctantly accepted that deviant or anti-social behaviour was biologically caused, and ceased to believe in Mary Carpenter's theories of social handicap. Social Darwinism gave a cloak of scientific respectability to the idea of innate biological inferiority, which

[4] *The Spectator*, 17th June 1877.
[5] Bristol Cathedral, memorial to Mary Carpenter. The inscription was composed, at the family's request, by James Martineau.

became fashionable among the intelligentsia of the late nineteenth century. A genuine concern for public health, housing, education and welfare was accompanied by a determination to weed out the failures and misfits of society, especially to prevent the birth of children to women and girls who might breed a 'parasitic and predatory class'. The reformatory movement, with its perhaps over-confident claims for the curative powers of good environment, care and training, fell out of favour.[6]

Nor were the schools themselves the happy places she had hoped. So long as conditions outside were utterly wretched, reformatory and industrial schools, however Spartan, offered a better life; it is accepted that two-thirds to three-quarters of their children did well. Then gradually, rising social standards overtook these schools, until some of them became little pockets of Victorian deprivation left behind in the twentieth century. The practical problems of these schools which beset Mary Carpenter in her lifetime had become acute by the beginning of the 1914–18 war. Difficulties of finance increased with higher standards and necessarily higher expenses. Staff were never numerous enough, seldom stayed long enough and rarely had the right personal qualities. There was never adequate staff or finance for essential aftercare. Since the Home Office inspectors, though devoted, were always overworked, the central problem of control was never solved; who could enforce humane conditions in these semi-independent institutions or provide for the emotional needs of individual children?[7] As public opinion swung away from them, voluntary subscriptions fell off steeply. The education rate was all that most citizens were prepared to pay. Sharp differences between managers on such points as preliminary imprisonment, not abolished until 1899 or corporal punishment, the subject of a series of 'reformatory scandals' in the new penny papers, made the public increasingly distrustful. By 1920 the claims once made for reformatory and industrial schools were being made, with equal confidence, for the newer methods of probation or Borstal training. In 1933 reformatory and industrial schools were abolished in favour of Senior and Junior Approved Schools. Not surprisingly, a change of name failed to produce a revolution. Such is the power of institutions, and of bricks and mortar, to survive, that children were often sent to the same schools, housed in the same, hastily converted buildings, managed by the descendants of the original management committees.

Red Lodge, Mary Carpenter's own creation, did not survive the vast social changes of the 1914–18 war. As early as 1896 an inspector noted how the committee 'still venerates the memory of Miss Mary Carpenter. There is consequently apt to be a tendency to rely too much on old methods' . . . these 'which may have been suitable and even advisable forty years ago may be the very reverse now'. The managers failed to respond to this criticism. By 1914 they were an elderly body, the chairman unable to attend meetings for two years 'by reason of advanced age and failing health', but it did not seem to occur

---

[6] Morris, P. *Put Away*, 9–10, 18, points out that rejected members of society, like the criminals of an earlier generation, were relegated to 'colonies'.

[7] Rose, G. *Schools for Young Offenders*, 8–10.

to anybody that he might resign.[8] They and the matron and teacher, both daughters of Mary's faithful Mr and Mrs Langabeer at the Boys Industrial School, ran Red Lodge as a pious memorial to its founder. In any doubt, they consulted the rules she had drafted in 1854, applying them sixty years later with no apparent sense of incongruity.

They were beset with problems. In 1916 they faced a deficit of over £80 on the previous year's working, owing to the increased cost of provisions and fuel. At the same time, they found their funds unequal to the demands of the new Home Office salaries and superannuation scale. The Inspectorate made bewildering demands, for hot water in the bathrooms, swimming lessons, seaside holidays, tennis and basketball, first-aid and baby welfare classes, plus Morris dancing, all of which the committee thought 'too expensive at present'. To suggestions of competitive sports with other schools, the managers replied primly that 'they did not think the competitive spirit desirable'. In a phrase eloquent of a vanished Victorian age, the matron asked for some outings for the girls, 'and that on the day of the outing there should be something extra for tea'.

With the best intentions, the care they offered was totally out of date. Girls were now seldom sent to the school under 15, as the younger offenders were usually on probation; yet the school made no provision for secondary education and continued to offer these lusty young women Mary Carpenter's treats of a visit to the Clifton Zoo and a Christmas tree with dressed dolls. Their training was directed entirely towards the nineteenth-century feminine occupation of domestic service, which during the war years an estimated total of 400,000 girls were leaving in favour of war work, and blessed independence at last. A pair of absconders from Red Lodge were found living quite respectably in a hostel, while earning a good living in a munitions factory; the police brought them back, but it was impossible to argue the school offered them a better chance in life. Others plainly needed specialized care; one was deaf, one partially sighted, two had fits and one 'did not know her letters at fourteen'. The new Chief Inspector of Reformatories, Dr A. H. Norris, warned the managers in May 1918 that the school had been given a 'severely censuring report'. Dr Norris before serving in the R.A.M.C. had specialized in tuberculosis among the children of the Manchester slums; he knew the social handicaps of the children and was determined to improve standards of health and education in the Home Office certificated schools. He told the committee bluntly that 'he could not advise local authorities to send girls to Red Lodge' and the members agreed rather helplessly that 'the training of girls at the present time required newer methods'. They had however no funds to move to modern premises or engage trained teachers; the two Misses Langabeer after long and faithful service gave notice of their retirement. Finally on 9th July 1919, in the presence of Dr Norris, the management committee resolved 'in view of the increasing difficulty of carrying on the work in accordance with modern requirements . . . the school to be closed at

[8] He was a member of the Worsley family, whose ancestors had been educated in Dr Carpenter's school.

the earliest possible date'. The remaining 44 girls were dispersed to other institutions. Red Lodge, a pioneer Victorian school, had failed to survive in the climate of the twentieth century.[9]

The need and the use of Day Feeding Industrial Schools lasted into the twentieth century, but they were never favoured by official opinion. The government had taken the decision, for better or worse, to promote efficient education by the yardstick of 'standards' measured by inspection in the three Rs, and 'payment by results'. The Day Industrial Schools were too often housed in the tumbledown relics of former ragged schools, and too often taught by the same pious eccentrics, with their warnings against the demon drink, and their fondness for juvenile death-bed scenes. They appeared increasingly out of date as old-fashioned Christianity, with its romantic love for the individual soul, gave way to the new enthusiasm for 'Social Darwinism'. This, referring all conditions to biological causes, looked for the stigmata of supposed degeneracy, the misshapen skull of congenital syphilis, physical defects, subnormal intelligence measured by fixed tests. The schools were attempting in their way to reclaim the educationally subnormal, the mal-adjusted, the children with behaviour problems, estimated at ten per cent of the school population.[10]

In the 1880s Galtonian eugenics proposed to improve the breed by checking the birth of the unfit. In aid of this, social policy weeded out these inefficient or non-conformist members of society and segregated them in large insti-tutions. It remains an open question which approach was more hopeful for the health of society or the well-being of children.[11]

The schools might, of course, have been very different if they had met with official support instead of the hostility of which they were painfully aware. An elderly relative of the writer, a teacher in a Bristol school, still popularly called "the Ragged", used to describe the panic of her children when the dreaded Inspector called. Asked sharply in an unfamiliar, educated voice, 'what's the colour of a black bag?' they would answer wildly at random "Brown", "Blue" or even "Red", although she knew they could answer the question sensibly whenever she herself asked it. The schools were especially needed where there was no policy of economic support for the family and no social services to prevent family breakdown. Had they been developed as an integral part of the education services, many children eventually sent to hospital or approved school might have been able to stay at home.

At the beginning of the twentieth century, the Day Industrial Schools were described as unnecessary, because the social need for them had passed. Today, many teachers of latch-key children, and many mothers driven to work by poverty, might question this comfortable assumption. A writer in 1967 recommended experimental day schools for young offenders, on the lines of the nineteenth-century Day Industrial Schools as 'at least worth trying'.[12]

[9] Bristol Archives 12693, No. 10.   [10] Rose, G. *Schools for Young Offenders*, 160.

[11] Family planning, which might have eased the burdens of poor families, developed first among the middle classes with an expensive standard of living. See Banks, J. A. *Prosperity and Parenthood*.

[12] Rose, G. *Schools for Young Offenders*, 204.

Nevertheless, with no indomitable Mary Carpenter to fight their battles, the schools which gave total day care to children in need were officially declared redundant and closed. Yet not everything was lost, for many of their provisions, free education from 1891, medical inspection from 1907, and—after a long battle—school meals from 1906, found a place in ordinary state school life.[13] Mary Carpenter's last campaign was not fought wholly in vain.

Forms of social service must change, as society itself changes. Yet its spirit and intention remain constant. Her pioneering institutions were overtaken by social change, yet Mary Carpenter's deeply thought out, passionately held principles have continued to guide work with children in need. She was the first person to argue that a child in trouble is first and foremost a child; 'we must not treat him as a man'. She maintained that for the deprived or delinquent, 'love is an absolute necessity . . . and when it is denied them they are no longer children'. Punishment, though it may satisfy the vindictive part of man's nature, is 'an utterly useless method' for reform. Finally, she laid responsibility upon the community: if society leaves children 'knowingly in a state of utter degradation, it absolutely owes them reparation, far more than they can be said to owe reparation to it'.

Slowly, these revolutionary principles won acceptance. A whole series of laws, from the Education Act of 1870 onwards, showed British society at last assuming responsibility for the care and protection of its most defenceless children. The 1889 Prevention of Cruelty to Children Act, popularly called the Children's Charter, allowed the custody of children to be transferred from cruel parents to other guardians, and the Custody of Children Act extended this to cases of serious neglect. It should not be assumed that these rights were easily won. So sacred was the home and family life to Victorians, that Lord Shaftesbury, archpriest of humanitarians, considered cruelty or neglect there 'of so private, internal and domestic a character, as to be beyond the reach of legislation'.[14] Both Acts were passed however. They were followed by the Infant Life Protection Act of 1897, after a Select Committee had reported 'there is a very considerable number of infants in this country who are starved to death each year, often to cash in on insurance policies'. At the same time the *British Medical Journal* conducted a campaign against large-scale baby-farming, and systematic infanticide as a form of birth control. A series of Poor Law Amendment Acts of 1889, 1899 and 1913, released children from the punitive aspects of the old Poor Law, in favour of cottage homes, fostering and special care for the physically or mentally handicapped. The Boer War, with its revelations of physical deterioration amongst recruits gave rise to school meals and medical inspections, the Great War, with its generation of illegitimate babies, to the Adoption Act.

Mary Carpenter's philosophy of social responsibility can be seen most clearly in the four great Children's Acts of the twentieth century. The first, of 1908, consolidated and developed no fewer than thirty-nine previous laws

[13] These social services followed the revelations of the 1903 Physical Deterioration Committee, investigating the low standard of recruits during the Boer War.

[14] Ashton, A. F. and Young, E. T. *British Social Work in the Nineteenth Century*, 149.

protecting children. It covered infant life, cruelty, neglect and the use of children for begging or prostitution. Child offenders received special attention; they were at last to be kept out of prison by the creation of remand homes, and were to be tried only in Juvenile Courts. The Act of 1933, which created the new Approved Schools in place of reformatory or industrial schools, stated that 'every court in dealing with a child or young person who is brought before it as being in need of care and protection, or as an offender, or otherwise, shall have regard to the welfare of the child . . . . and for securing that proper provision is made for his education and training'. This Act still proposed to remove the child from 'undesirable surroundings'. The importance of home and the 'family tie' of which Mary Carpenter had so often written, was fully recognized for the first time in the Act of 1948, which followed the Curtis Committee's inquiry into provision for children 'deprived of a normal home life'. This Act created a new local authority official, the Children's Officer, covering the duties of Mary Carpenter's voluntary Children's Agent. The Act emphasized first and foremost every child's need for a family background.[15] The most recent, the Children and Young Persons Act of 1969, finally abolished any legal distinction between the deprived and depraved, those children of social neglect whom Mary Carpenter had described as 'the perishing and dangerous classes'. In face of continuing criticism, the act prescribed for all children in trouble, a care order to the local authority social service department. Responsibility for them now rests where Mary Carpenter always claimed that it belonged, to their own local community.[16] Experiment shows no sign of ending. In the U.S.A., Massachusetts and Illinois have now closed all correctional institutions for young people, and offer instead a wide range of individual treatment. Social reforms have reduced the scale of deprivation, but have not made it disappear. Ironically, Mary Carpenter who saw no need to vote herself, was inclined to over-estimate the power of political action. General standards of living rose over the last hundred years, yet suffering and deprivation obstinately refused to be abolished by law. Photographs of the 1890s and 1900s still show the same ragged, wild children roaming the streets. Cross-streets and alleys reveal long vistas of misery, in which figures grope among garbage and rags. Child mortality figures show how precarious was the hold on life of these narrow-chested listless urchins. Compulsory school attendance, of which Mary Carpenter had such hopes, merely imprisoned them for a few hours of inky boredom, without touching their real lives. The second half of the twentieth century shows less open neglect, at least in Europe, but a pervasive emotional poverty.

Workers among children in trouble or need, still paint a picture which Mary Carpenter would have recognized. On one day in 1975, 174 children between 14 and 16 were in adult prisons.[17] Community homes, psychological testing, remedial education or family casework remain useless to personalities

---

[15] Bruce, M. *The Coming of the Welfare State*, 4th ed., 225, 289, 304.

[16] *The Guardian*, 26th March 1973. Courts can still sentence serious offenders over 15 to Detention Centre or Borstal; some observers claim this is increasingly done.

[17] *The Guardian*, 18th April 1975.

deeply scarred by failure and loss of hope. Some families seem predestined to go slowly, inevitably downhill, deteriorating before the eyes of willing helpers. Success or failure are equally hard to estimate in these troubled lives. Honouring Mary Carpenter where she succeeded, we are most concerned with her failures. Many of the problems which defeated her remain unsolved to this day. Society still offers no constructive alternative to prison for women offenders. To find a school for a disturbed and difficult adolescent girl is a hard task, while schools find their work disrupted by frustrated, violent young offenders of either sex. Long periods of confinement still erode the character and will-power of prisoners. Technology cannot create a home for children who have lost their own. Most offenders, child or adult, still come from the most deeply deprived social setting. Competitive society itself creates a growing heap of failures, frustrated, angry, resentful rejects of society. No hopeful change in the name of the institutions, to which so many find their way, seems likely to change their essential problems. The roots of social disease, which the Victorian reformers weeded out with such self-confident vigour and enthusiasm, still elude the twentieth century. In spite of committees and Blue Books, in spite of Social Service Departments and genuine goodwill, deprivation persists like twitch-grass. For the most enlightened institution cannot replace a happy home, nor the most liberal welfare policy take the place of a just society. The individual, like Mary Carpenter, must still hope against hope.

APPENDIX I

Mary Carpenter in Account with Red Lodge Reformatory

Dr. — December 31st 1864

	£	s.	d.
Balance from 1863	48	18	7
Payments from Treasury	953	13	0
Do. from Parents per H.M. Inspector	54	2	3
Do. from Magistrates of Bristol	71	8	0
Do. —— Worcester	40	12	0
Do. —— Sussex	30	18	0
Do. —— for Rouse	7	16	0
Do. for Outfits & Discharge of Girls	19	0	0
Profits of Industrial Work	106	9	10
Interest of Money Vested	108	14	7
	£1441	12	3

Cr. — December 31st 1864

	£	s.	d.
Rent	73	0	0
Repairs and Alterations	58	9	11
Furniture & House Linen	35	2	11
Salaries	207	9	6
Food Red Lodge	337	0	10
Do. Red Lodge Cottage	67	17	1
House Expenses Red Lodge	7	19	5
Red Lodge Cottage	4	16	1
Fuel, Lighting } Red Lodge	61	4	9
& Washing } Red Lodge Cottage	15	15	3
Cost of 2 Girls at Red Lodge House	36	0	0
Clothing & Outfit	126	8	4
Medicine	2	9	9
Gratuities to Girls	14	7	6
Books Stationery & Printing	17	12	9
Postage & Stamps	3	15	5
Miscellaneous	4	15	1
Money Vested	350	0	0
Supervision of Girls after discharge	12	18	3
Journeys	3	17	7
Balance in hand		11	10
	£1441	12	3

1865, February 4th.

Audited this account and found it correct

Arthur A. Wansey,
Herbert Thomas.

APPENDIX II

Contributions by Mary Carpenter to the Annual Conferences of the National Association for the Promotion of Social Science

1857	Birmingham	The relation of ragged schools to the Educational Movement
		Reformatories for convicted girls
1858	Liverpool	The relation of ragged and industrial schools to the Parliamentary Educational Grant
		The disposal of girls from reformatory schools
1859	Bradford	The claims of ragged schools to a full share of the Parliamentary Educational Grant
		On Certified Industrial Schools: their principle and operation
1860	Glasgow	On the principles of education
		Supplementary measures needed for the diminution of juvenile crime
1861	Dublin	What shall we do with our pauper children?
		Voluntary aid and its relation to institutions supported by Government
1862	London	National education and the Revised Code
		On the education of pauper girls
		On the essential principles of the reformatory movement
1863	Edinburgh	On the treatment of female convicts
		Refuges for female convicts [at a special meeting]
1864	York	On the non-imprisonment of children
		The duty of Government to aid the education of children of the neglected classes
1865	Sheffield	On the consolidation of the Reformatory and Industrial Schools Acts
		On neglected and destitute children
1866	Manchester	On the nature of the educational aid required for the destitute and neglected portion of the community
1867	Belfast	On prison discipline in India
		On female education in India
1868	Birmingham	On the condition of Indian prisons
		On the inefficiency of pauper schools
1869	Bristol	[At this meeting the Council of the National Association for the Promotion of Social Science elected

Mary Carpenter an honorary member]

Children's agents

Female education

Results of the Industrial Schools and Reformatory Schools Acts

1870 *Newcastle upon Tyne* [Mary Carpenter was in India, but sent a letter demanding repeal of the Contagious Diseases Acts]

1871 *Leeds* Certified Industrial Schools and their relation to School Boards

How may the education of neglected children be best provided ?

1872 *Plymouth* On Day Industrial Schools for neglected and destitute children

The need for trained women teachers in secondary schools for girls

1873 *Norwich* On the treatment of life-sentenced prisoners

How can education be brought to the hitherto untouched portions of the population ?

The need for women teachers and inspectors in elementary and high schools

1874 *Glasgow* How far is it desirable that the Industrial Schools Act should be extended to day schools ?

On reformatory and industrial schools in India

1875 *Brighton* [Mary Carpenter was in India; before she left she had read a paper on Day Industrial Schools to the British Association meeting in Bristol]

1876 *Liverpool* Female education in India

Day Industrial Schools

1877 *Aberdeen* [The President of the Council gave a memorial address on Mary Carpenter's life and work]

SOURCES

I MANUSCRIPT AND PRIVATELY PRINTED

Boston, Mass., by courtesy of the Trustees of the Boston Public Library:

Fifty-five letters of Mary Carpenter to William Lloyd Garrison, A. A. Livermore, Samuel May, Mrs Follen, Mrs Chapman, etc.

San Marino, Cal., by permission of the Huntington Library:
Twenty-five letters of Mary Carpenter to Frances Power Cobbe.

Bristol Council House Archives, Accession number 12693:

Red Lodge Journal, 2 vols., 1855–60

Principles, rules and regulations of the school 1854

Account books, 1854–84

Minute books, 4 vols., 1878–1918

Visitors' book of Red Lodge

Red Lodge Girls' Reformatory School, its history, principles and working. Privately printed, Bristol 1875

Certificate of Red Lodge, signed by Lord Palmerston as Secretary of State, 9th December 1854

Folder labelled by Mary Carpenter 'Autograph letters on Public Work' containing numerous letters from 'public and official gentlemen'

Album labelled by Mary Carpenter 'Records of India 1866'

Album labelled by Mary Carpenter 'Records of India 1875–1877' (the last three items contain letters from Florence Nightingale, Lord Shaftesbury, Lord Salisbury, etc.)

Scrapbook entitled 'Miscellaneous papers', containing numerous pamphlets and newspaper cuttings relating to Mary Carpenter, her books, her schools, press controversies, etc.

Album containing Mary Carpenter's personal visitors' book, 1836–75

'Interview with the Queen' dated 20th May 1868, Mary Carpenter's own manuscript account

Album containing Mary Carpenter's own poems, manuscript and printed

Bristol Council House Archives, Accession number 28776:

Visitors' book and official inspections of Kingswood School

Scrapbook of press cuttings relating to Kingswood and reformatory controversies generally

Bristol Council House Archives, Accession number 6687 (1–4):

Lewin's Mead Meeting

Accession number 5535 (1–66):

Documents relating to Red Lodge and adjoining property

Accession number 09683 (1–3):

Documents relating to St James' Back Certified Day Industrial School

Bristol Red Lodge Museum:

Water-colours, photographs, presentation copies and personal possessions of Mary Carpenter

Bristol City Art Gallery:

Maps, topographical paintings and engravings, portraits, etc. relating to old Bristol, Bristol institutions, Lewin's Mead Meeting, the Carpenter family, etc.

Oxford Manchester College Library, by permission of the Principal:

Eighty-six letters from James Martineau to members of the Carpenter family, including Mary Carpenter, 1821–80

Album of letters to or from Mary Carpenter and Florence Nightingale, Theodore Parker, Joseph Tuckerman, J. S. Mill, A. H. Clough, Charles Dickens, Charles Darwin, Matthew Arnold, R. W. Emerson, Harriet Martineau, Lady Byron, etc.

Cambridge Trinity College Library, by permission of the Master and Fellows:

Eight letters from Mary Carpenter to R. Monckton Milnes, 1861–76

Liverpool University by permission of the Librarian:

Letters from Mary Carpenter to the Rathbone family

Birmingham University, by permission of the Rare Book Librarian:

Letters from Mary Carpenter to Harriet Martineau

Victoria and Albert Museum

Letters from Mary Carpenter to John Forster

II STATE PAPERS

Public Record Office. Foreign Office, Class 43, piece 32:

Correspondence between the British Consul at Rome and the Foreign Office, concerning the mysterious death of Lant Carpenter at sea

Parliamentary Papers

Report of Select Committee on Criminal and Destitute Children

1852 (515) VII 1
1853 XXIII 1

Report of Select Committee on the Education of Destitute Children

1861 VII (895)

Reports of Commissions on Reformatory and Industrial Schools

1884 XLV 1
1896 C 8240

Bill for the Provision of Reformatory Schools 1854

Bill for the Provision of Industrial Schools 1857

Bill for the Provision of Industrial and Reformatory Schools 1861

Education Act 1870

Education Act 1876 (Lord Sandon's Act)

Reports of Joseph Fletcher, H.M.I., on St James' Back Ragged School

1849–50 XLIII–IV
1851–52 XXXIX–XL

Reports by the Rev. Sydney Turner, H.M.I. of Reformatory and Industrial Schools:

1857-8	XXIX 811	1868-9	XXX 579
1859	XIII sess. 2, 1	1870	XXXVI 663
1860	XXXV 765	1872	XXX 385
1861	XXX 29	1873	XXXL 457
1862	XXVI 523	1874	XXVIII 479
1863	XXIV 497	1875	XXXVI 467
1864	XXVII	1876	XXXIV 469
1865	XXV 341	1877	XLII 471
1866	XXXVIII 367	1878	XLII 253
1867	XXVI 637	1879	XXXVI

III   BOOKS AND PAMPHLETS BY MARY CARPENTER

Morning and Evening Meditations 1845 London
Ragged Schools 1849 London
Life of Tuckerman 1849 London
Reformatory Schools 1851 London
Juvenile Delinquents 1853 London
On Reformatory Schools 1855 Bristol
The Claims of Ragged Schools 1859 Bristol
On the Principles of Education 1860 Bristol
Reformatories for the Diminution of Juvenile Crime 1861 London
What shall we do with our Pauper Children? 1861 London
On the Education of Pauper Girls 1862 Bristol
A Day at Red Lodge 1864 Bristol
The Management of Reformatories 1864 Bristol
Our Convicts II Vols. 1864 London
Last Days in England of the Rajah Rammohun Roy 1866 London
Six Months in India II Vols. 1868 London
Day Industrial Schools 1874 Bristol
Prison Discipline and Juvenile Reformatories 1876 Calcutta

see also Appendix 2 Contributions by Mary Carpenter to the Annual Conferences of the National Association for the Promotion of Social Science. Only those papers separately published as pamphlets have been listed above.

IV   PERIODICALS

The Bristol Mercury 1811-64
The Bristol Mirror 1811-64
The Christian Reformer First Series 1834-44
                            New Series 1845-63
The Contemporary Review August-December 1870
The Cornhill Magazine April 1861-October 1874
The Edinburgh Review 1849-74
The Home and Foreign Review 1860-2
The Inquirer 1842-77
Macmillan's Magazine 1860-73
The Modern Review 1880
The Monthly Repository First Series 1806-26
                            New Series 1827-37

The North British Review November 1848–February 1861
The Quarterly Review 1861–73
The Ragged School Union Magazine 1849–75
The Reformatory and Refuge Journal 1861–99
The Western Daily Press 1858–77

V   PRINTED BOOKS

anon., A New History, Survey and Description of Bristol 1794. Bristol.
—— The late Riots in Bristol. 1831. Bristol.
Baker, T. B. L., Report on the Childrens Friend Reformatory. 1855. Gloucester.
—— War with Crime, 1889. London.
Bamford, T. W., The Rise of the Public Schools. 1967. London.
Banerji, Sir S. N., A Nation in the Making. 1925. Calcutta.
Banks, J. A., Prosperity and Parenthood. 1954. London.
Barrett, —, The History and Antiquities of Bristol. 1789. Bristol.
Beggs, T., An Inquiry into the extent and causes of Juvenile Depravity. 1849. London.
Bristol City Art Gallery, Bristol Scenery 1714–1858. Bristol.
—— Views of Bristol and Clifton. 1864. Bristol.
—— The Red Lodge. 1951. Bristol.
British Association, Bristol and its Environs. 1875. London and Bristol.
Bruce, M., The Coming of the Welfare State. (fourth edition) 1968. London.
Burgess, T., The Divinity of Christ. 1820. London.
Burt, Sir C., The Young Delinquent. (fourth edition) 1944. Bickley.
Carlebach, J., Caring for Children in Trouble. 1969. London.
Carpenter, J. E., Life and Work of Mary Carpenter. (second edition) 1881. London.
—— James Martineau. 1905. London.
Carpenter, L., Introductory Catechism 1826. London.
—— Sermons on Practical Subjects. 1840. Bristol.
—— with Shepherd, W. and Joyce, J., Systematic Education. 1817. London.
Carpenter, R. L., Memoir of Lant Carpenter. 1842. Bristol and London.
—— Memoir of Philip Pearsall Carpenter. 1880. London.
—— Personal and Social Christianity. 1893. London.
Chance, W., Children under the Poor Law. 1897. London.
—— Our Treatment of the Poor. 1899. London.
Channing, W. E., Life and Character of J. Tuckerman. 1841. Boston.
Chesney, K., The Victorian Underworld. 1970. London.
Clay, W. L., The Prison Chaplain. 1861. Cambridge.
Cobbe, F. P., Life of Frances Power Cobbe. (second edition) 1904. London.
Collins, P., Dickens and Education. 1963. London.
—— Dickens and Crime (second edition) 1963. London.
Coombs, C. F., Rheumatic Heart Disease. 1924. Bristol.
Dickens, C., Reprinted Pieces. 1868. London.
—— The Uncommercial Traveller. 1860–1869. London.
Escott, T. H., Social Transformation of the Victorian Age. 1897. London.
Fletcher, J., The Farm School System of the Continent. 1851. London.
Gaskell, E., ed. Pollard, A., and Chapple, J. A. V., Letters. 1966. Manchester.
Glueck, S., The Problem of Delinquency. 1959. New York.
Hart, M., The Children of the Streets. 1880. London.
Herford, C. H., J. E. Carpenter. 1929. London.

Hill, F., Children of the State. (second edition) 1889. Edinburgh.

Hill, R. and F., Matthew Davenport Hill. 1878. Birmingham.

Hinde, R. S. E., The British Penal System. 1951. London.

Holt, R., The Unitarian Contribution to Social Progress in England. (second edition) 1952. London.

Hunter, R. and Macalpine, I., Three Hundred Years of Psychiatry. 1963. London.

Jones, H., Crime and the Penal System. (third edition) 1965. London.

Jones, M. G., Hannah More. 1952. Cambridge.

McLachlan, H., Education under the Test Act. 1932. Manchester.

―― The Unitarian Movement in the Religious Life of England. 1934. London.

McColgan, D., Joseph Tuckerman: Pioneer in American social work. 1940. Boston, Mass.

Madison, A., Hints on Rescue Work. 1898. Portsmouth.

Majumdar, R. C., Rayachaudhari, H. and Datta, K. An Advanced History of India. (second edition) 1951. London.

Majumdar, R. C. (ed.), History and Culture of the Indian People. X 1950. Calcutta.

Manton, J., Elizabeth Garrett Anderson. 1965. London.

―― Sister Dora. 1971. London.

Martineau, H., Autobiography. 1877. London.

Mayhew, A., Education of India, 1935–1920. 1926. London.

Mayne, E. C., Life of Lady Byron. 1929. London.

Mays, J. B., Juvenile Delinquency in an Urban Neighbourhood. 1964. New York.

Neale, W. B., Juvenile Delinquency. 1846. Manchester.

Pinchbeck, I. and Hewitt, M., Children in English Society. II 1974. London.

Radzinowicz, Sir L., A History of English Criminal Law and its administration from 1750. I–IV 1948. London.

Richardson, H., Adolescent Girls in Approved Schools. 1969. London.

Rose, G., Schools for Young Offenders. 1967. London.

Rotch, B., Suggestions for the Prevention of Juvenile Depravity. 1846. London.

Spate, O. H. K. and Learmonth, A. T. A., An Advanced Geography of India and Pakistan. 1972. London.

Tobias, J. J., Crime and Industrial Society in the nineteenth century. 1967. London.

Waugh, B., The Gaol Cradle. 1873. London.

Webb, B. and S., English Prisons under Local Government. 1929. London.

Wines, E. C., (ed.) Report of the International Penitentiary Congress. 1872. New York.

Woodruff, P., Men who ruled India. I–II 1963. London.

Young, A. F. and Ashton, E. T., British Social Work in the nineteenth century. 1956. London.

INDEX